Little
nster

6

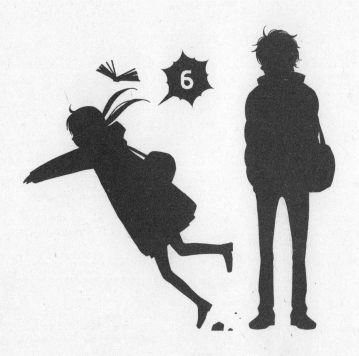

Robico

C O N T E N T S

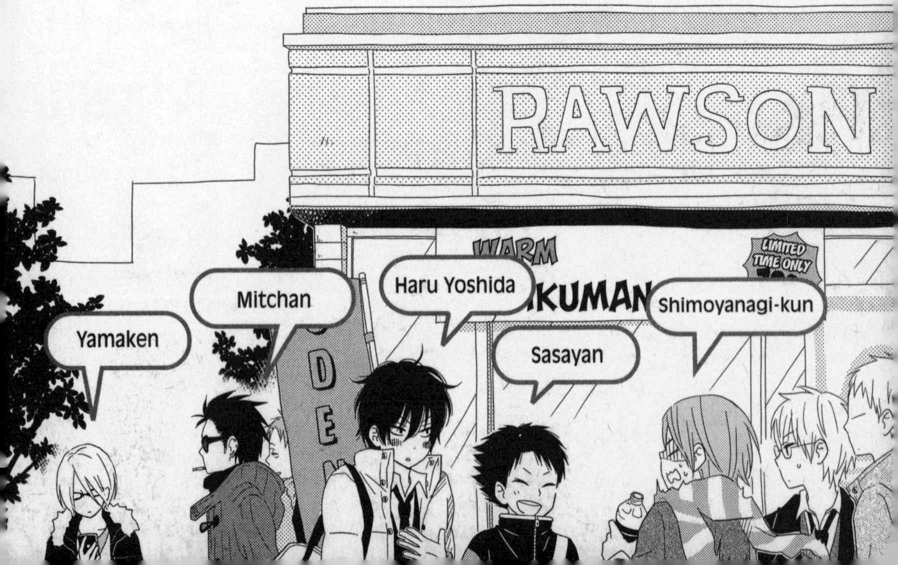

RAWSON
LIMITED TIME ONLY
WARM
Haru Yoshida
Shimoyanagi-kun
Mitchan
Sasayan
Yamaken

S T O R Y

When Shizuku Mizutani does a favor for problem child Haru Yoshida, who sits next to her in school, he develops a huge crush on her. Attracted to his innocence, she eventually falls for him, too, but when she asks him out, he inexplicably turns her down. Shizuku temporarily locks away her romantic feelings, but then she starts to change by facing people more assertively. She again tells Haru that she likes him, but her confession goes right over his head! The two just cannot get on the same page, but on a snowboarding trip, Haru starts to see that Shizuku is trying to make him happy, and finally begins his own transformation.

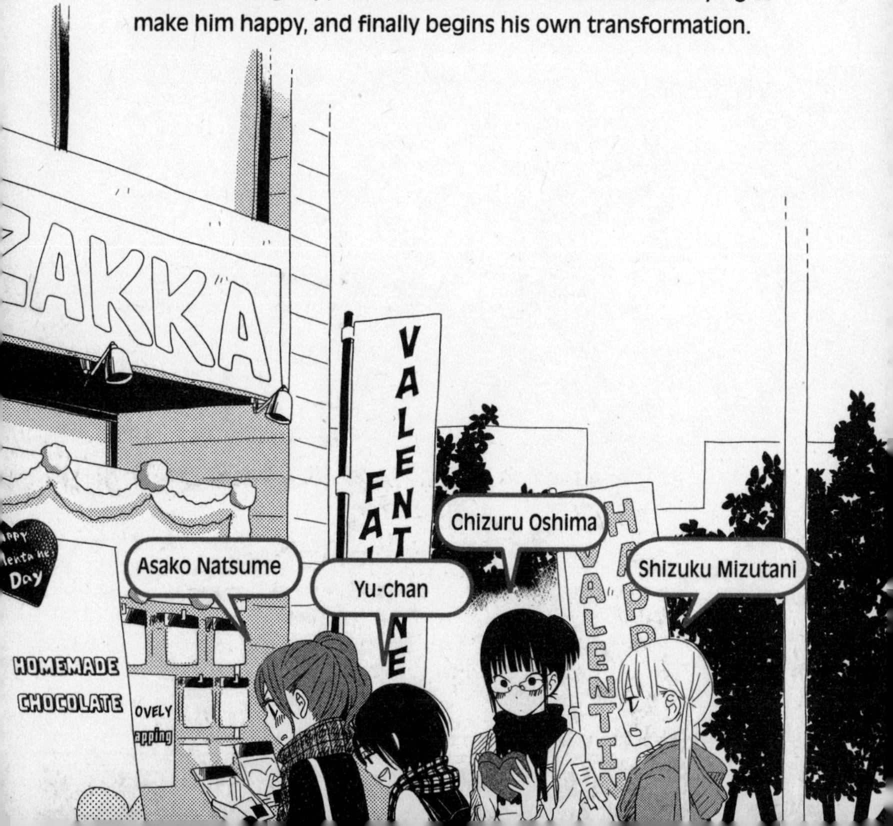
Shizuku Mizutani
Chizuru Oshima
Yu-chan
Asako Natsume
HOMEMADE
CHOCOLATE

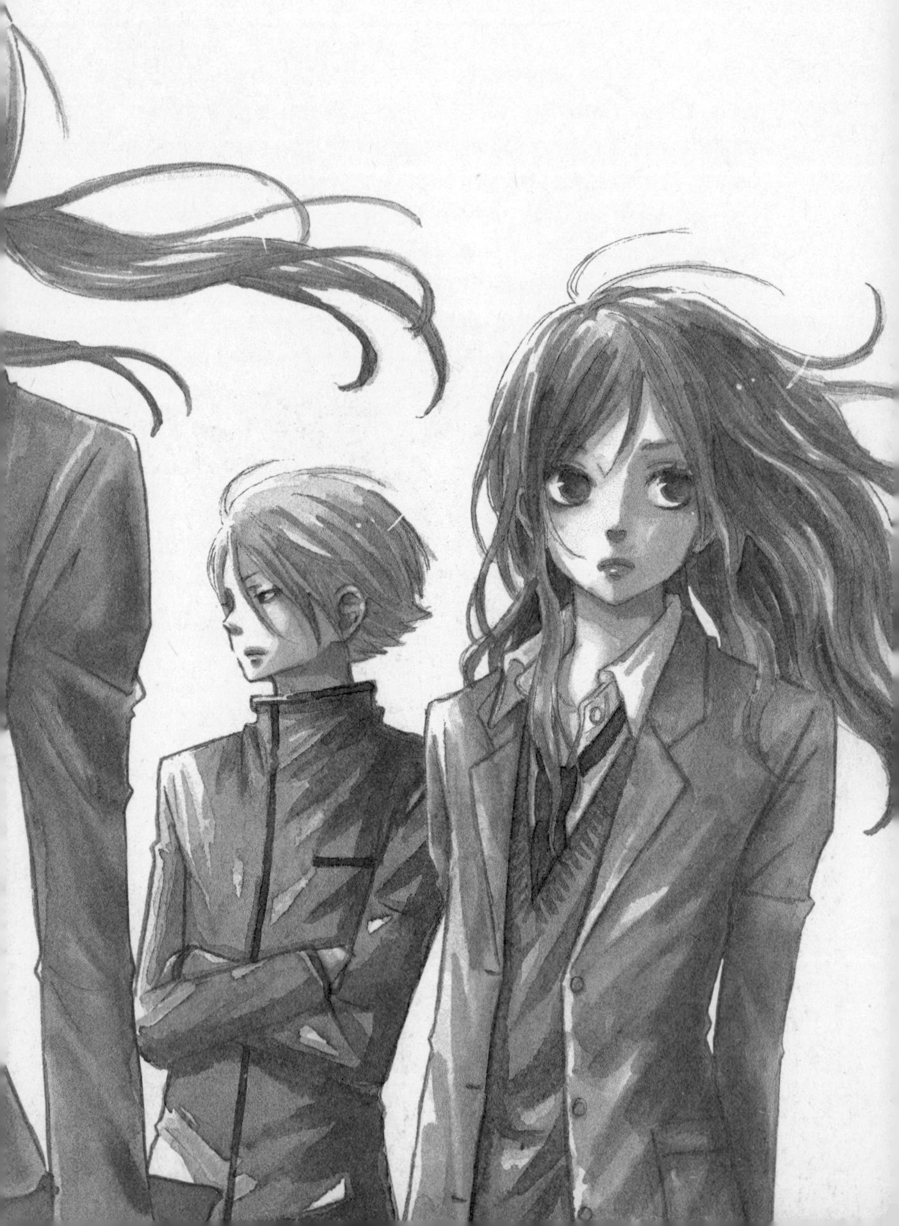

Chapter 21 Sasayan and Haru

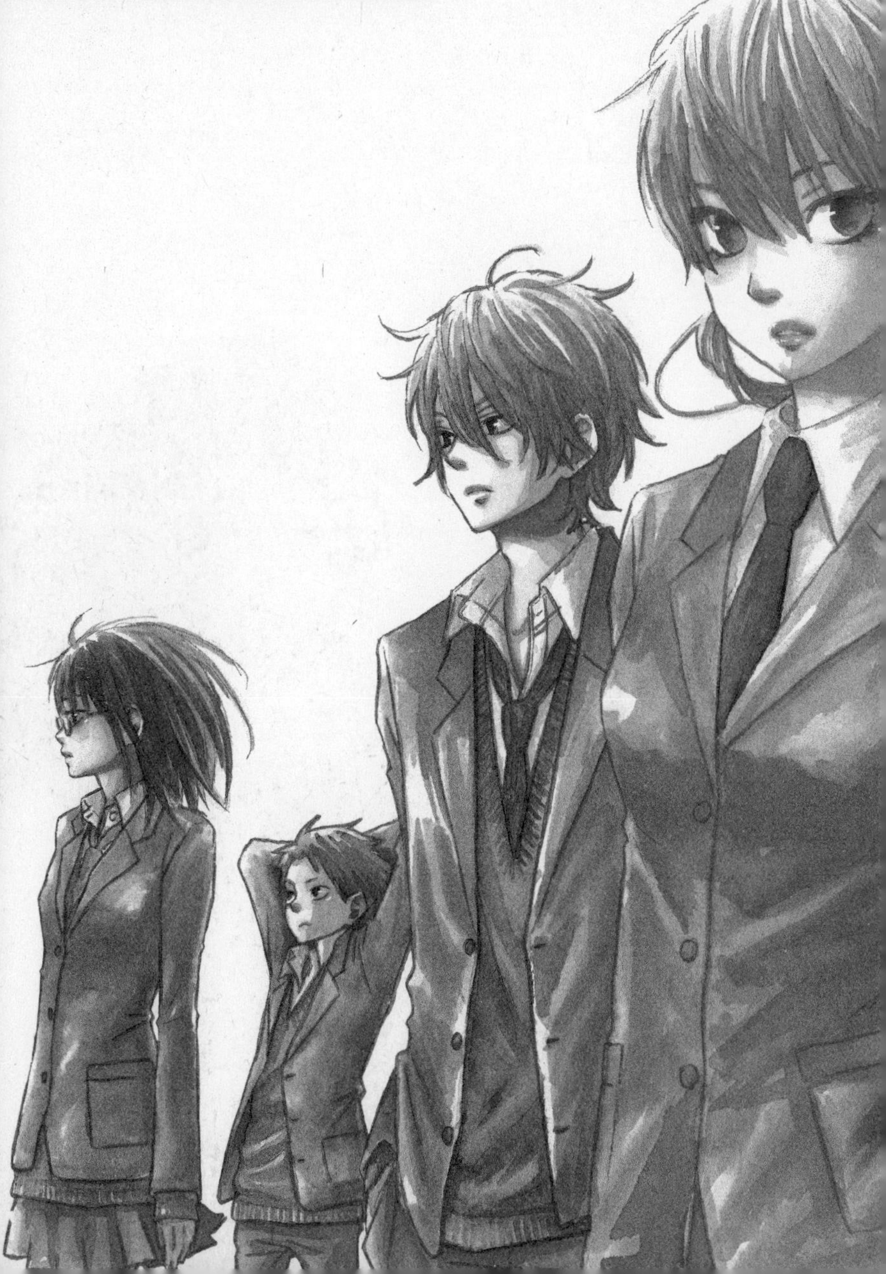

On the way home.

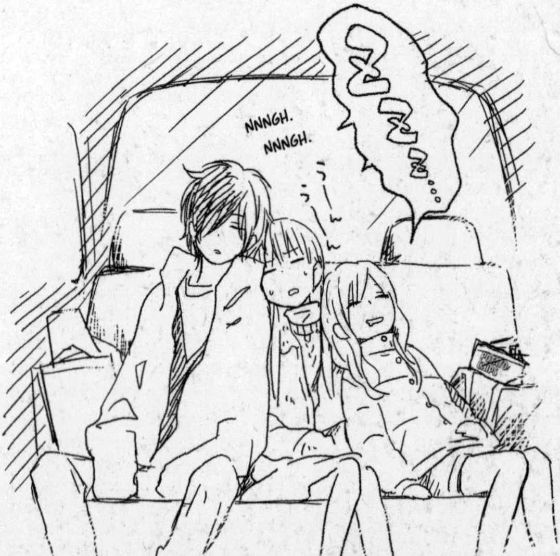
ZZZZ...
NNNGH.
NNNGH.
うーん
うーん
POTATO CHIPS

I ALWAYS THOUGHT THAT SOMEONE HAD WHAT I WANT.

THE MORE I STRUGGLED FOR IT, THE FARTHER AWAY IT GOT.

THE MORE I WISHED FOR IT, THE MORE IM-POSSIBLE IT WAS TO OBTAIN.

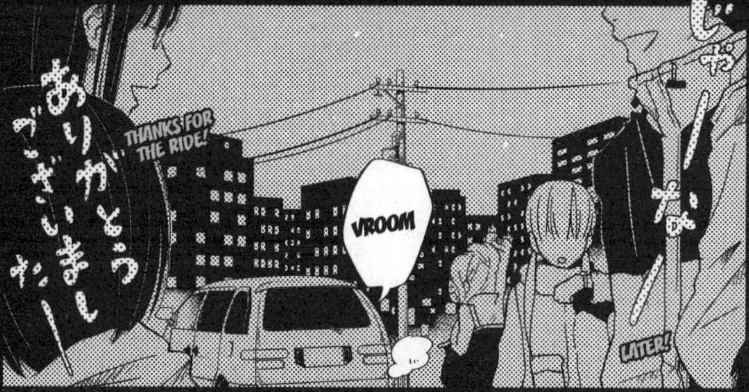
LATER!
VROOM
THANKS FOR THE RIDE!

BUT IF...

IF I, TOO,

COULD GIVE SOMETHING TO SOMEONE ELSE...

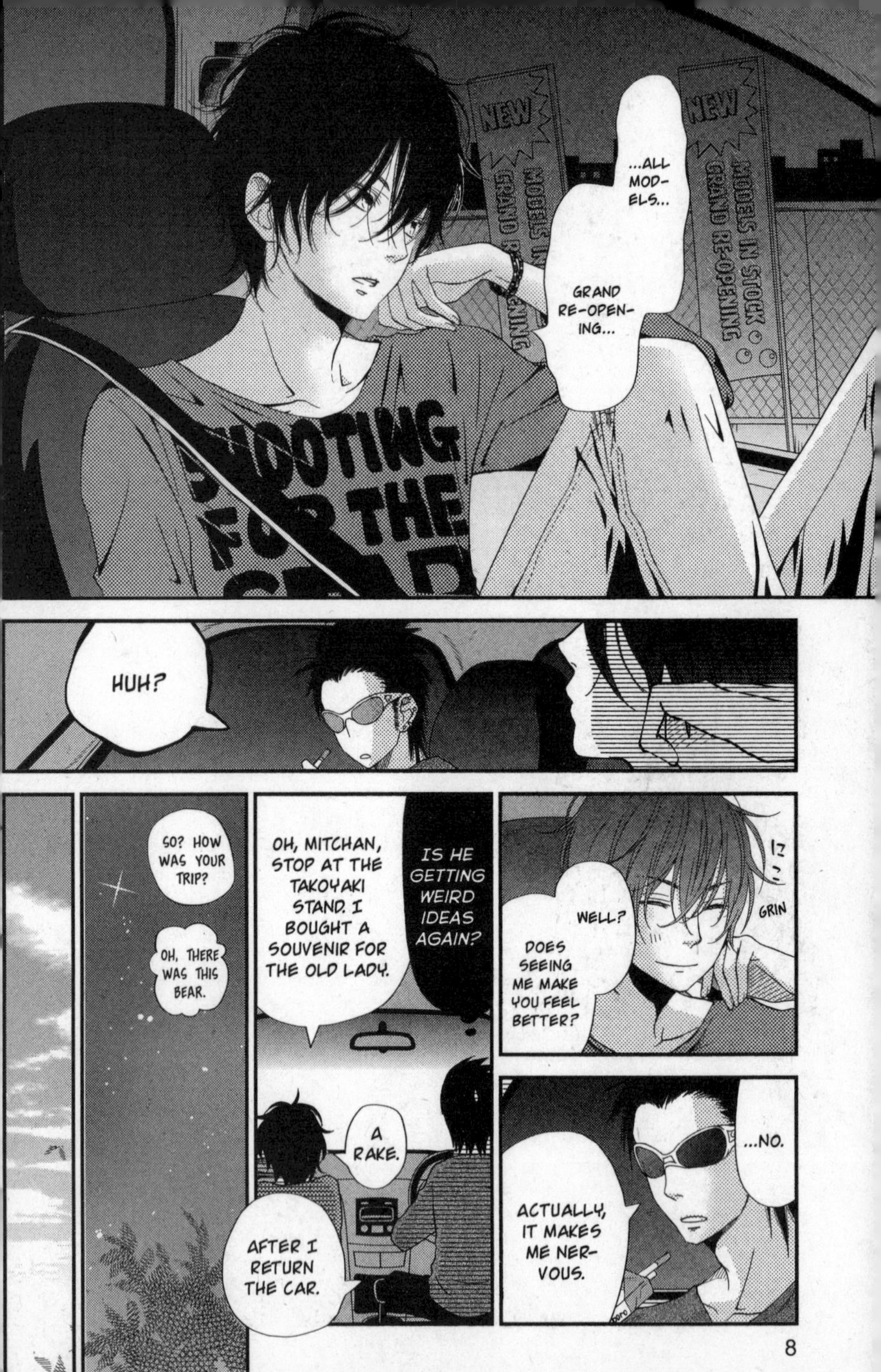
NEW
MODELS IN STOCK
GRAND RE-OPENING
...ALL MOD-ELS...
GRAND RE-OPENING...
HUH?
GRIN
WELL?
DOES SEEING ME MAKE YOU FEEL BETTER?
...NO.
ACTUALLY, IT MAKES ME NERVOUS.
IS HE GETTING WEIRD IDEAS AGAIN?
OH, MITCHAN, STOP AT THE TAKOYAKI STAND. I BOUGHT A SOUVENIR FOR THE OLD LADY.
A RAKE.
AFTER I RETURN THE CAR.
SO? HOW WAS YOUR TRIP?
OH, THERE WAS THIS BEAR.

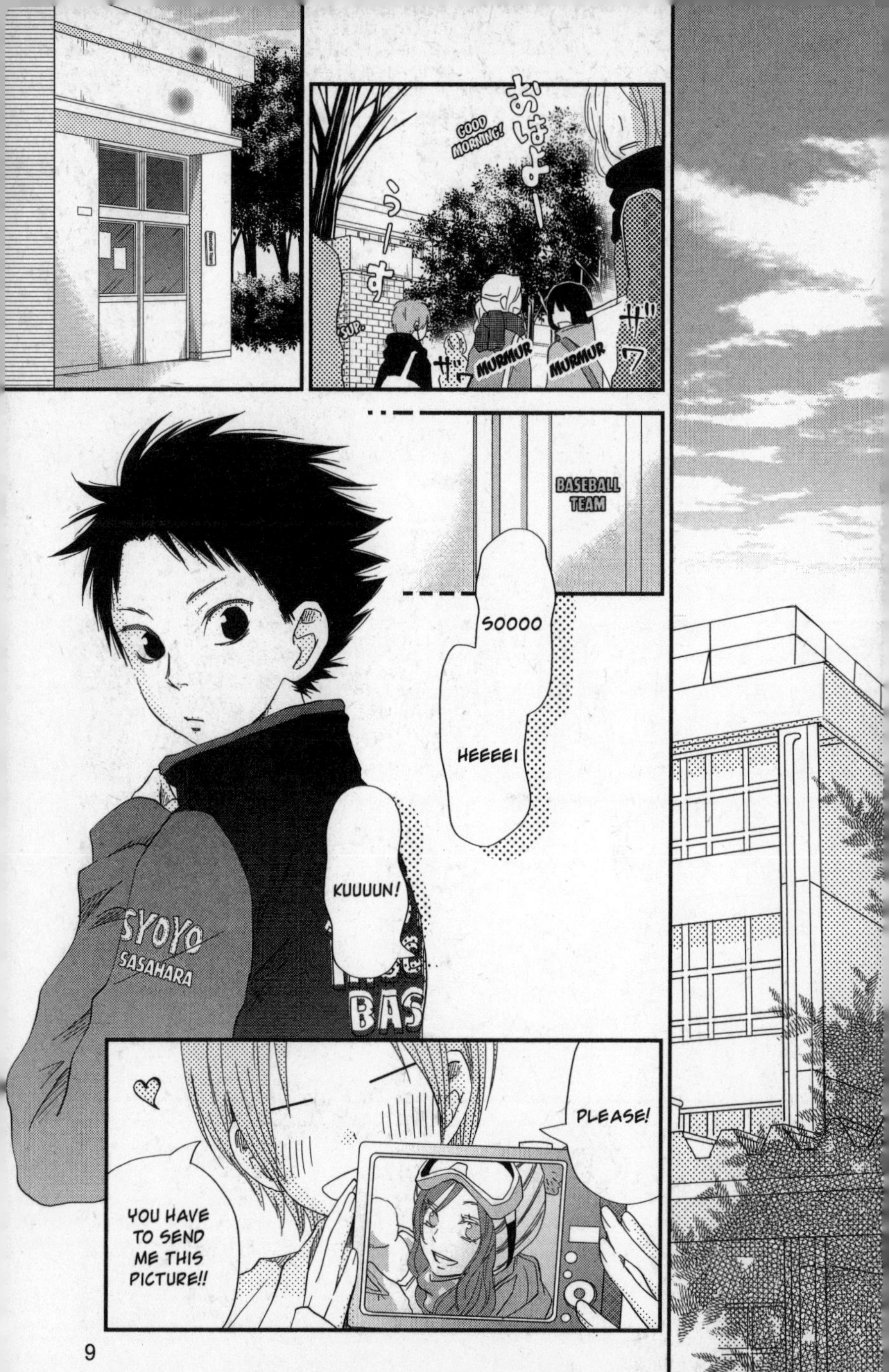

おはよー
GOOD MORNING!
うーす
SUP.
ザワ
MURMUR
ザワ
MURMUR
BASEBALL TEAM
SOOOO
HEEEEI
KUUUUN!
SYOYO SASAHARA
BAS
PLEASE!
YOU HAVE TO SEND ME THIS PICTURE!!

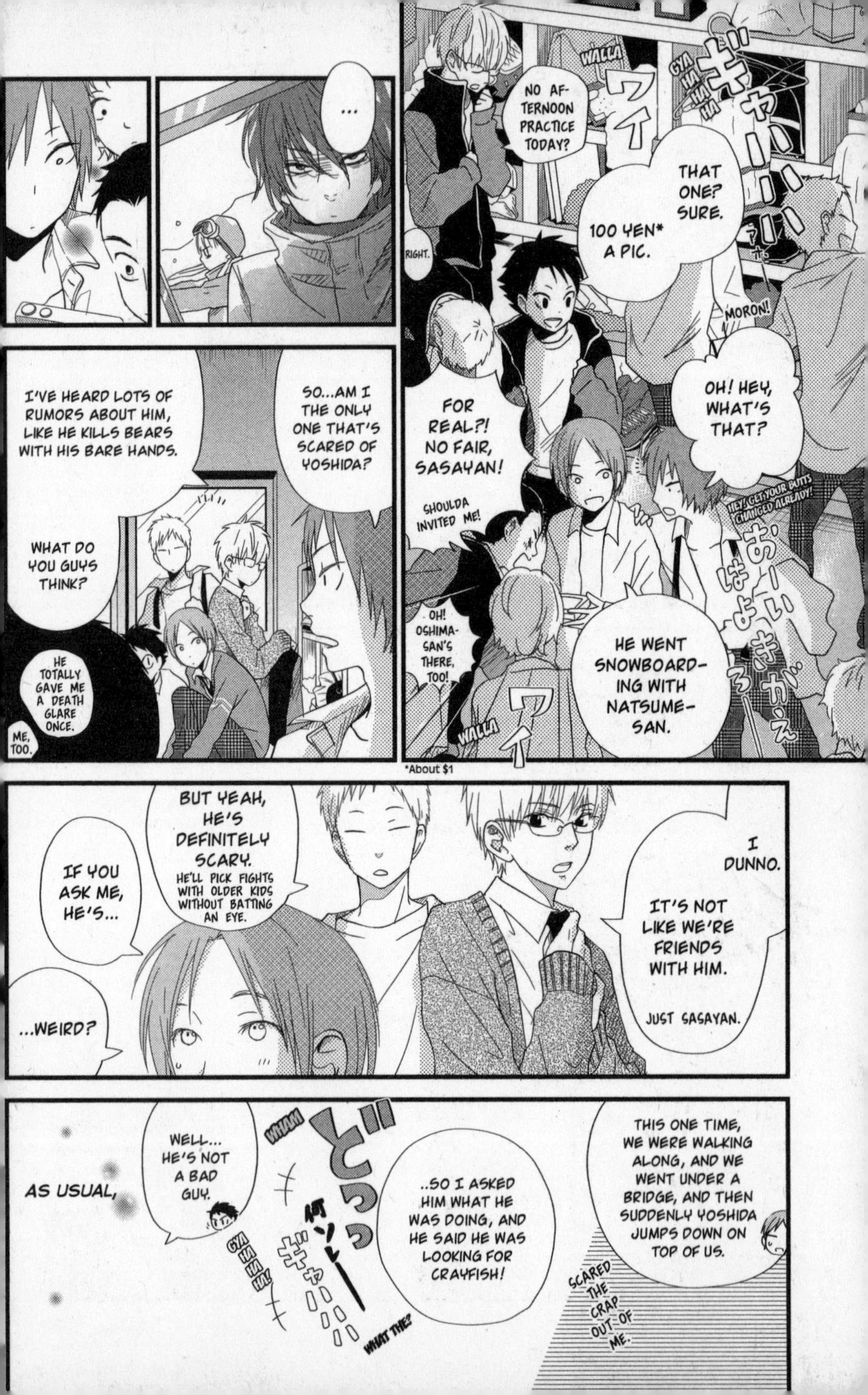
GYA HA HA HA
WALLA
NO AFTERNOON PRACTICE TODAY?
THAT ONE? SURE.
100 YEN* A PIC.
RIGHT.
MORON!
OH! HEY, WHAT'S THAT?
FOR REAL?! NO FAIR, SASAYAN!
HEY! GET YOUR BUTTS CHANGED ALREADY!
SHOULDA INVITED ME!
HE WENT SNOWBOARDING WITH NATSUME-SAN.
OH! OSHIMA-SAN'S THERE, TOO!
WALLA
...
SO...AM I THE ONLY ONE THAT'S SCARED OF YOSHIDA?
I'VE HEARD LOTS OF RUMORS ABOUT HIM, LIKE HE KILLS BEARS WITH HIS BARE HANDS.
WHAT DO YOU GUYS THINK?
HE TOTALLY GAVE ME A DEATH GLARE ONCE.
ME, TOO.
I DUNNO.
IT'S NOT LIKE WE'RE FRIENDS WITH HIM.
JUST SASAYAN.
BUT YEAH, HE'S DEFINITELY SCARY.
HE'LL PICK FIGHTS WITH OLDER KIDS WITHOUT BATTING AN EYE.
IF YOU ASK ME, HE'S...
...WEIRD?
THIS ONE TIME, WE WERE WALKING ALONG, AND WE WENT UNDER A BRIDGE, AND THEN SUDDENLY YOSHIDA JUMPS DOWN ON TOP OF US.
SCARED THE CRAP OUT OF ME.
..SO I ASKED HIM WHAT HE WAS DOING, AND HE SAID HE WAS LOOKING FOR CRAYFISH!
WHAM
WHAT THE?
GYA HA HA HA!
WELL... HE'S NOT A BAD GUY.
AS USUAL,
*About $1

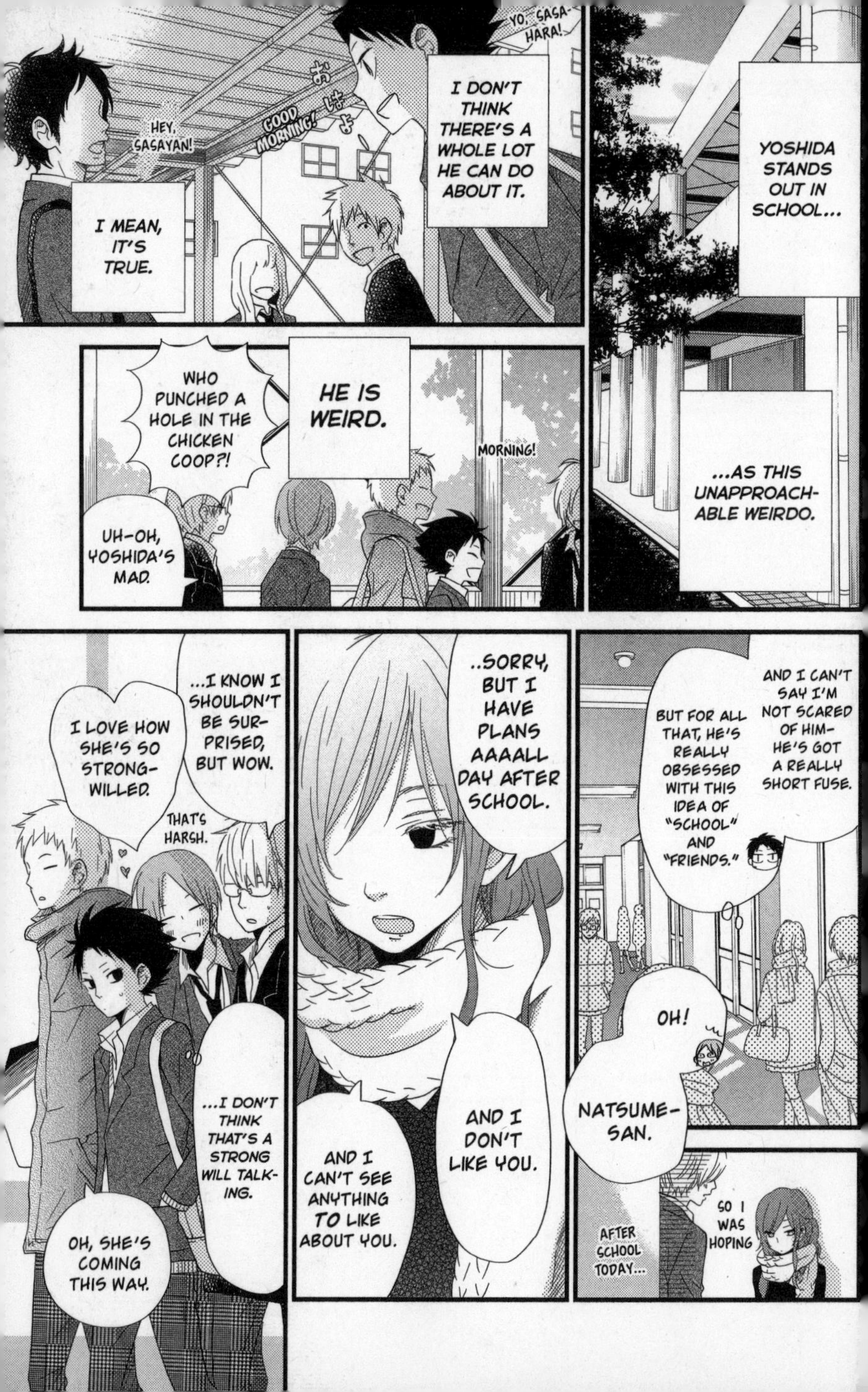
YOSHIDA STANDS OUT IN SCHOOL...
...AS THIS UNAPPROACHABLE WEIRDO.
YO, SASA-HARA!
I DON'T THINK THERE'S A WHOLE LOT HE CAN DO ABOUT IT.
おはよ
GOOD MORNING!
HEY, SASAYAN!
I MEAN, IT'S TRUE.
MORNING!
HE IS WEIRD.
WHO PUNCHED A HOLE IN THE CHICKEN COOP?!
UH-OH, YOSHIDA'S MAD.
AND I CAN'T SAY I'M NOT SCARED OF HIM-HE'S GOT A REALLY SHORT FUSE.
BUT FOR ALL THAT, HE'S REALLY OBSESSED WITH THIS IDEA OF "SCHOOL" AND "FRIENDS."
OH!
NATSUME-SAN.
SO I WAS HOPING
AFTER SCHOOL TODAY...
..SORRY, BUT I HAVE PLANS AAAALL DAY AFTER SCHOOL.
AND I DON'T LIKE YOU.
AND I CAN'T SEE ANYTHING TO LIKE ABOUT YOU.
...I KNOW I SHOULDN'T BE SUR-PRISED, BUT WOW.
I LOVE HOW SHE'S SO STRONG-WILLED.
THAT'S HARSH.
...I DON'T THINK THAT'S A STRONG WILL TALK-ING.
OH, SHE'S COMING THIS WAY.

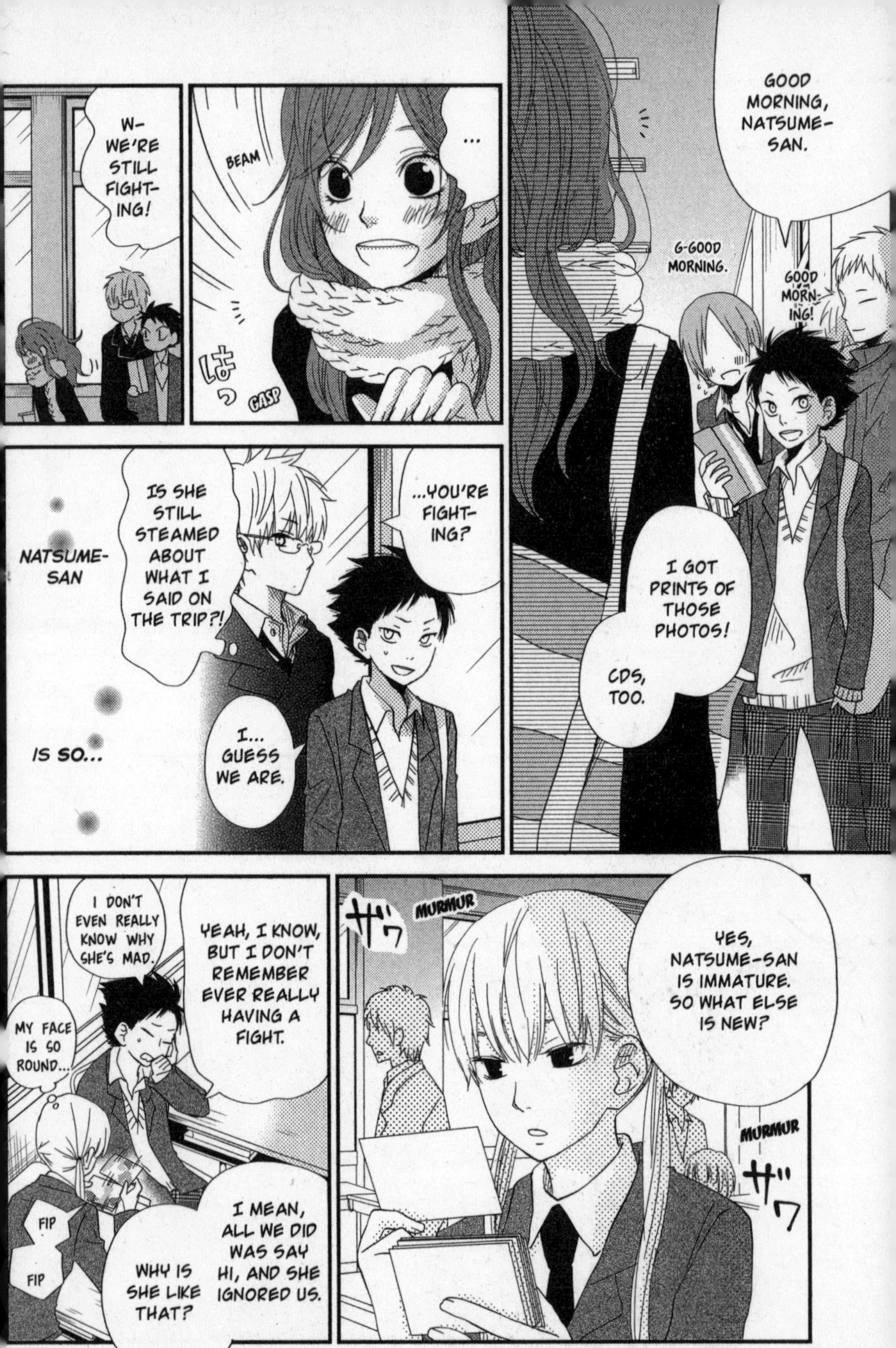
GOOD MORNING, NATSUME-SAN.
G-GOOD MORNING.
GOOD MORN-ING!
I GOT PRINTS OF THOSE PHOTOS!
CDS, TOO.
...
BEAM
はっ
GASP
W-WE'RE STILL FIGHT-ING!
...YOU'RE FIGHT-ING?
IS SHE STILL STEAMED ABOUT WHAT I SAID ON THE TRIP?!
I... GUESS WE ARE.
NATSUME-SAN
IS SO...
ザワ
MURMUR
YES, NATSUME-SAN IS IMMATURE. SO WHAT ELSE IS NEW?
MURMUR
ザワ
YEAH, I KNOW, BUT I DON'T REMEMBER EVER REALLY HAVING A FIGHT.
I DON'T EVEN REALLY KNOW WHY SHE'S MAD.
MY FACE IS SO ROUND...
I MEAN, ALL WE DID WAS SAY HI, AND SHE IGNORED US.
WHY IS SHE LIKE THAT?
FIP
FIP

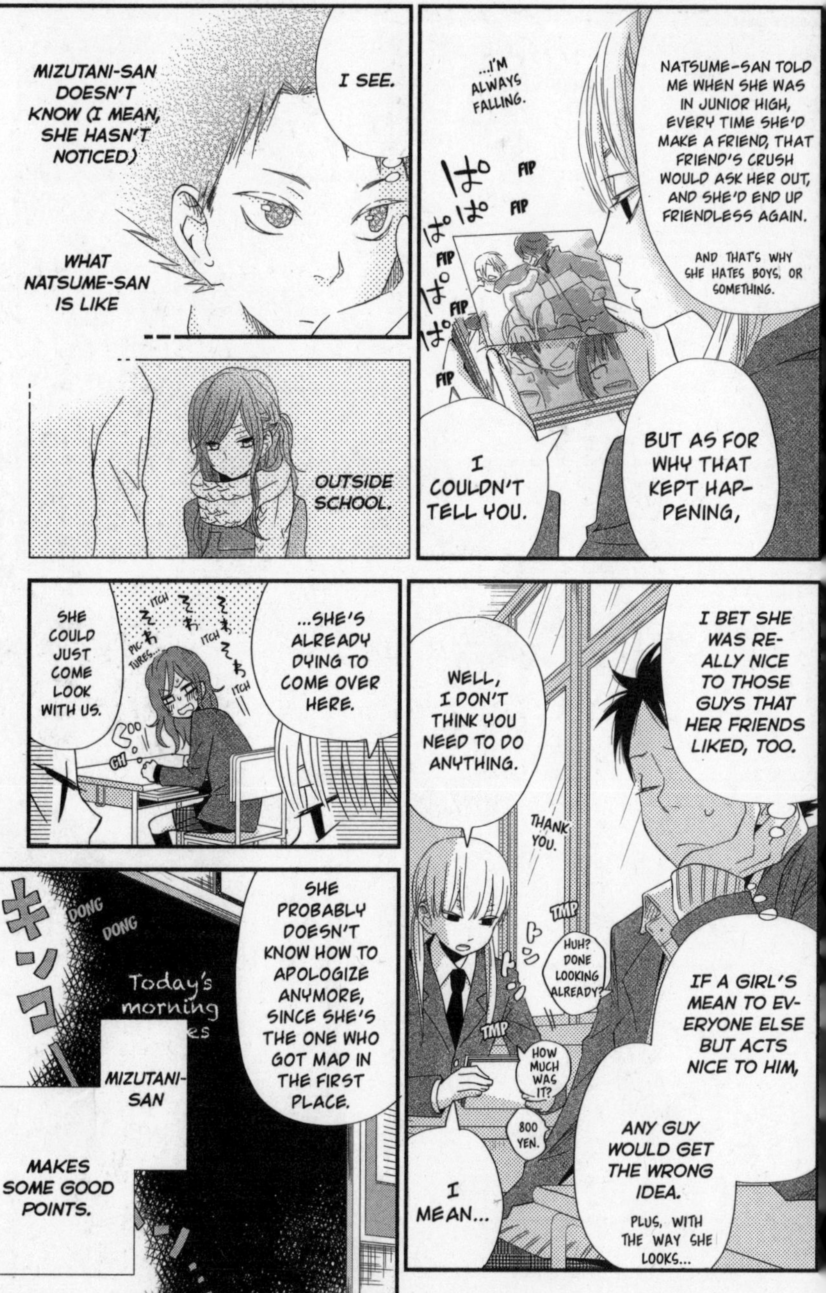
NATSUME-SAN TOLD ME WHEN SHE WAS IN JUNIOR HIGH, EVERY TIME SHE'D MAKE A FRIEND, THAT FRIEND'S CRUSH WOULD ASK HER OUT, AND SHE'D END UP FRIENDLESS AGAIN.
AND THAT'S WHY SHE HATES BOYS, OR SOMETHING.
...I'M ALWAYS FALLING.
ぱ FIP
ぱ FIP
ぱ FIP
ぱ FIP
ぱ FIP
BUT AS FOR WHY THAT KEPT HAP-PENING,
I COULDN'T TELL YOU.
I SEE.
MIZUTANI-SAN DOESN'T KNOW (I MEAN, SHE HASN'T NOTICED)
WHAT NATSUME-SAN IS LIKE
OUTSIDE SCHOOL.
I BET SHE WAS RE-ALLY NICE TO THOSE GUYS THAT HER FRIENDS LIKED, TOO.
WELL, I DON'T THINK YOU NEED TO DO ANYTHING.
THANK YOU.
IF A GIRL'S MEAN TO EV-ERYONE ELSE BUT ACTS NICE TO HIM,
ANY GUY WOULD GET THE WRONG IDEA.
PLUS, WITH THE WAY SHE LOOKS...
TMP
HUH? DONE LOOKING ALREADY?
TMP
HOW MUCH WAS IT?
800 YEN.
I MEAN...
...SHE'S ALREADY DYING TO COME OVER HERE.
SHE COULD JUST COME LOOK WITH US.
ITCH
ITCH
ITCH
ITCH
PIC-TURES...
SHE PROBABLY DOESN'T KNOW HOW TO APOLOGIZE ANYMORE, SINCE SHE'S THE ONE WHO GOT MAD IN THE FIRST PLACE.
キンコ DONG DONG
MIZUTANI-SAN
MAKES SOME GOOD POINTS.

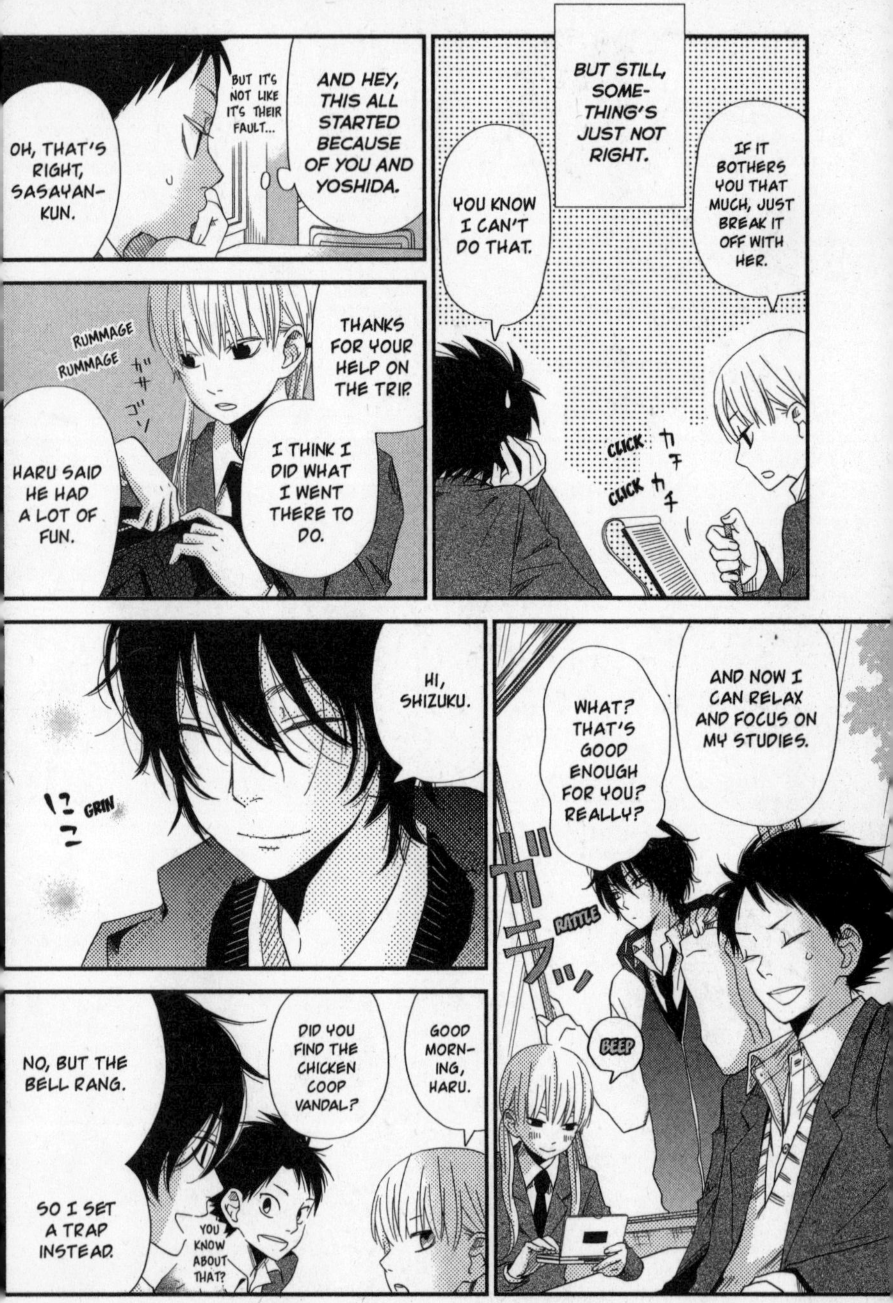
BUT STILL, SOME-THING'S JUST NOT RIGHT.
IF IT BOTHERS YOU THAT MUCH, JUST BREAK IT OFF WITH HER.
YOU KNOW I CAN'T DO THAT.
CLICK
CLICK
AND HEY, THIS ALL STARTED BECAUSE OF YOU AND YOSHIDA.
BUT IT'S NOT LIKE IT'S THEIR FAULT...
OH, THAT'S RIGHT, SASAYAN-KUN.
THANKS FOR YOUR HELP ON THE TRIP.
I THINK I DID WHAT I WENT THERE TO DO.
RUMMAGE
RUMMAGE
HARU SAID HE HAD A LOT OF FUN.
AND NOW I CAN RELAX AND FOCUS ON MY STUDIES.
WHAT? THAT'S GOOD ENOUGH FOR YOU? REALLY?
RATTLE
BEEP
HI, SHIZUKU.
GRIN
GOOD MORN-ING, HARU.
DID YOU FIND THE CHICKEN COOP VANDAL?
NO, BUT THE BELL RANG.
SO I SET A TRAP INSTEAD.
YOU KNOW ABOUT THAT?

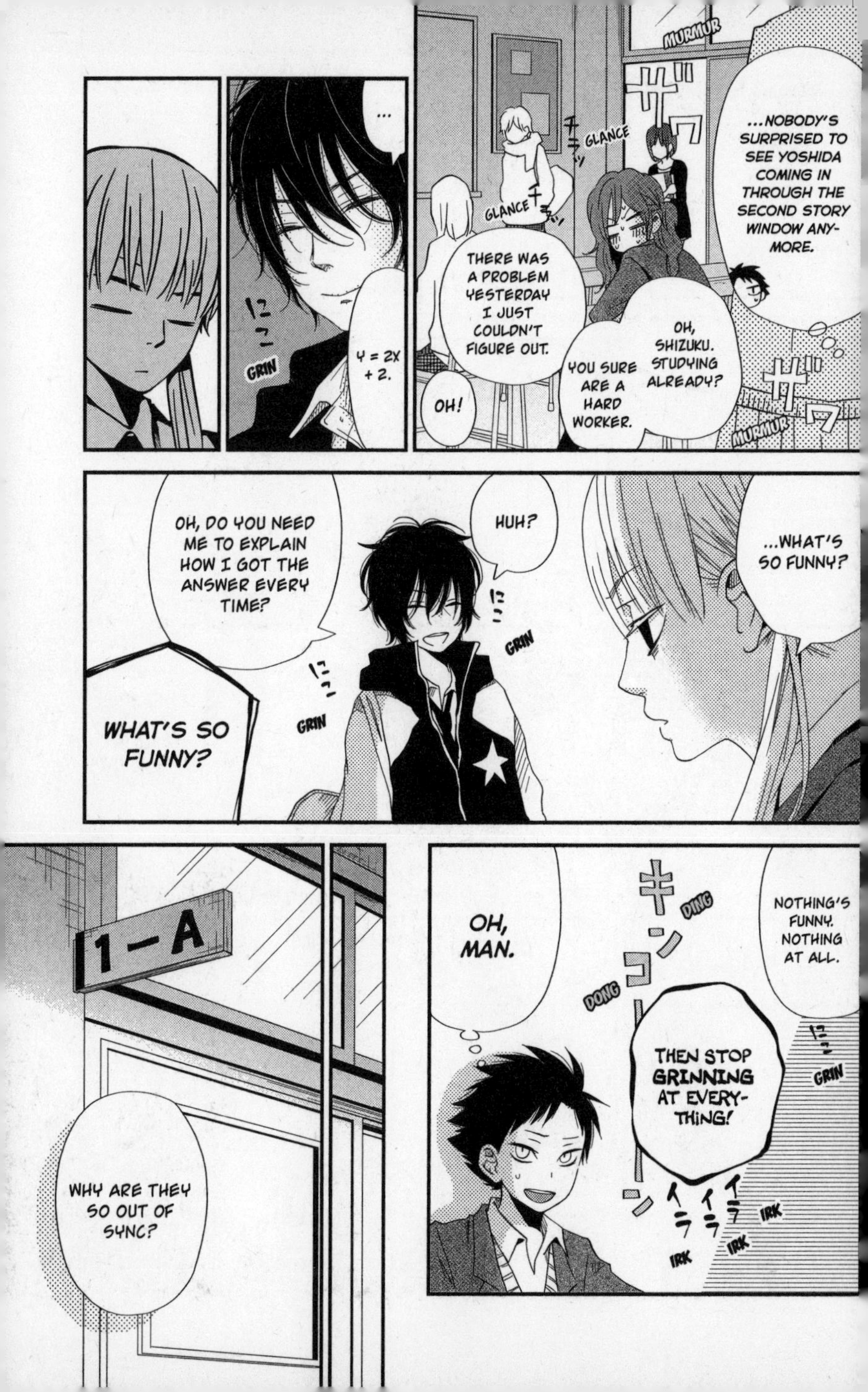
MURMUR
...NOBODY'S SURPRISED TO SEE YOSHIDA COMING IN THROUGH THE SECOND STORY WINDOW ANYMORE.
GLANCE
GLANCE
OH, SHIZUKU. STUDYING ALREADY?
YOU SURE ARE A HARD WORKER.
THERE WAS A PROBLEM YESTERDAY I JUST COULDN'T FIGURE OUT.
OH!
MURMUR
...
Y = 2X + 2.
GRIN
...WHAT'S SO FUNNY?
HUH?
GRIN
OH, DO YOU NEED ME TO EXPLAIN HOW I GOT THE ANSWER EVERY TIME?
GRIN
WHAT'S SO FUNNY?
NOTHING'S FUNNY. NOTHING AT ALL.
GRIN
DING
DONG
OH, MAN.
THEN STOP GRINNING AT EVERYTHING!
IRK
IRK
IRK
1-A
WHY ARE THEY SO OUT OF SYNC?

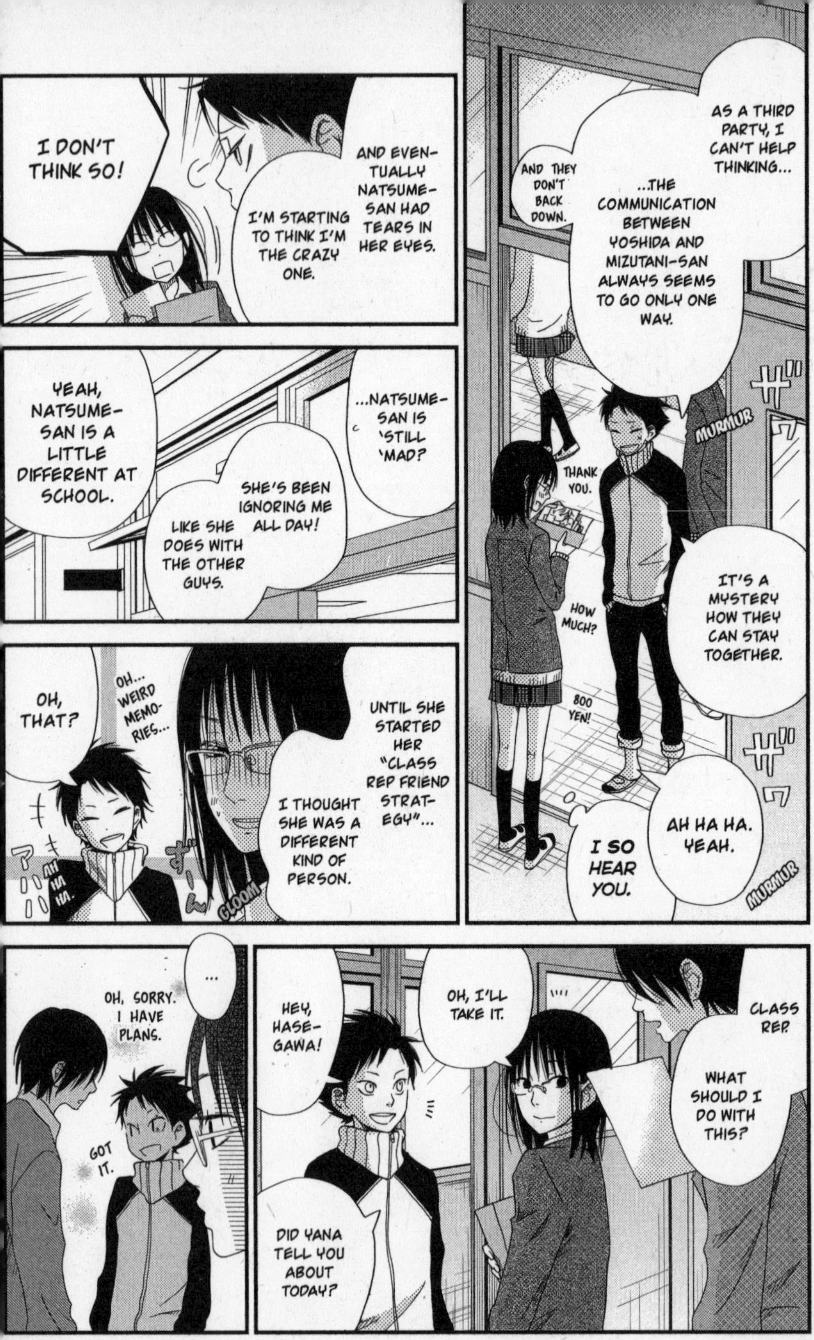
AS A THIRD PARTY, I CAN'T HELP THINKING...
...THE COMMUNICATION BETWEEN YOSHIDA AND MIZUTANI-SAN ALWAYS SEEMS TO GO ONLY ONE WAY.
AND THEY DON'T BACK DOWN.
MURMUR
THANK YOU.
IT'S A MYSTERY HOW THEY CAN STAY TOGETHER.
HOW MUCH?
800 YEN!
AH HA HA. YEAH.
I SO HEAR YOU.
MURMUR
AND EVEN-TUALLY NATSUME-SAN HAD TEARS IN HER EYES.
I'M STARTING TO THINK I'M THE CRAZY ONE.
I DON'T THINK SO!
...NATSUME-SAN IS 'STILL 'MAD?
SHE'S BEEN IGNORING ME ALL DAY!
LIKE SHE DOES WITH THE OTHER GUYS.
YEAH, NATSUME-SAN IS A LITTLE DIFFERENT AT SCHOOL.
UNTIL SHE STARTED HER "CLASS REP FRIEND STRAT-EGY"...
I THOUGHT SHE WAS A DIFFERENT KIND OF PERSON.
GLOOM
OH... WEIRD MEMO-RIES...
OH, THAT?
AH HA HA.
CLASS REP
WHAT SHOULD I DO WITH THIS?
OH, I'LL TAKE IT.
HEY, HASE-GAWA!
DID YANA TELL YOU ABOUT TODAY?
...
OH, SORRY. I HAVE PLANS.
GOT IT.

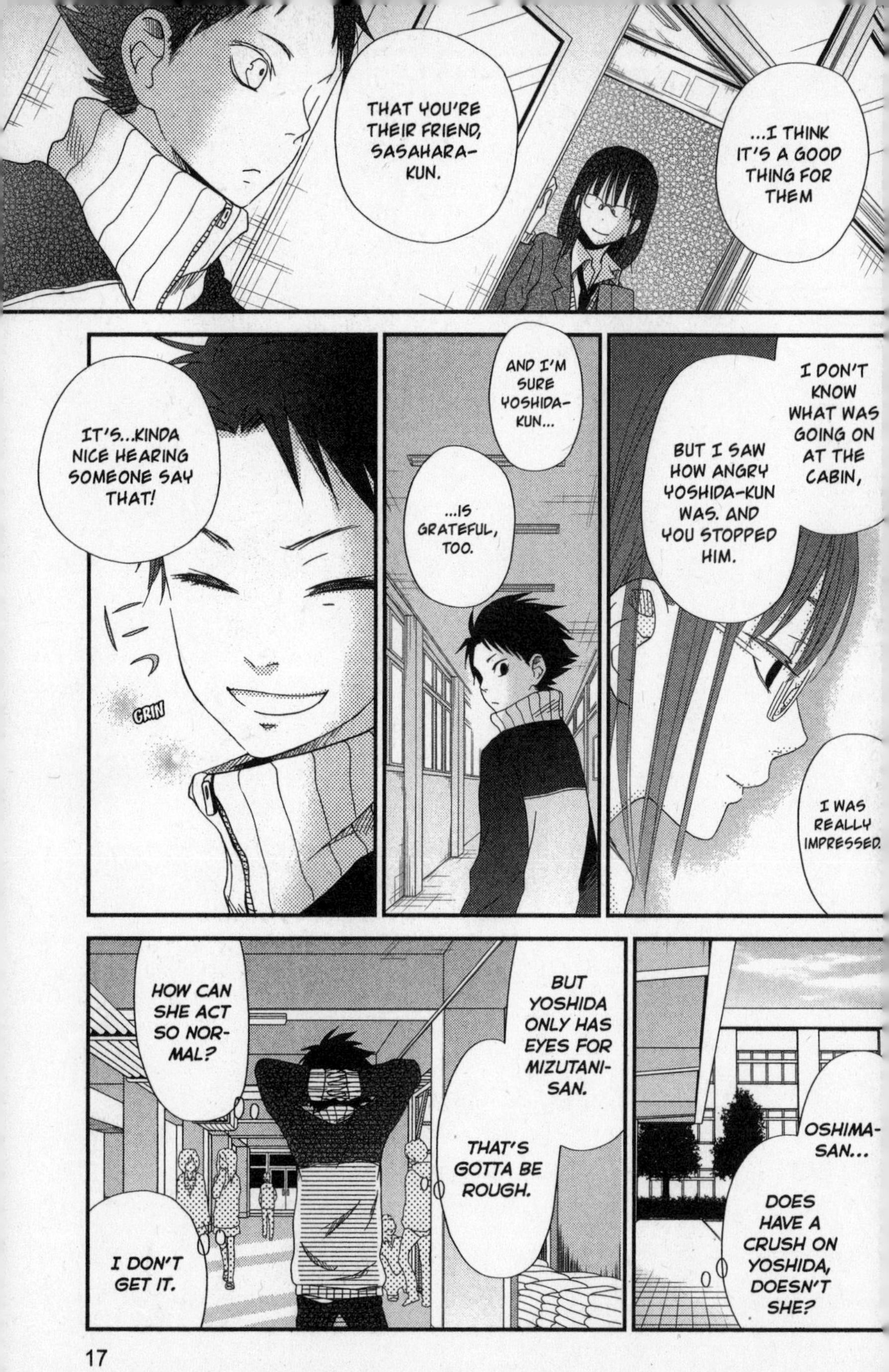
...I THINK IT'S A GOOD THING FOR THEM
THAT YOU'RE THEIR FRIEND, SASAHARA-KUN.
I DON'T KNOW WHAT WAS GOING ON AT THE CABIN,
BUT I SAW HOW ANGRY YOSHIDA-KUN WAS. AND YOU STOPPED HIM.
I WAS REALLY IMPRESSED.
AND I'M SURE YOSHIDA-KUN...
...IS GRATEFUL, TOO.
IT'S...KINDA NICE HEARING SOMEONE SAY THAT!
GRIN
OSHIMA-SAN...
DOES HAVE A CRUSH ON YOSHIDA, DOESN'T SHE?
BUT YOSHIDA ONLY HAS EYES FOR MIZUTANI-SAN.
THAT'S GOTTA BE ROUGH.
HOW CAN SHE ACT SO NOR-MAL?
I DON'T GET IT.

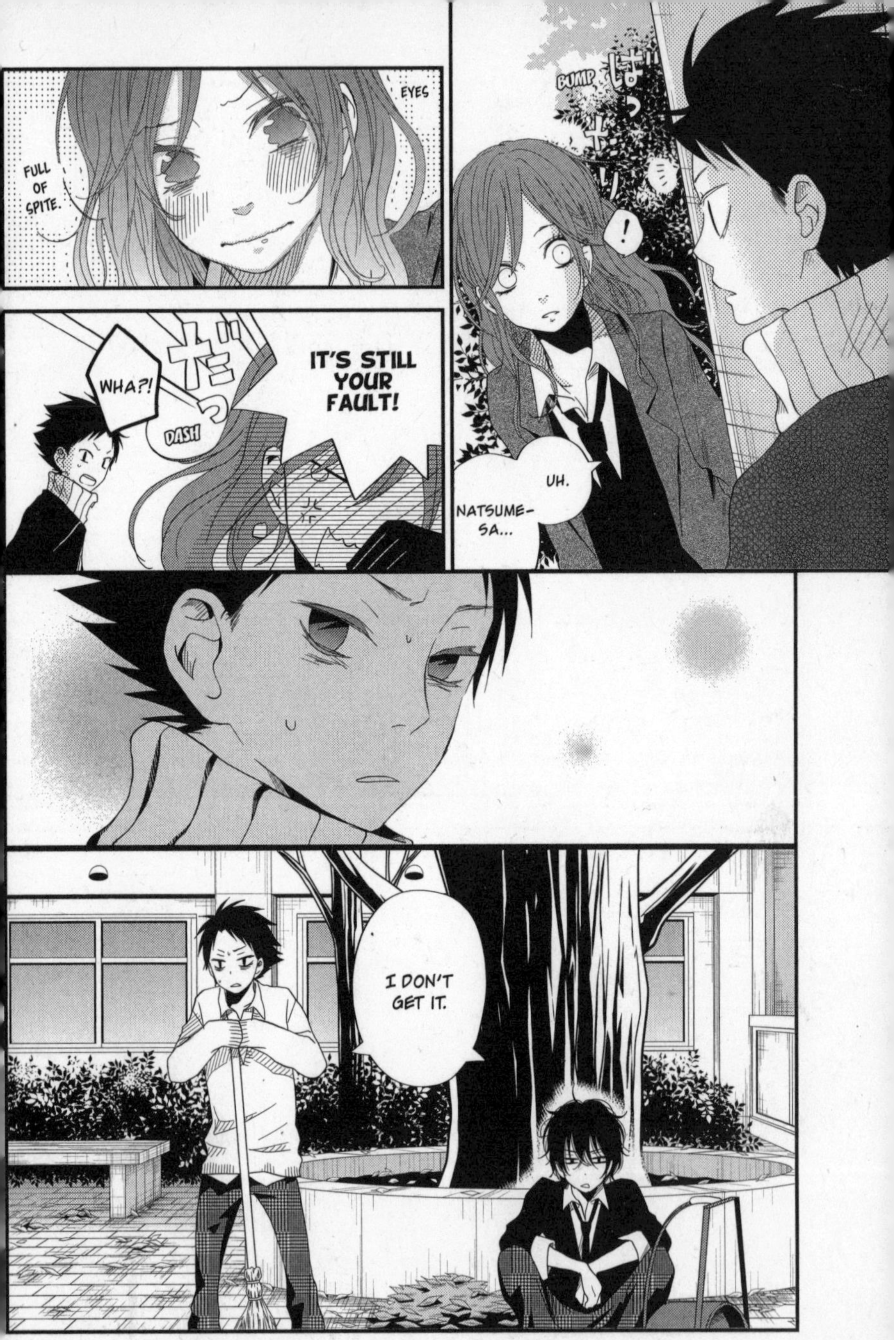
BUMP
!
UH.
NATSUME-SA...
EYES
FULL OF SPITE.
IT'S STILL YOUR FAULT!
DASH
WHA?!
I DON'T GET IT.

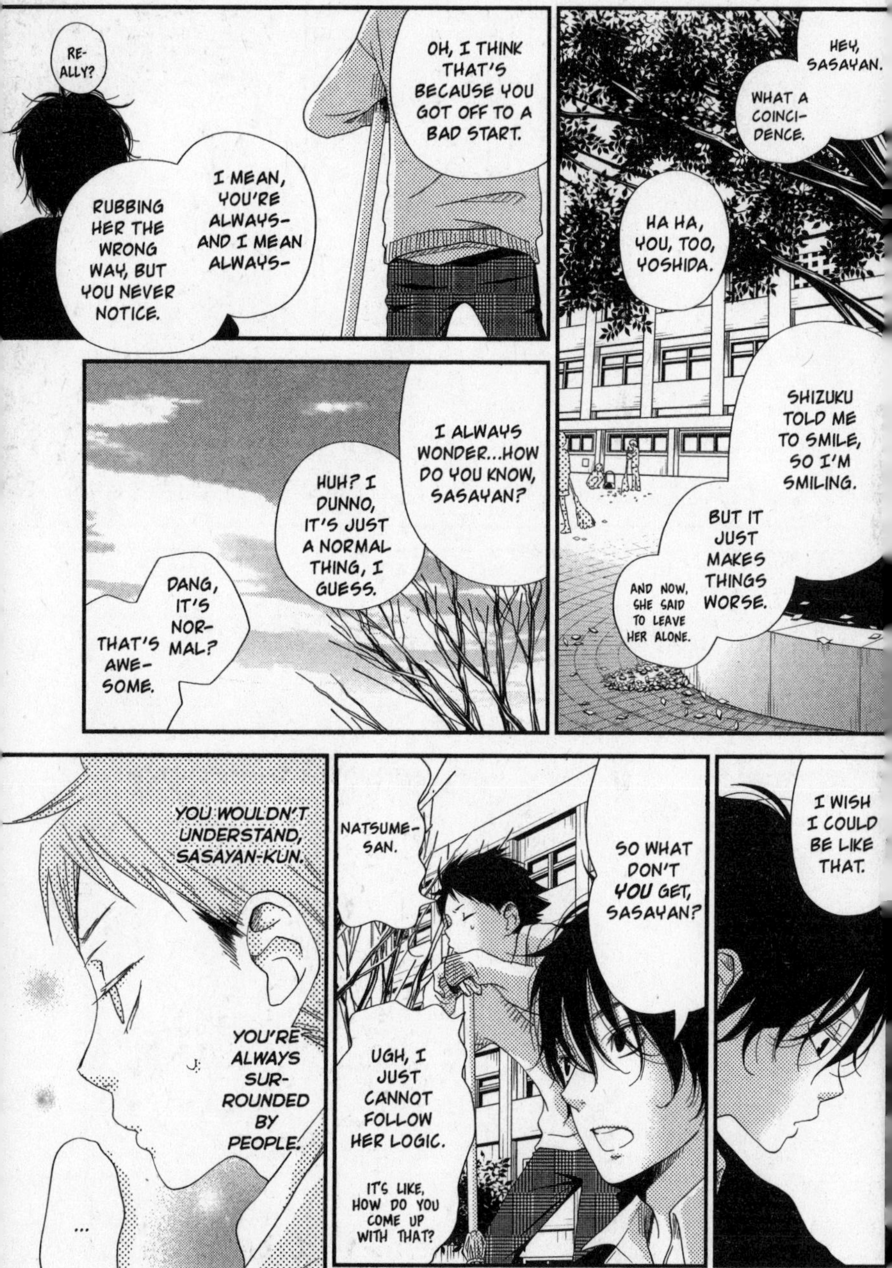
HEY, SASAYAN.
WHAT A COINCIDENCE.
HA HA, YOU, TOO, YOSHIDA.
SHIZUKU TOLD ME TO SMILE, SO I'M SMILING.
BUT IT JUST MAKES THINGS WORSE.
AND NOW, SHE SAID TO LEAVE HER ALONE.
OH, I THINK THAT'S BECAUSE YOU GOT OFF TO A BAD START.
I MEAN, YOU'RE ALWAYS-AND I MEAN ALWAYS-
RUBBING HER THE WRONG WAY, BUT YOU NEVER NOTICE.
RE-ALLY?
I ALWAYS WONDER...HOW DO YOU KNOW, SASAYAN?
HUH? I DUNNO, IT'S JUST A NORMAL THING, I GUESS.
DANG, IT'S NOR-MAL?
THAT'S AWE-SOME.
I WISH I COULD BE LIKE THAT.
SO WHAT DON'T YOU GET, SASAYAN?
NATSUME-SAN.
UGH, I JUST CANNOT FOLLOW HER LOGIC.
IT'S LIKE, HOW DO YOU COME UP WITH THAT?
YOU WOULDN'T UNDERSTAND, SASAYAN-KUN.
YOU'RE ALWAYS SUR-ROUNDED BY PEOPLE.
...

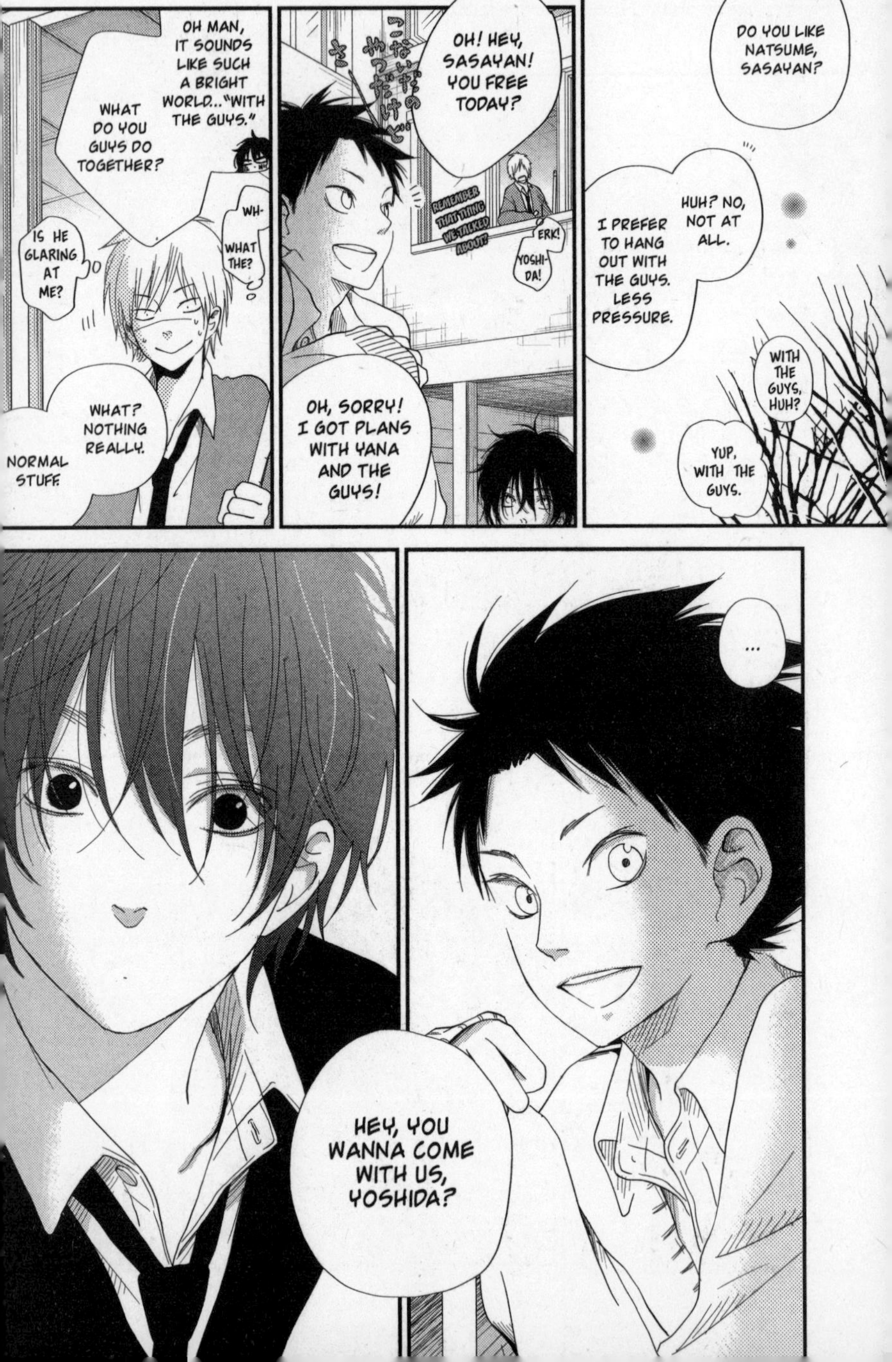
DO YOU LIKE NATSUME, SASAYAN?
HUH? NO, NOT AT ALL.
I PREFER TO HANG OUT WITH THE GUYS. LESS PRESSURE.
WITH THE GUYS, HUH?
YUP, WITH THE GUYS.
OH! HEY, SASAYAN! YOU FREE TODAY?
REMEMBER THAT THING WE TALKED ABOUT?
ERK!
YOSHI-DA!
OH, SORRY! I GOT PLANS WITH YANA AND THE GUYS!
OH MAN, IT SOUNDS LIKE SUCH A BRIGHT WORLD... "WITH THE GUYS."
WHAT DO YOU GUYS DO TOGETHER?
WH-
WHAT THE?
IS HE GLARING AT ME?
WHAT? NOTHING REALLY.
NORMAL STUFF.
...
HEY, YOU WANNA COME WITH US, YOSHIDA?

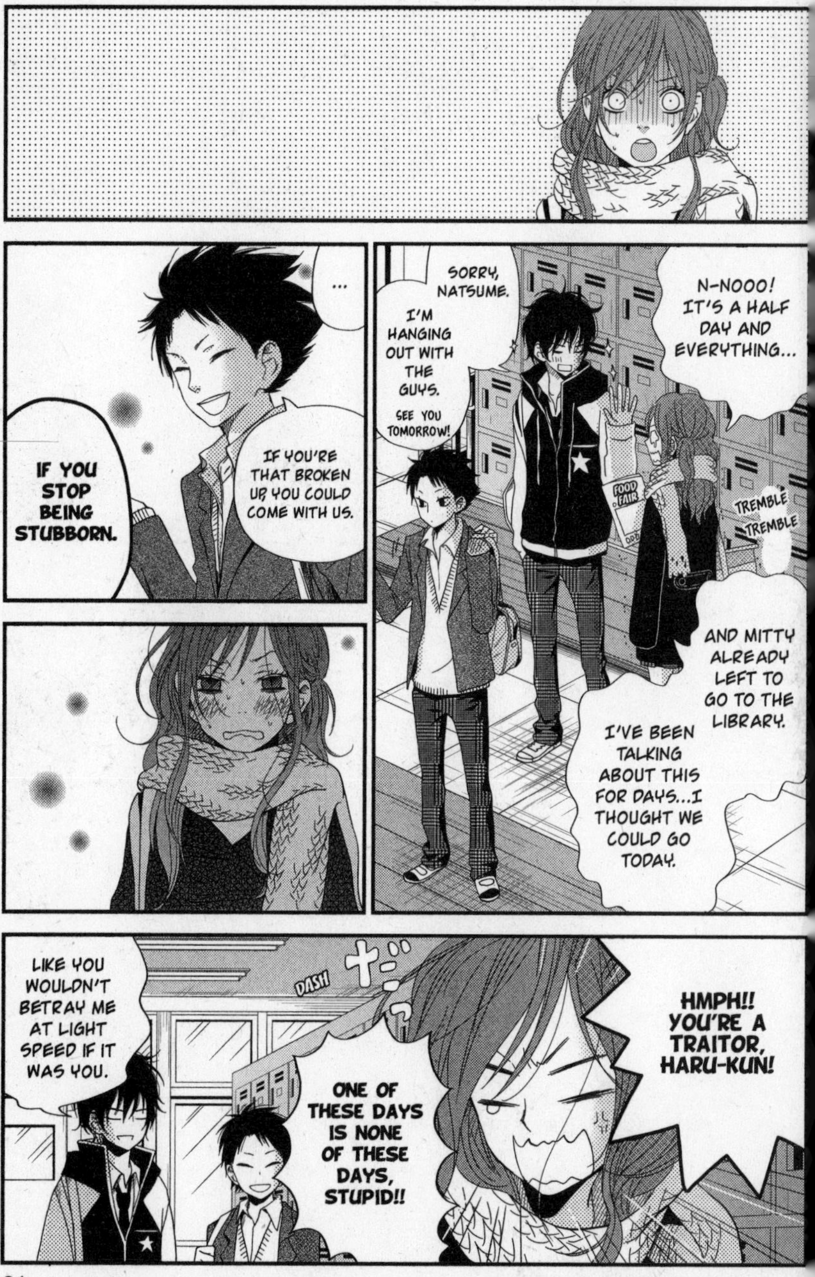
N-NOOO! IT'S A HALF DAY AND EVERYTHING...
SORRY, NATSUME.
I'M HANGING OUT WITH THE GUYS.
SEE YOU TOMORROW!
FOOD FAIR
TREMBLE TREMBLE
AND MITTY ALREADY LEFT TO GO TO THE LIBRARY.
I'VE BEEN TALKING ABOUT THIS FOR DAYS...I THOUGHT WE COULD GO TODAY.
...
IF YOU'RE THAT BROKEN UP, YOU COULD COME WITH US.
IF YOU STOP BEING STUBBORN.
HMPH!! YOU'RE A TRAITOR, HARU-KUN!
DASH
ONE OF THESE DAYS IS NONE OF THESE DAYS, STUPID!!
LIKE YOU WOULDN'T BETRAY ME AT LIGHT SPEED IF IT WAS YOU.

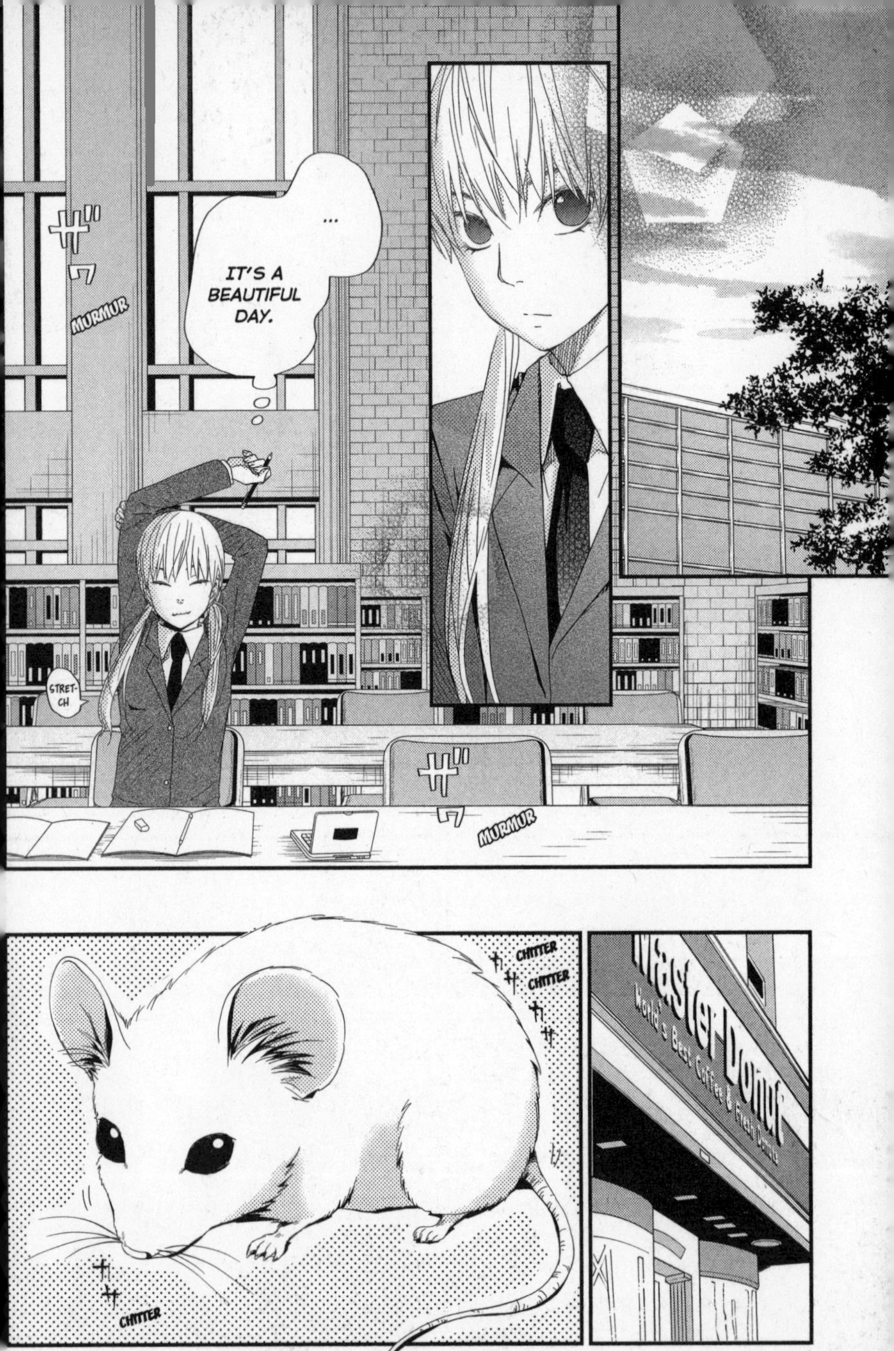
...
IT'S A BEAUTIFUL DAY.
ザワ
MURMUR
STRET-CH
ザワ
MURMUR
Master Donut
CHITTER
CHITTER
CHITTER

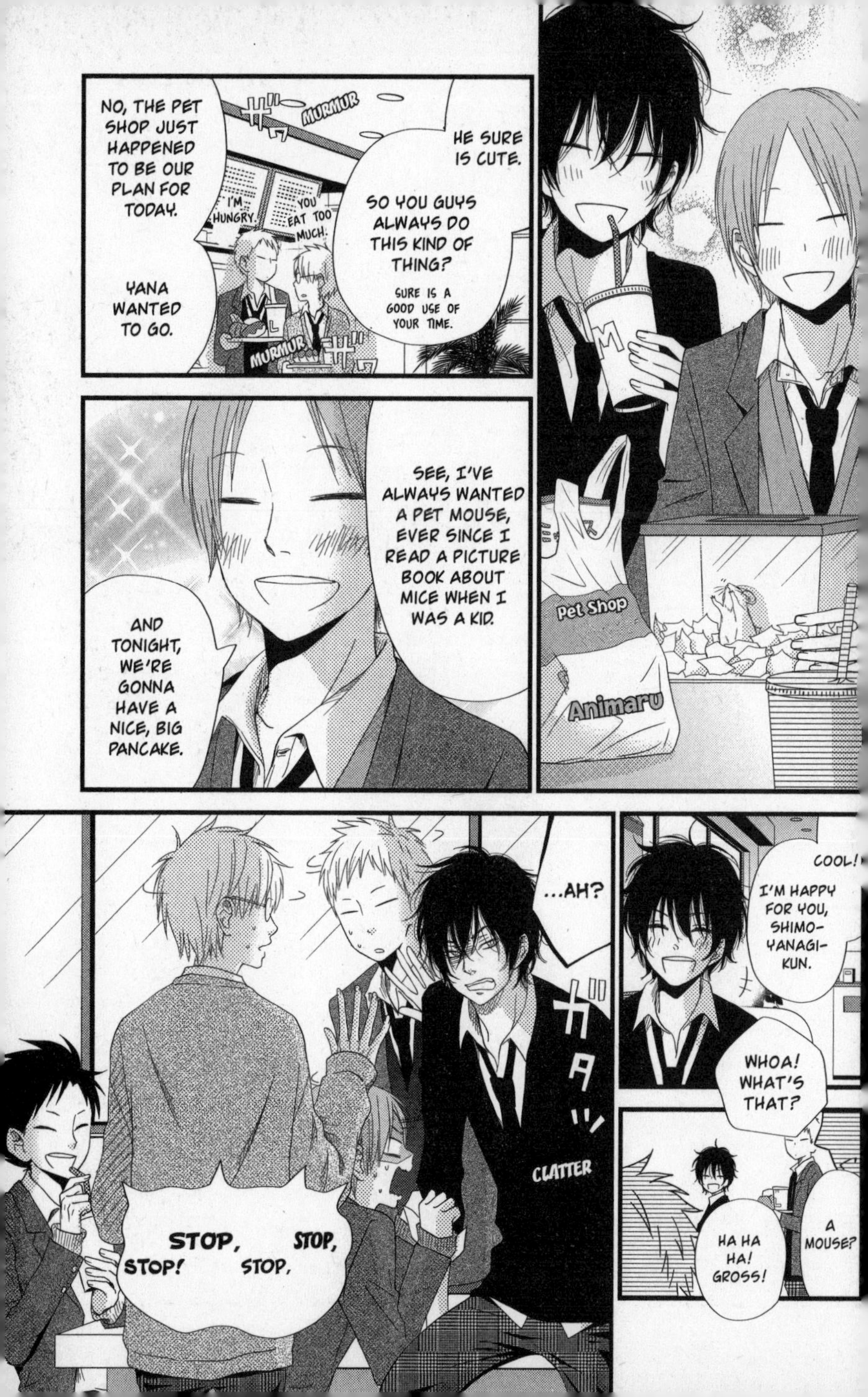
Pet Shop
Animaru
HE SURE IS CUTE.
SO YOU GUYS ALWAYS DO THIS KIND OF THING?
SURE IS A GOOD USE OF YOUR TIME.
MURMUR
YOU EAT TOO MUCH.
I'M HUNGRY.
NO, THE PET SHOP JUST HAPPENED TO BE OUR PLAN FOR TODAY.
YANA WANTED TO GO.
MURMUR
SEE, I'VE ALWAYS WANTED A PET MOUSE, EVER SINCE I READ A PICTURE BOOK ABOUT MICE WHEN I WAS A KID.
AND TONIGHT, WE'RE GONNA HAVE A NICE, BIG PANCAKE.
COOL!
I'M HAPPY FOR YOU, SHIMO-YANAGI-KUN.
WHOA! WHAT'S THAT?
A MOUSE?
HA HA HA! GROSS!
...AH?
CLATTER
STOP, STOP, STOP, STOP!

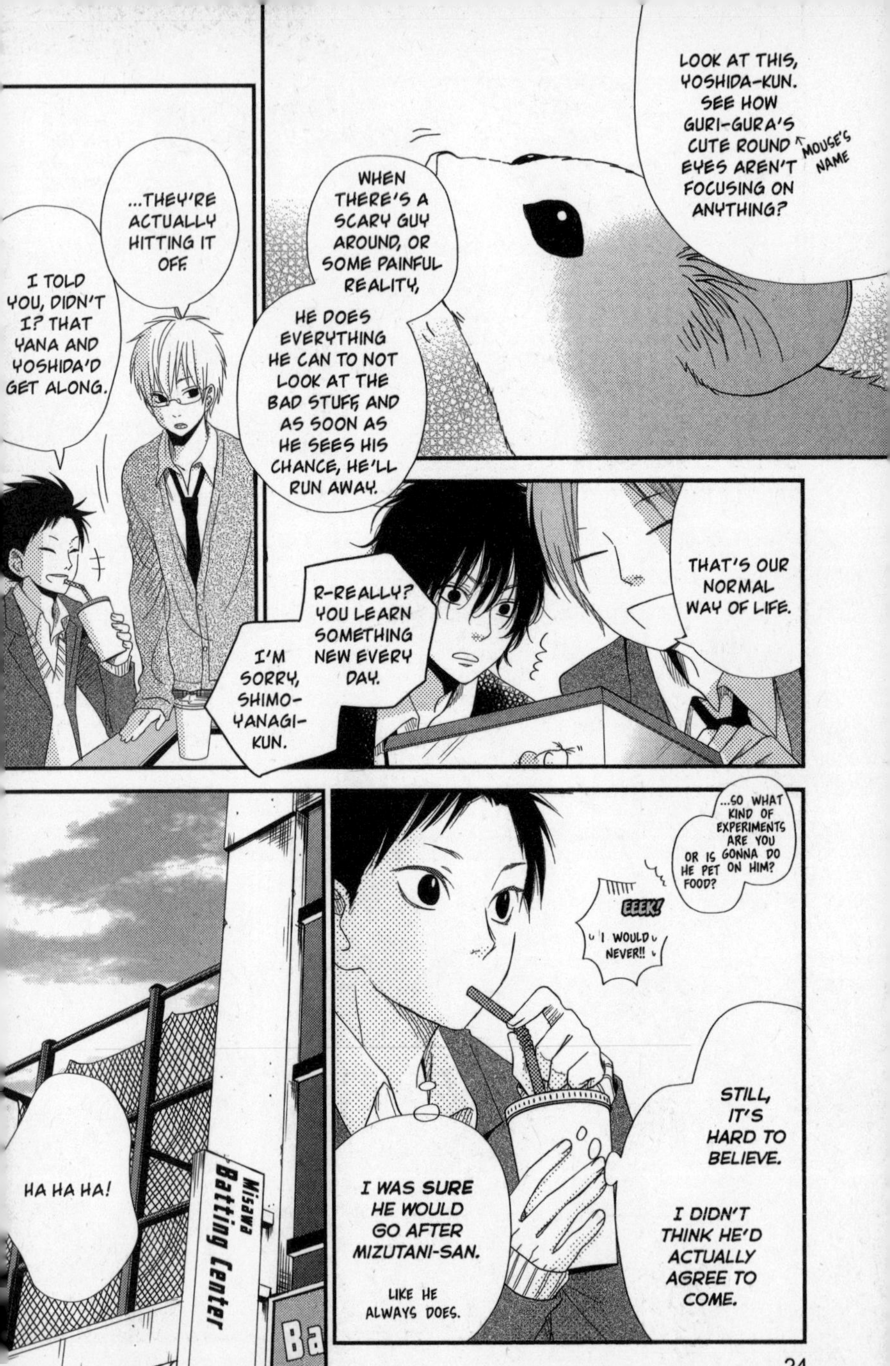
LOOK AT THIS, YOSHIDA-KUN. SEE HOW GURI-GURA'S CUTE ROUND EYES AREN'T FOCUSING ON ANYTHING?
MOUSE'S NAME
WHEN THERE'S A SCARY GUY AROUND, OR SOME PAINFUL REALITY,
HE DOES EVERYTHING HE CAN TO NOT LOOK AT THE BAD STUFF, AND AS SOON AS HE SEES HIS CHANCE, HE'LL RUN AWAY.
THAT'S OUR NORMAL WAY OF LIFE.
R-REALLY? YOU LEARN SOMETHING NEW EVERY DAY.
I'M SORRY, SHIMO-YANAGI-KUN.
...THEY'RE ACTUALLY HITTING IT OFF.
I TOLD YOU, DIDN'T I? THAT YANA AND YOSHIDA'D GET ALONG.
...SO WHAT KIND OF EXPERIMENTS ARE YOU GONNA DO ON HIM? OR IS HE PET FOOD?
EEEK!
I WOULD NEVER!!
STILL, IT'S HARD TO BELIEVE.
I DIDN'T THINK HE'D ACTUALLY AGREE TO COME.
I WAS SURE HE WOULD GO AFTER MIZUTANI-SAN.
LIKE HE ALWAYS DOES.
HA HA HA!
Misawa Batting Center
Ba

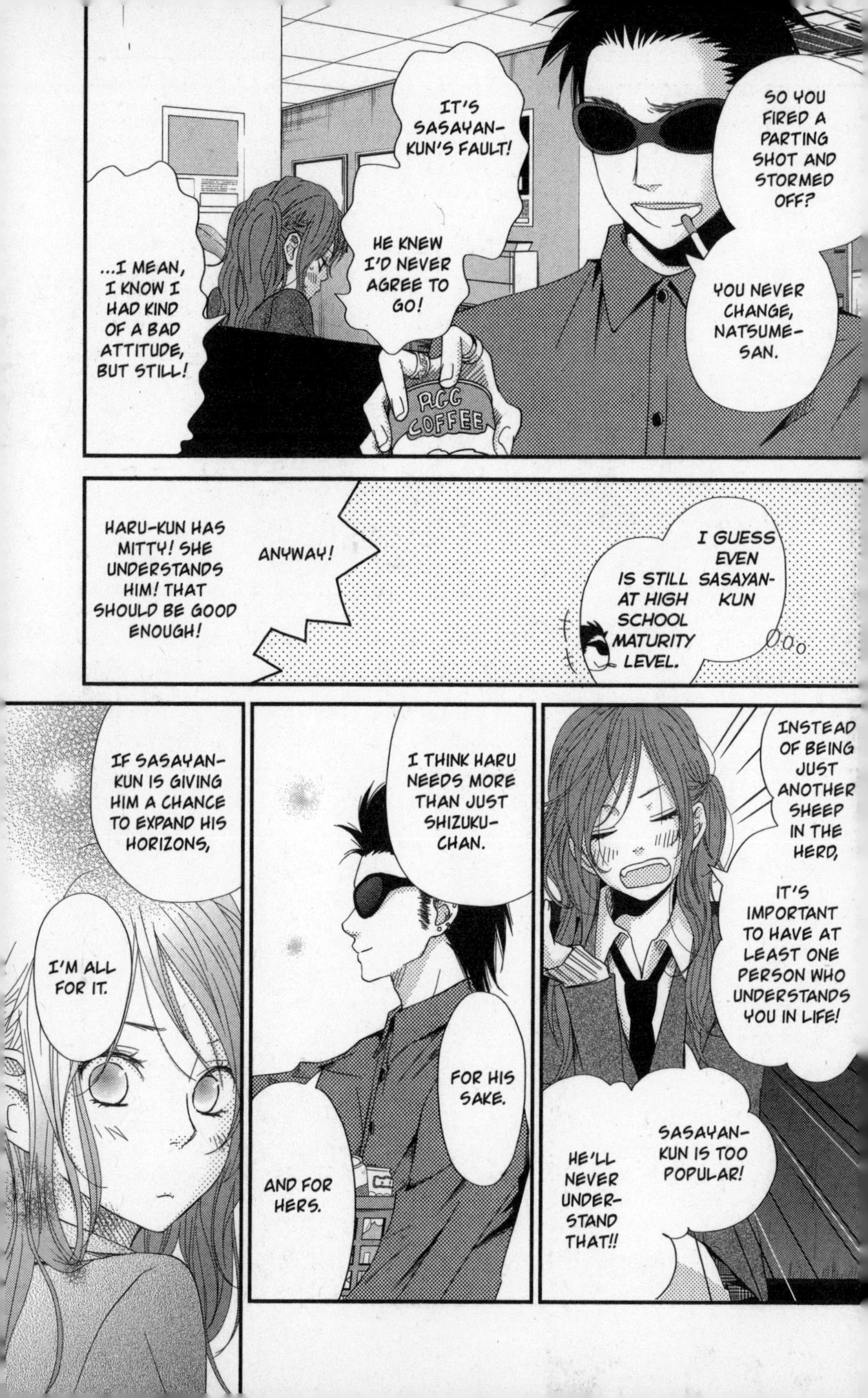
SO YOU FIRED A PARTING SHOT AND STORMED OFF?
YOU NEVER CHANGE, NATSUME-SAN.
IT'S SASAYAN-KUN'S FAULT!
HE KNEW I'D NEVER AGREE TO GO!
...I MEAN, I KNOW I HAD KIND OF A BAD ATTITUDE, BUT STILL!
RGG COFFEE
I GUESS EVEN SASAYAN-KUN IS STILL AT HIGH SCHOOL MATURITY LEVEL.
ANYWAY!
HARU-KUN HAS MITTY! SHE UNDERSTANDS HIM! THAT SHOULD BE GOOD ENOUGH!
INSTEAD OF BEING JUST ANOTHER SHEEP IN THE HERD,
IT'S IMPORTANT TO HAVE AT LEAST ONE PERSON WHO UNDERSTANDS YOU IN LIFE!
SASAYAN-KUN IS TOO POPULAR!
HE'LL NEVER UNDERSTAND THAT!!
I THINK HARU NEEDS MORE THAN JUST SHIZUKU-CHAN.
FOR HIS SAKE.
AND FOR HERS.
IF SASAYAN-KUN IS GIVING HIM A CHANCE TO EXPAND HIS HORIZONS,
I'M ALL FOR IT.

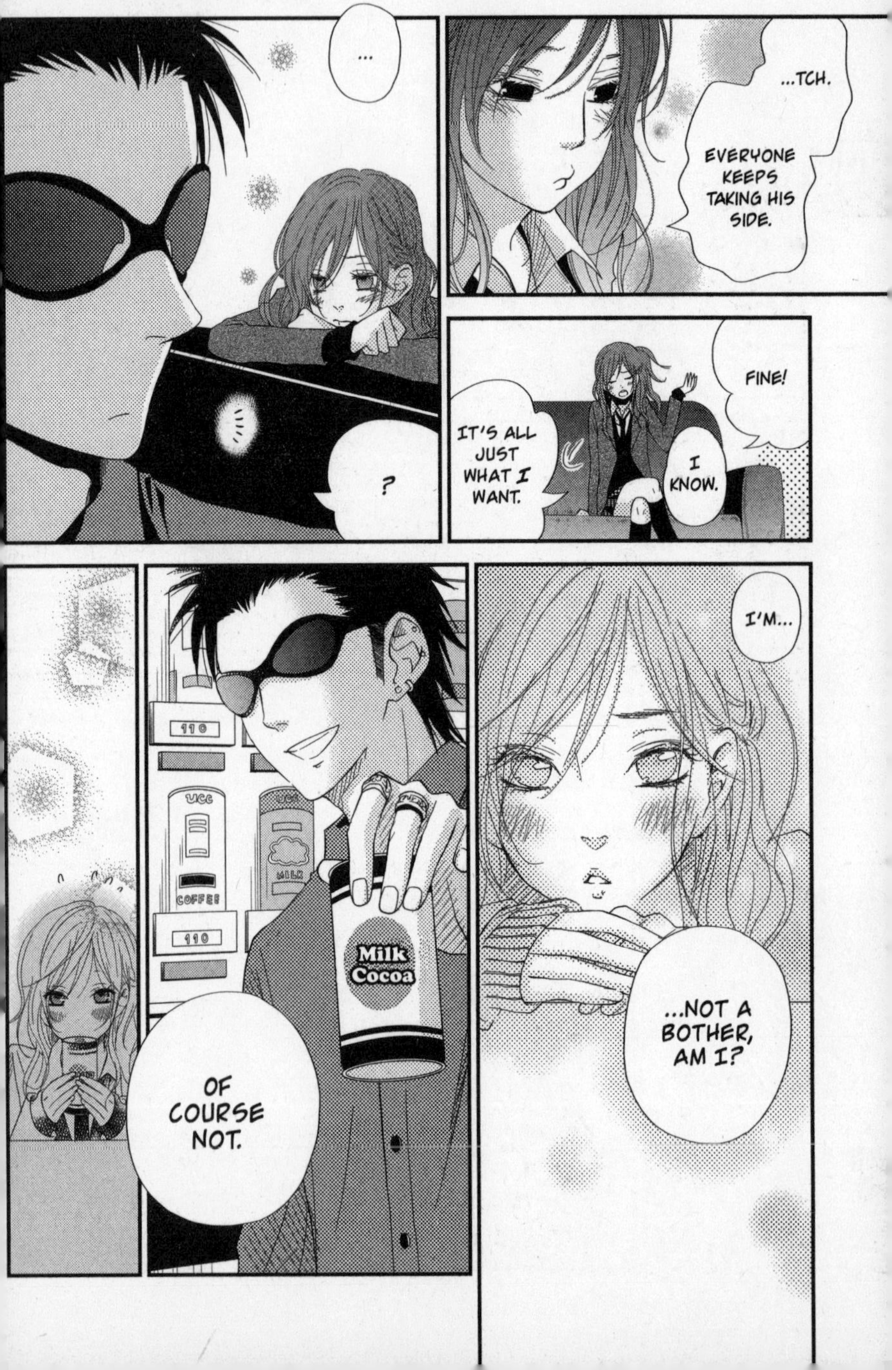
...TCH.
EVERYONE KEEPS TAKING HIS SIDE.
FINE!
I KNOW.
IT'S ALL JUST WHAT I WANT.
...
?
I'M...
...NOT A BOTHER, AM I?
110
UCC
COFFEE
MILK
110
Milk Cocoa
OF COURSE NOT.

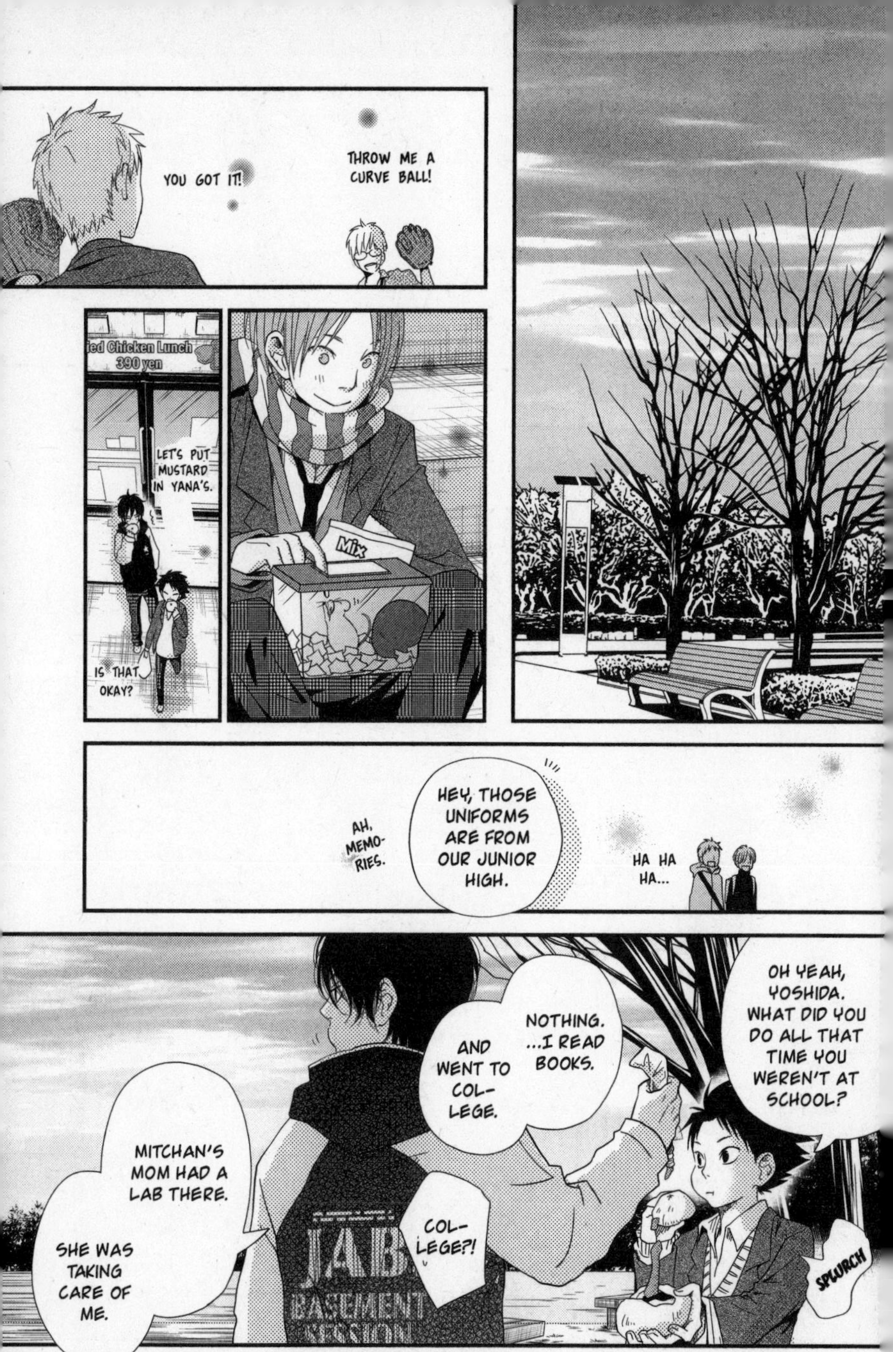
THROW ME A CURVE BALL!
YOU GOT IT!
Mix
Chicken Lunch
390 yen
LET'S PUT MUSTARD IN YANA'S.
IS THAT OKAY?
HA HA HA...
HEY, THOSE UNIFORMS ARE FROM OUR JUNIOR HIGH.
AH, MEMORIES.
OH YEAH, YOSHIDA. WHAT DID YOU DO ALL THAT TIME YOU WEREN'T AT SCHOOL?
SPLURCH
NOTHING. ...I READ BOOKS.
AND WENT TO COL-LEGE.
COL-LEGE?!
MITCHAN'S MOM HAD A LAB THERE.
SHE WAS TAKING CARE OF ME.

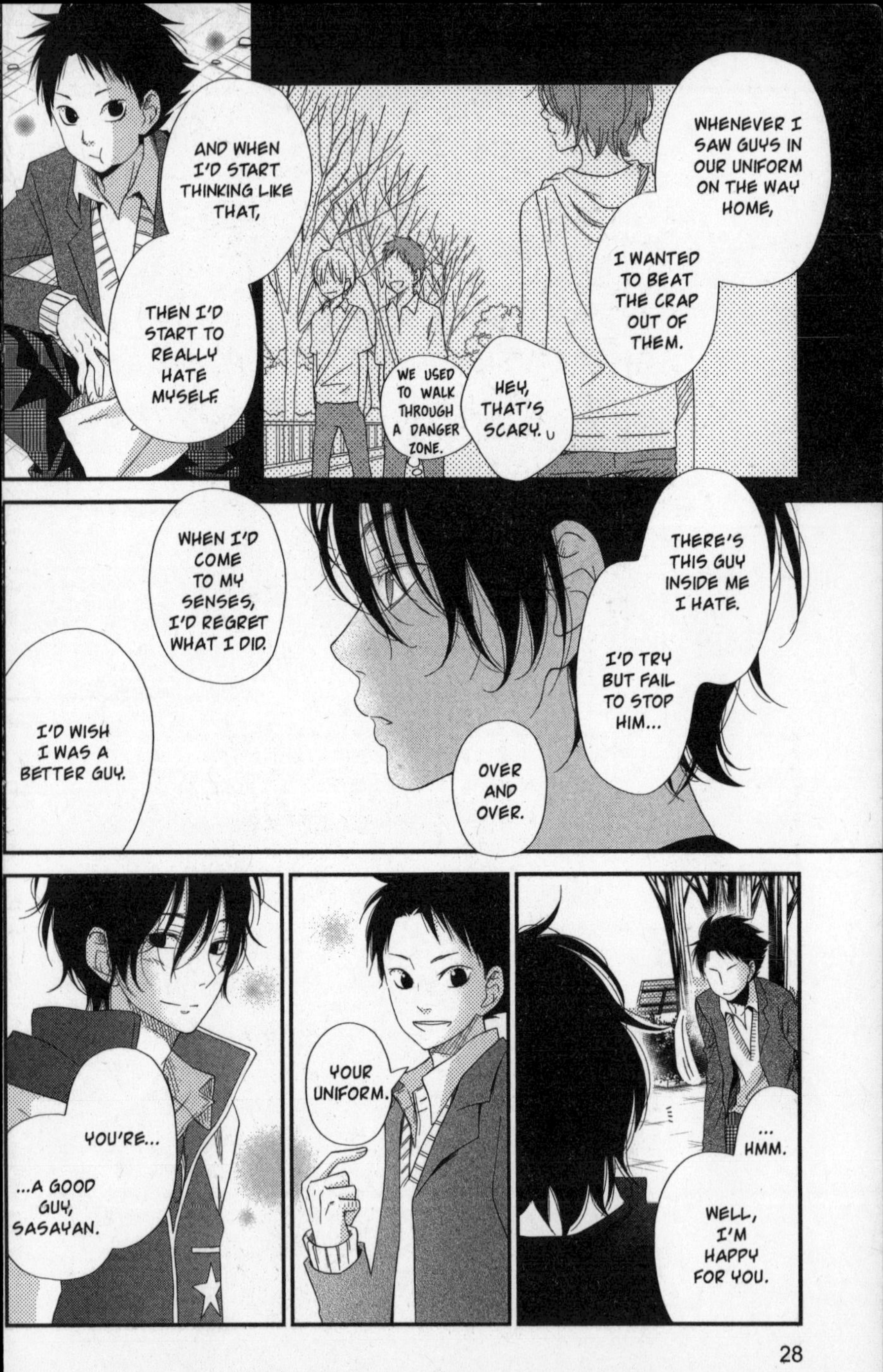
WHENEVER I SAW GUYS IN OUR UNIFORM ON THE WAY HOME,
I WANTED TO BEAT THE CRAP OUT OF THEM.
HEY, THAT'S SCARY.
WE USED TO WALK THROUGH A DANGER ZONE.
AND WHEN I'D START THINKING LIKE THAT,
THEN I'D START TO REALLY HATE MYSELF.
THERE'S THIS GUY INSIDE ME I HATE.
I'D TRY BUT FAIL TO STOP HIM...
OVER AND OVER.
WHEN I'D COME TO MY SENSES, I'D REGRET WHAT I DID.
I'D WISH I WAS A BETTER GUY.
... HMM.
WELL, I'M HAPPY FOR YOU.
YOUR UNIFORM.
YOU'RE...
...A GOOD GUY, SASAYAN.

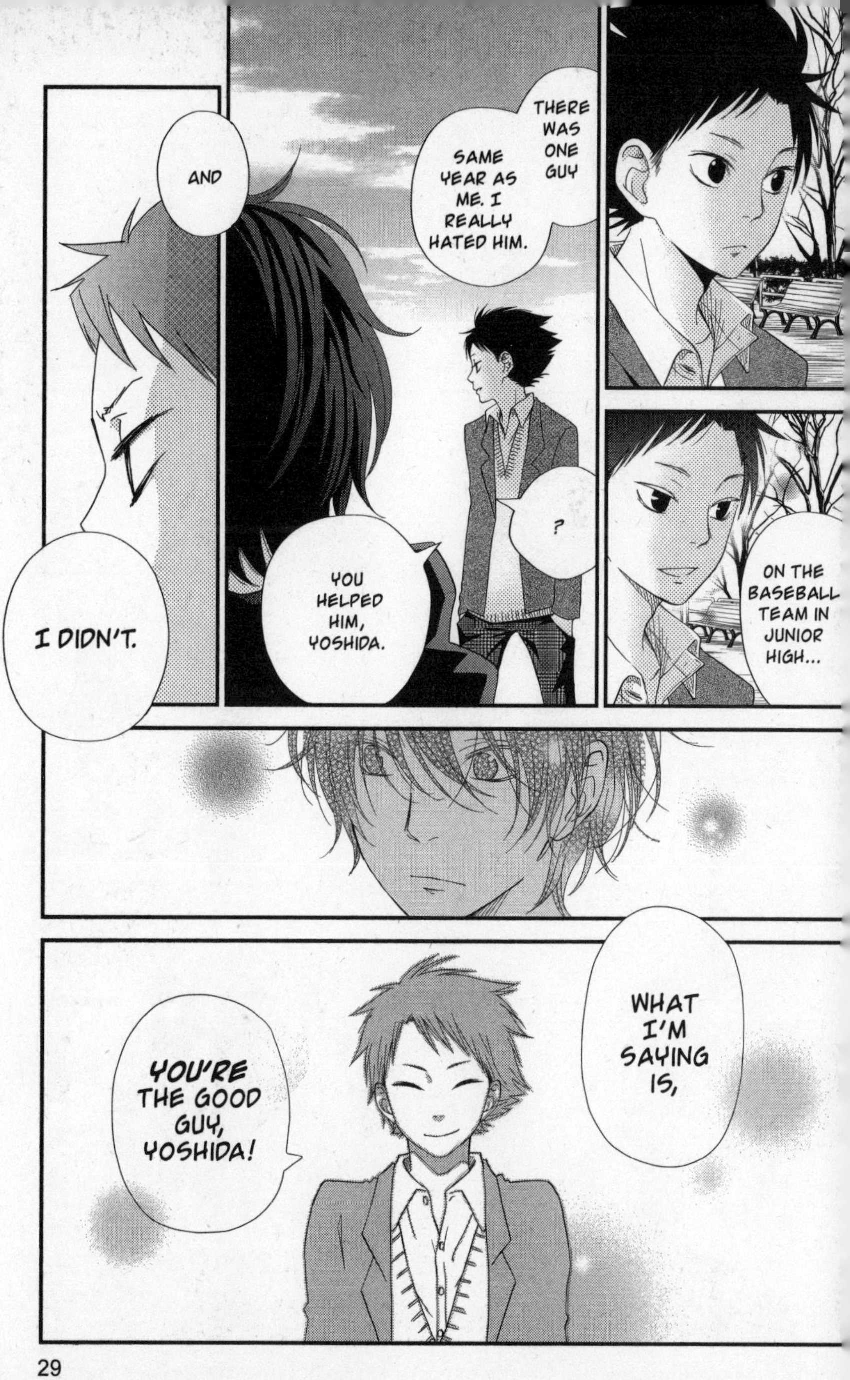
ON THE BASEBALL TEAM IN JUNIOR HIGH...
THERE WAS ONE GUY
SAME YEAR AS ME. I REALLY HATED HIM.
?
YOU HELPED HIM, YOSHIDA.
AND
I DIDN'T.
WHAT I'M SAYING IS,
YOU'RE THE GOOD GUY, YOSHIDA!

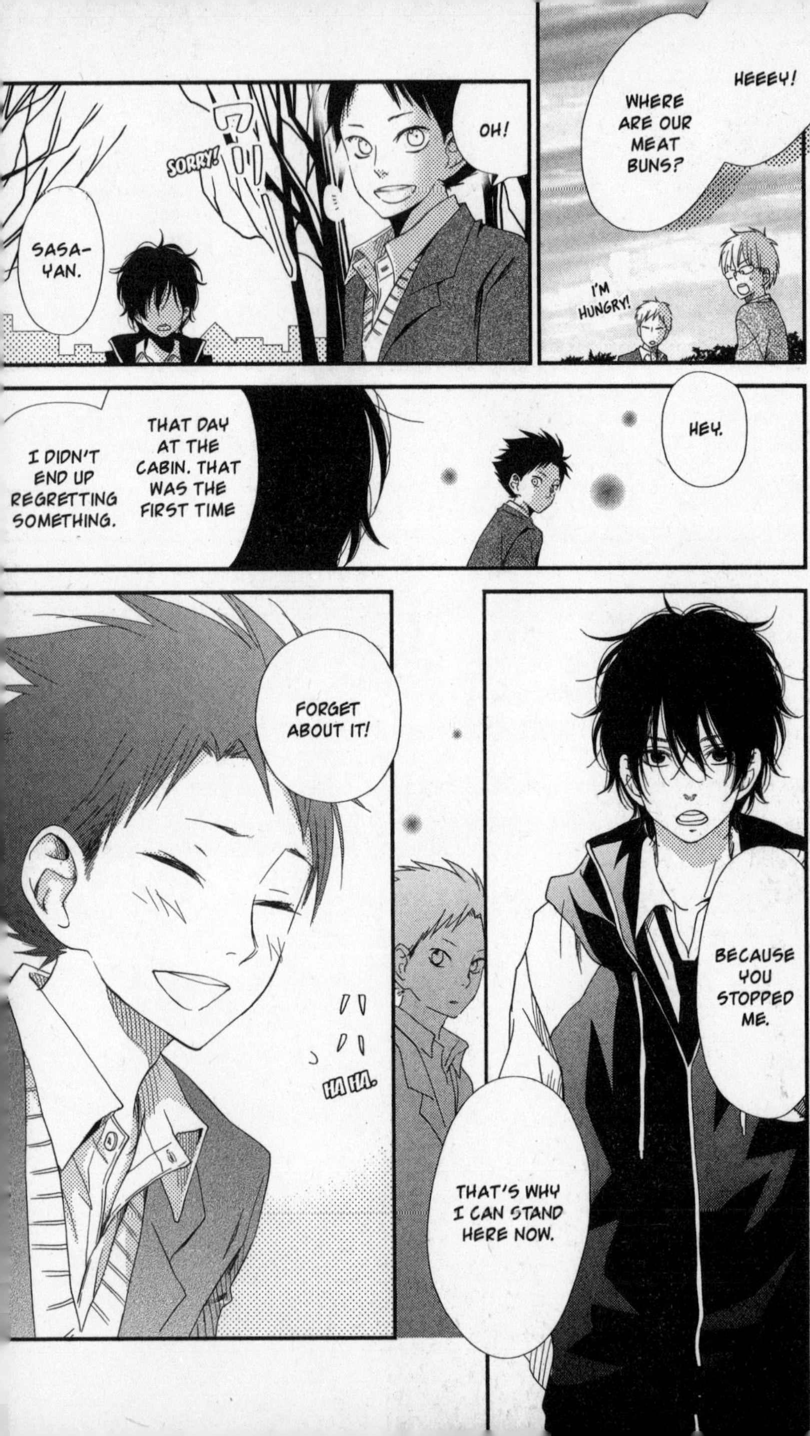
HEEEY!
WHERE ARE OUR MEAT BUNS?
I'M HUNGRY!
OH!
SORRY!
SASA-YAN.
HEY.
THAT DAY AT THE CABIN. THAT WAS THE FIRST TIME
I DIDN'T END UP REGRETTING SOMETHING.
BECAUSE YOU STOPPED ME.
THAT'S WHY I CAN STAND HERE NOW.
FORGET ABOUT IT!
HA HA.

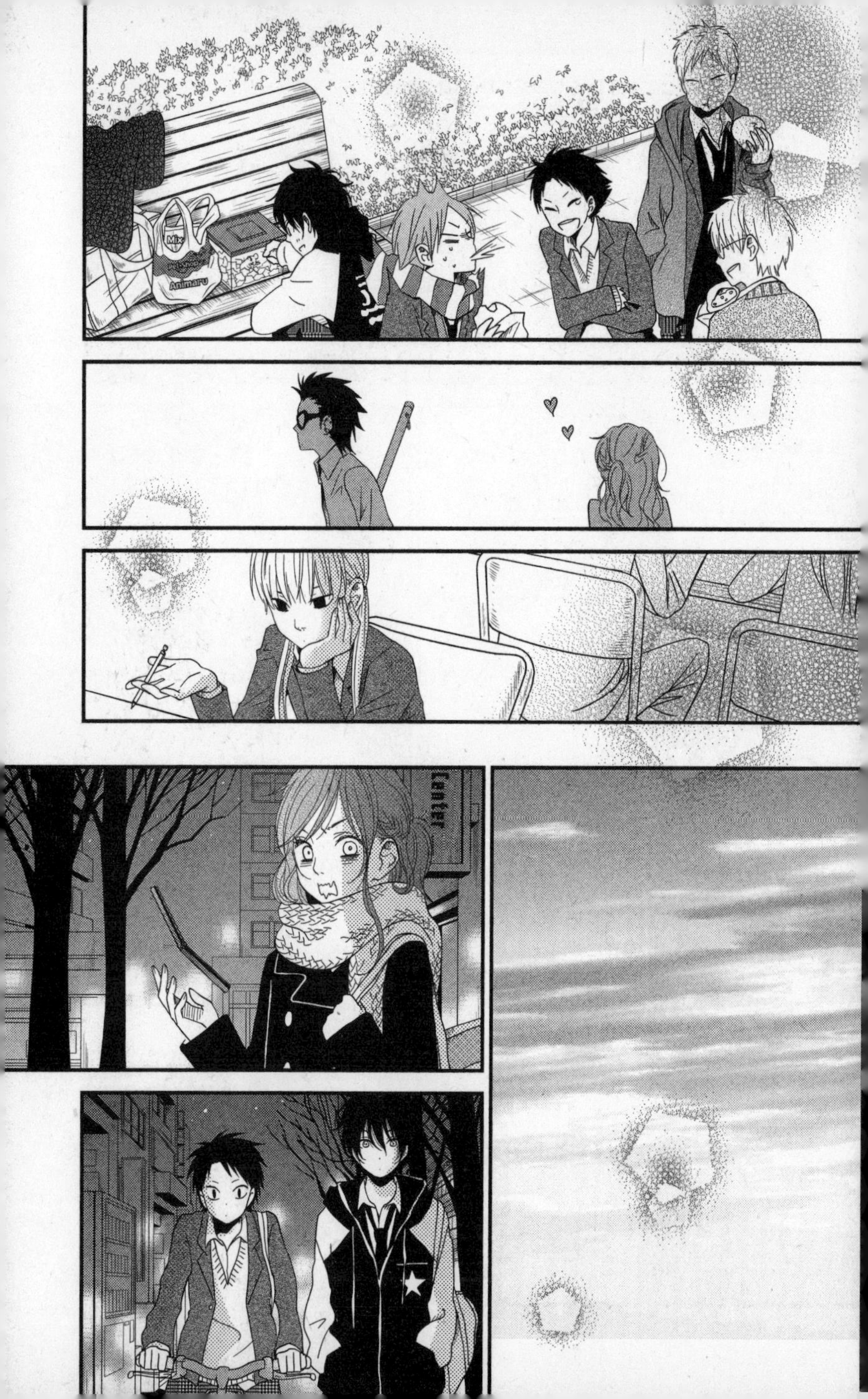
Animaru
Center

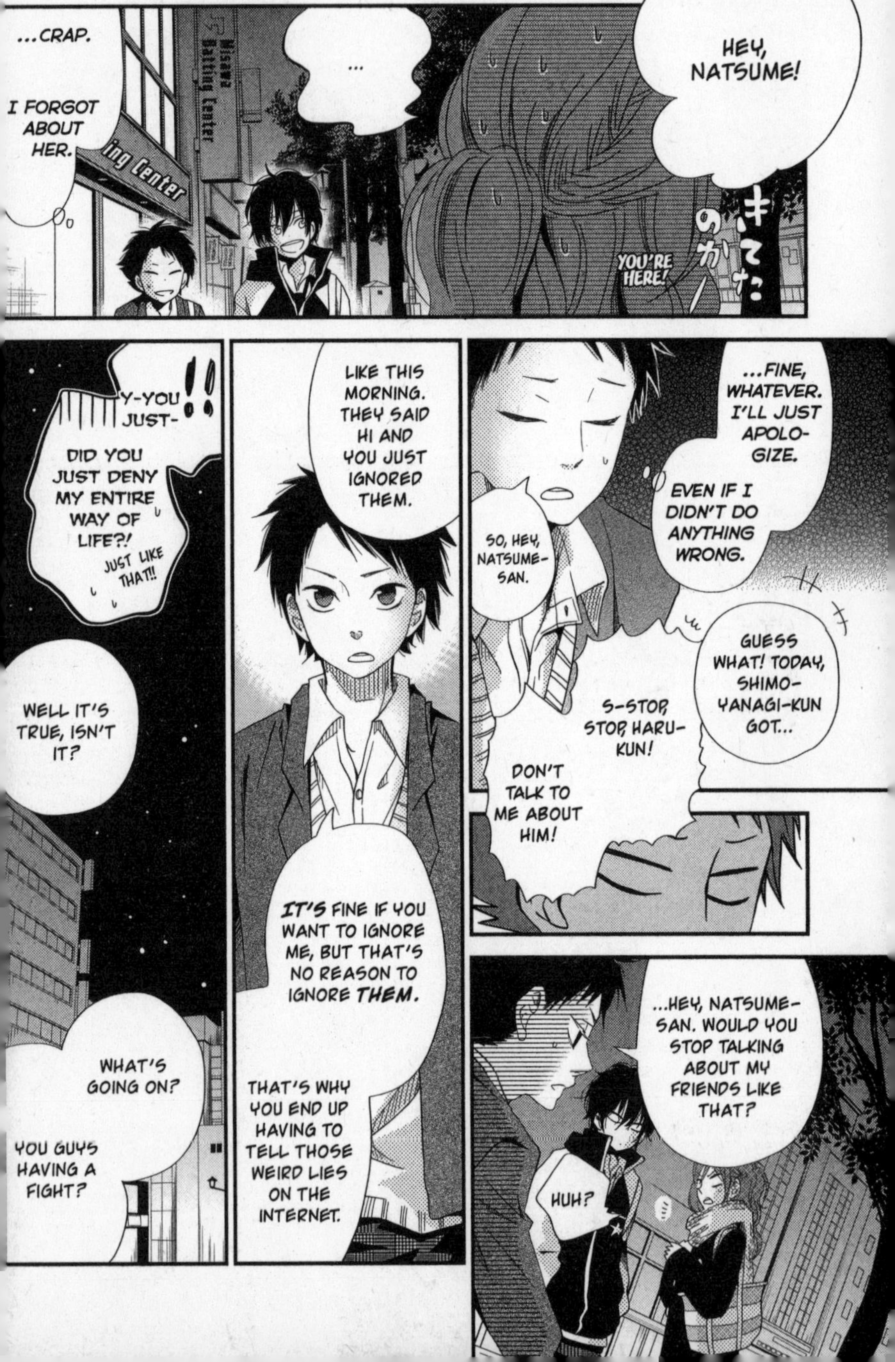
HEY, NATSUME!
YOU'RE HERE!
キてたのか
...
Misawa Batting Center
ing Center
...CRAP.
I FORGOT ABOUT HER.
...FINE, WHATEVER. I'LL JUST APOLOGIZE.
EVEN IF I DIDN'T DO ANYTHING WRONG.
SO, HEY, NATSUME-SAN.
GUESS WHAT! TODAY, SHIMO-YANAGI-KUN GOT...
S-STOP, STOP, HARU-KUN!
DON'T TALK TO ME ABOUT HIM!
...HEY, NATSUME-SAN. WOULD YOU STOP TALKING ABOUT MY FRIENDS LIKE THAT?
HUH?
...
LIKE THIS MORNING. THEY SAID HI AND YOU JUST IGNORED THEM.
IT'S FINE IF YOU WANT TO IGNORE ME, BUT THAT'S NO REASON TO IGNORE THEM.
THAT'S WHY YOU END UP HAVING TO TELL THOSE WEIRD LIES ON THE INTERNET.
Y-YOU JUST-!!
DID YOU JUST DENY MY ENTIRE WAY OF LIFE?!
JUST LIKE THAT!!
WELL IT'S TRUE, ISN'T IT?
WHAT'S GOING ON?
YOU GUYS HAVING A FIGHT?

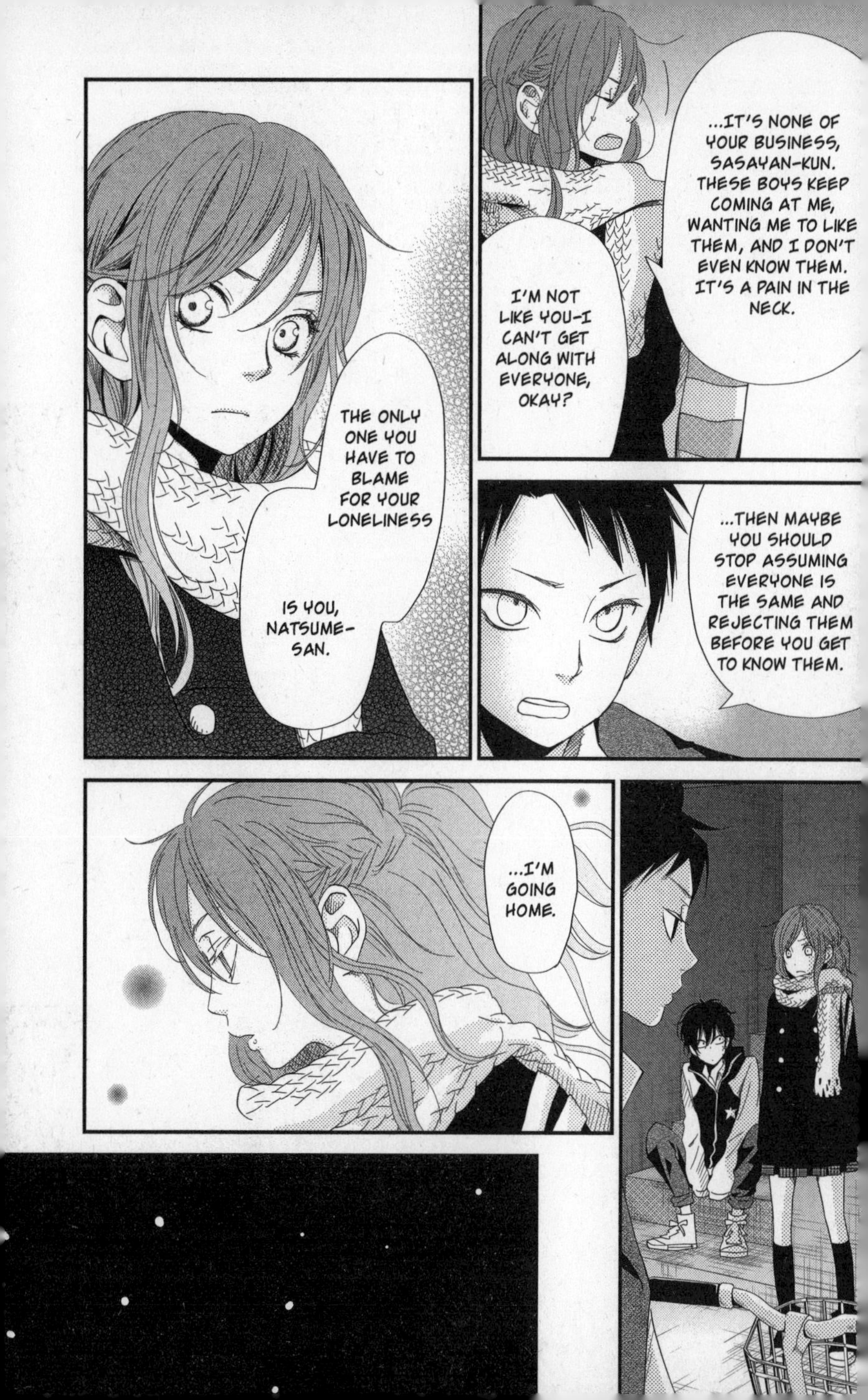
...IT'S NONE OF YOUR BUSINESS, SASAYAN-KUN. THESE BOYS KEEP COMING AT ME, WANTING ME TO LIKE THEM, AND I DON'T EVEN KNOW THEM. IT'S A PAIN IN THE NECK.
I'M NOT LIKE YOU–I CAN'T GET ALONG WITH EVERYONE, OKAY?
...THEN MAYBE YOU SHOULD STOP ASSUMING EVERYONE IS THE SAME AND REJECTING THEM BEFORE YOU GET TO KNOW THEM.
THE ONLY ONE YOU HAVE TO BLAME FOR YOUR LONELINESS
IS YOU, NATSUME-SAN.
...I'M GOING HOME.

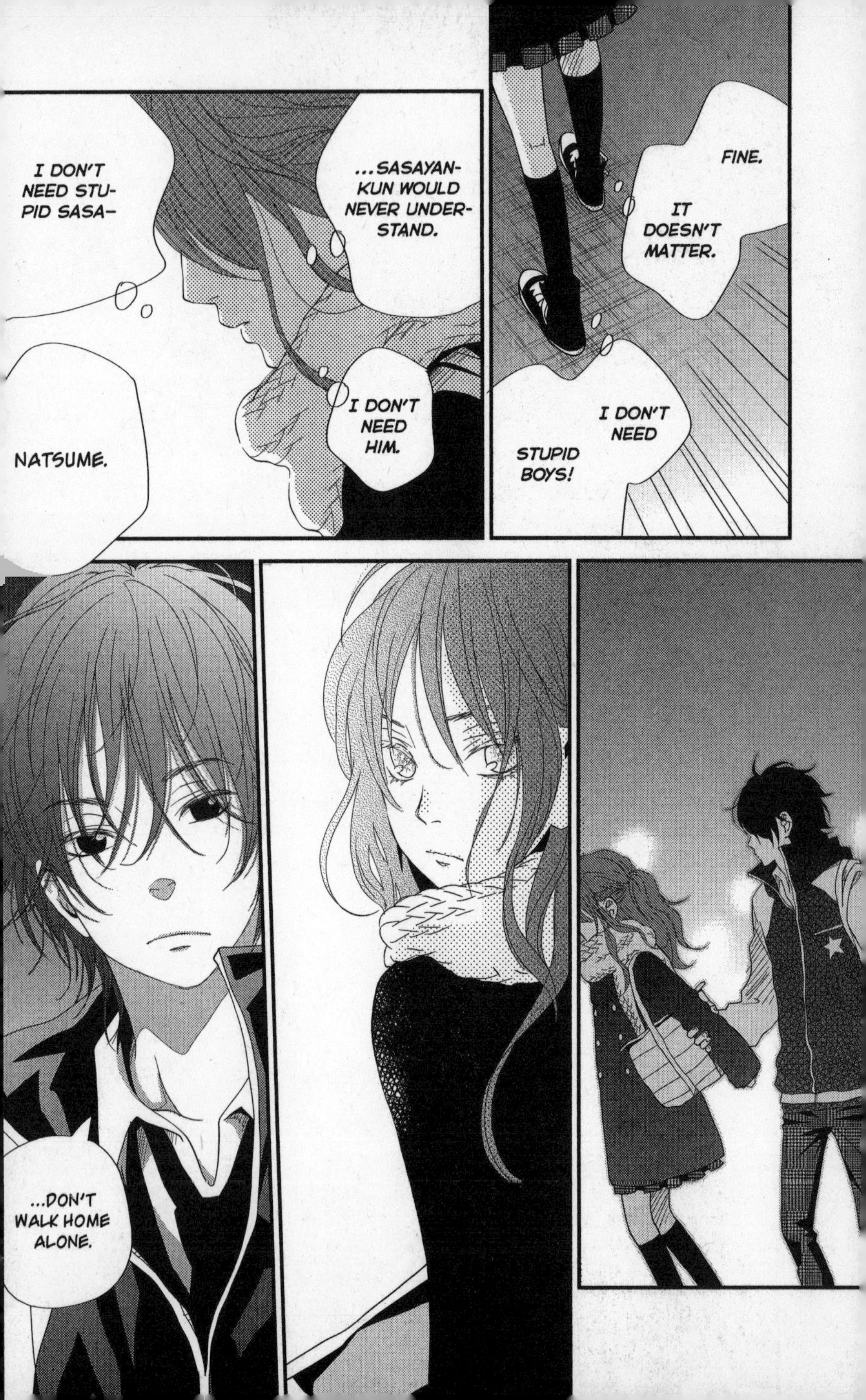
FINE.
IT DOESN'T MATTER.
I DON'T NEED
STUPID BOYS!
...SASAYAN-KUN WOULD NEVER UNDER-STAND.
I DON'T NEED HIM.
I DON'T NEED STU-PID SASA-
NATSUME.
...DON'T WALK HOME ALONE.

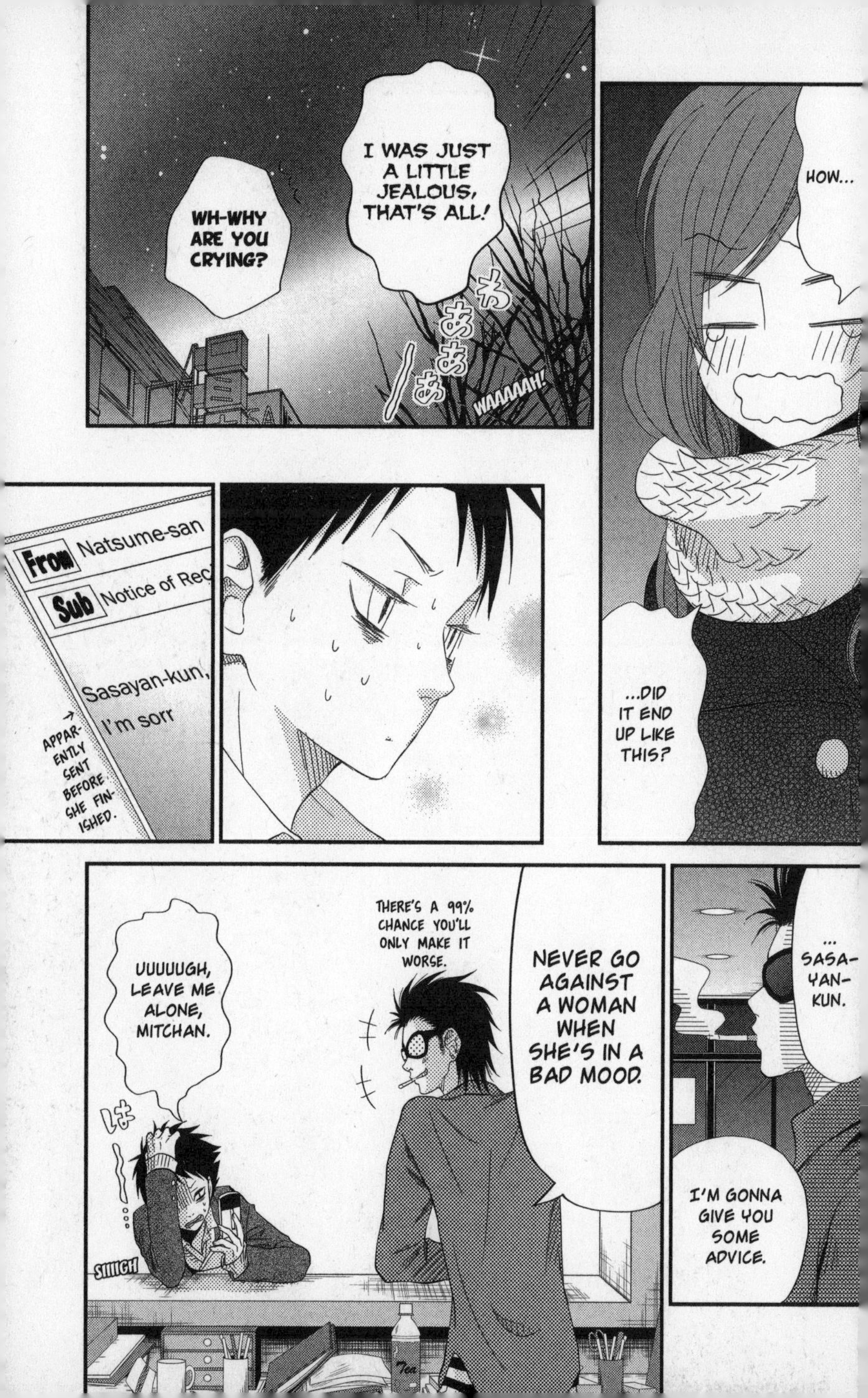
HOW...
...DID IT END UP LIKE THIS?
WH-WHY ARE YOU CRYING?
I WAS JUST A LITTLE JEALOUS, THAT'S ALL!
WAAAAAH!
From Natsume-san
Sub Notice of Rec
Sasayan-kun,
I'm sorr
APPARENTLY SENT BEFORE SHE FINISHED.
... SASAYAN-KUN.
I'M GONNA GIVE YOU SOME ADVICE.
NEVER GO AGAINST A WOMAN WHEN SHE'S IN A BAD MOOD.
THERE'S A 99% CHANCE YOU'LL ONLY MAKE IT WORSE.
UUUUUGH, LEAVE ME ALONE, MITCHAN.
SIIIIGH
Tea

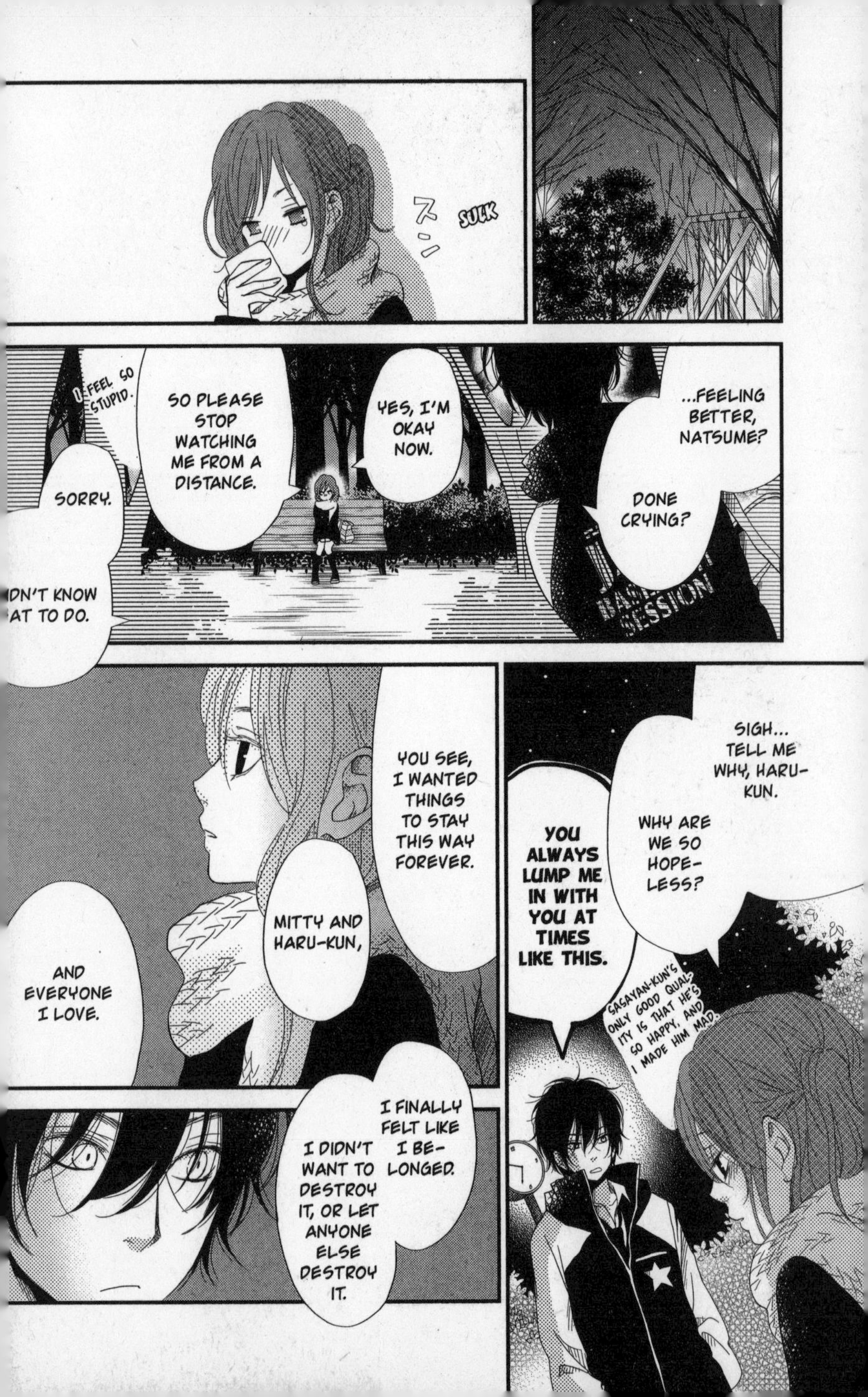
SULK
...FEELING BETTER, NATSUME?
DONE CRYING?
YES, I'M OKAY NOW.
SO PLEASE STOP WATCHING ME FROM A DISTANCE.
I FEEL SO STUPID.
SORRY.
DN'T KNOW AT TO DO.
SIGH... TELL ME WHY, HARU-KUN.
WHY ARE WE SO HOPE-LESS?
YOU ALWAYS LUMP ME IN WITH YOU AT TIMES LIKE THIS.
GASAYAN-KUN'S ONLY GOOD QUALITY IS THAT HE'S SO HAPPY, AND I MADE HIM MAD.
YOU SEE, I WANTED THINGS TO STAY THIS WAY FOREVER.
MITTY AND HARU-KUN,
AND EVERYONE I LOVE.
I FINALLY FELT LIKE I BE-LONGED.
I DIDN'T WANT TO DESTROY IT, OR LET ANYONE ELSE DESTROY IT.

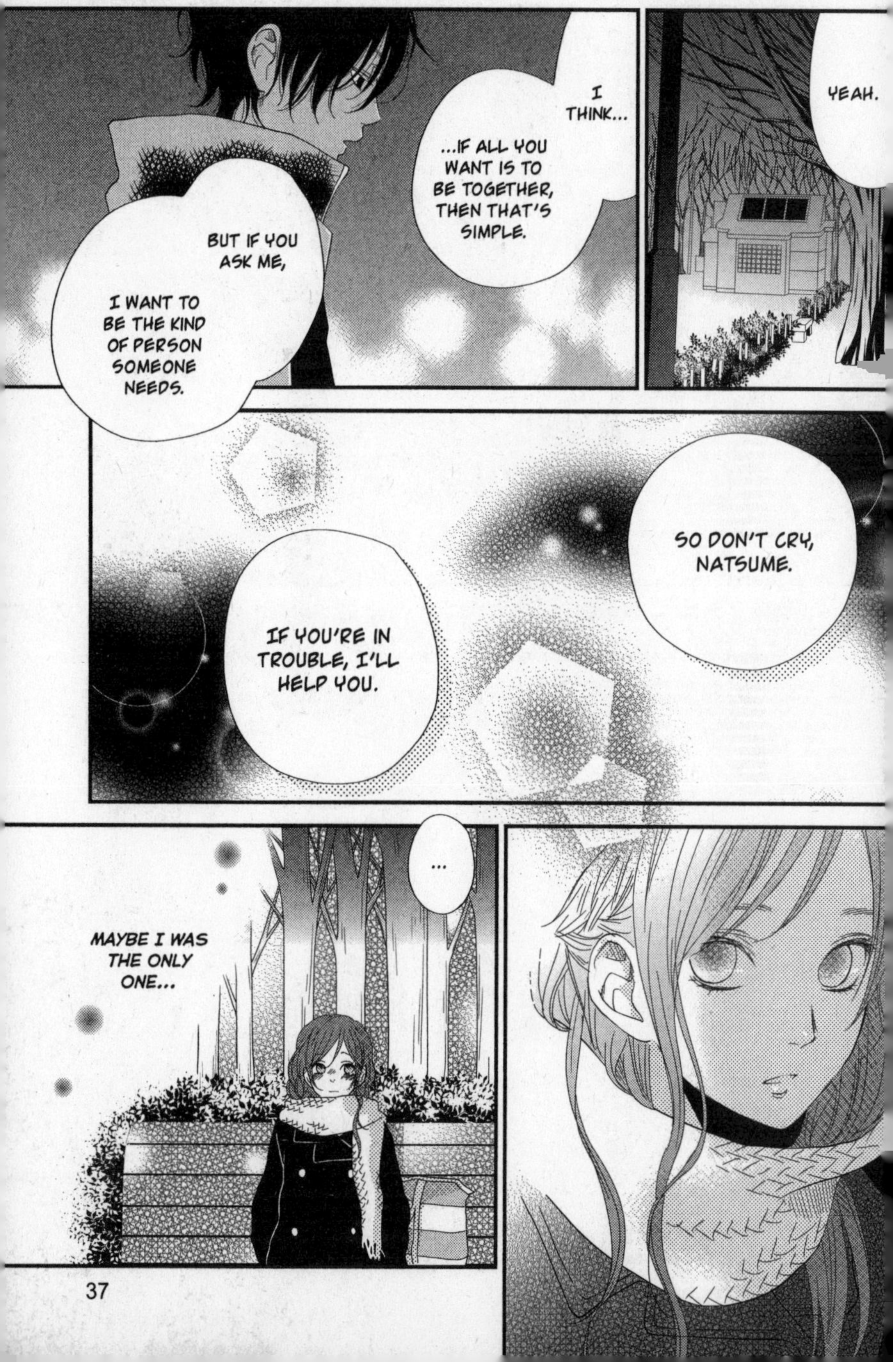
YEAH.
I THINK...
...IF ALL YOU WANT IS TO BE TOGETHER, THEN THAT'S SIMPLE.
BUT IF YOU ASK ME,
I WANT TO BE THE KIND OF PERSON SOMEONE NEEDS.
SO DON'T CRY, NATSUME.
IF YOU'RE IN TROUBLE, I'LL HELP YOU.
...
MAYBE I WAS THE ONLY ONE...

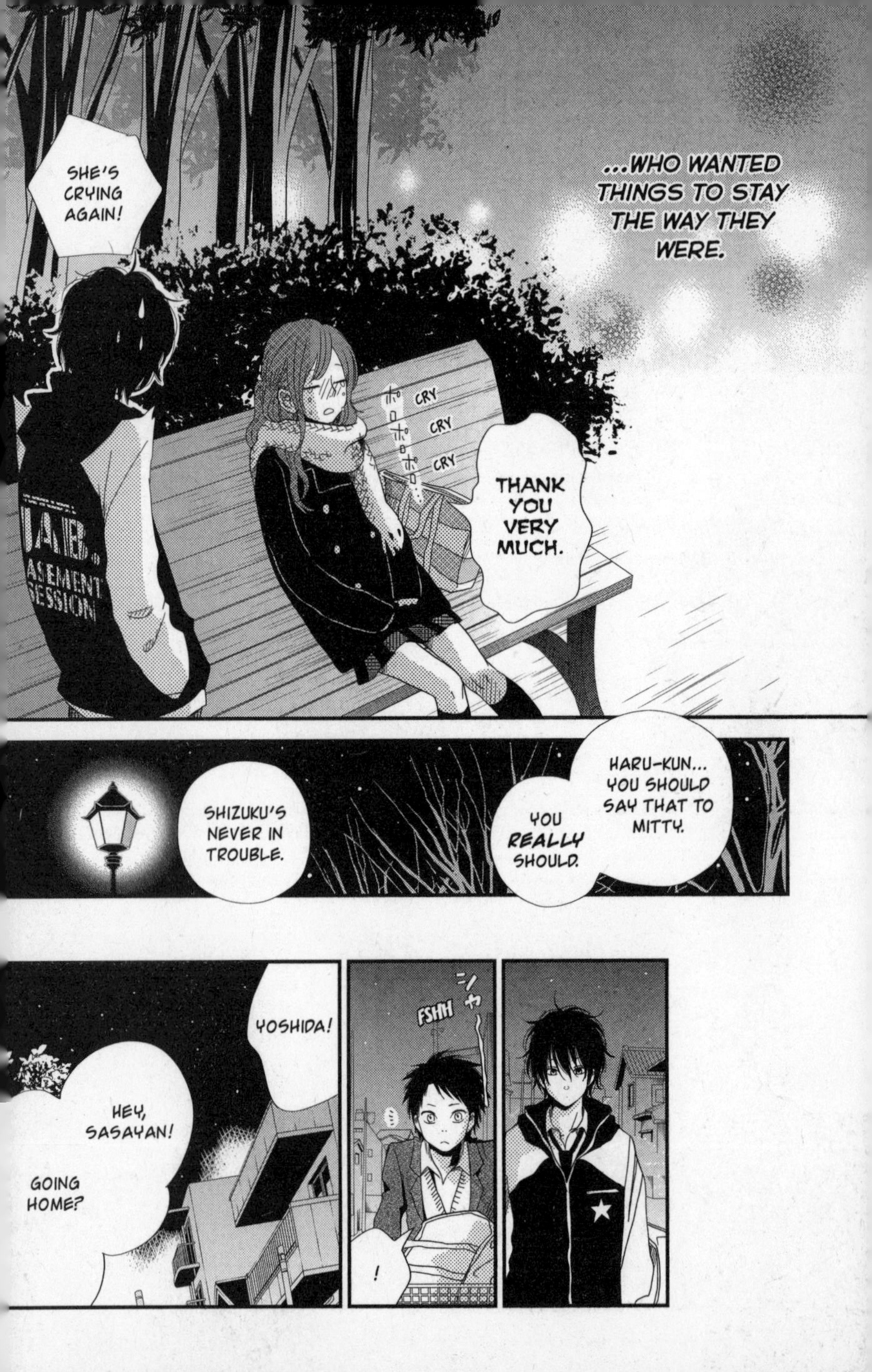
...WHO WANTED THINGS TO STAY THE WAY THEY WERE.
SHE'S CRYING AGAIN!
ポロポロポロ
CRY CRY CRY
THANK YOU VERY MUCH.
HARU-KUN... YOU SHOULD SAY THAT TO MITTY.
YOU REALLY SHOULD.
SHIZUKU'S NEVER IN TROUBLE.
ニヤ~
FSHH
!
YOSHIDA!
HEY, SASAYAN!
GOING HOME?

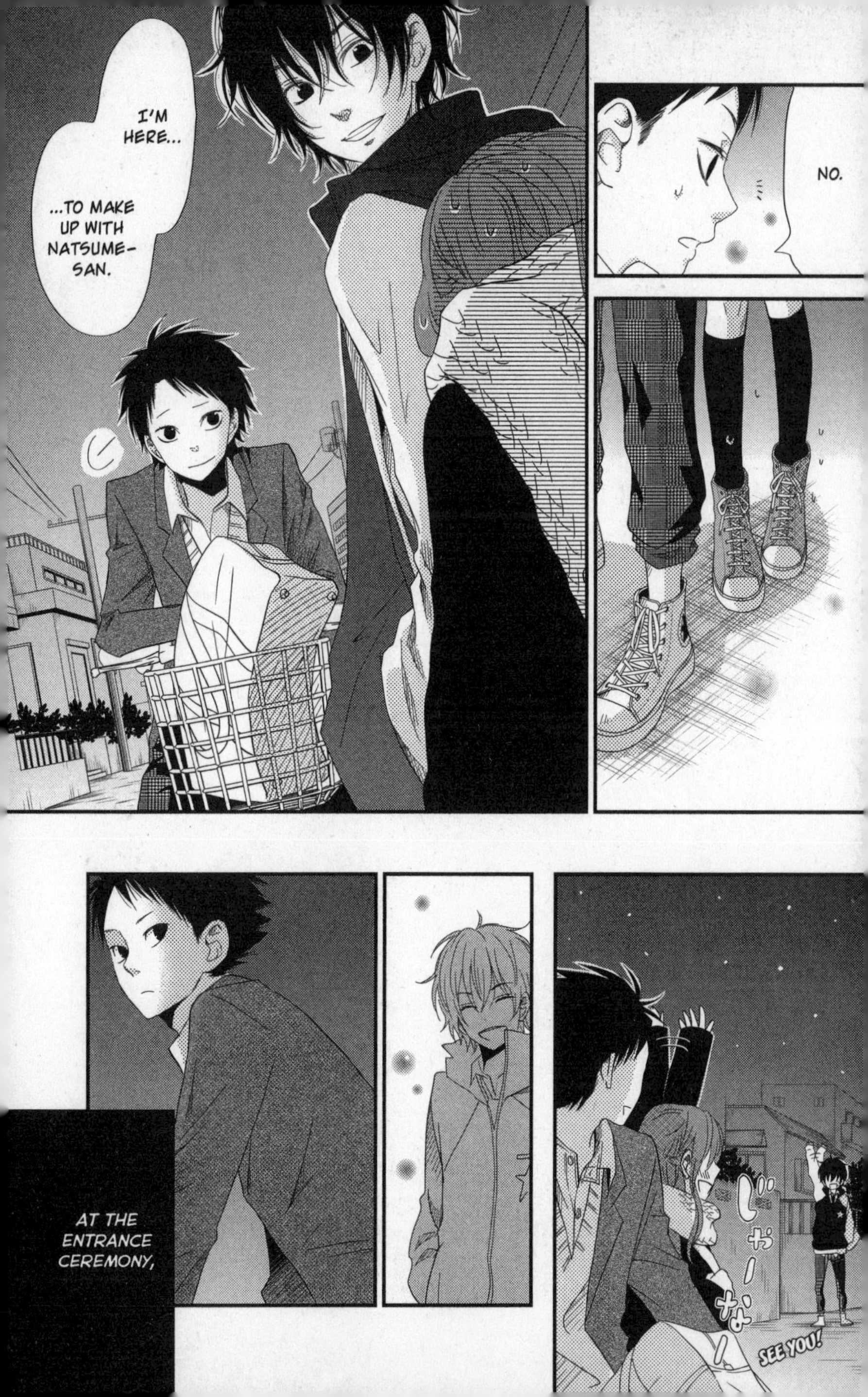
NO.
I'M HERE...
...TO MAKE UP WITH NATSUME-SAN.
SEE YOU!
AT THE ENTRANCE CEREMONY,

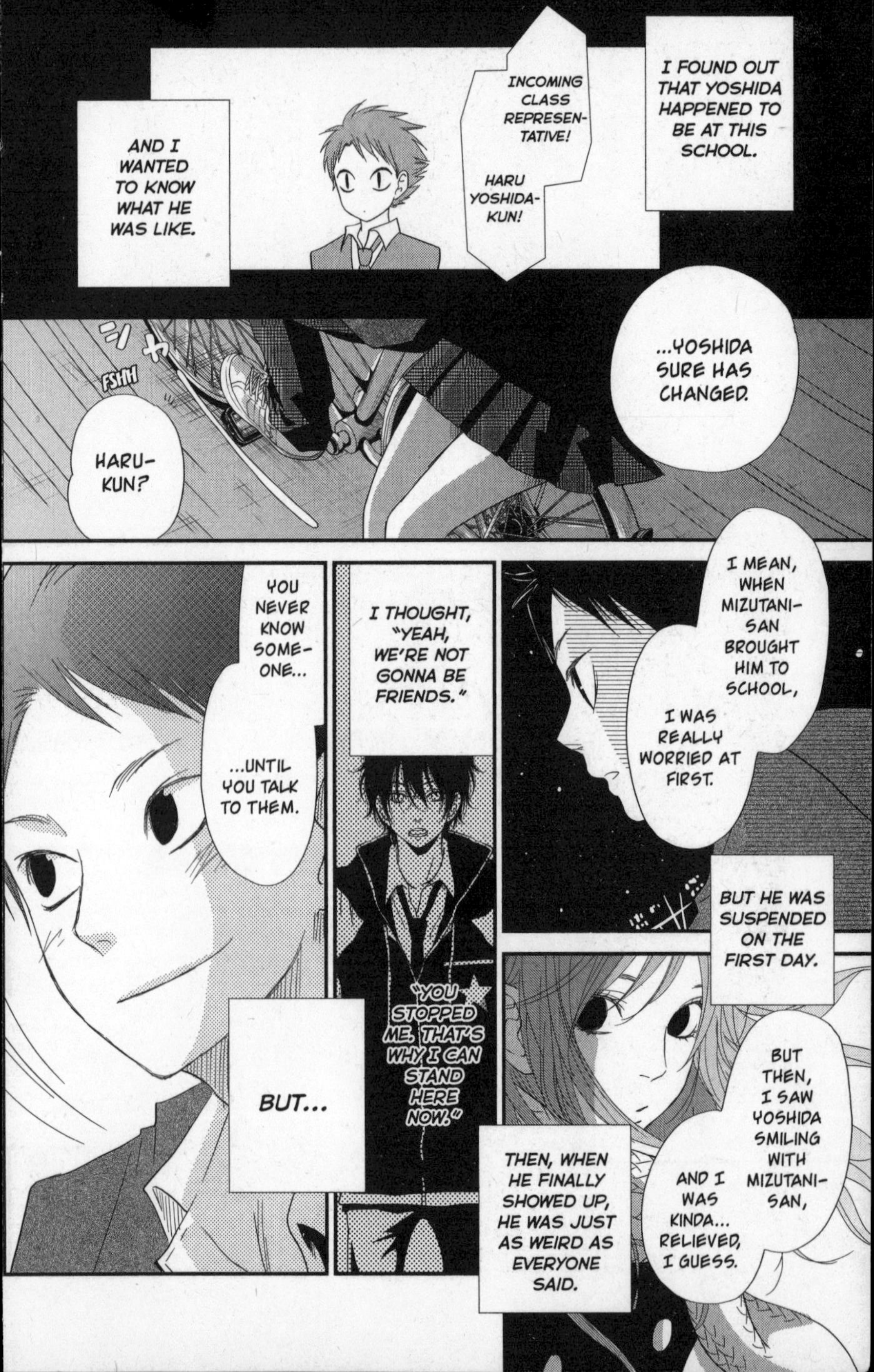
I FOUND OUT THAT YOSHIDA HAPPENED TO BE AT THIS SCHOOL.
INCOMING CLASS REPRESEN-TATIVE!
HARU YOSHIDA-KUN!
AND I WANTED TO KNOW WHAT HE WAS LIKE.
...YOSHIDA SURE HAS CHANGED.
FSHH
HARU-KUN?
I MEAN, WHEN MIZUTANI-SAN BROUGHT HIM TO SCHOOL,
I WAS REALLY WORRIED AT FIRST.
BUT HE WAS SUSPENDED ON THE FIRST DAY.
THEN, WHEN HE FINALLY SHOWED UP, HE WAS JUST AS WEIRD AS EVERYONE SAID.
I THOUGHT, "YEAH, WE'RE NOT GONNA BE FRIENDS."
"YOU STOPPED ME. THAT'S WHY I CAN STAND HERE NOW."
BUT THEN, I SAW YOSHIDA SMILING WITH MIZUTANI-SAN,
AND I WAS KINDA... RELIEVED, I GUESS.
YOU NEVER KNOW SOME-ONE...
...UNTIL YOU TALK TO THEM.
BUT...

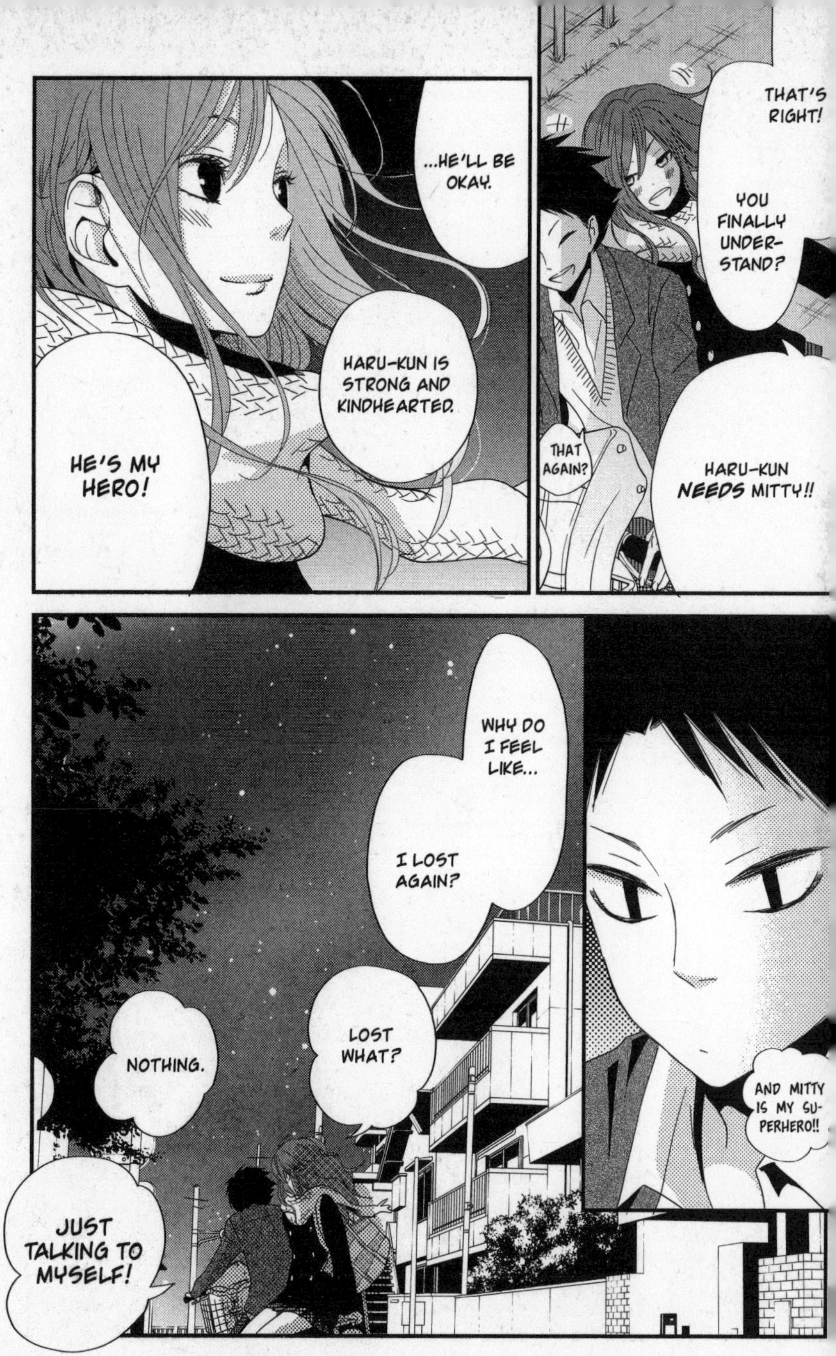
THAT'S RIGHT!
YOU FINALLY UNDERSTAND?
THAT AGAIN?
HARU-KUN **NEEDS** MITTY!!
...HE'LL BE OKAY.
HARU-KUN IS STRONG AND KINDHEARTED.
HE'S MY HERO!
AND MITTY IS MY SUPERHERO!!
WHY DO I FEEL LIKE...
I LOST AGAIN?
LOST WHAT?
NOTHING.
JUST TALKING TO MYSELF!

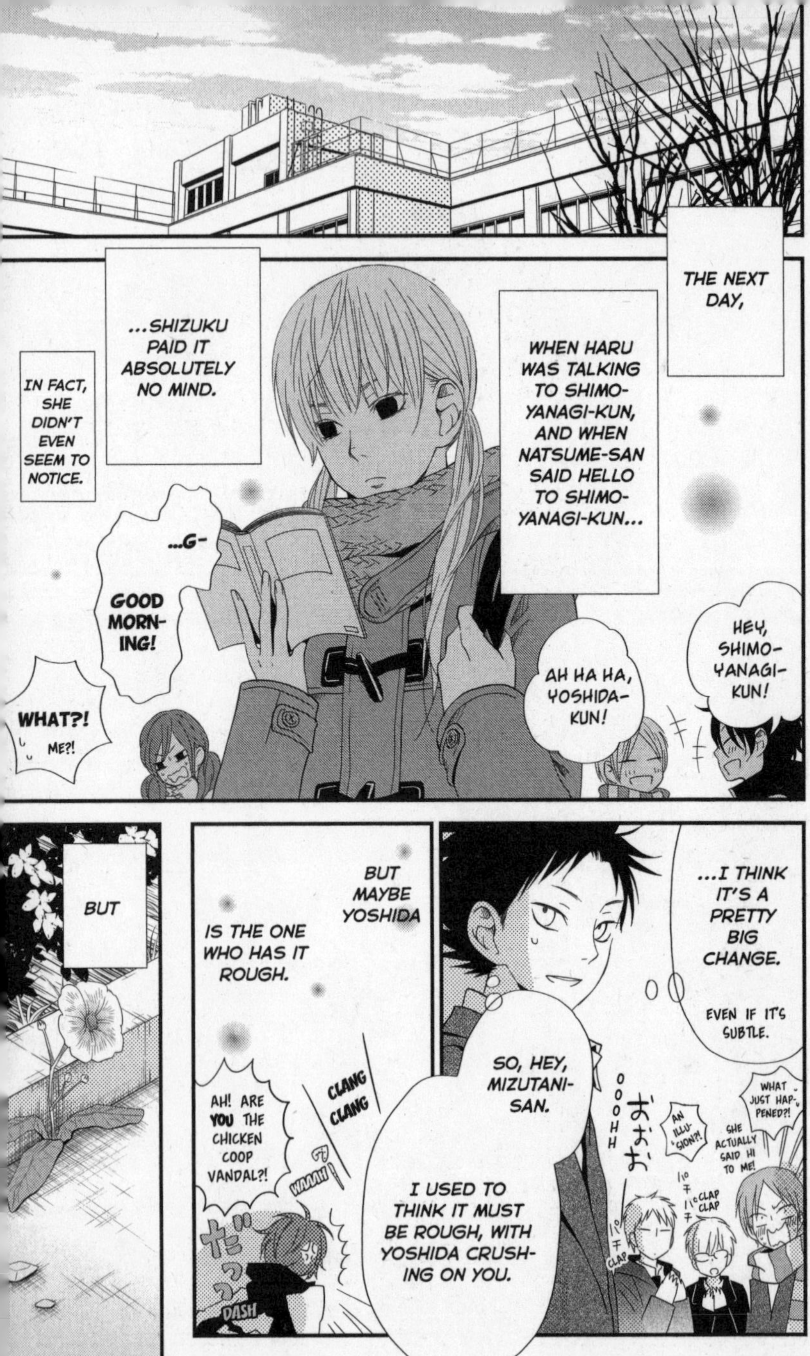
THE NEXT DAY,
WHEN HARU WAS TALKING TO SHIMO-YANAGI-KUN, AND WHEN NATSUME-SAN SAID HELLO TO SHIMO-YANAGI-KUN...
HEY, SHIMO-YANAGI-KUN!
AH HA HA, YOSHIDA-KUN!
...SHIZUKU PAID IT ABSOLUTELY NO MIND.
IN FACT, SHE DIDN'T EVEN SEEM TO NOTICE.
...G- GOOD MORNING!
WHAT?! ME?!
...I THINK IT'S A PRETTY BIG CHANGE.
EVEN IF IT'S SUBTLE.
WHAT JUST HAPPENED?!
SHE ACTUALLY SAID HI TO ME!
AN ILLUSION?!
OOOHH
CLAP CLAP
CLAP
SO, HEY, MIZUTANI-SAN.
I USED TO THINK IT MUST BE ROUGH, WITH YOSHIDA CRUSHING ON YOU.
BUT MAYBE YOSHIDA
IS THE ONE WHO HAS IT ROUGH.
CLANG CLANG
AH! ARE YOU THE CHICKEN COOP VANDAL?!
WAAAH
DASH
BUT

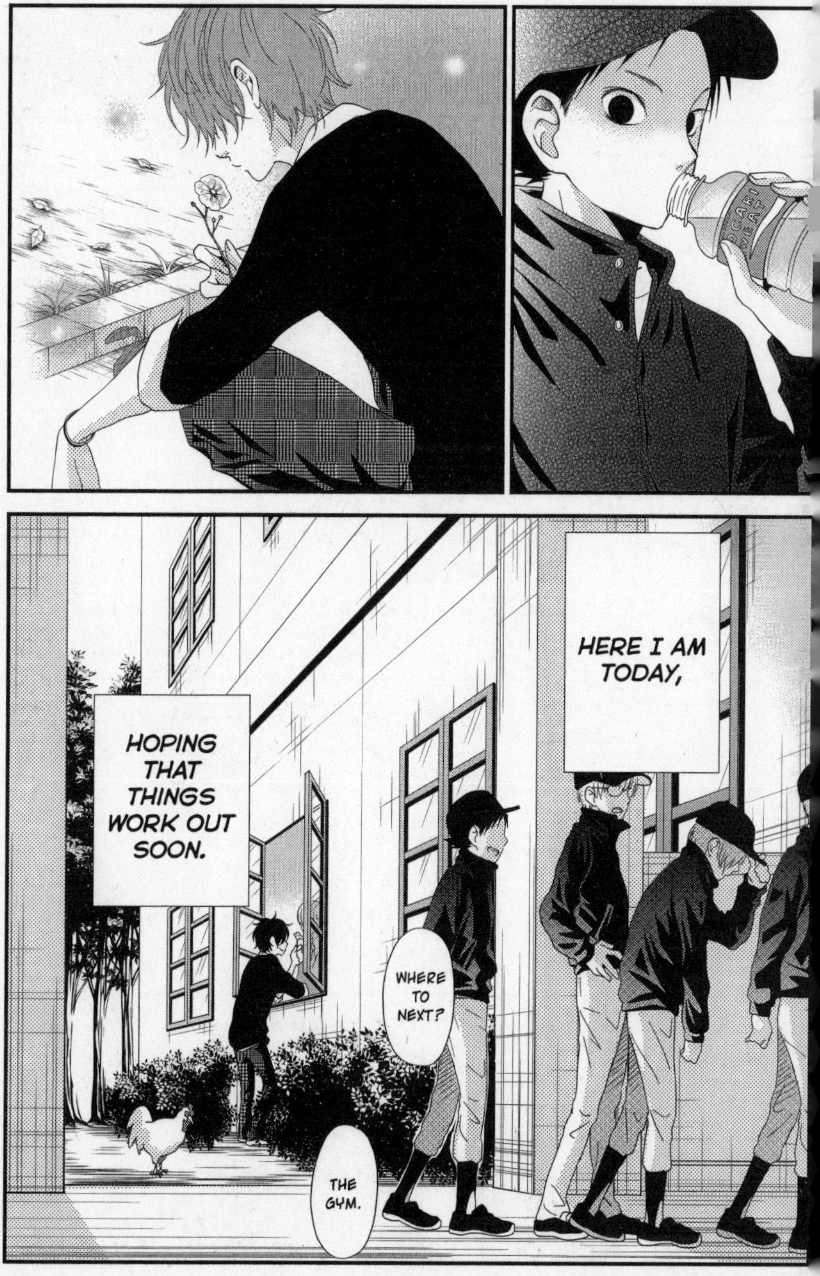
HERE I AM TODAY,
HOPING THAT THINGS WORK OUT SOON.
WHERE TO NEXT?
THE GYM.

Shimoyanagi-kun and Haru, Part One

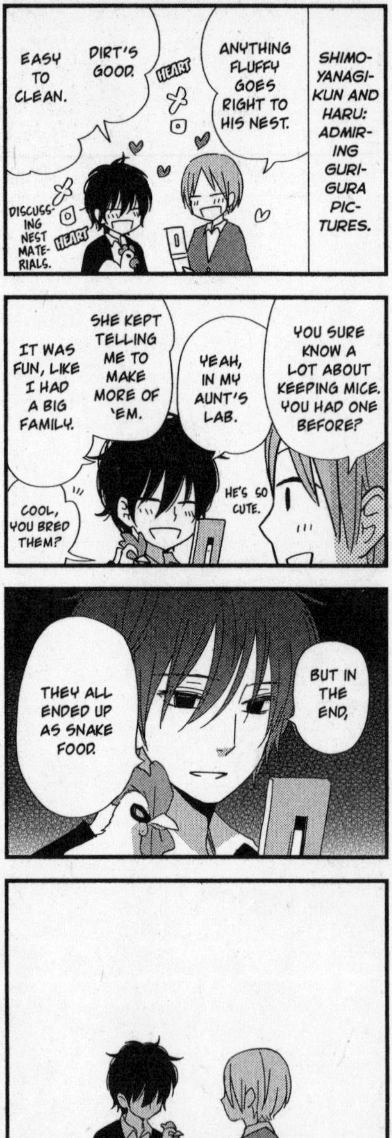
SHIMO-YANAGI-KUN AND HARU: ADMIRING GURI-GURA PICTURES.
ANYTHING FLUFFY GOES RIGHT TO HIS NEST.
HEART
DIRT'S GOOD.
EASY TO CLEAN.
HEART
DISCUSSING NEST MATERIALS.
YOU SURE KNOW A LOT ABOUT KEEPING MICE. YOU HAD ONE BEFORE?
YEAH, IN MY AUNT'S LAB.
SHE KEPT TELLING ME TO MAKE MORE OF 'EM.
IT WAS FUN, LIKE I HAD A BIG FAMILY.
HE'S SO CUTE.
COOL, YOU BRED THEM?
BUT IN THE END,
THEY ALL ENDED UP AS SNAKE FOOD.

Shimoyanagi-kun and Haru, Part Two

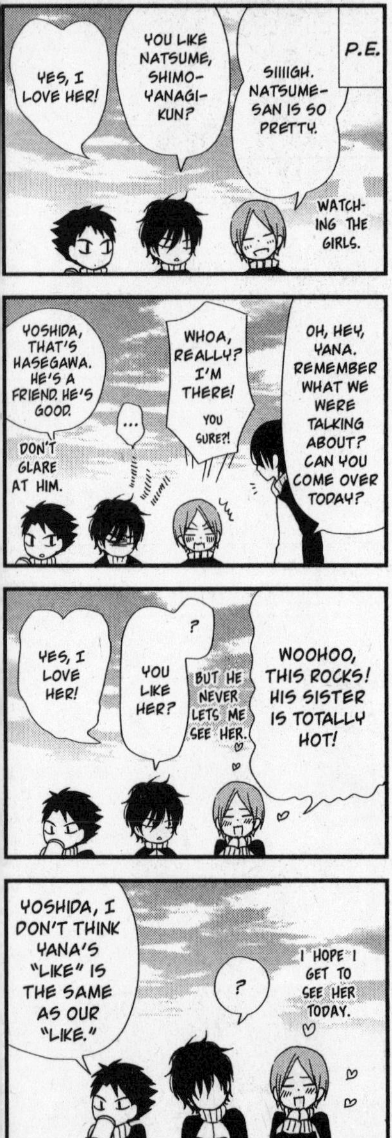
P.E.
SIIIIGH. NATSUME-SAN IS SO PRETTY.
YOU LIKE NATSUME, SHIMO-YANAGI-KUN?
YES, I LOVE HER!
WATCHING THE GIRLS.
OH, HEY, YANA. REMEMBER WHAT WE WERE TALKING ABOUT? CAN YOU COME OVER TODAY?
WHOA, REALLY? I'M THERE!
YOU SURE?!
...
YOSHIDA, THAT'S HASEGAWA. HE'S A FRIEND. HE'S GOOD.
DON'T GLARE AT HIM.
WOOHOO, THIS ROCKS! HIS SISTER IS TOTALLY HOT!
BUT HE NEVER LETS ME SEE HER.
?
YOU LIKE HER?
YES, I LOVE HER!
I HOPE I GET TO SEE HER TODAY.
?
YOSHIDA, I DON'T THINK YANA'S "LIKE" IS THE SAME AS OUR "LIKE."

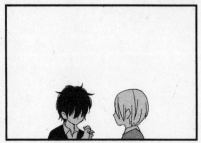

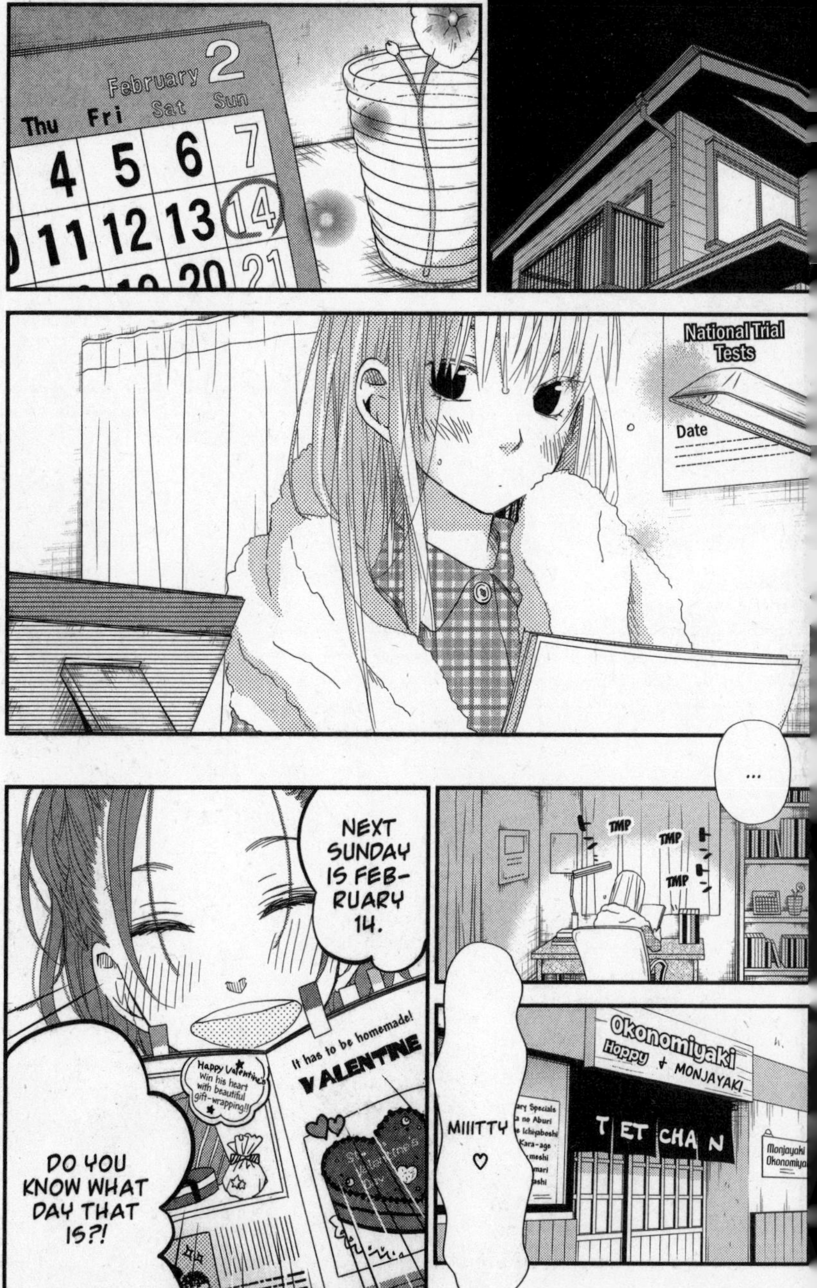

February 2
Thu Fri Sat Sun
4 5 6 7
11 12 13 14
20 21
National Trial Tests
Date
...
TMP
TMP
TMP
Okonomiyaki
Hoppy + MONJAYAKI
T ET CHA N
Monjayaki Okonomiya
MIIITTY ♡
NEXT SUNDAY IS FEB-RUARY 14.
It has to be homemade!
VALENTINE
Happy Valentine's Win his heart with beautiful gift-wrapping!!
DO YOU KNOW WHAT DAY THAT IS?!

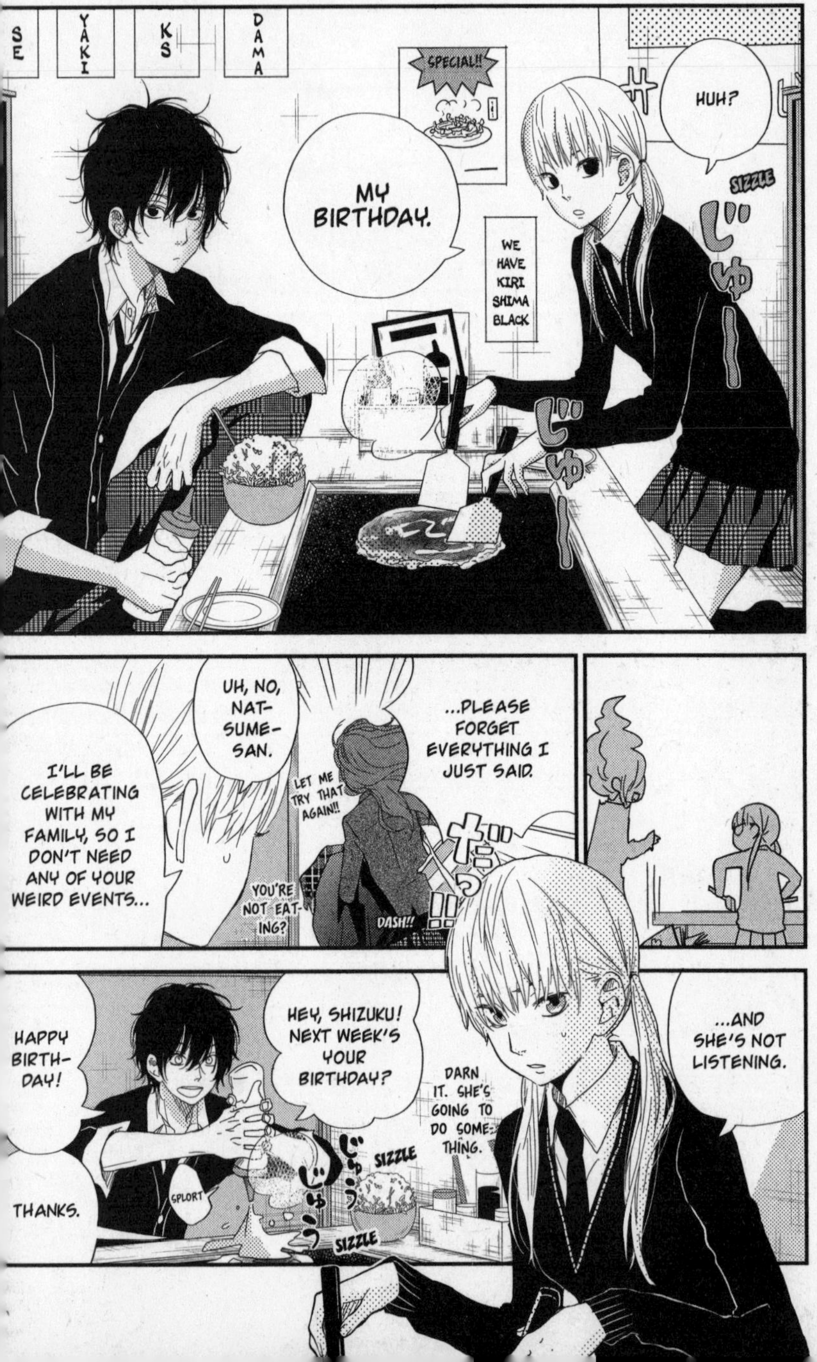
HUH?
SIZZLE
じゅー
じゅー
WE HAVE KIRISHIMA BLACK
SPECIAL!!
MY BIRTHDAY.
DAMA
KS
YAKI
SE
...PLEASE FORGET EVERYTHING I JUST SAID.
ダッ!!
DASH!!
UH, NO, NAT-SUME-SAN.
LET ME TRY THAT AGAIN!!
YOU'RE NOT EATING?
I'LL BE CELEBRATING WITH MY FAMILY, SO I DON'T NEED ANY OF YOUR WEIRD EVENTS...
...AND SHE'S NOT LISTENING.
DARN IT. SHE'S GOING TO DO SOME-THING.
じゅう
SIZZLE
じゅう
SIZZLE
HEY, SHIZUKU! NEXT WEEK'S YOUR BIRTHDAY?
HAPPY BIRTH-DAY!
SPLORT
THANKS.

Chapter 22 Les Filles Cuisinent le Chocolat

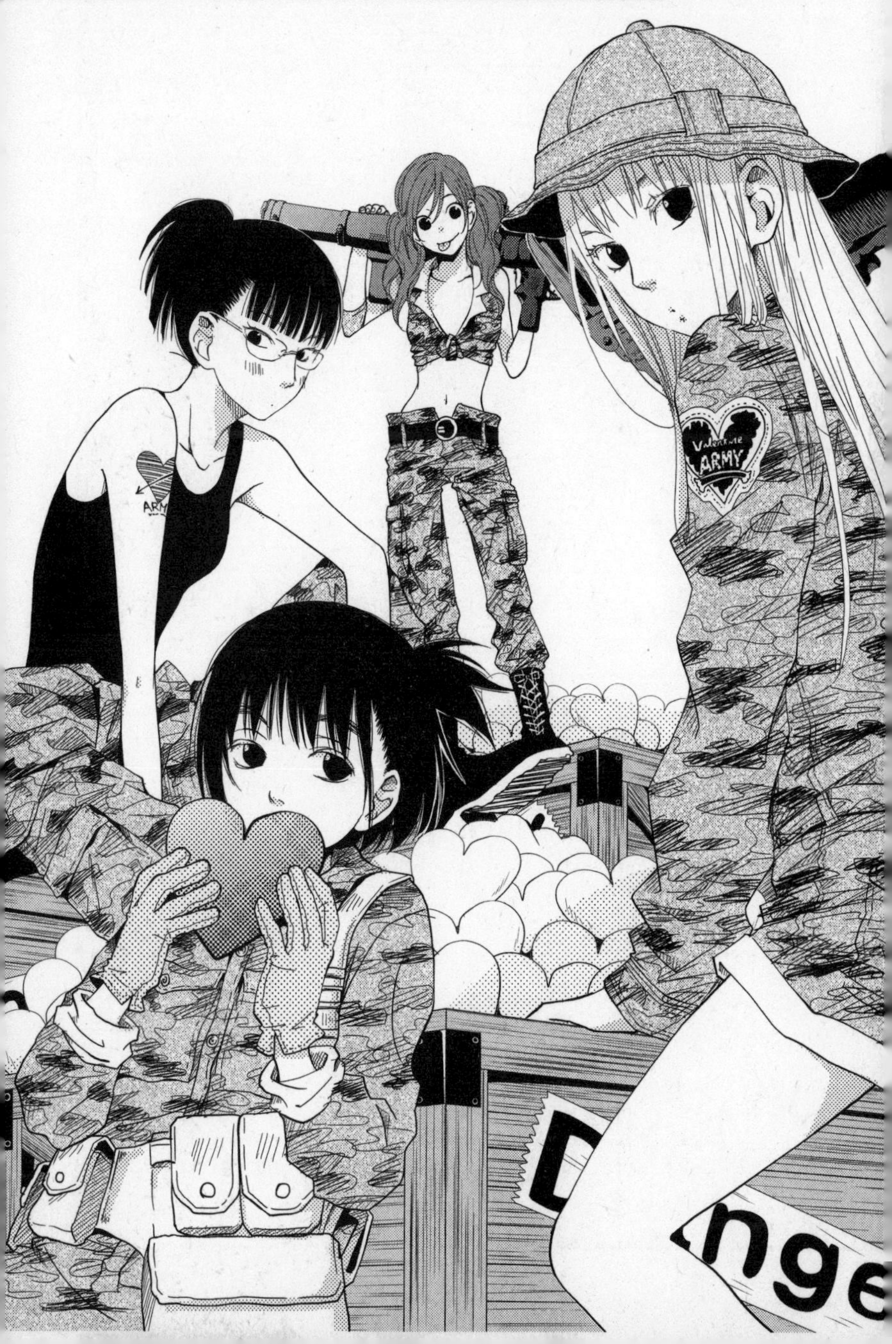
Valentine ARMY
ARMY

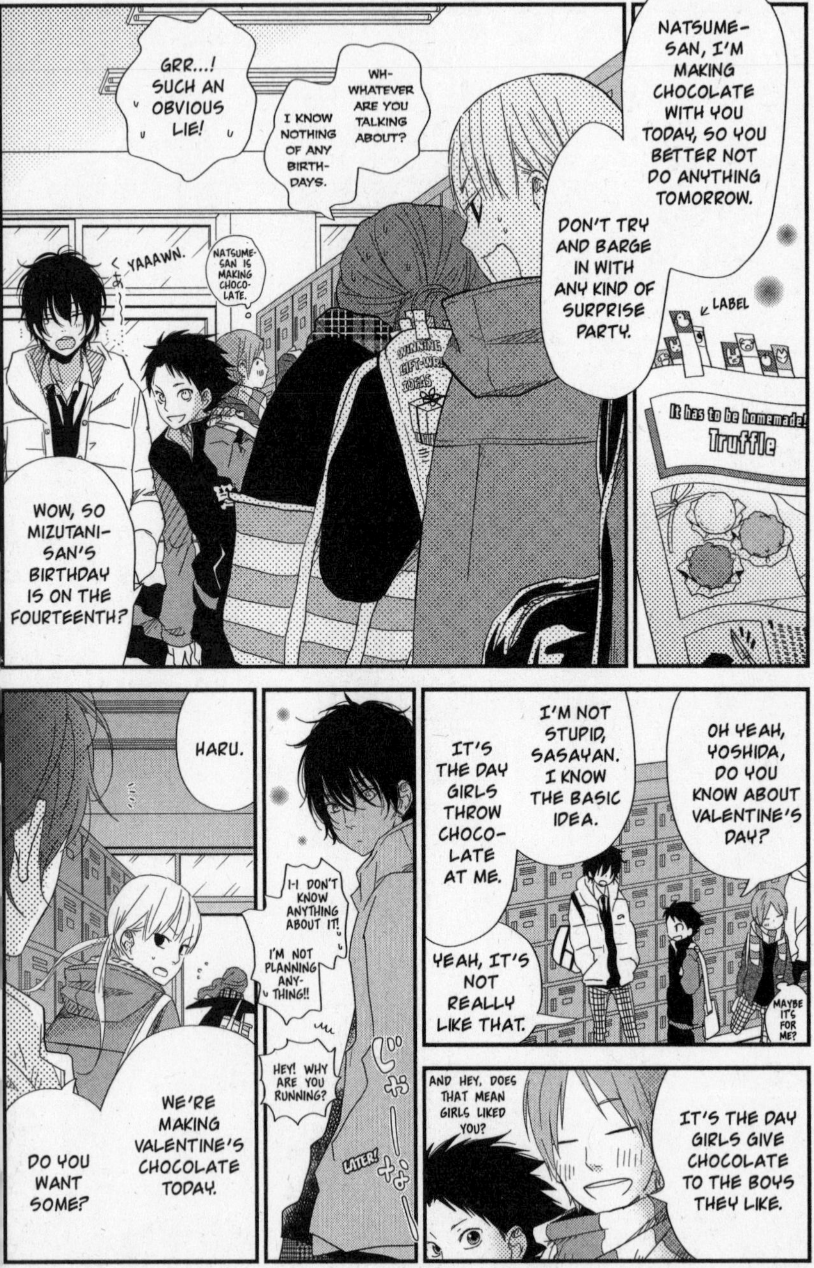
NATSUME-SAN, I'M MAKING CHOCOLATE WITH YOU TODAY, SO YOU BETTER NOT DO ANYTHING TOMORROW.
DON'T TRY AND BARGE IN WITH ANY KIND OF SURPRISE PARTY.
LABEL
It has to be homemade!
Truffle
WH-WHATEVER ARE YOU TALKING ABOUT?
GRR...! SUCH AN OBVIOUS LIE!
I KNOW NOTHING OF ANY BIRTHDAYS.
NATSUME-SAN IS MAKING CHOCOLATE.
YAAAWN.
WOW, SO MIZUTANI-SAN'S BIRTHDAY IS ON THE FOURTEENTH?
OH YEAH, YOSHIDA, DO YOU KNOW ABOUT VALENTINE'S DAY?
I'M NOT STUPID, SASAYAN. I KNOW THE BASIC IDEA.
IT'S THE DAY GIRLS THROW CHOCOLATE AT ME.
MAYBE IT'S FOR ME?
YEAH, IT'S NOT REALLY LIKE THAT.
IT'S THE DAY GIRLS GIVE CHOCOLATE TO THE BOYS THEY LIKE.
AND HEY, DOES THAT MEAN GIRLS LIKED YOU?
HEY! WHY ARE YOU RUNNING?
I-I DON'T KNOW ANYTHING ABOUT IT!
I'M NOT PLANNING ANYTHING!!
LATER!
HARU.
WE'RE MAKING VALENTINE'S CHOCOLATE TODAY.
DO YOU WANT SOME?

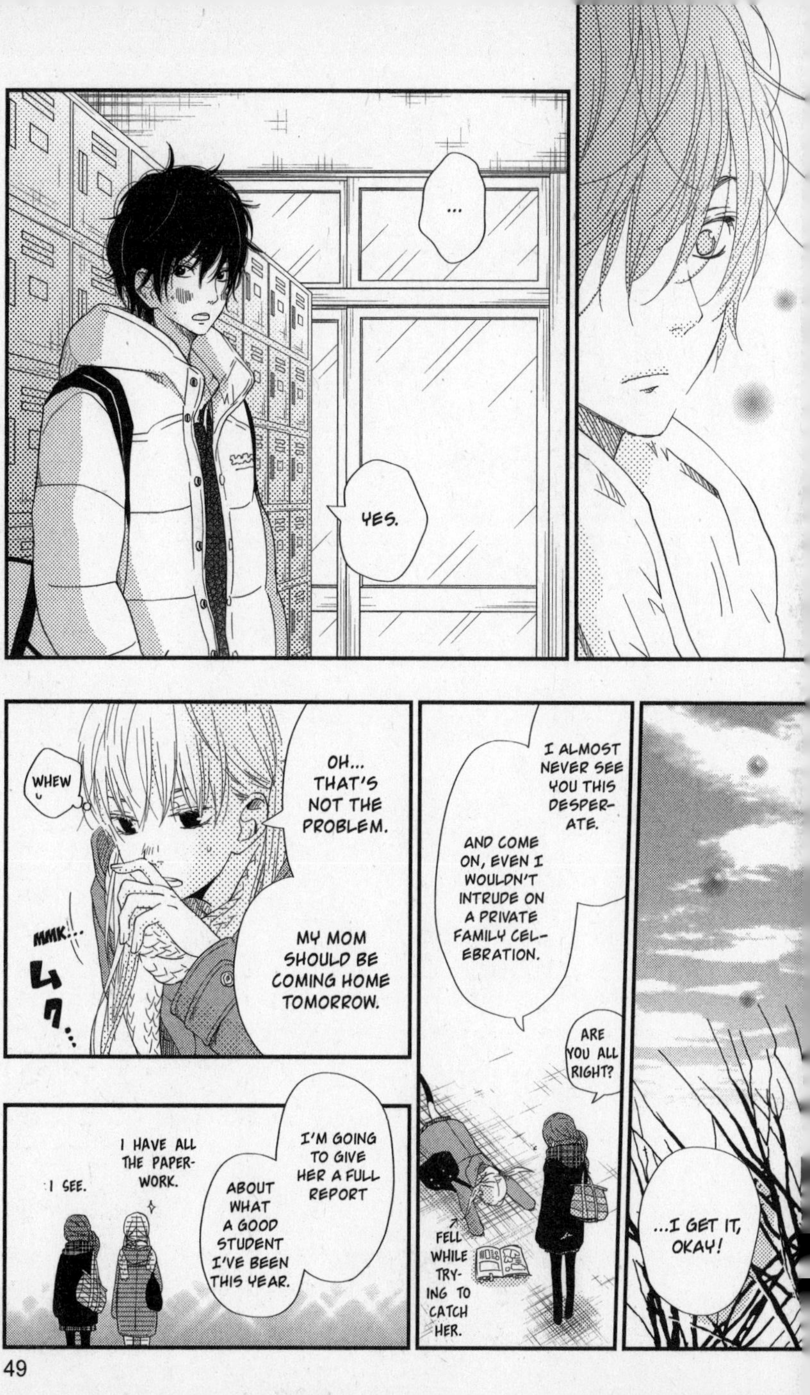
...
YES.
...I GET IT, OKAY!
I ALMOST NEVER SEE YOU THIS DESPERATE.
AND COME ON, EVEN I WOULDN'T INTRUDE ON A PRIVATE FAMILY CELEBRATION.
ARE YOU ALL RIGHT?
FELL WHILE TRYING TO CATCH HER.
OH... THAT'S NOT THE PROBLEM.
WHEW
MY MOM SHOULD BE COMING HOME TOMORROW.
MMK...
ムク...
I'M GOING TO GIVE HER A FULL REPORT
ABOUT WHAT A GOOD STUDENT I'VE BEEN THIS YEAR.
I HAVE ALL THE PAPERWORK.
I SEE.

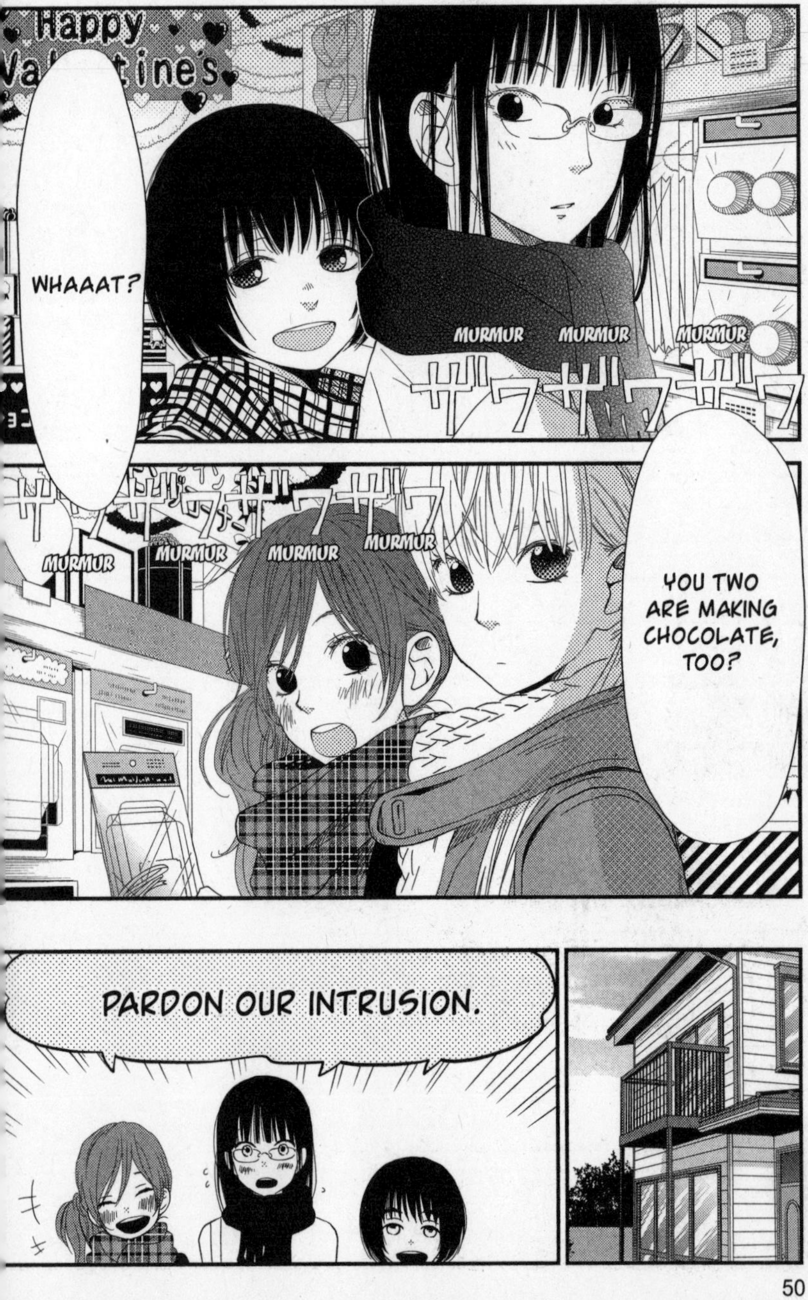
Happy
WHAAAT?
MURMUR
MURMUR
MURMUR
ザワザワザワ
YOU TWO ARE MAKING CHOCOLATE, TOO?
ザワザワザワザワ
MURMUR
MURMUR
MURMUR
MURMUR
PARDON OUR INTRUSION.

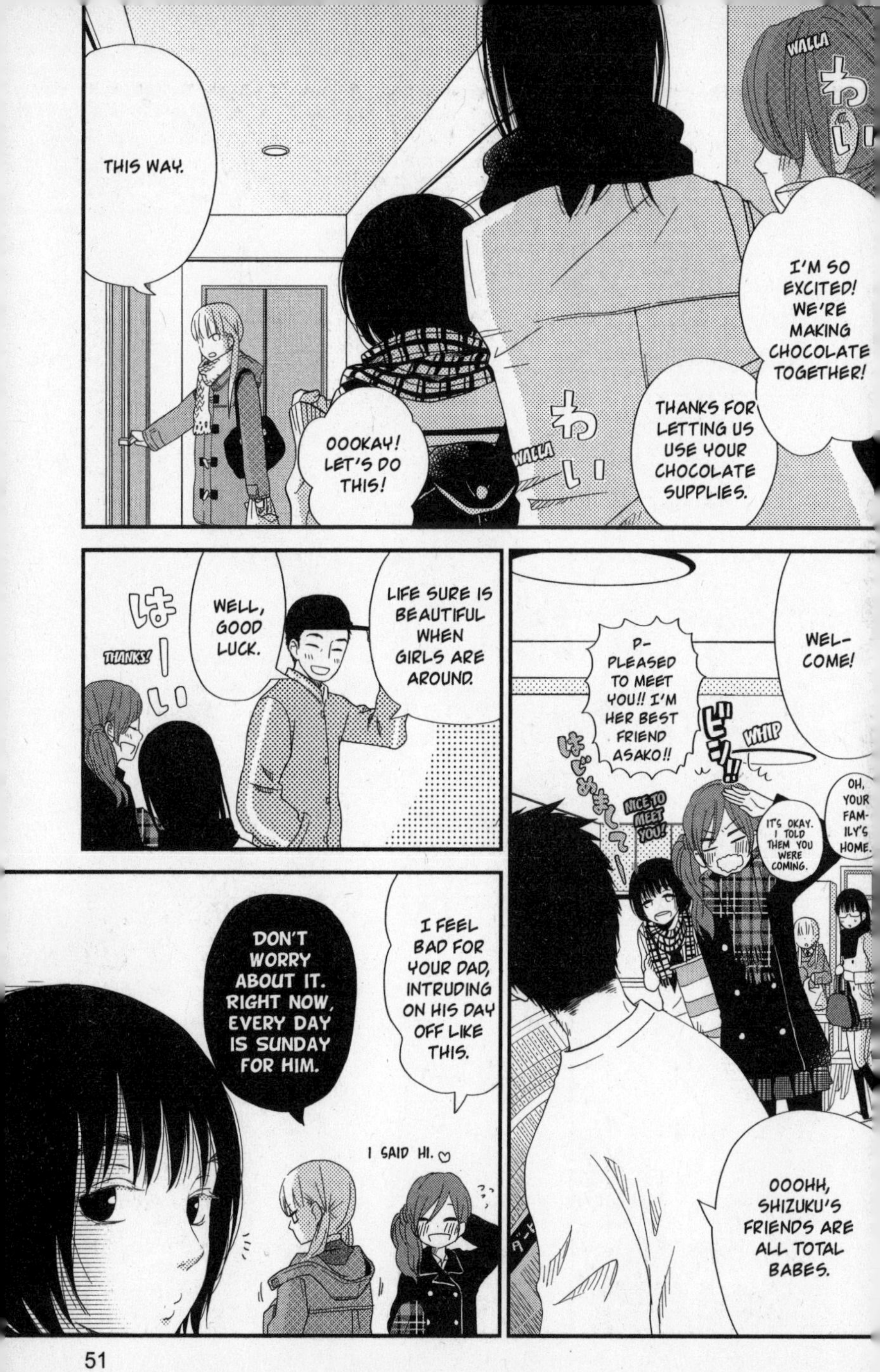
WALLA
わい
I'M SO EXCITED! WE'RE MAKING CHOCOLATE TOGETHER!
THANKS FOR LETTING US USE YOUR CHOCOLATE SUPPLIES.
わい
WALLA
OOOKAY! LET'S DO THIS!
THIS WAY.
WEL-COME!
OH, YOUR FAM-ILY'S HOME.
IT'S OKAY. I TOLD THEM YOU WERE COMING.
ビシッ!!
WHIP
P-PLEASED TO MEET YOU!! I'M HER BEST FRIEND ASAKO!!
はじめまして～
NICE TO MEET YOU!
OOOHH, SHIZUKU'S FRIENDS ARE ALL TOTAL BABES.
LIFE SURE IS BEAUTIFUL WHEN GIRLS ARE AROUND.
WELL, GOOD LUCK.
はーい
THANKS!
I FEEL BAD FOR YOUR DAD, INTRUDING ON HIS DAY OFF LIKE THIS.
DON'T WORRY ABOUT IT. RIGHT NOW, EVERY DAY IS SUNDAY FOR HIM.
I SAID HI. ♡

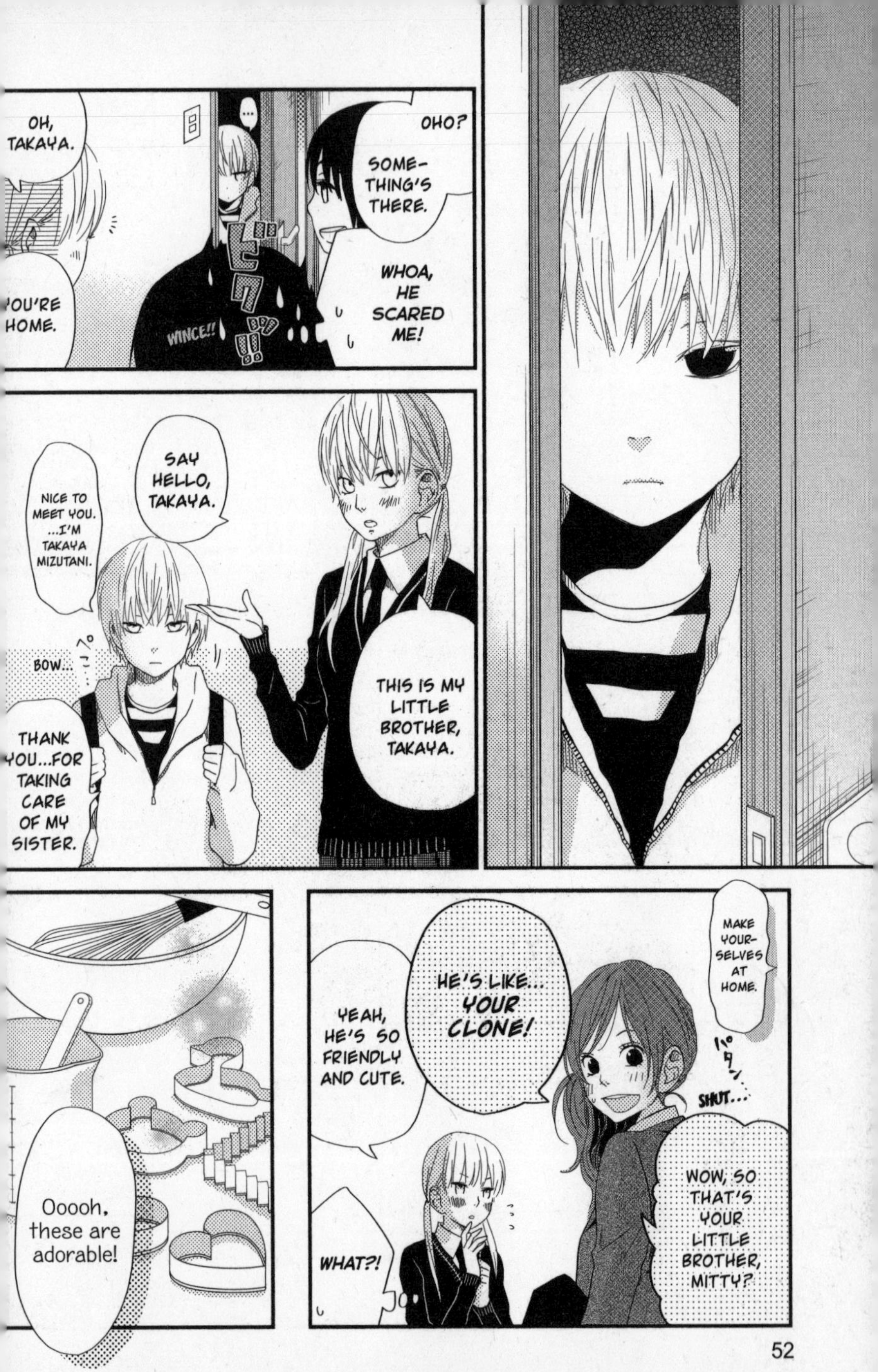
OHO?
SOME-THING'S THERE.
...
WHOA, HE SCARED ME!
WINCE!!
OH, TAKAYA.
OU'RE HOME.
SAY HELLO, TAKAYA.
THIS IS MY LITTLE BROTHER, TAKAYA.
NICE TO MEET YOU. ...I'M TAKAYA MIZUTANI.
BOW...
THANK YOU...FOR TAKING CARE OF MY SISTER.
MAKE YOUR-SELVES AT HOME.
SHUT...
WOW, SO THAT'S YOUR LITTLE BROTHER, MITTY?
YEAH, HE'S SO FRIENDLY AND CUTE.
HE'S LIKE... YOUR CLONE!
WHAT?!
Ooooh, these are adorable!

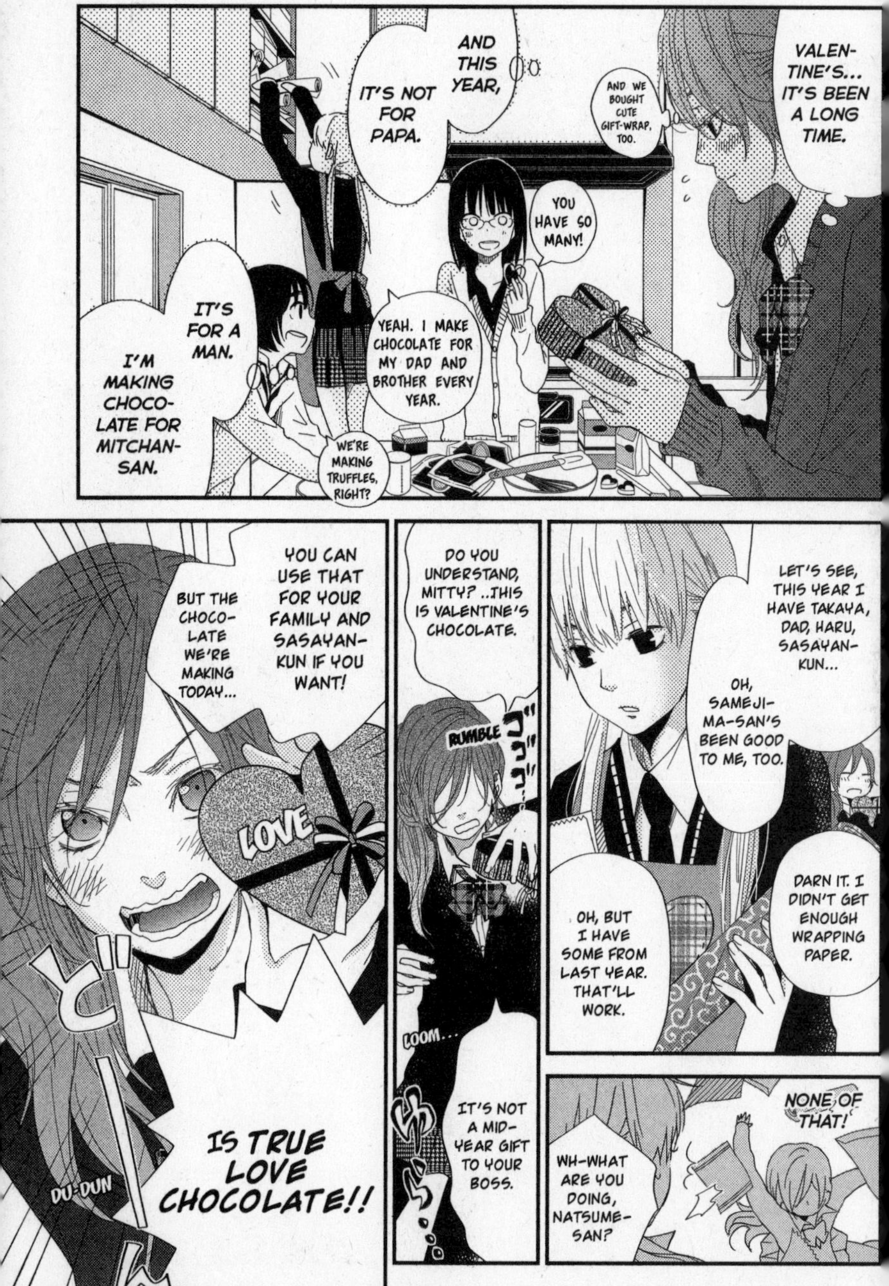
VALENTINE'S... IT'S BEEN A LONG TIME.
AND WE BOUGHT CUTE GIFT-WRAP, TOO.
AND THIS YEAR,
IT'S NOT FOR PAPA.
YOU HAVE SO MANY!
YEAH. I MAKE CHOCOLATE FOR MY DAD AND BROTHER EVERY YEAR.
IT'S FOR A MAN.
I'M MAKING CHOCOLATE FOR MITCHAN-SAN.
WE'RE MAKING TRUFFLES, RIGHT?
LET'S SEE, THIS YEAR I HAVE TAKAYA, DAD, HARU, SASAYAN-KUN...
OH, SAMEJIMA-SAN'S BEEN GOOD TO ME, TOO.
DARN IT. I DIDN'T GET ENOUGH WRAPPING PAPER.
OH, BUT I HAVE SOME FROM LAST YEAR. THAT'LL WORK.
NONE OF THAT!
WH-WHAT ARE YOU DOING, NATSUME-SAN?
DO YOU UNDERSTAND, MITTY? ..THIS IS VALENTINE'S CHOCOLATE.
RUMBLE
LOOM...
IT'S NOT A MID-YEAR GIFT TO YOUR BOSS.
YOU CAN USE THAT FOR YOUR FAMILY AND SASAYAN-KUN IF YOU WANT!
BUT THE CHOCOLATE WE'RE MAKING TODAY...
LOVE
IS TRUE LOVE CHOCOLATE!!
DU-DUN

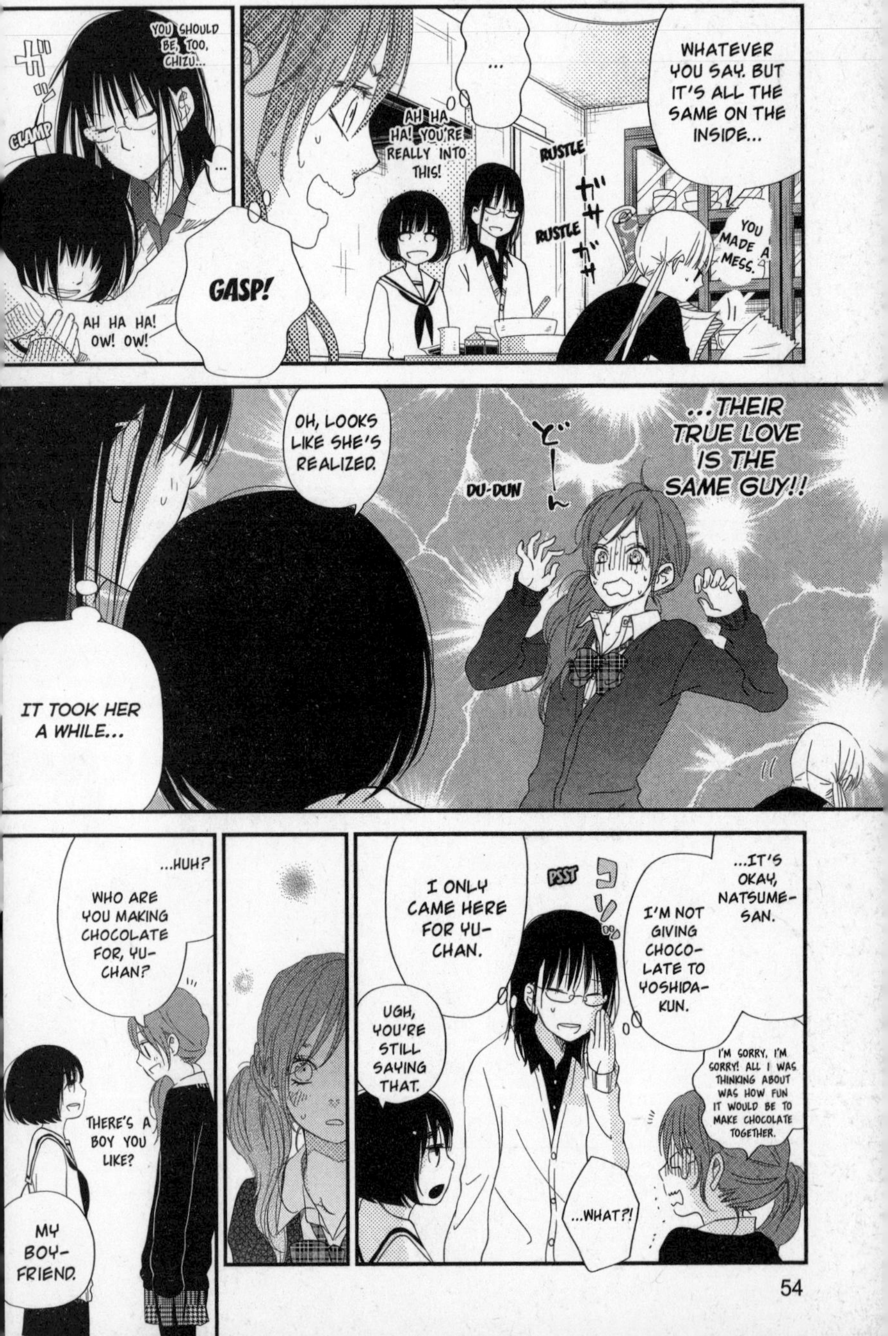

WHATEVER YOU SAY. BUT IT'S ALL THE SAME ON THE INSIDE...
YOU MADE A MESS.
RUSTLE
ガサ
RUSTLE
ガサ
...
AH HA HA! YOU'RE REALLY INTO THIS!
GASP!
YOU SHOULD BE, TOO, CHIZU...
ガ
CLAMP
...
AH HA HA! OW! OW!
...THEIR TRUE LOVE IS THE SAME GUY!!
どーん
DU-DUN
OH, LOOKS LIKE SHE'S REALIZED.
IT TOOK HER A WHILE...
...IT'S OKAY, NATSUME-SAN.
I'M NOT GIVING CHOCO-LATE TO YOSHIDA-KUN.
PSST
コソ
I ONLY CAME HERE FOR YU-CHAN.
I'M SORRY, I'M SORRY! ALL I WAS THINKING ABOUT WAS HOW FUN IT WOULD BE TO MAKE CHOCOLATE TOGETHER.
UGH, YOU'RE STILL SAYING THAT.
...WHAT?!
...HUH?
WHO ARE YOU MAKING CHOCOLATE FOR, YU-CHAN?
THERE'S A BOY YOU LIKE?
MY BOY-FRIEND.

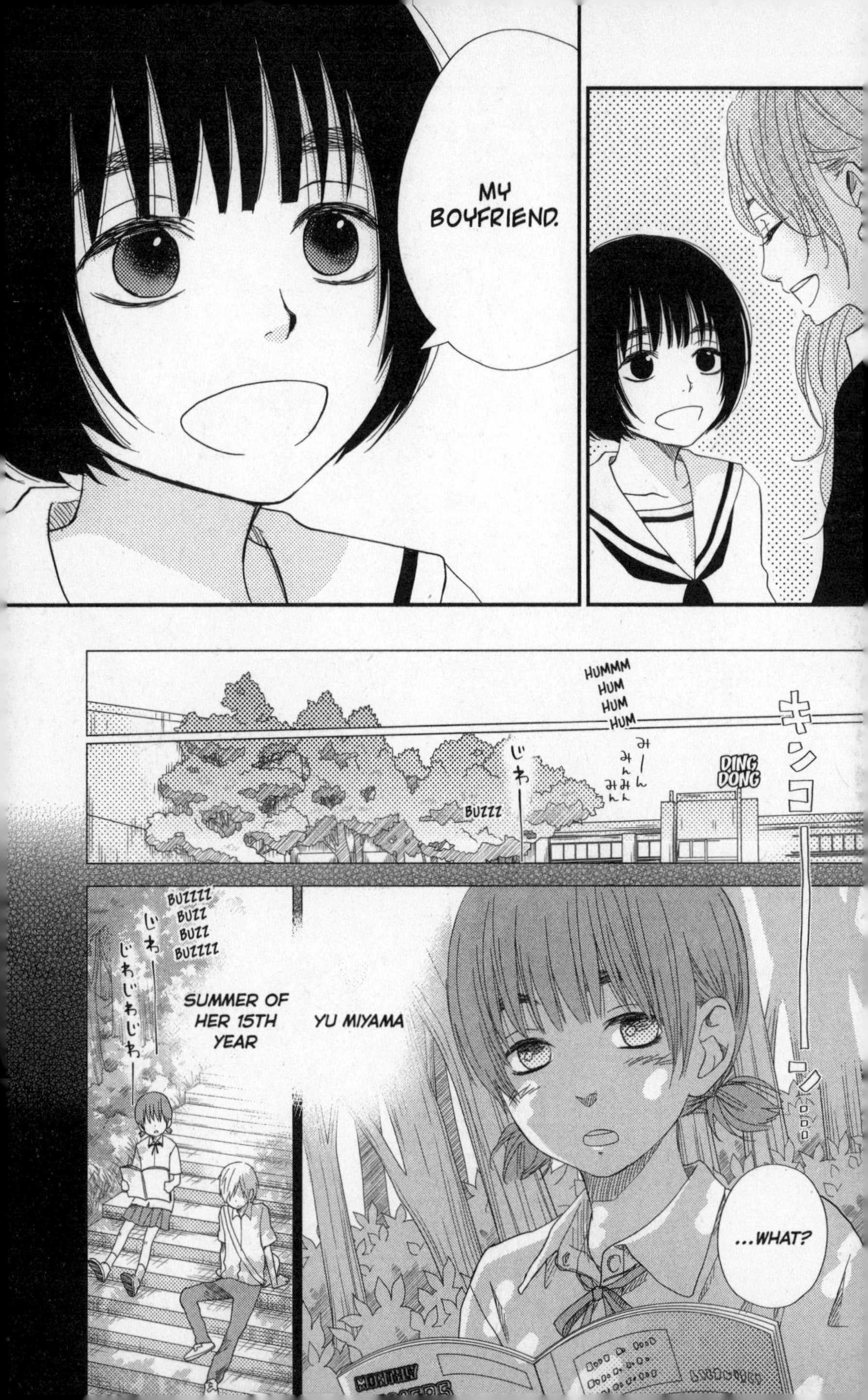
MY BOYFRIEND.
HUMMM HUM HUM HUM
キンコーン
DING DONG
みーんみんみんみん
じわー
BUZZZ
...WHAT?
YU MIYAMA
BUZZZZ BUZZ BUZZ BUZZZZ
じわー じわじわじわー
SUMMER OF HER 15TH YEAR

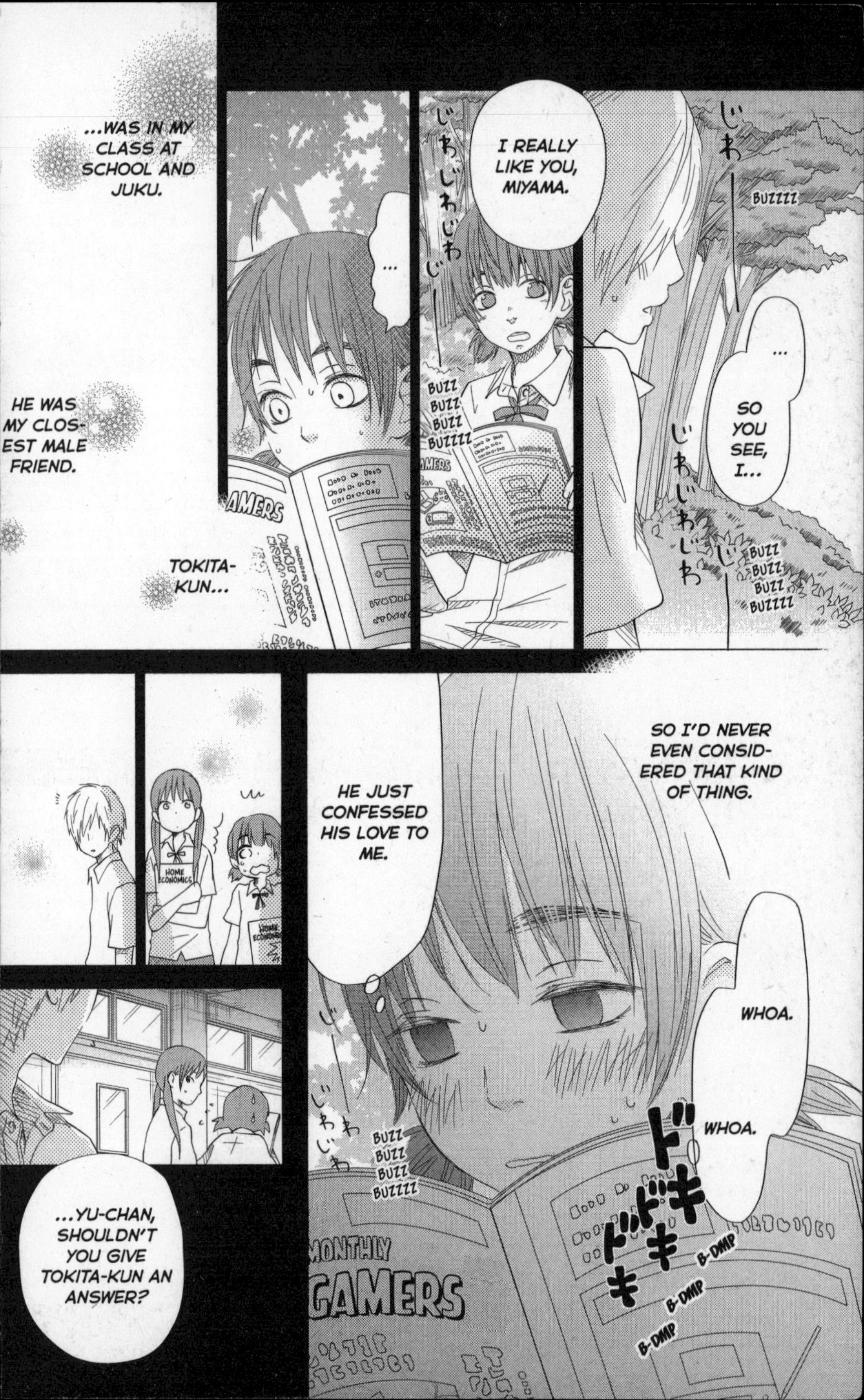

じわ—
BUZZZZ
...
SO YOU SEE, I...
じわじわじわじ—
BUZZ BUZZ BUZZ BUZZZZ
I REALLY LIKE YOU, MIYAMA.
じわじわじわじ—
BUZZ BUZZ BUZZ BUZZZZ
...
...WAS IN MY CLASS AT SCHOOL AND JUKU.
HE WAS MY CLOSEST MALE FRIEND.
TOKITA-KUN...
SO I'D NEVER EVEN CONSIDERED THAT KIND OF THING.
HE JUST CONFESSED HIS LOVE TO ME.
WHOA.
WHOA.
ドキドキドキ
B-DMP B-DMP B-DMP
じわじわ
BUZZ BUZZ BUZZ BUZZZZ
MONTHLY GAMERS
HOME ECONOMICS
HOME ECONOMICS
...YU-CHAN, SHOULDN'T YOU GIVE TOKITA-KUN AN ANSWER?

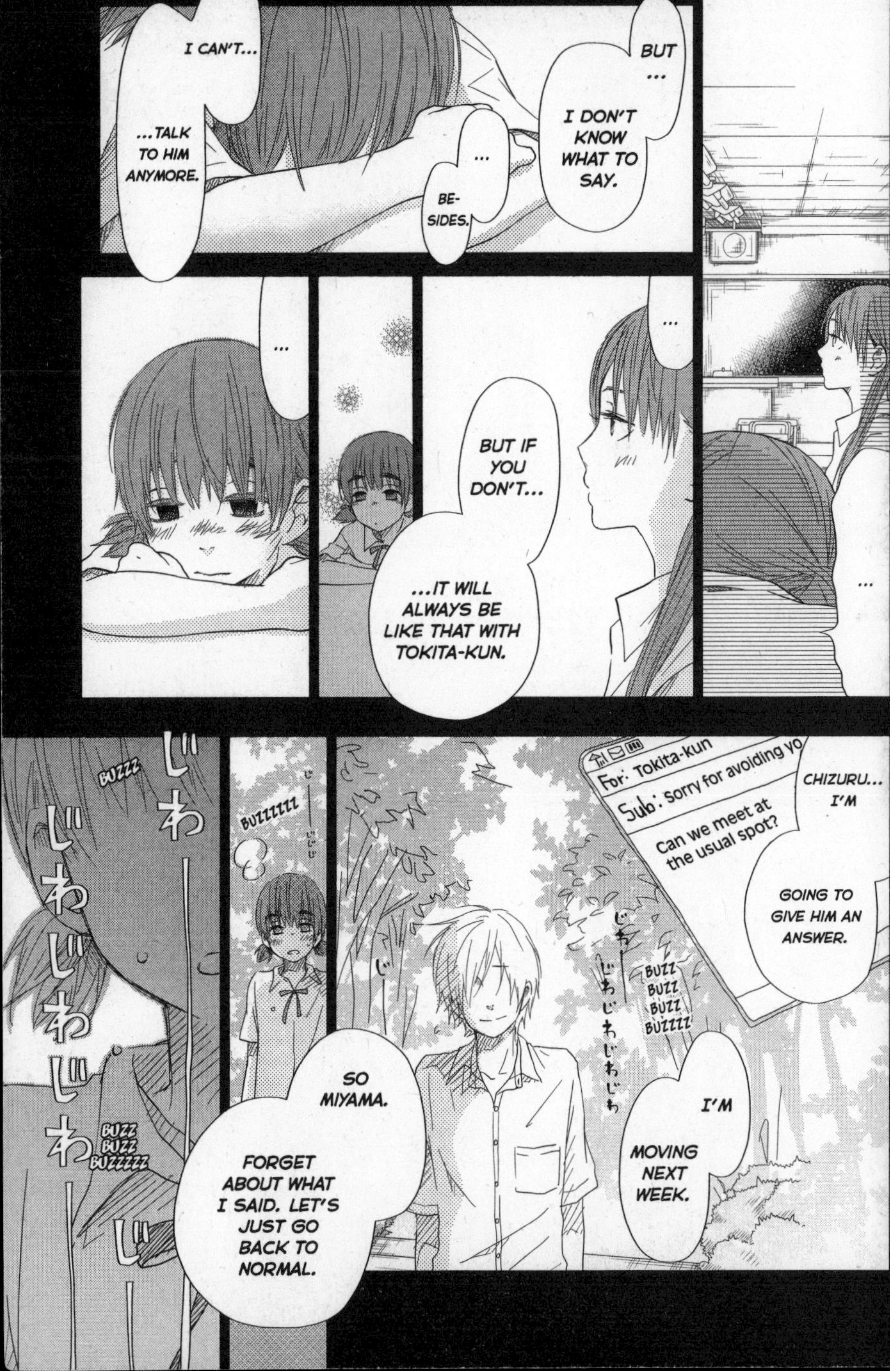
...
BUT ... I DON'T KNOW WHAT TO SAY.
... BE-SIDES.
I CAN'T...
...TALK TO HIM ANYMORE.
...
BUT IF YOU DON'T...
...IT WILL ALWAYS BE LIKE THAT WITH TOKITA-KUN.
...
For: Tokita-kun
Sub: Sorry for avoiding yo
Can we meet at the usual spot?
CHIZURU... I'M
GOING TO GIVE HIM AN ANSWER.
BUZZ BUZZ BUZZ BUZZZZ
I'M
MOVING NEXT WEEK.
SO MIYAMA.
FORGET ABOUT WHAT I SAID. LET'S JUST GO BACK TO NORMAL.
BUZZZZZZ
BUZZZ
じわ
じわじわじわ
BUZZ BUZZ BUZZZZZZ

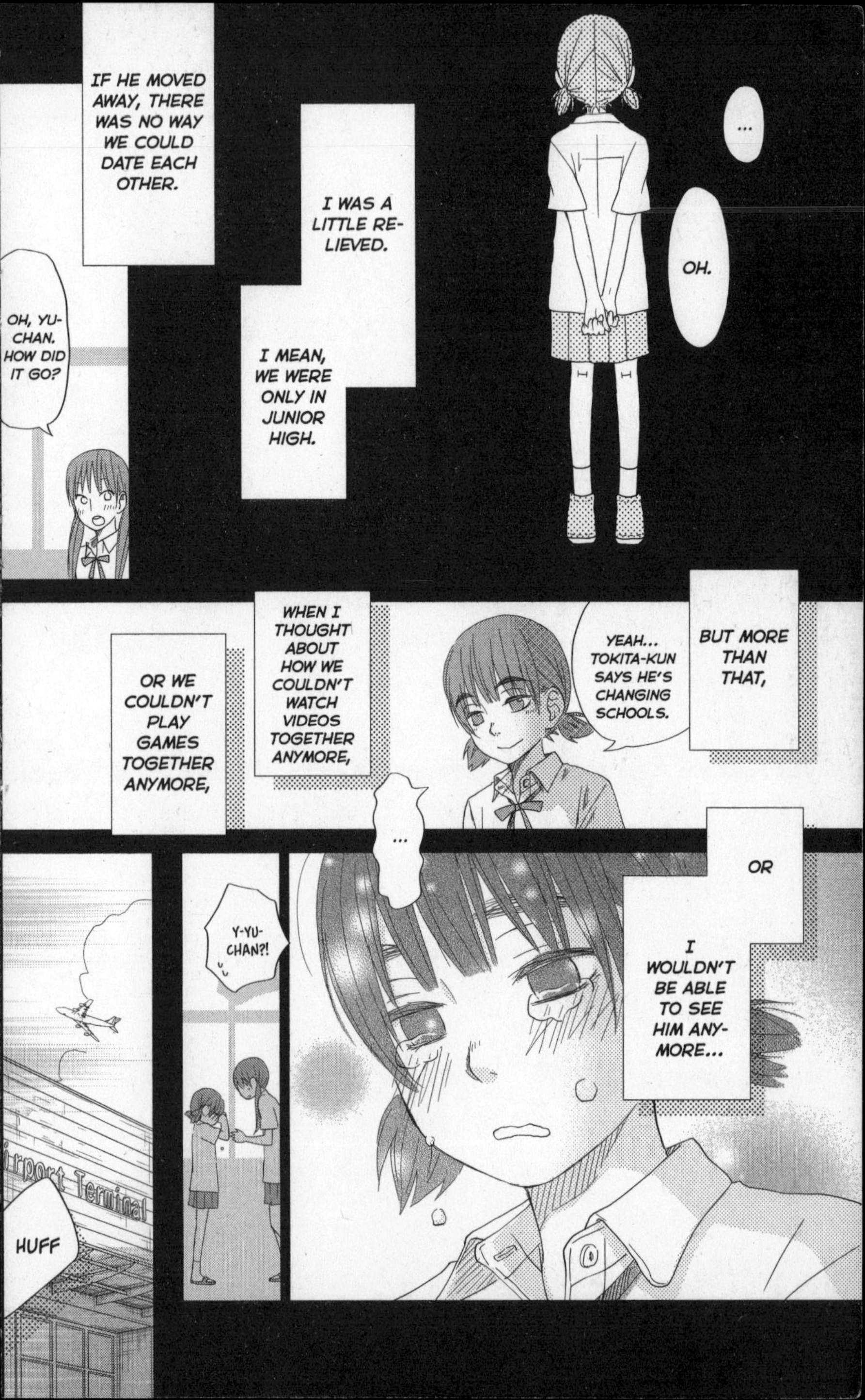
...
OH.
IF HE MOVED AWAY, THERE WAS NO WAY WE COULD DATE EACH OTHER.
I WAS A LITTLE RE-LIEVED.
I MEAN, WE WERE ONLY IN JUNIOR HIGH.
OH, YU-CHAN. HOW DID IT GO?
BUT MORE THAN THAT,
YEAH... TOKITA-KUN SAYS HE'S CHANGING SCHOOLS.
WHEN I THOUGHT ABOUT HOW WE COULDN'T WATCH VIDEOS TOGETHER ANYMORE,
OR WE COULDN'T PLAY GAMES TOGETHER ANYMORE,
...
OR
I WOULDN'T BE ABLE TO SEE HIM ANY-MORE...
Y-YU-CHAN?!
irport Terminal
HUFF

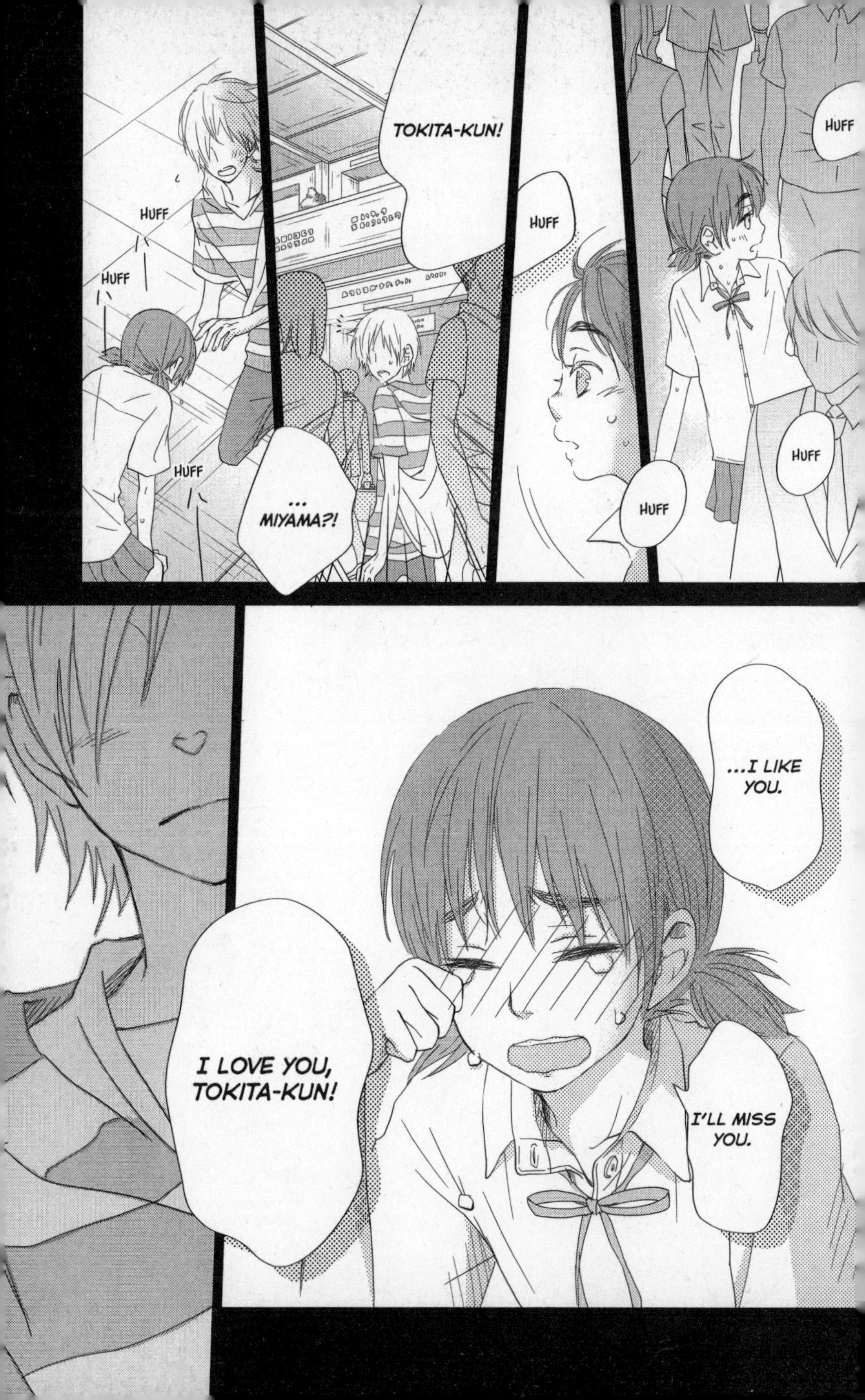
HUFF
HUFF
HUFF
HUFF
TOKITA-KUN!
...MIYAMA?!
HUFF
HUFF
HUFF
...I LIKE YOU.
I'LL MISS YOU.
I LOVE YOU, TOKITA-KUN!

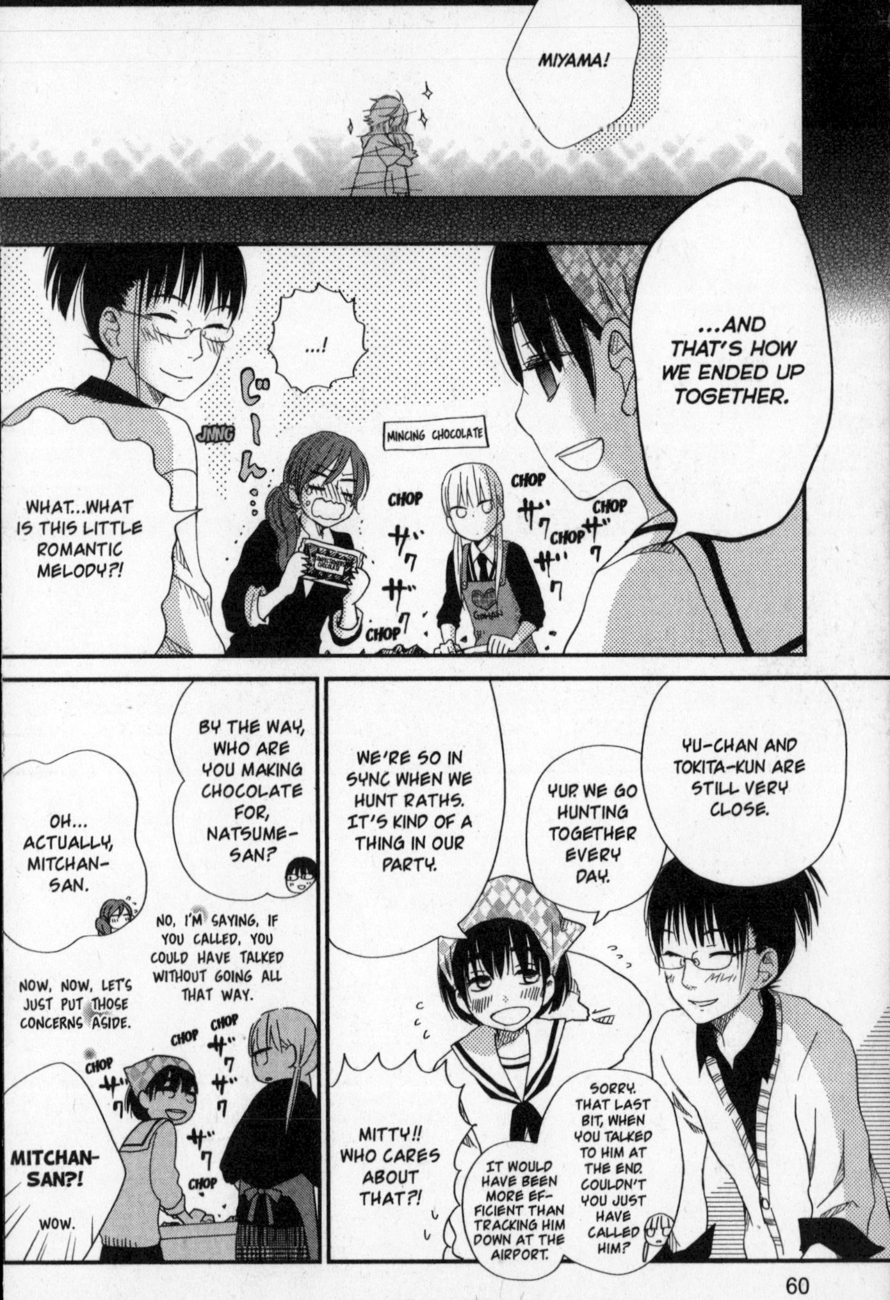
MIYAMA!
...AND THAT'S HOW WE ENDED UP TOGETHER.
...!
JNNG
MINCING CHOCOLATE
CHOP
CHOP
CHOP
CHOP
CHOP
WHAT...WHAT IS THIS LITTLE ROMANTIC MELODY?!
YU-CHAN AND TOKITA-KUN ARE STILL VERY CLOSE.
YUP. WE GO HUNTING TOGETHER EVERY DAY.
WE'RE SO IN SYNC WHEN WE HUNT RATHS. IT'S KIND OF A THING IN OUR PARTY.
SORRY. THAT LAST BIT, WHEN YOU TALKED TO HIM AT THE END. COULDN'T YOU JUST HAVE CALLED HIM?
IT WOULD HAVE BEEN MORE EF-FICIENT THAN TRACKING HIM DOWN AT THE AIRPORT.
MITTY!! WHO CARES ABOUT THAT?!
BY THE WAY, WHO ARE YOU MAKING CHOCOLATE FOR, NATSUME-SAN?
OH... ACTUALLY, MITCHAN-SAN.
NO, I'M SAYING, IF YOU CALLED, YOU COULD HAVE TALKED WITHOUT GOING ALL THAT WAY.
NOW, NOW, LET'S JUST PUT THOSE CONCERNS ASIDE.
CHOP
CHOP
CHOP
CHOP
MITCHAN-SAN?!
WOW.

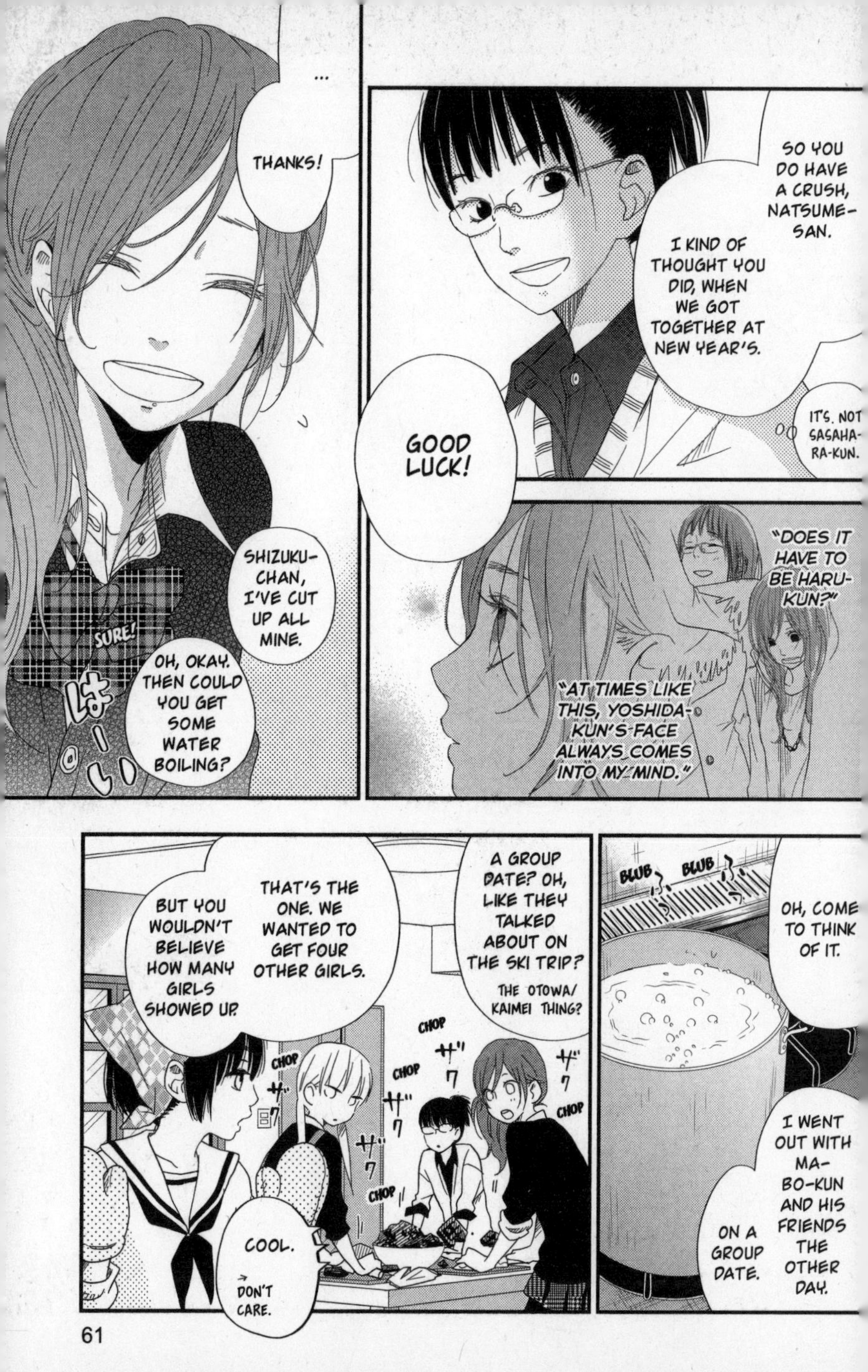
SO YOU DO HAVE A CRUSH, NATSUME-SAN.
I KIND OF THOUGHT YOU DID, WHEN WE GOT TOGETHER AT NEW YEAR'S.
IT'S NOT SASAHARA-KUN.
GOOD LUCK!
"DOES IT HAVE TO BE HARU-KUN?"
"AT TIMES LIKE THIS, YOSHIDA-KUN'S FACE ALWAYS COMES INTO MY MIND."
...
THANKS!
SHIZUKU-CHAN, I'VE CUT UP ALL MINE.
OH, OKAY. THEN COULD YOU GET SOME WATER BOILING?
SURE!
はーい
BLUB
BLUB
OH, COME TO THINK OF IT.
I WENT OUT WITH MA-BO-KUN AND HIS FRIENDS THE OTHER DAY.
ON A GROUP DATE.
A GROUP DATE? OH, LIKE THEY TALKED ABOUT ON THE SKI TRIP?
THE OTOWA/KAIMEI THING?
THAT'S THE ONE. WE WANTED TO GET FOUR OTHER GIRLS.
BUT YOU WOULDN'T BELIEVE HOW MANY GIRLS SHOWED UP.
CHOP
ザク
CHOP
ザク
CHOP
ザク
CHOP
ザク
CHOP
COOL.
DON'T CARE.

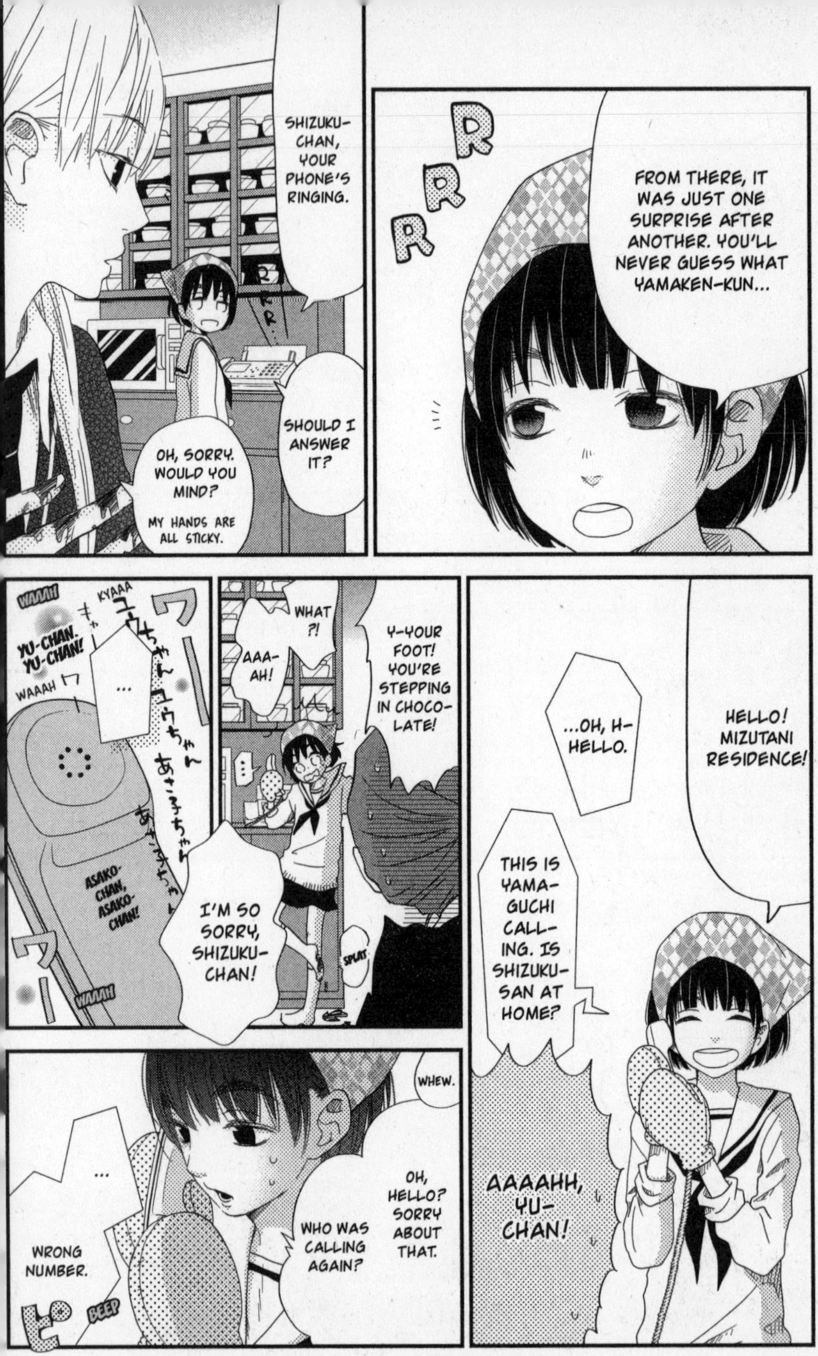
FROM THERE, IT WAS JUST ONE SURPRISE AFTER ANOTHER. YOU'LL NEVER GUESS WHAT YAMAKEN-KUN...
RRR
SHIZUKU-CHAN, YOUR PHONE'S RINGING.
SHOULD I ANSWER IT?
OH, SORRY. WOULD YOU MIND?
MY HANDS ARE ALL STICKY.
HELLO! MIZUTANI RESIDENCE!
...OH, H-HELLO.
THIS IS YAMAGUCHI CALLING. IS SHIZUKU-SAN AT HOME?
AAAAHH, YU-CHAN!
WHAT?!
Y-YOUR FOOT! YOU'RE STEPPING IN CHOCOLATE!
AAA-AH!
I'M SO SORRY, SHIZUKU-CHAN!
SPLAT
KYAAA
WAAAH
YU-CHAN. YU-CHAN!
...
ASAKO-CHAN, ASAKO-CHAN!
WAAAH
WHEW.
OH, HELLO? SORRY ABOUT THAT.
WHO WAS CALLING AGAIN?
...
WRONG NUMBER.
BEEP

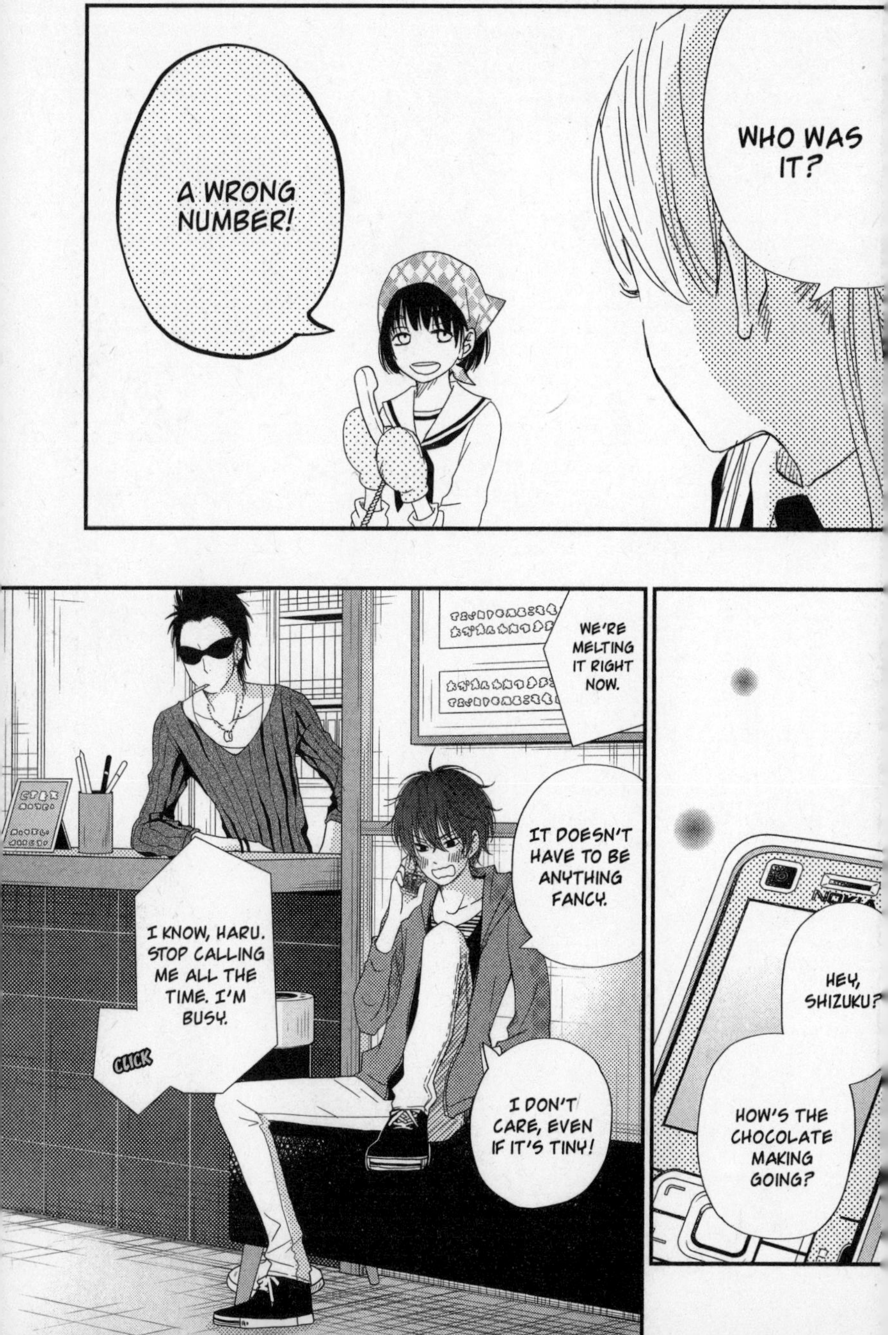
WHO WAS IT?
A WRONG NUMBER!
HEY, SHIZUKU?
HOW'S THE CHOCOLATE MAKING GOING?
WE'RE MELTING IT RIGHT NOW.
IT DOESN'T HAVE TO BE ANYTHING FANCY.
I DON'T CARE, EVEN IF IT'S TINY!
I KNOW, HARU. STOP CALLING ME ALL THE TIME. I'M BUSY.
CLICK

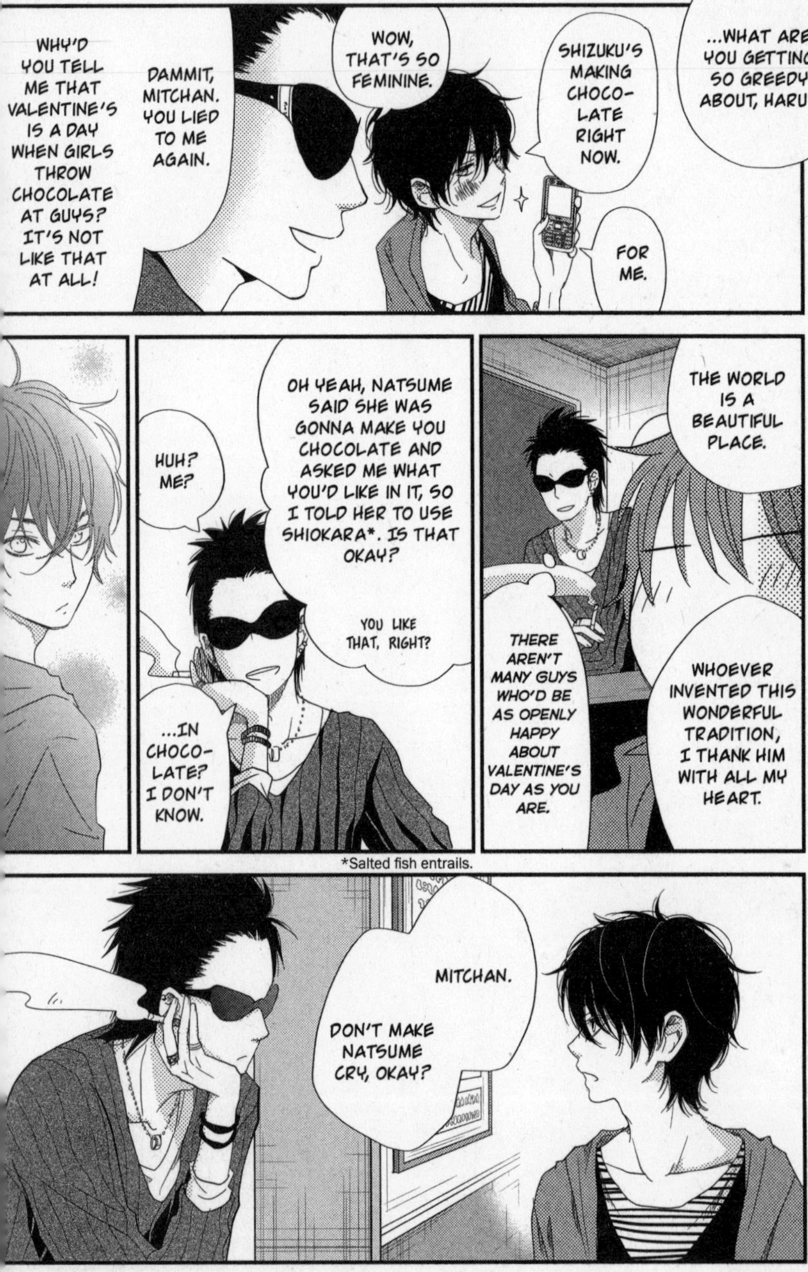
...WHAT ARE YOU GETTING SO GREEDY ABOUT, HARU?
SHIZUKU'S MAKING CHOCOLATE RIGHT NOW.
FOR ME.
WOW, THAT'S SO FEMININE.
DAMMIT, MITCHAN. YOU LIED TO ME AGAIN.
WHY'D YOU TELL ME THAT VALENTINE'S IS A DAY WHEN GIRLS THROW CHOCOLATE AT GUYS? IT'S NOT LIKE THAT AT ALL!
THE WORLD IS A BEAUTIFUL PLACE.
WHOEVER INVENTED THIS WONDERFUL TRADITION, I THANK HIM WITH ALL MY HEART.
THERE AREN'T MANY GUYS WHO'D BE AS OPENLY HAPPY ABOUT VALENTINE'S DAY AS YOU ARE.
OH YEAH, NATSUME SAID SHE WAS GONNA MAKE YOU CHOCOLATE AND ASKED ME WHAT YOU'D LIKE IN IT, SO I TOLD HER TO USE SHIOKARA*. IS THAT OKAY?
YOU LIKE THAT, RIGHT?
HUH? ME?
...IN CHOCOLATE? I DON'T KNOW.
MITCHAN.
DON'T MAKE NATSUME CRY, OKAY?

*Salted fish entrails.

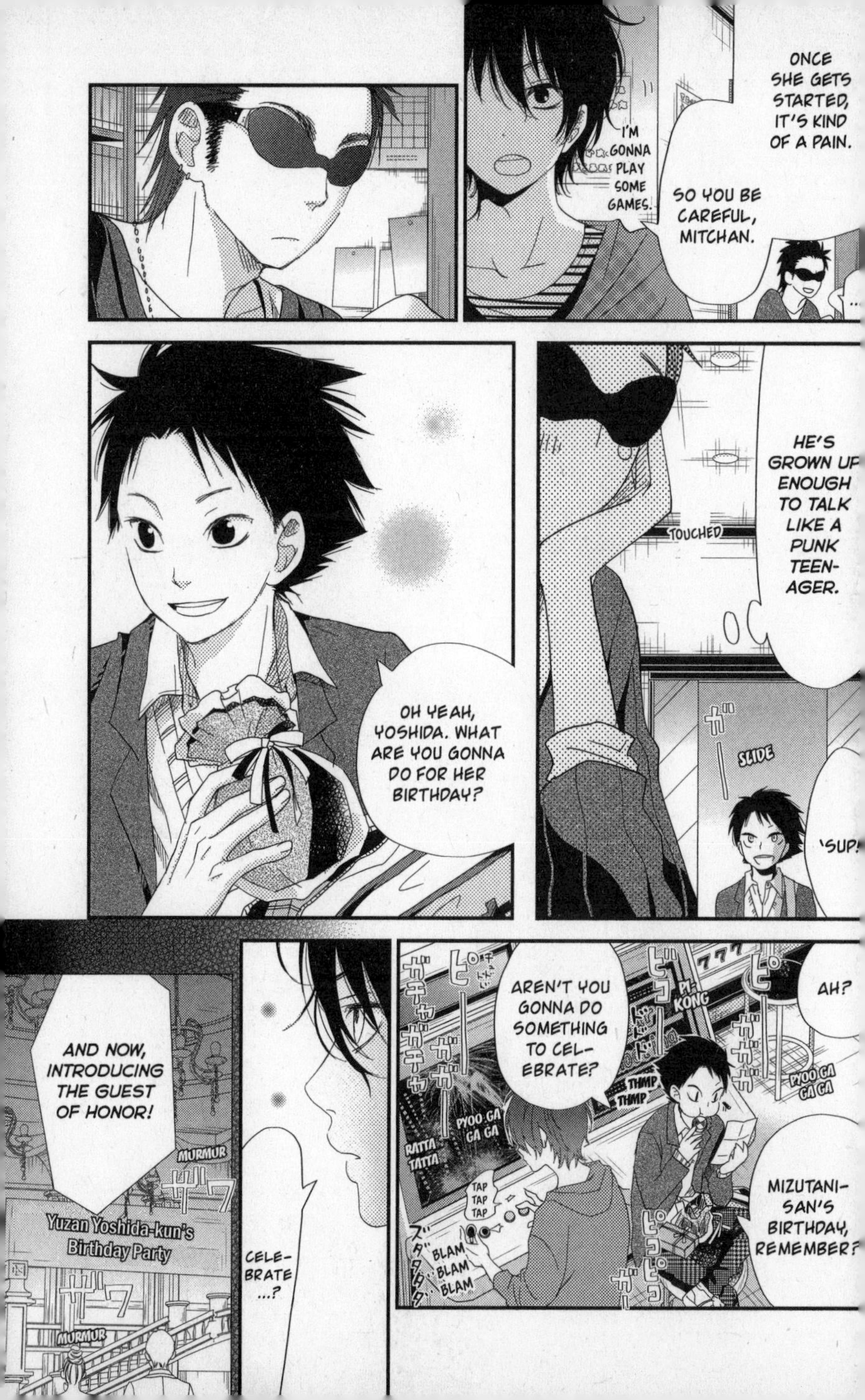
ONCE SHE GETS STARTED, IT'S KIND OF A PAIN.
SO YOU BE CAREFUL, MITCHAN.
I'M GONNA PLAY SOME GAMES.
HE'S GROWN UP ENOUGH TO TALK LIKE A PUNK TEEN-AGER.
TOUCHED
SLIDE
'SUP!
OH YEAH, YOSHIDA. WHAT ARE YOU GONNA DO FOR HER BIRTHDAY?
AH?
PYOO GA GA GA
PI-KONG
AREN'T YOU GONNA DO SOMETHING TO CEL-EBRATE?
THMP THMP
PYOO GA GA GA
RATTA TATTA
TAP TAP TAP
BLAM BLAM BLAM
MIZUTANI-SAN'S BIRTHDAY, REMEMBER?
CELE-BRATE ...?
AND NOW, INTRODUCING THE GUEST OF HONOR!
MURMUR
Yuzan Yoshida-kun's Birthday Party
MURMUR

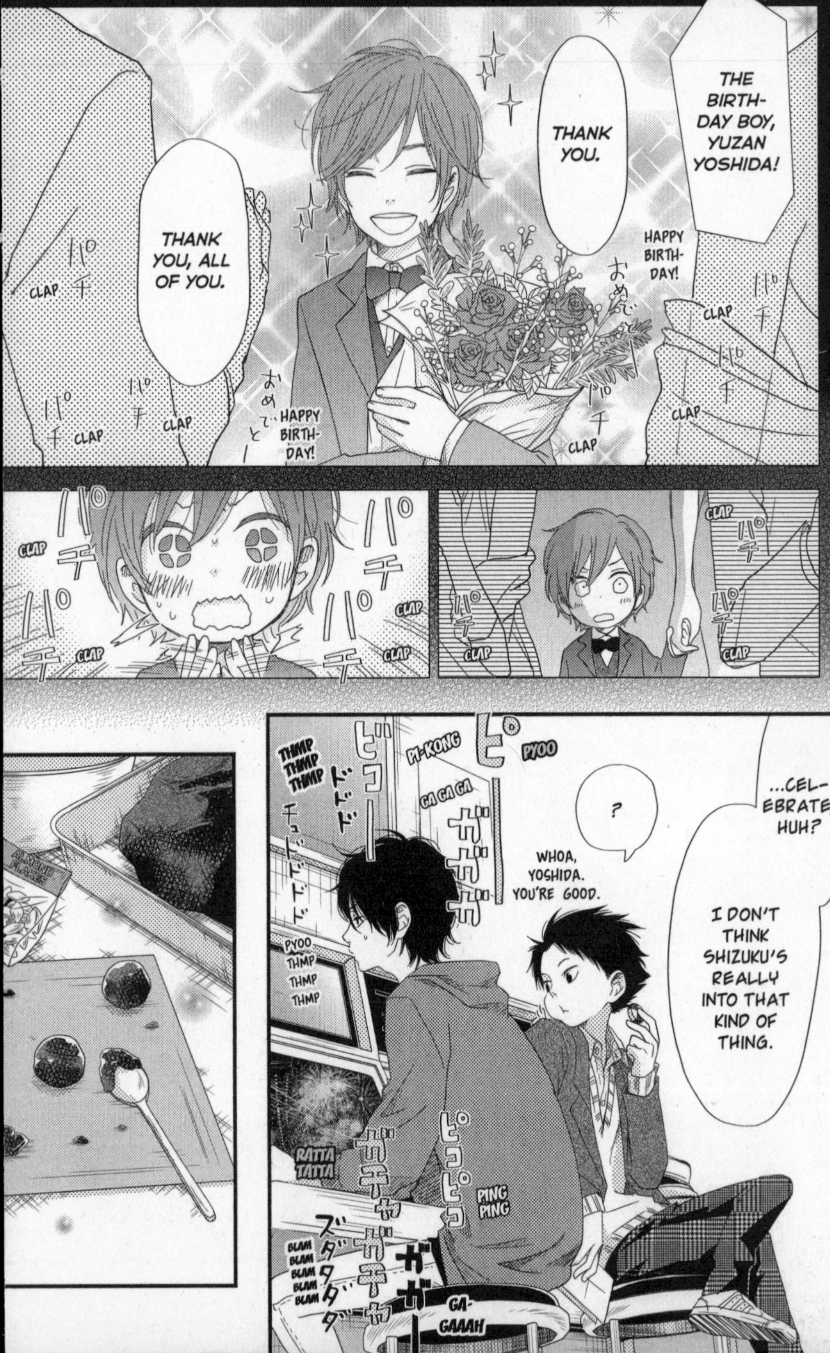

THE BIRTH-DAY BOY, YUZAN YOSHIDA!
THANK YOU.
HAPPY BIRTH-DAY!
CLAP
CLAP
THANK YOU, ALL OF YOU.
HAPPY BIRTH-DAY!
CLAP
CLAP
CLAP
CLAP
CLAP
CLAP
CLAP
CLAP
CLAP
CLAP
CLAP
PI-KONG
PYOO
...CEL-EBRATE, HUH?
I DON'T THINK SHIZUKU'S REALLY INTO THAT KIND OF THING.
?
WHOA, YOSHIDA. YOU'RE GOOD.
GA GA GA
THMP THMP THMP
PYOO THMP THMP THMP
PING PING
RATTA TATTA
BLAM BLAM BLAM BLAM BLAM
GA-GAAAH
ALMOND FLAKES

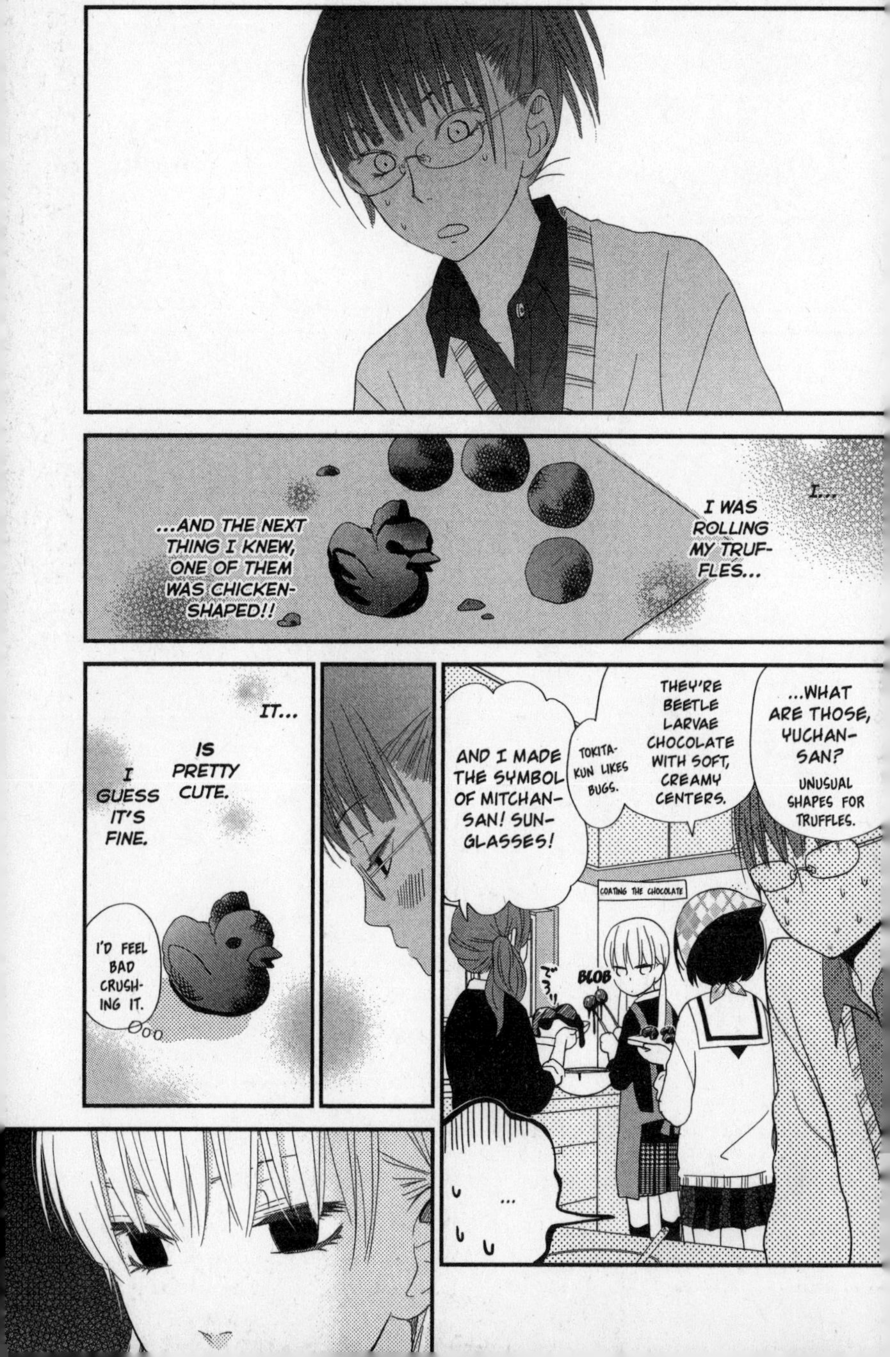
I...
I WAS ROLLING MY TRUFFLES...
...AND THE NEXT THING I KNEW, ONE OF THEM WAS CHICKEN-SHAPED!!
...WHAT ARE THOSE, YUCHAN-SAN?
UNUSUAL SHAPES FOR TRUFFLES.
THEY'RE BEETLE LARVAE CHOCOLATE WITH SOFT, CREAMY CENTERS.
TOKITA-KUN LIKES BUGS.
AND I MADE THE SYMBOL OF MITCHAN-SAN! SUN-GLASSES!
COATING THE CHOCOLATE
BLOB
...
IT...
IS PRETTY CUTE.
I GUESS IT'S FINE.
I'D FEEL BAD CRUSHING IT.

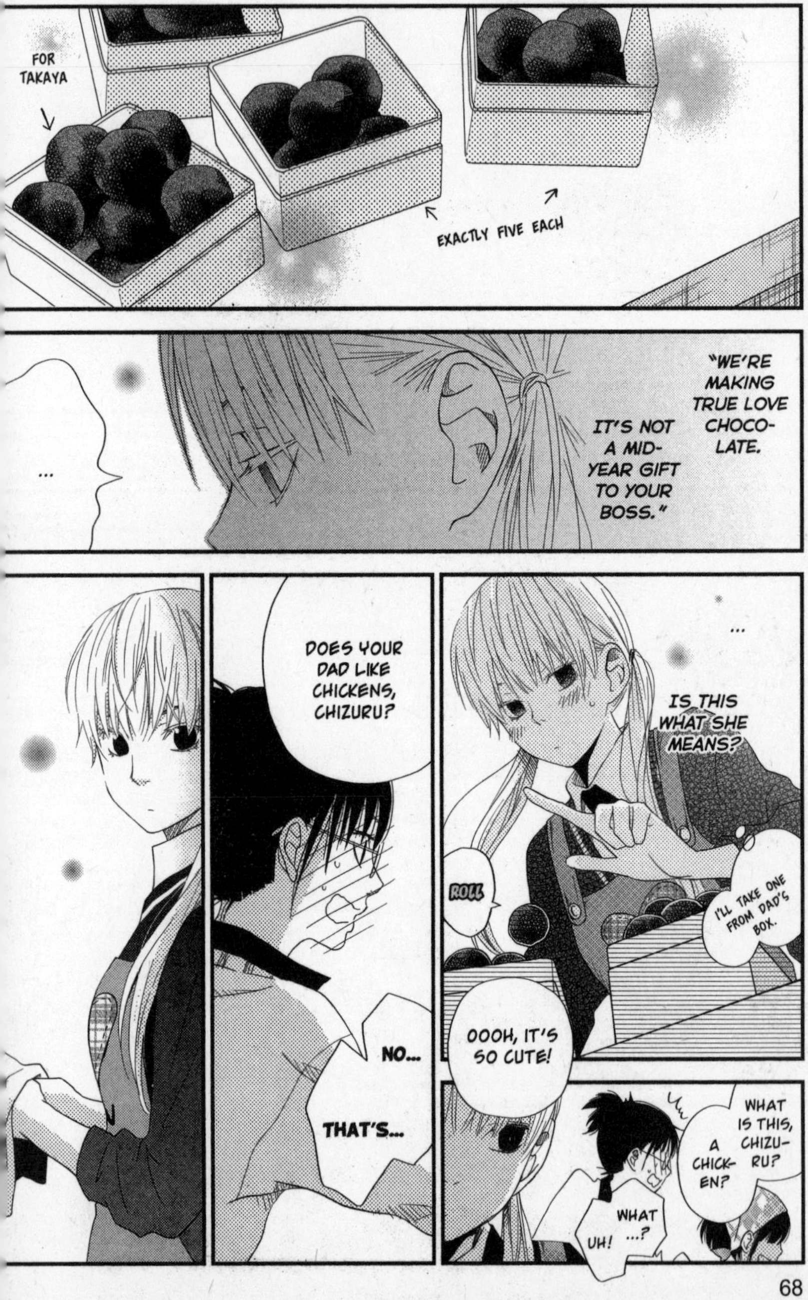
FOR TAKAYA
EXACTLY FIVE EACH
"WE'RE MAKING TRUE LOVE CHOCO-LATE.
IT'S NOT A MID-YEAR GIFT TO YOUR BOSS."
...
...
IS THIS WHAT SHE MEANS?
I'LL TAKE ONE FROM DAD'S BOX.
ROLL
WHAT IS THIS, CHIZU-RU?
A CHICK-EN?
OOOH, IT'S SO CUTE!
WHAT ...?
UH!
DOES YOUR DAD LIKE CHICKENS, CHIZURU?
NO...
THAT'S...

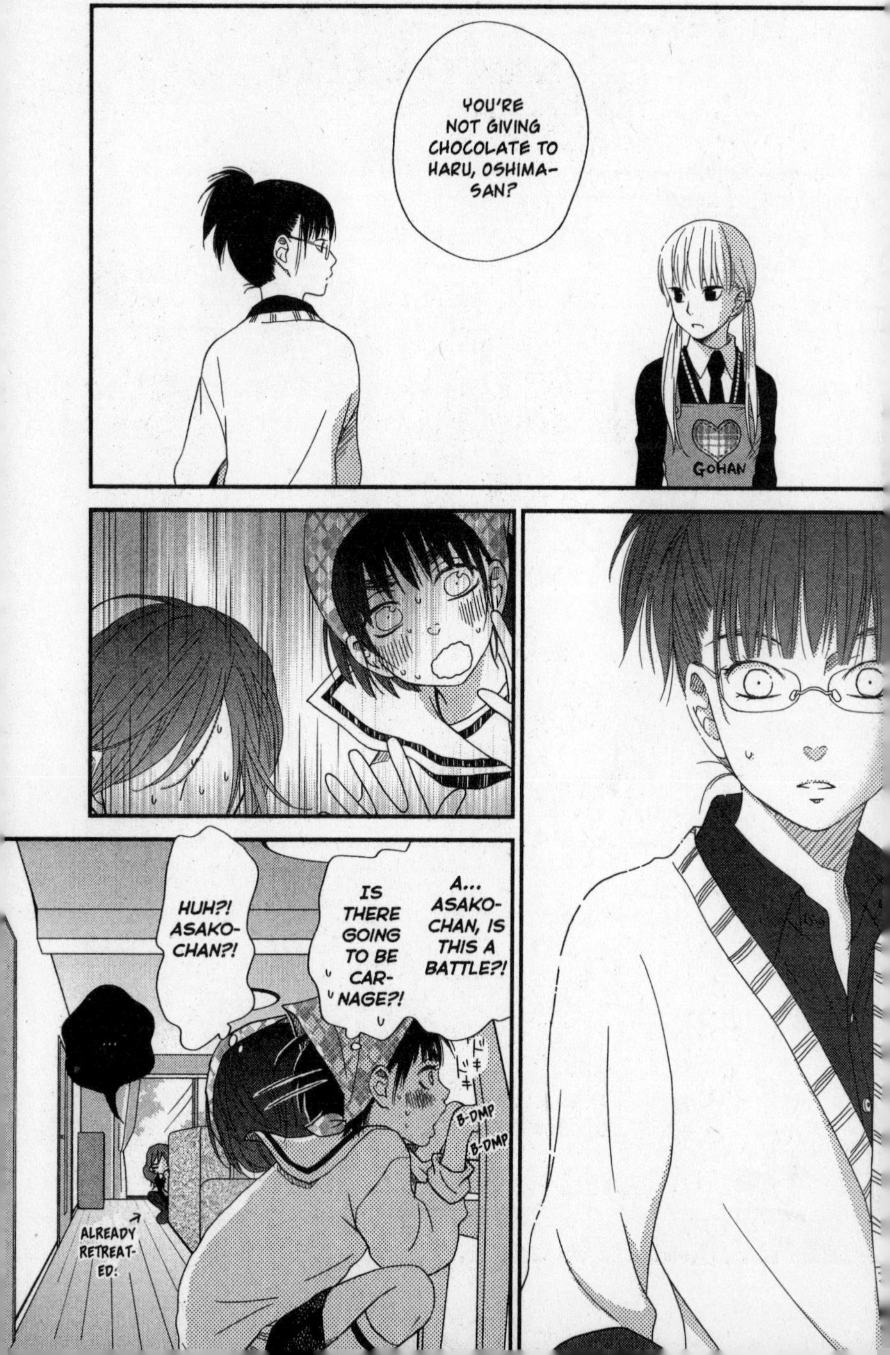
YOU'RE NOT GIVING CHOCOLATE TO HARU, OSHIMA-SAN?
GOHAN
A... ASAKO-CHAN, IS THIS A BATTLE?!
IS THERE GOING TO BE CAR-NAGE?!
HUH?! ASAKO-CHAN?!
B-DMP
B-DMP
ALREADY RETREAT-ED.

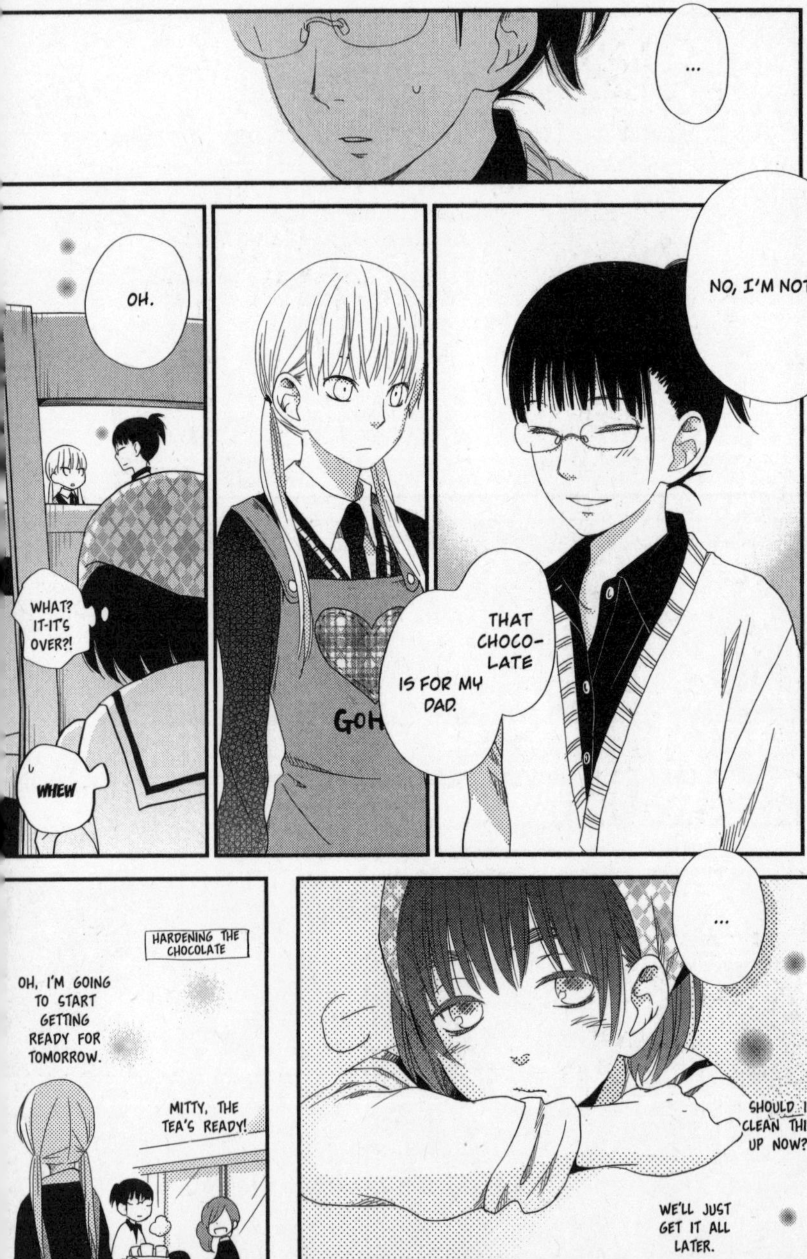
...
NO, I'M NOT.
THAT CHOCOLATE IS FOR MY DAD.
OH.
WHAT? IT-IT'S OVER?!
WHEW
...
SHOULD I CLEAN THIS UP NOW?
WE'LL JUST GET IT ALL LATER.
HARDENING THE CHOCOLATE
OH, I'M GOING TO START GETTING READY FOR TOMORROW.
MITTY, THE TEA'S READY!
GOH

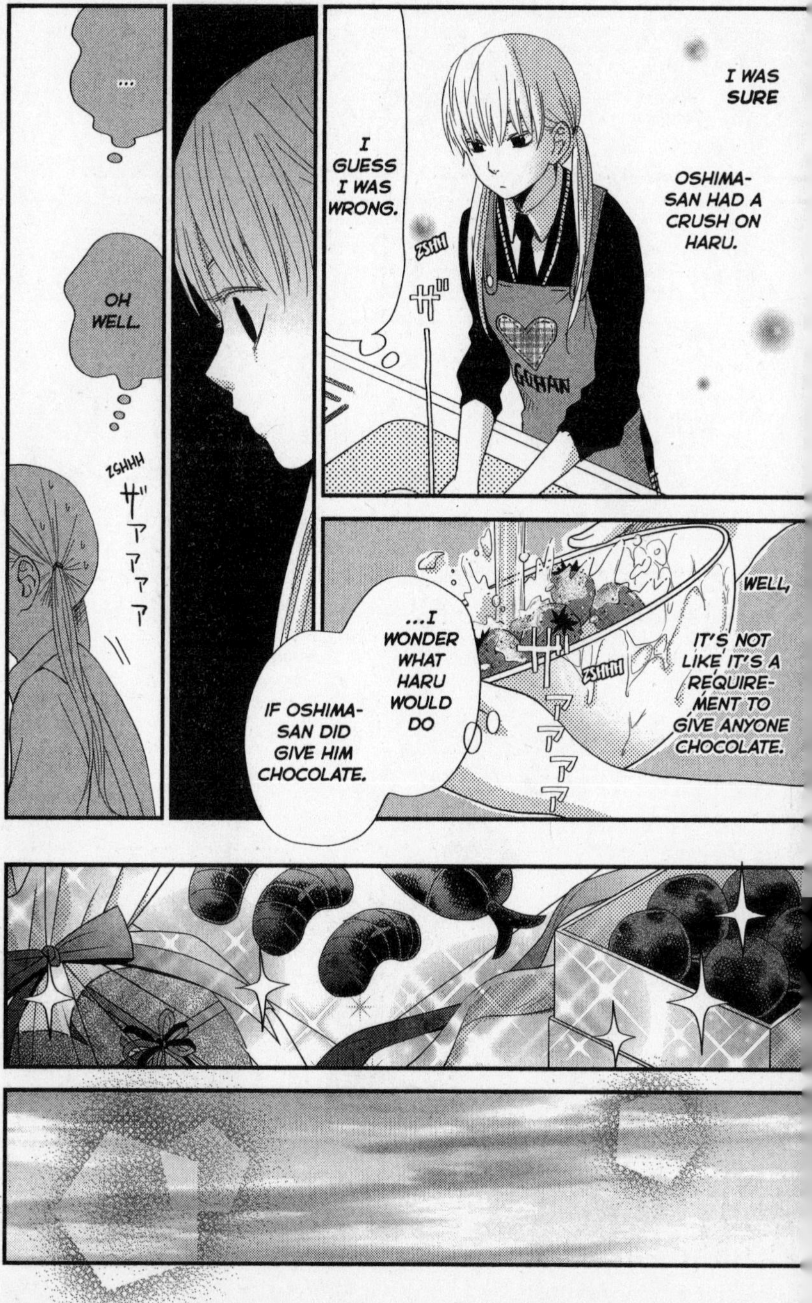
I WAS SURE
OSHIMA-SAN HAD A CRUSH ON HARU.
I GUESS I WAS WRONG.
ZSHH
ザ
WELL,
IT'S NOT LIKE IT'S A REQUIREMENT TO GIVE ANYONE CHOCOLATE.
ZSHHH
ザァァァ
...I WONDER WHAT HARU WOULD DO
IF OSHIMA-SAN DID GIVE HIM CHOCOLATE.
...
OH WELL.
ZSHHH
ザァァァァ

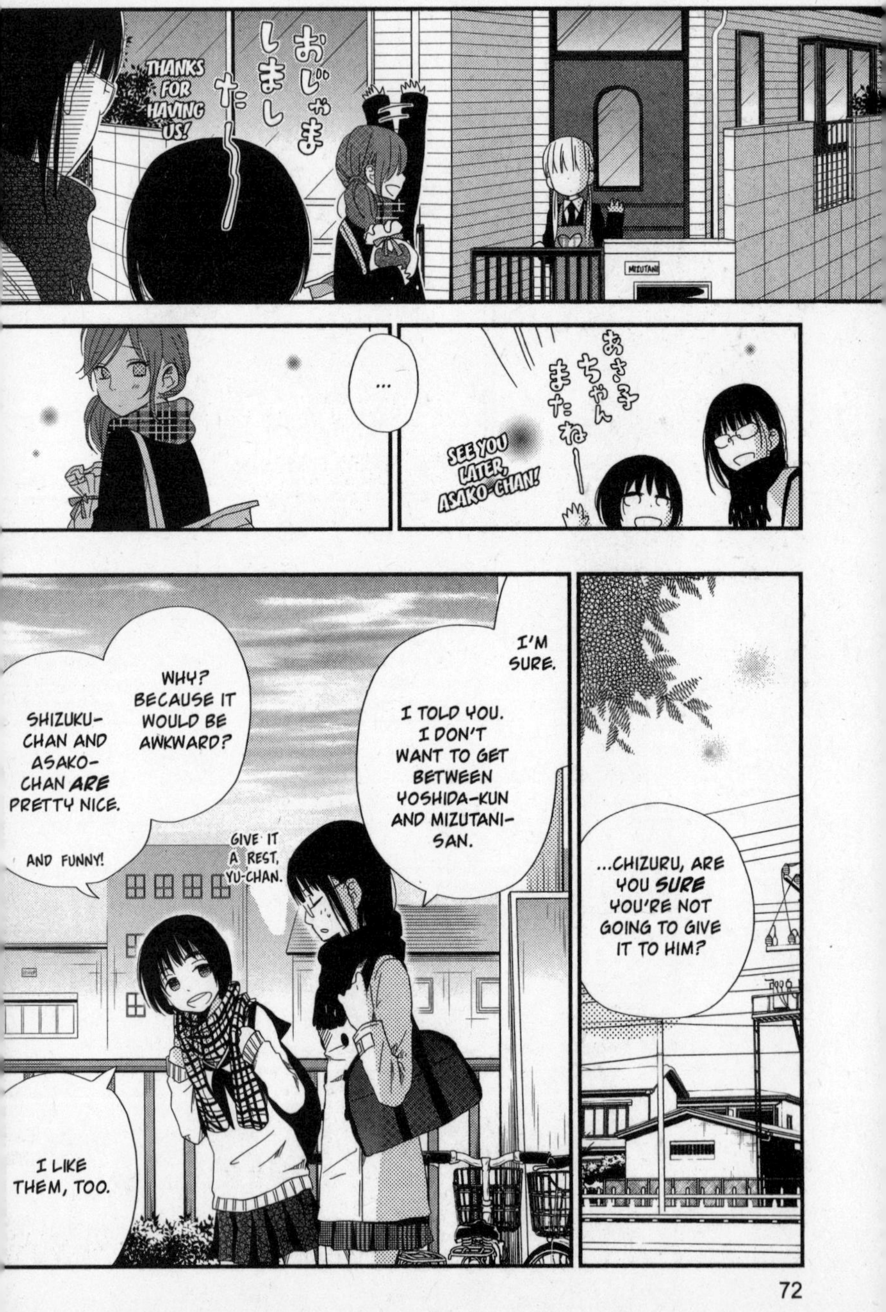
おじゃましました～
THANKS FOR HAVING US!
MIZUTANI
あさ子ちゃんまたね～
SEE YOU LATER, ASAKO-CHAN!
...
...CHIZURU, ARE YOU SURE YOU'RE NOT GOING TO GIVE IT TO HIM?
I'M SURE.
I TOLD YOU. I DON'T WANT TO GET BETWEEN YOSHIDA-KUN AND MIZUTANI-SAN.
WHY? BECAUSE IT WOULD BE AWKWARD?
GIVE IT A REST, YU-CHAN.
SHIZUKU-CHAN AND ASAKO-CHAN ARE PRETTY NICE.
AND FUNNY!
I LIKE THEM, TOO.

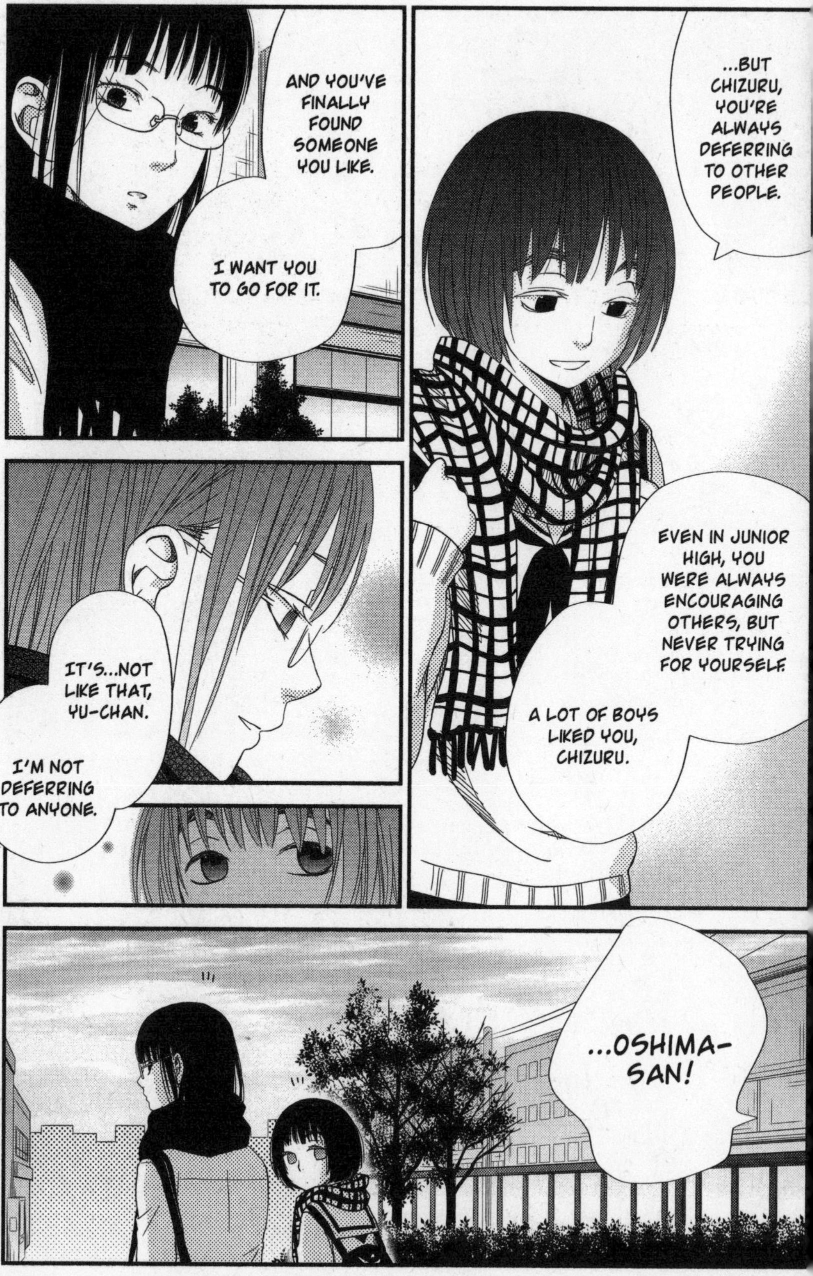
...BUT CHIZURU, YOU'RE ALWAYS DEFERRING TO OTHER PEOPLE.
EVEN IN JUNIOR HIGH, YOU WERE ALWAYS ENCOURAGING OTHERS, BUT NEVER TRYING FOR YOURSELF.
A LOT OF BOYS LIKED YOU, CHIZURU.
AND YOU'VE FINALLY FOUND SOMEONE YOU LIKE.
I WANT YOU TO GO FOR IT.
IT'S...NOT LIKE THAT, YU-CHAN.
I'M NOT DEFERRING TO ANYONE.
...OSHIMA-SAN!

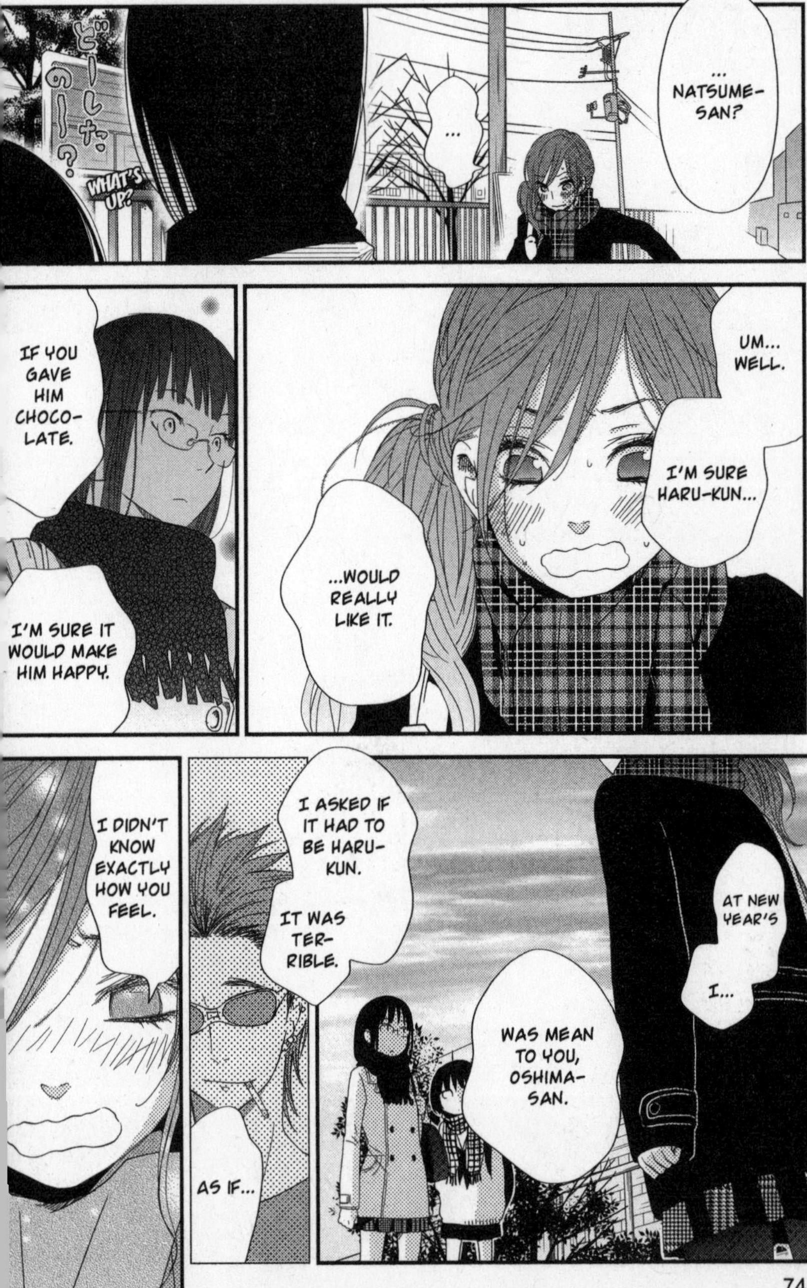
... NATSUME-SAN?
...
どーしたのー?
WHAT'S UP?
UM... WELL.
I'M SURE HARU-KUN...
...WOULD REALLY LIKE IT.
IF YOU GAVE HIM CHOCOLATE.
I'M SURE IT WOULD MAKE HIM HAPPY.
AT NEW YEAR'S
I...
WAS MEAN TO YOU, OSHIMA-SAN.
I ASKED IF IT HAD TO BE HARU-KUN.
IT WAS TERRIBLE.
AS IF...
I DIDN'T KNOW EXACTLY HOW YOU FEEL.

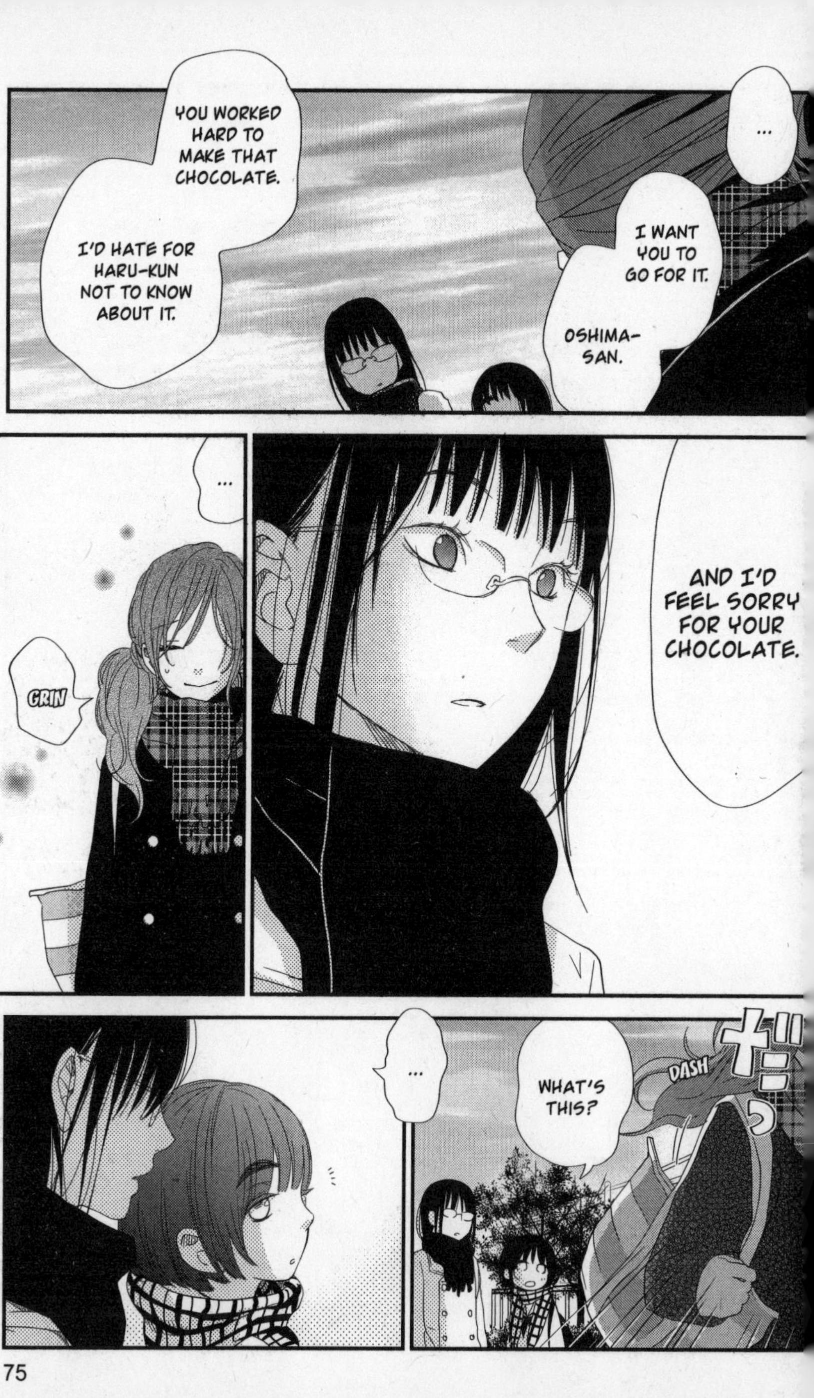
...
I WANT YOU TO GO FOR IT.
OSHIMA-SAN.
YOU WORKED HARD TO MAKE THAT CHOCOLATE.
I'D HATE FOR HARU-KUN NOT TO KNOW ABOUT IT.
AND I'D FEEL SORRY FOR YOUR CHOCOLATE.
...
GRIN
DASH
WHAT'S THIS?
...

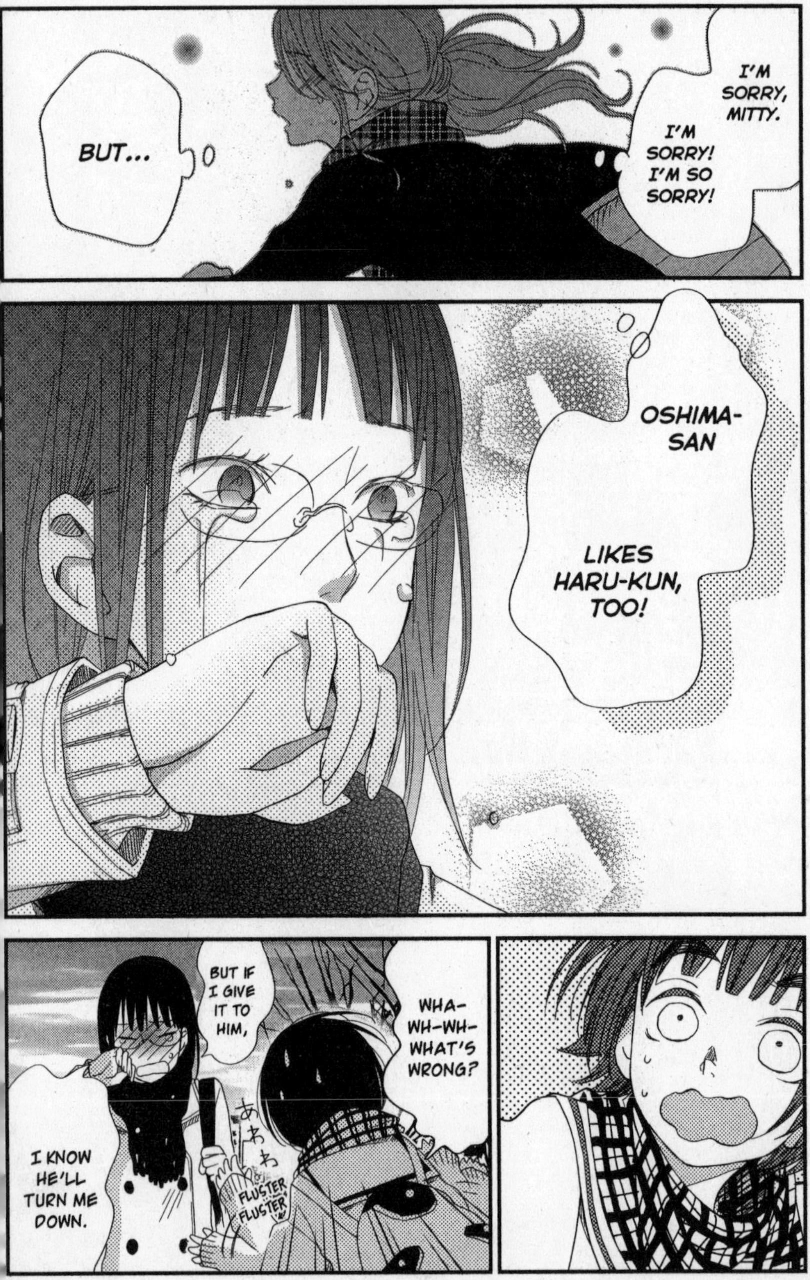
I'M SORRY, MITTY.
I'M SORRY! I'M SO SORRY!
BUT...
OSHIMA-SAN
LIKES HARU-KUN, TOO!
WHA-WH-WH-WHAT'S WRONG?
BUT IF I GIVE IT TO HIM,
FLUSTER FLUSTER
I KNOW HE'LL TURN ME DOWN.

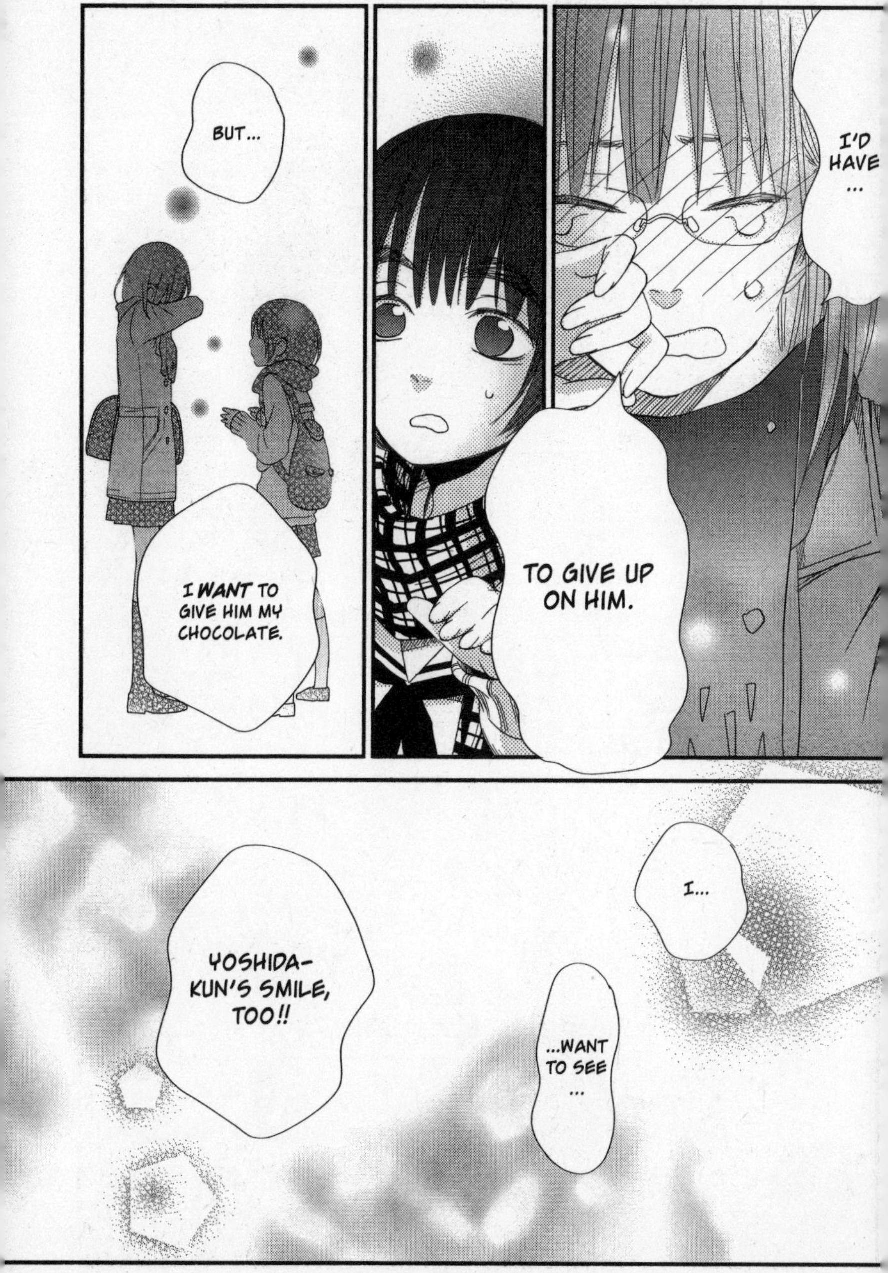
I'D HAVE ...
TO GIVE UP ON HIM.
BUT...
I WANT TO GIVE HIM MY CHOCOLATE.
I...
...WANT TO SEE ...
YOSHIDA-KUN'S SMILE, TOO!!

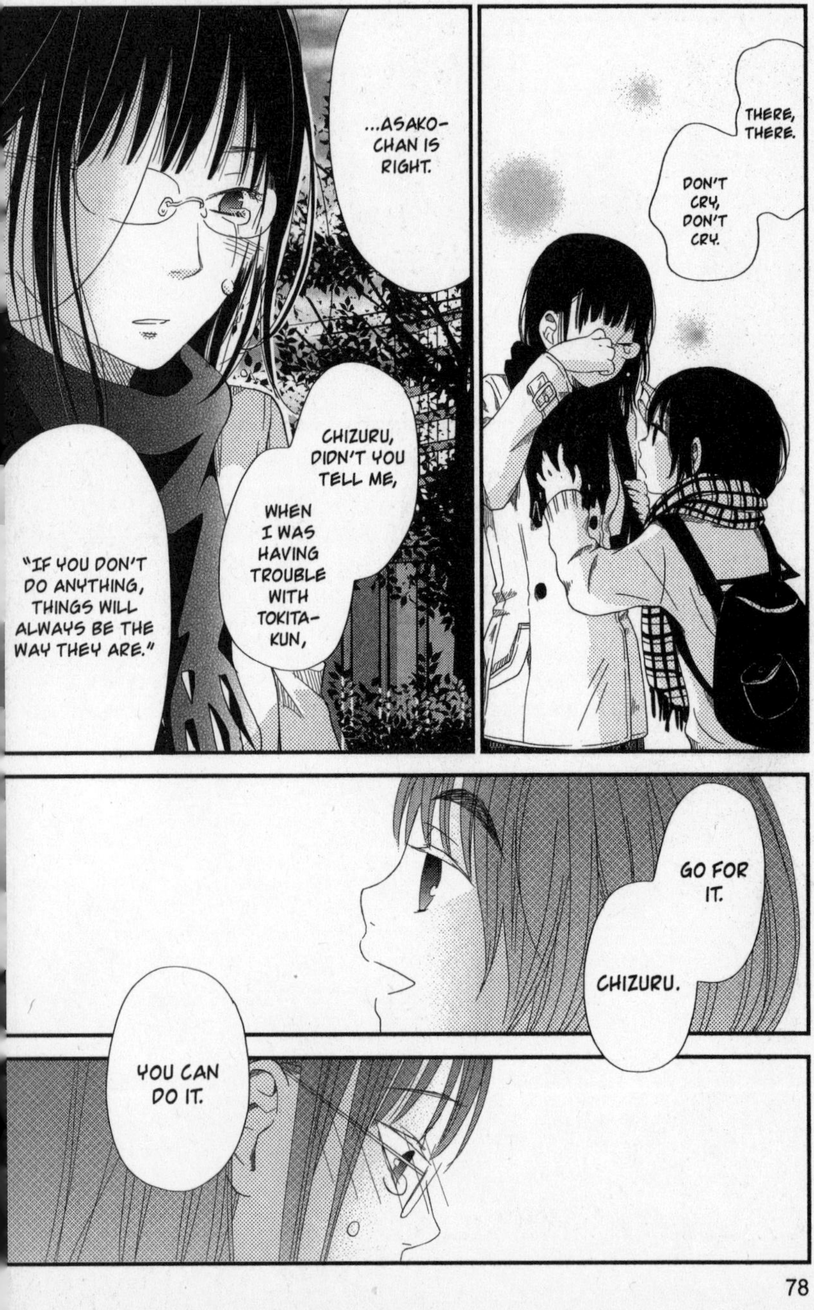
THERE, THERE.
DON'T CRY, DON'T CRY.
...ASAKO-CHAN IS RIGHT.
CHIZURU, DIDN'T YOU TELL ME,
WHEN I WAS HAVING TROUBLE WITH TOKITA-KUN,
"IF YOU DON'T DO ANYTHING, THINGS WILL ALWAYS BE THE WAY THEY ARE."
GO FOR IT.
CHIZURU.
YOU CAN DO IT.

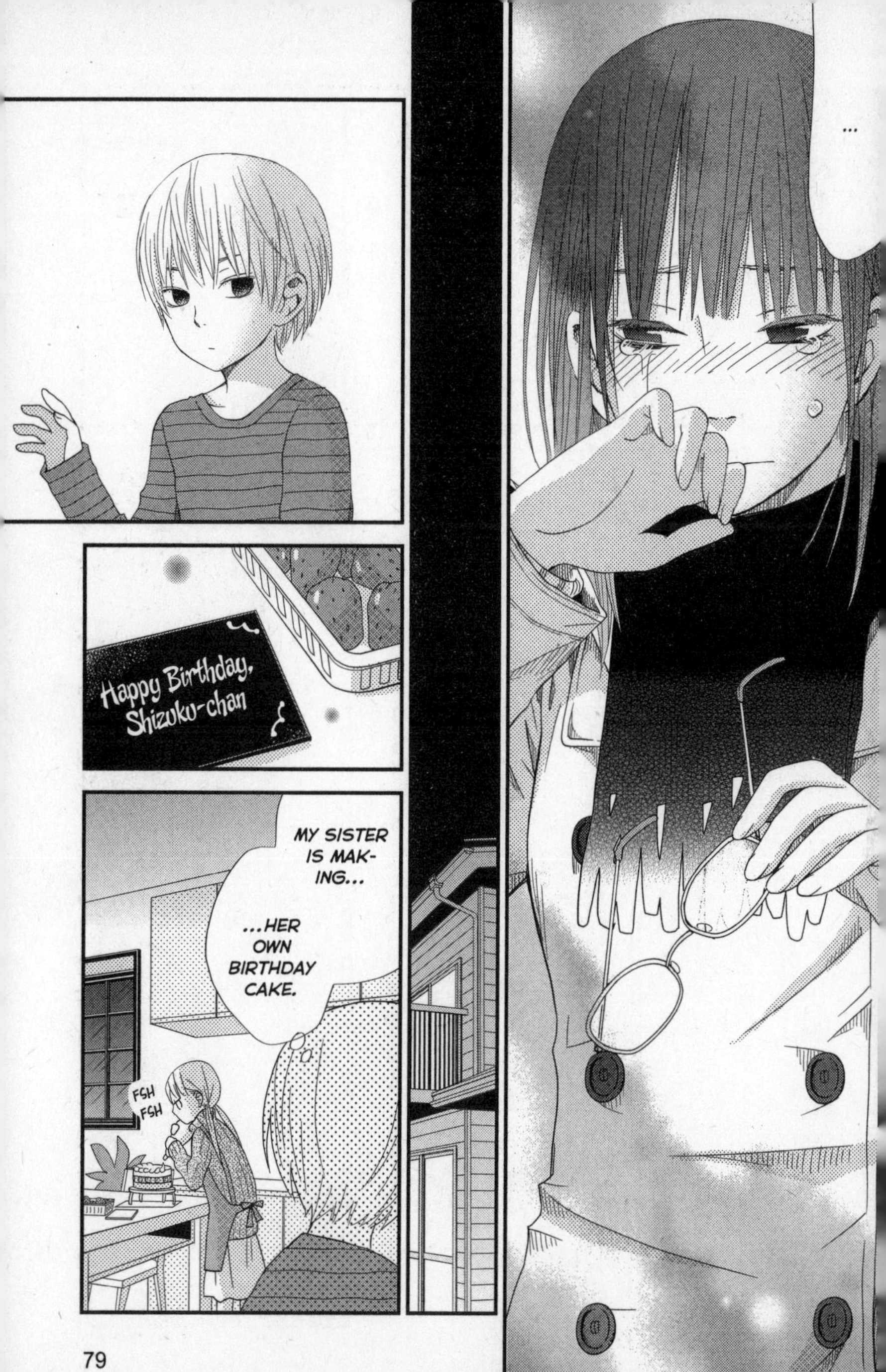
...
Happy Birthday, Shizuku-chan
MY SISTER IS MAK-ING...
...HER OWN BIRTHDAY CAKE.
FSH FSH

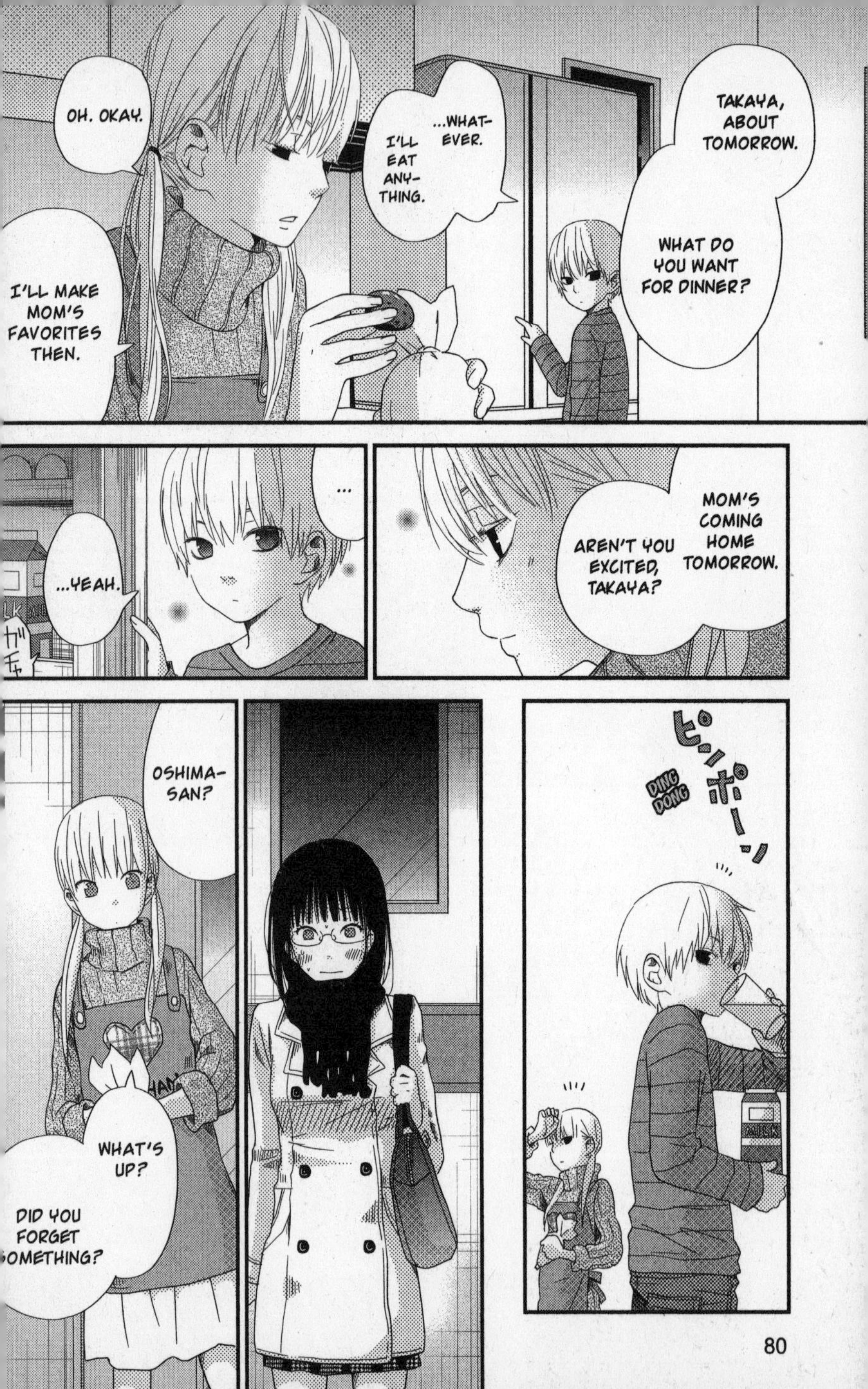
TAKAYA, ABOUT TOMORROW.
WHAT DO YOU WANT FOR DINNER?
...WHATEVER. I'LL EAT ANYTHING.
OH. OKAY.
I'LL MAKE MOM'S FAVORITES THEN.
MOM'S COMING HOME TOMORROW.
AREN'T YOU EXCITED, TAKAYA?
...
...YEAH.
ピンポーン
DING DONG
OSHIMA-SAN?
WHAT'S UP?
DID YOU FORGET SOMETHING?

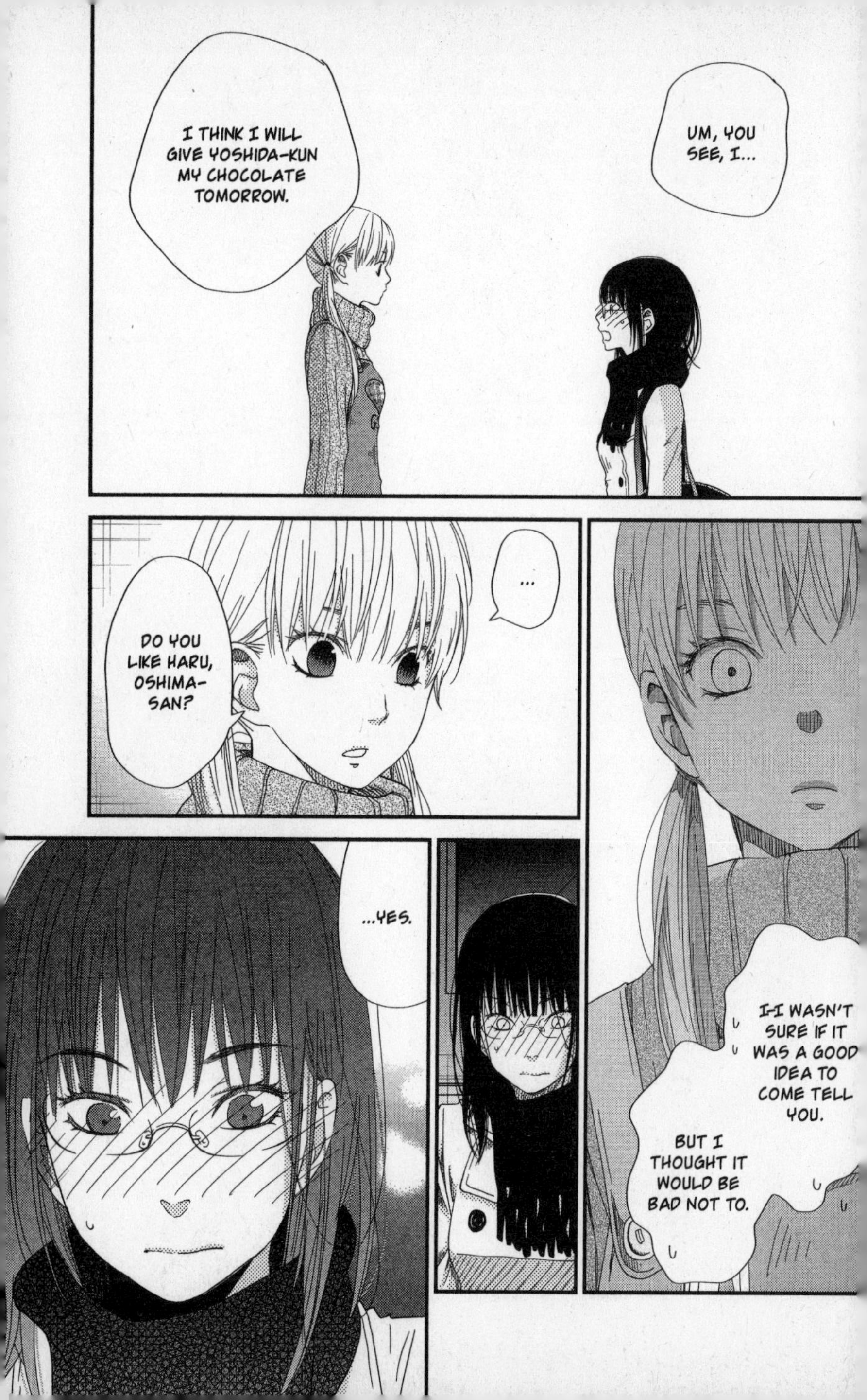
UM, YOU SEE, I...
I THINK I WILL GIVE YOSHIDA-KUN MY CHOCOLATE TOMORROW.
I-I WASN'T SURE IF IT WAS A GOOD IDEA TO COME TELL YOU.
BUT I THOUGHT IT WOULD BE BAD NOT TO.
...
DO YOU LIKE HARU, OSHIMA-SAN?
...YES.

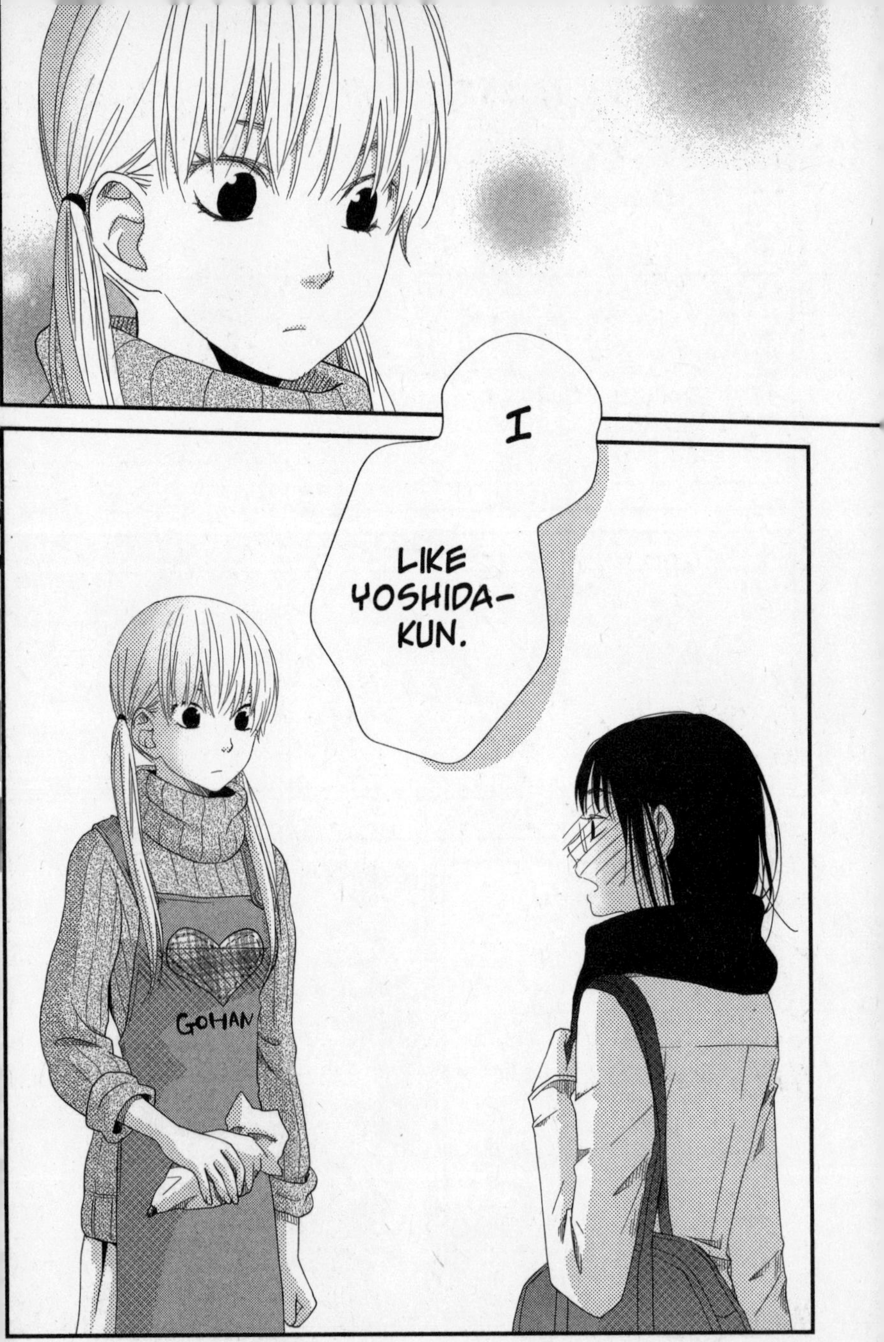
I
LIKE YOSHIDA-KUN.
GOHAN

Takaya Mizutani

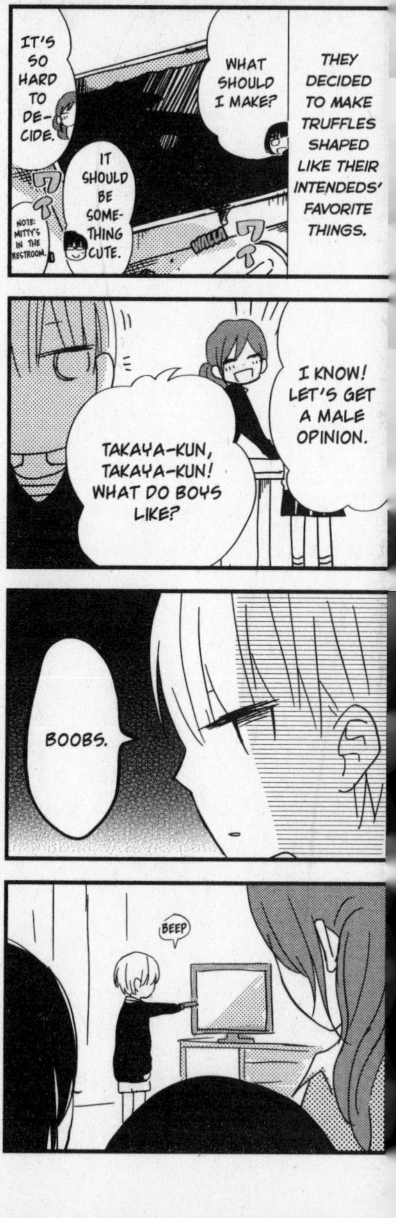
THEY DECIDED TO MAKE TRUFFLES SHAPED LIKE THEIR INTENDEDS' FAVORITE THINGS.
WHAT SHOULD I MAKE?
IT'S SO HARD TO DECIDE.
IT SHOULD BE SOMETHING CUTE.
WALLA
NOTE: MITTY'S IN THE RESTROOM.
I KNOW! LET'S GET A MALE OPINION.
TAKAYA-KUN, TAKAYA-KUN! WHAT DO BOYS LIKE?
BOOBS.
BEEP

Mysterious Objects

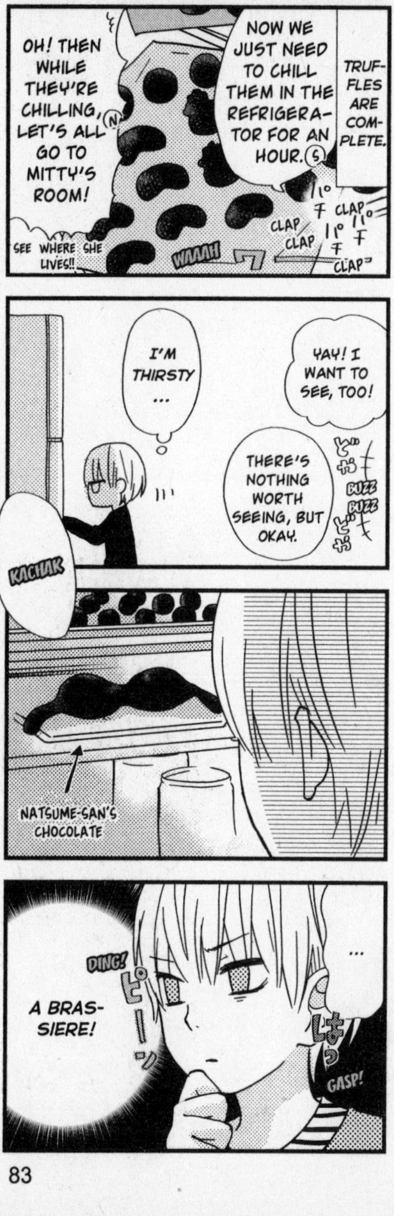
TRUFFLES ARE COMPLETE.
NOW WE JUST NEED TO CHILL THEM IN THE REFRIGERATOR FOR AN HOUR.
OH! THEN WHILE THEY'RE CHILLING, LET'S ALL GO TO MITTY'S ROOM!
CLAP CLAP CLAP CLAP
WAAAH
SEE WHERE SHE LIVES!!
YAY! I WANT TO SEE, TOO!
I'M THIRSTY...
BUZZ BUZZ
THERE'S NOTHING WORTH SEEING, BUT OKAY.
KACHAK
NATSUME-SAN'S CHOCOLATE
...
DING!
A BRASSIERE!
GASP!

NET DISTRIBUTION MAP
FOR GAMING
PC USERS
MOBILE DEVICE USERS
FOR COMMUNITIES, BLOGS, AND SOCIAL NETWORKING

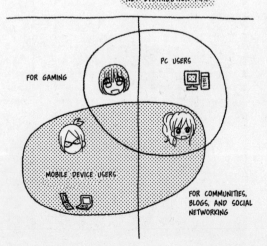

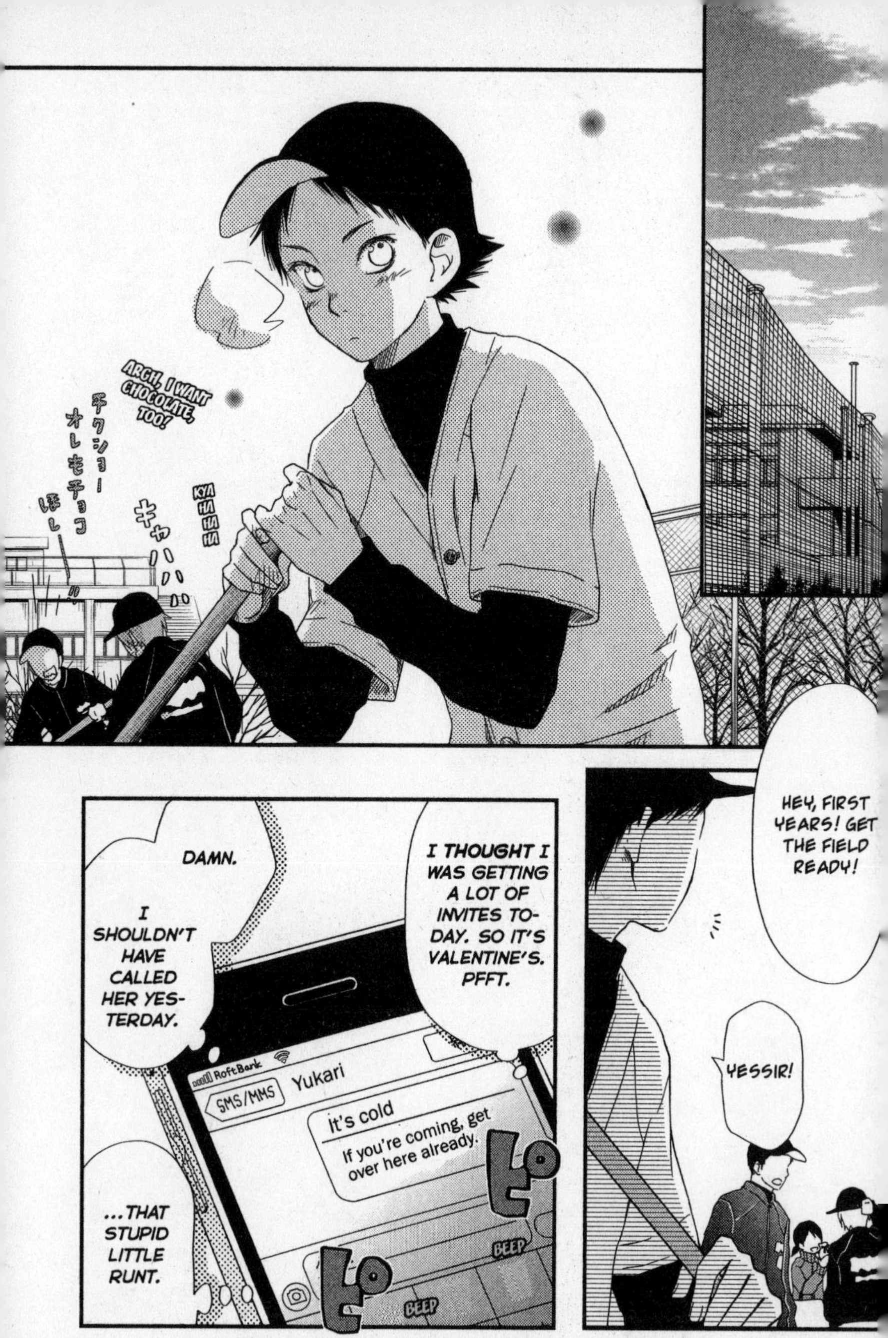

ARGH, I WANT CHOCOLATE, TOO!
チクショー
オレもチョコほしー
KYA HA HA HA
キャハハハ
HEY, FIRST YEARS! GET THE FIELD READY!
YESSIR!
I THOUGHT I WAS GETTING A LOT OF INVITES TO-DAY. SO IT'S VALENTINE'S. PFFT.
DAMN.
I SHOULDN'T HAVE CALLED HER YES-TERDAY.
RoftBank
Yukari
SMS/MMS
It's cold
If you're coming, get over here already.
ピ
BEEP
ピ
BEEP
...THAT STUPID LITTLE RUNT.

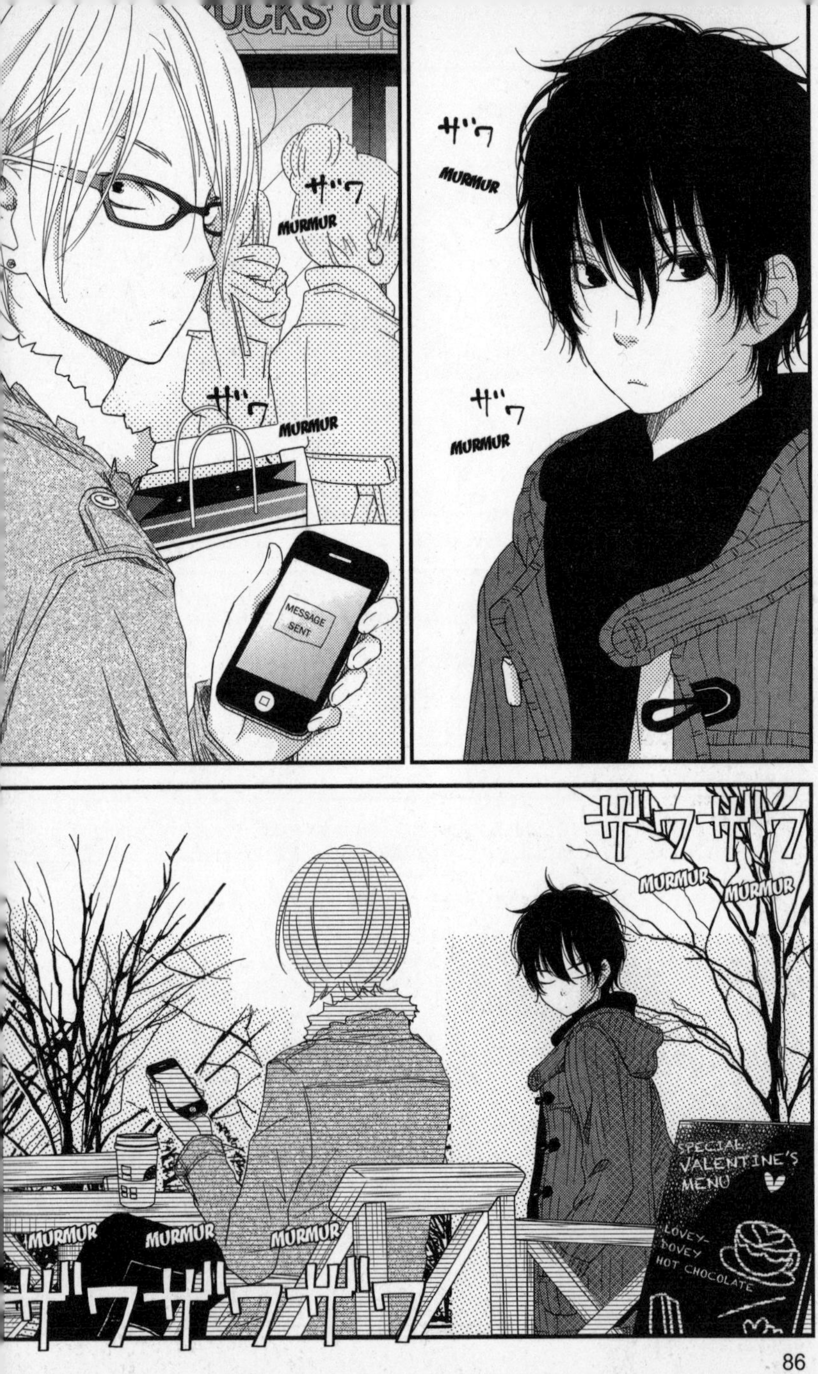
ザワ
MURMUR
ザワ
MURMUR
ザワ
MURMUR
ザワ
MURMUR
MESSAGE SENT
ザワザワ
MURMUR
MURMUR
SPECIAL VALENTINE'S MENU
LOVEY-DOVEY HOT CHOCOLATE
MURMUR
MURMUR
MURMUR
ザワザワザワ

Chapter 23 Birthday (Part One)

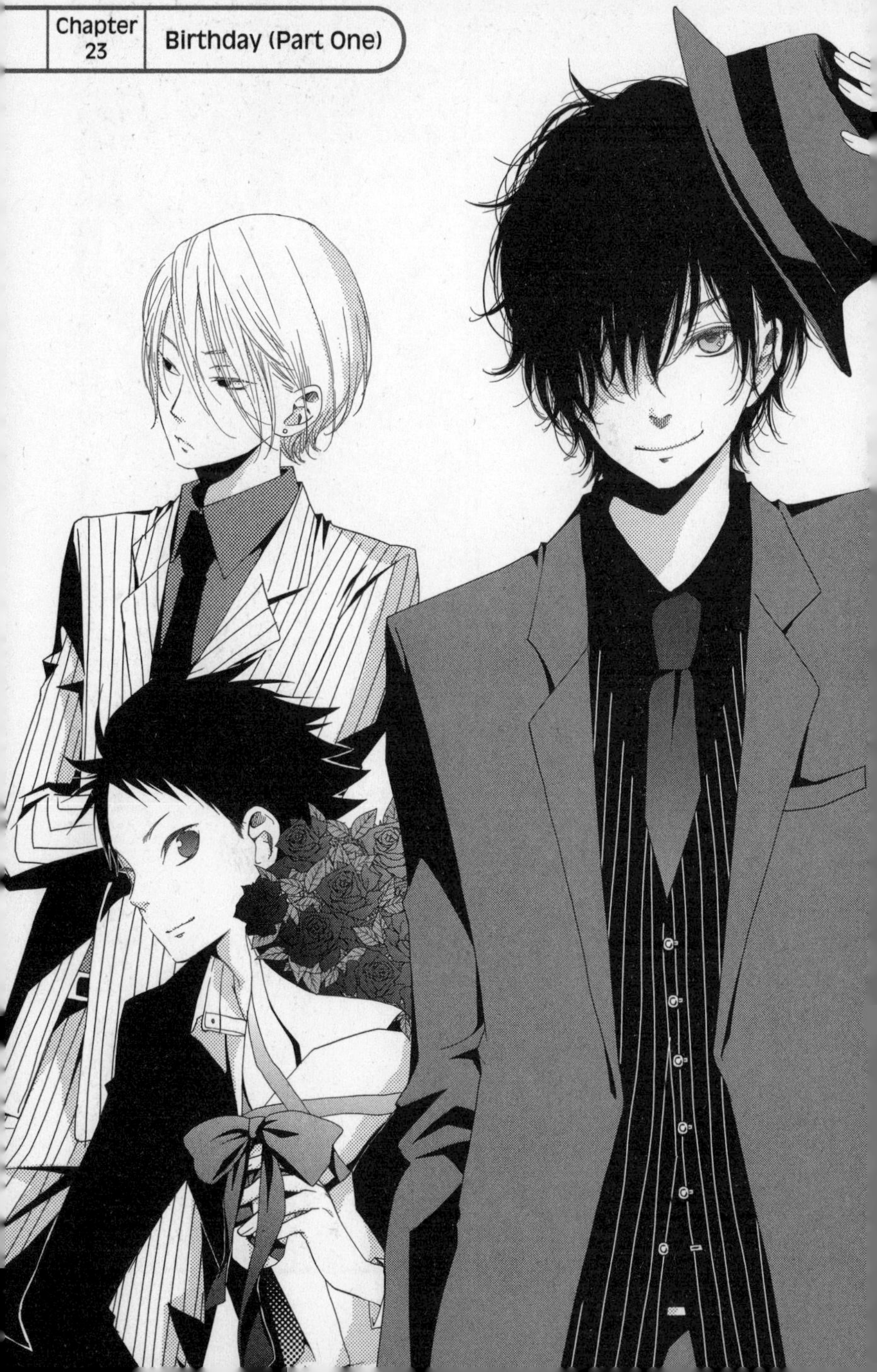

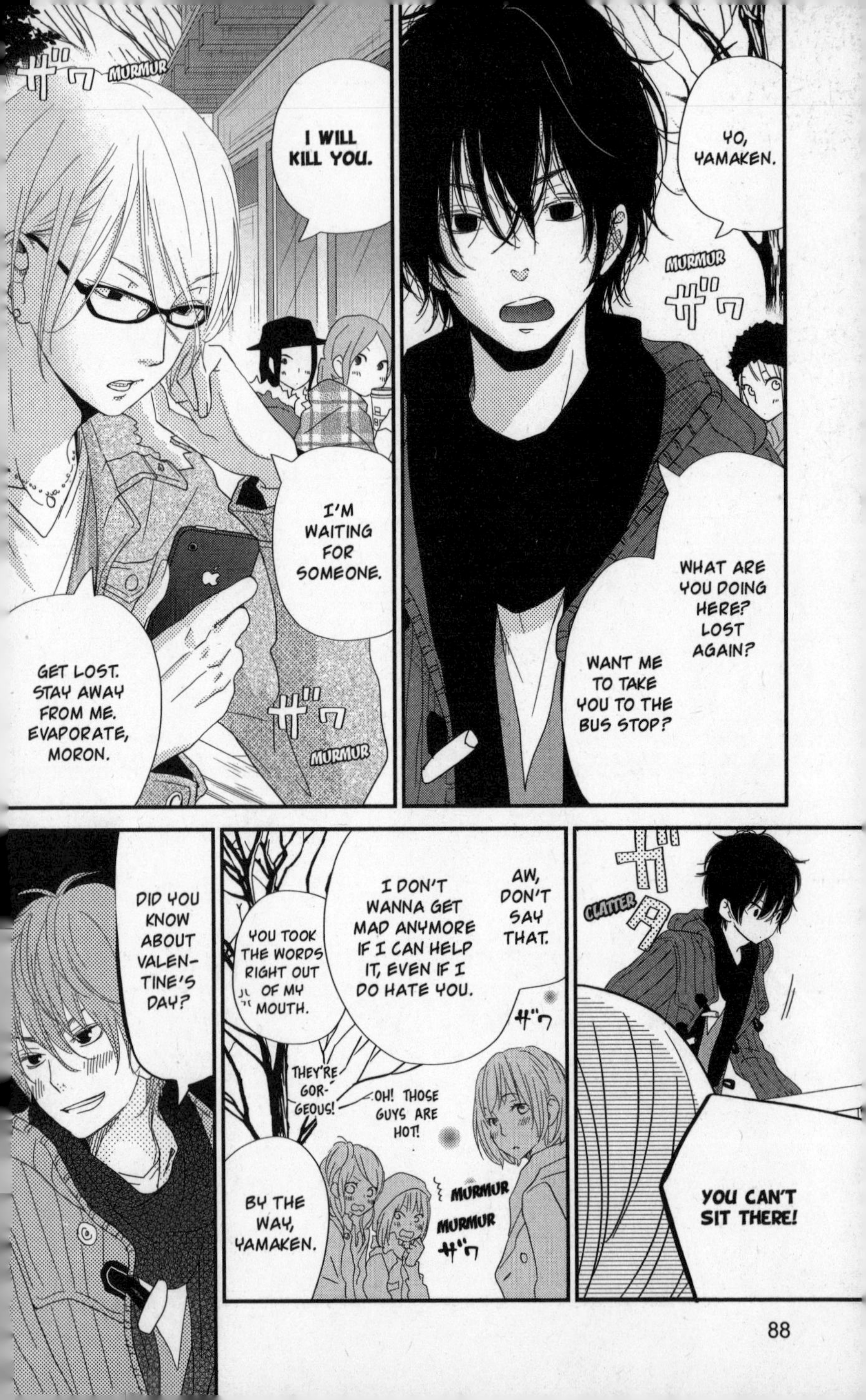
ザワ MURMUR
YO, YAMAKEN.
WHAT ARE YOU DOING HERE? LOST AGAIN?
WANT ME TO TAKE YOU TO THE BUS STOP?
ザワ MURMUR
I WILL KILL YOU.
I'M WAITING FOR SOMEONE.
GET LOST. STAY AWAY FROM ME. EVAPORATE, MORON.
ザワ MURMUR
ガタ CLATTER
YOU CAN'T SIT THERE!
AW, DON'T SAY THAT.
I DON'T WANNA GET MAD ANYMORE IF I CAN HELP IT, EVEN IF I DO HATE YOU.
YOU TOOK THE WORDS RIGHT OUT OF MY MOUTH.
OH! THOSE GUYS ARE HOT!
THEY'RE GOR-GEOUS!
MURMUR MURMUR ザワ
BY THE WAY, YAMAKEN.
DID YOU KNOW ABOUT VALEN-TINE'S DAY?

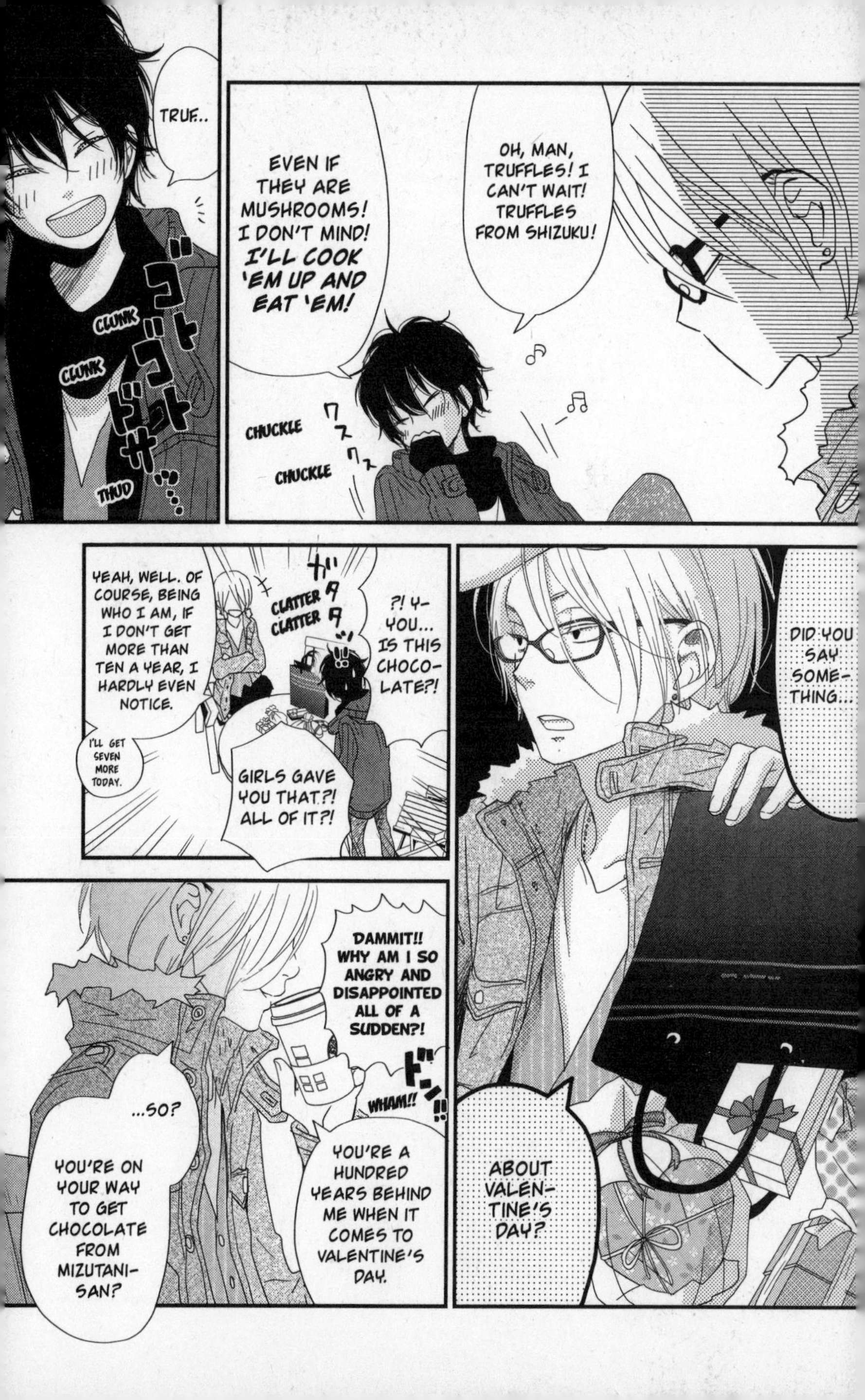

OH, MAN, TRUFFLES! I CAN'T WAIT! TRUFFLES FROM SHIZUKU!
EVEN IF THEY ARE MUSHROOMS! I DON'T MIND! I'LL COOK 'EM UP AND EAT 'EM!
CHUCKLE
CHUCKLE
TRUF...
CLUNK
CLUNK
THUD
DID YOU SAY SOMETHING...
ABOUT VALENTINE'S DAY?
?! Y-YOU... IS THIS CHOCOLATE?!
CLATTER
CLATTER
GIRLS GAVE YOU THAT?! ALL OF IT?!
YEAH, WELL. OF COURSE, BEING WHO I AM, IF I DON'T GET MORE THAN TEN A YEAR, I HARDLY EVEN NOTICE.
I'LL GET SEVEN MORE TODAY.
DAMMIT!! WHY AM I SO ANGRY AND DISAPPOINTED ALL OF A SUDDEN?!
WHAM!!
YOU'RE A HUNDRED YEARS BEHIND ME WHEN IT COMES TO VALENTINE'S DAY.
...SO?
YOU'RE ON YOUR WAY TO GET CHOCOLATE FROM MIZUTANI-SAN?

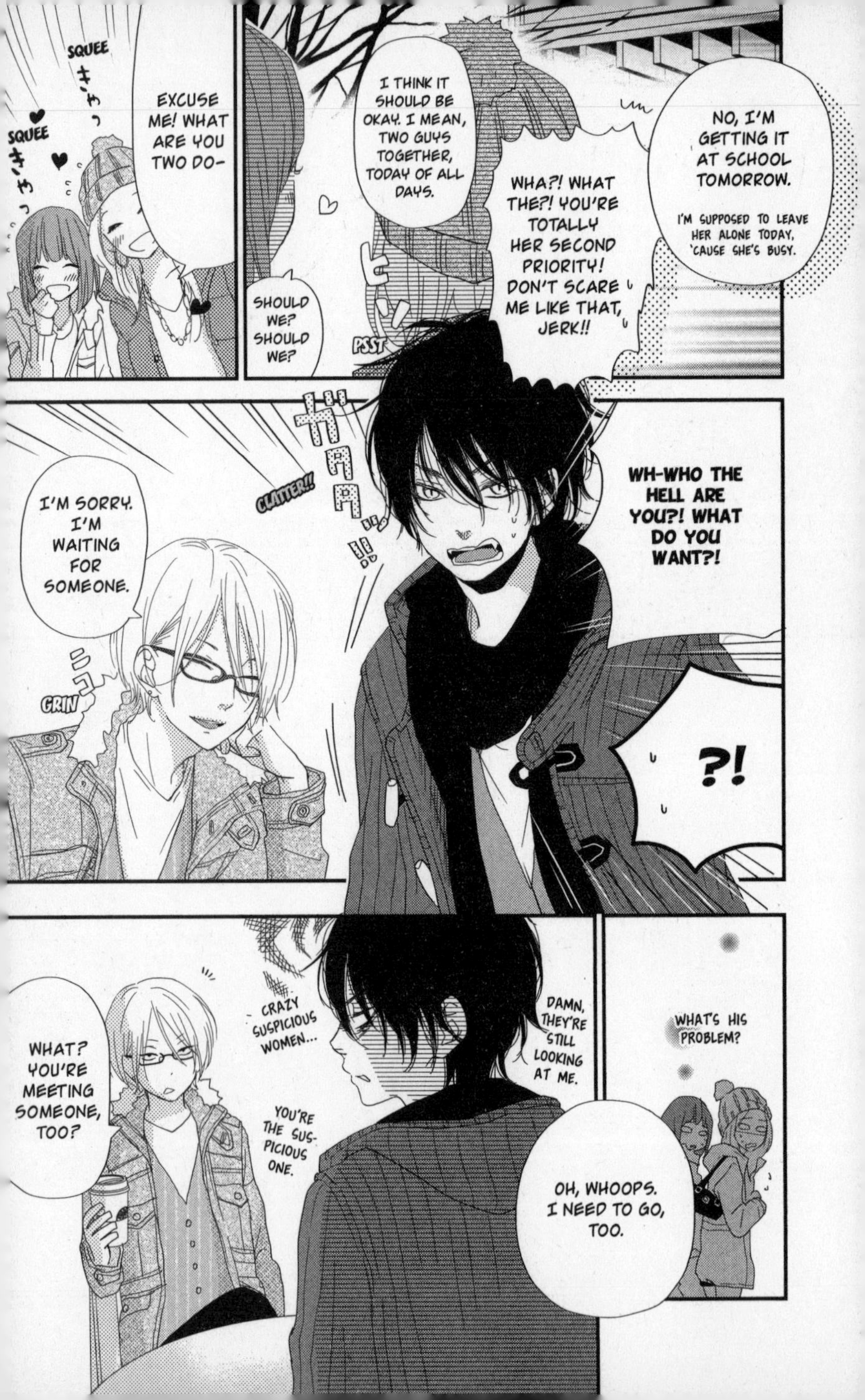
NO, I'M GETTING IT AT SCHOOL TOMORROW.
I'M SUPPOSED TO LEAVE HER ALONE TODAY, 'CAUSE SHE'S BUSY.
WHA?! WHAT THE?! YOU'RE TOTALLY HER SECOND PRIORITY! DON'T SCARE ME LIKE THAT, JERK!!
I THINK IT SHOULD BE OKAY. I MEAN, TWO GUYS TOGETHER, TODAY OF ALL DAYS.
SHOULD WE? SHOULD WE?
PSST
SQUEE
SQUEE
EXCUSE ME! WHAT ARE YOU TWO DO-
?!
WH-WHO THE HELL ARE YOU?! WHAT DO YOU WANT?!
CLATTER!!
I'M SORRY. I'M WAITING FOR SOMEONE.
GRIN
WHAT'S HIS PROBLEM?
DAMN, THEY'RE STILL LOOKING AT ME.
CRAZY SUSPICIOUS WOMEN...
OH, WHOOPS. I NEED TO GO, TOO.
YOU'RE THE SUS-PICIOUS ONE.
WHAT? YOU'RE MEETING SOMEONE, TOO?

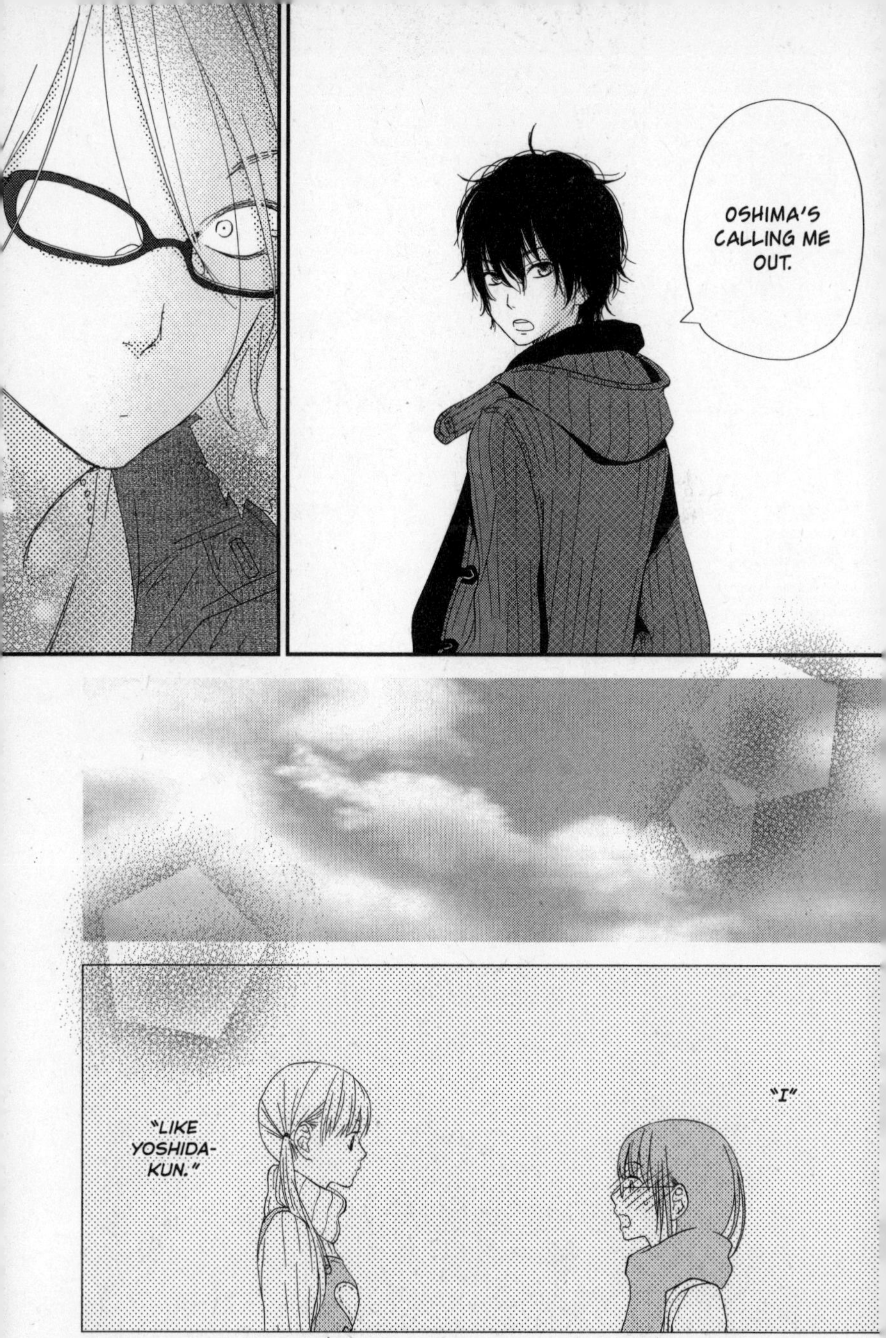
OSHIMA'S CALLING ME OUT.
"I"
"LIKE YOSHIDA-KUN."

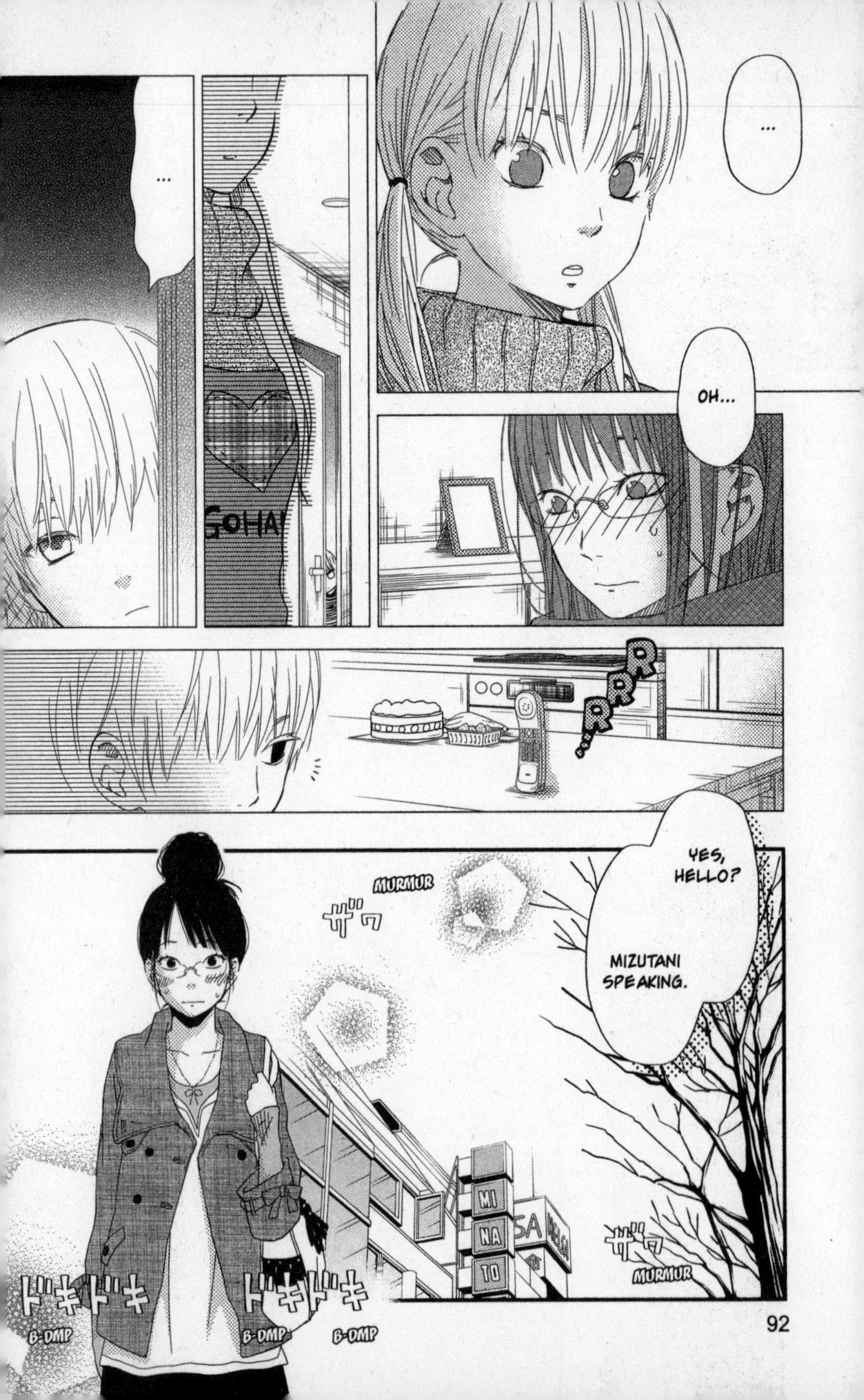
...
OH...
GOHA
...
RRRR...
YES, HELLO?
MIZUTANI SPEAKING.
ザワ
MURMUR
ザワ
MURMUR
MI NA TO
SA
ドキドキ
B-DMP
ドキドキ
B-DMP
B-DMP

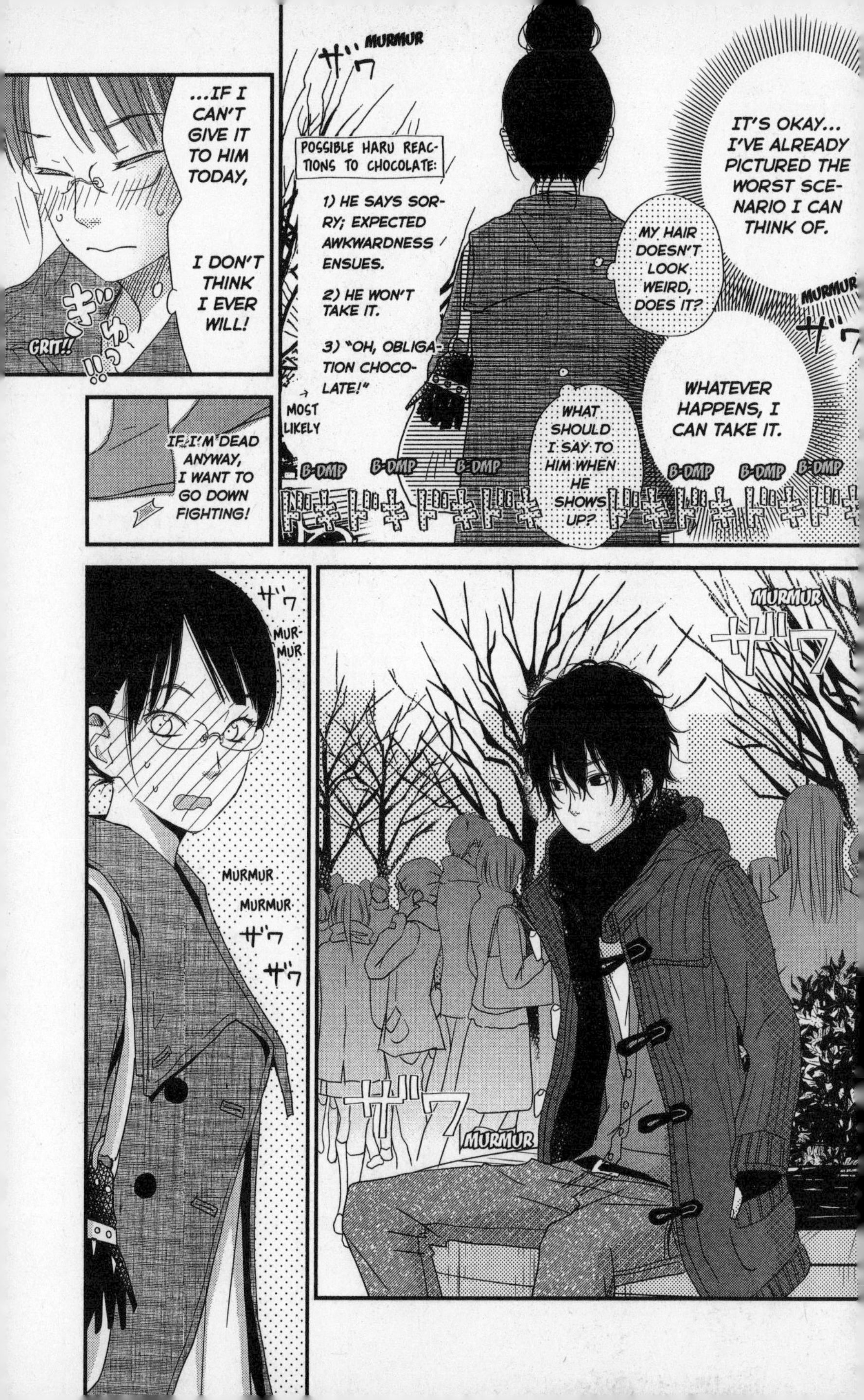
IT'S OKAY... I'VE ALREADY PICTURED THE WORST SCENARIO I CAN THINK OF.
MURMUR
ザワ
MY HAIR DOESN'T LOOK WEIRD, DOES IT?
WHATEVER HAPPENS, I CAN TAKE IT.
WHAT SHOULD I SAY TO HIM WHEN HE SHOWS UP?
B-DMP B-DMP B-DMP
MURMUR
ザワ
POSSIBLE HARU REACTIONS TO CHOCOLATE:
1) HE SAYS SORRY; EXPECTED AWKWARDNESS ENSUES.
2) HE WON'T TAKE IT.
3) "OH, OBLIGATION CHOCOLATE!"
→ MOST LIKELY
B-DMP B-DMP B-DMP
...IF I CAN'T GIVE IT TO HIM TODAY,
I DON'T THINK I EVER WILL!
ぎゅっ!!
GRIT!!
IF I'M DEAD ANYWAY, I WANT TO GO DOWN FIGHTING!
MURMUR
ザワ
ザワ
MURMUR
ザワ
MUR-MUR
MURMUR
MURMUR
ザワ
ザワ

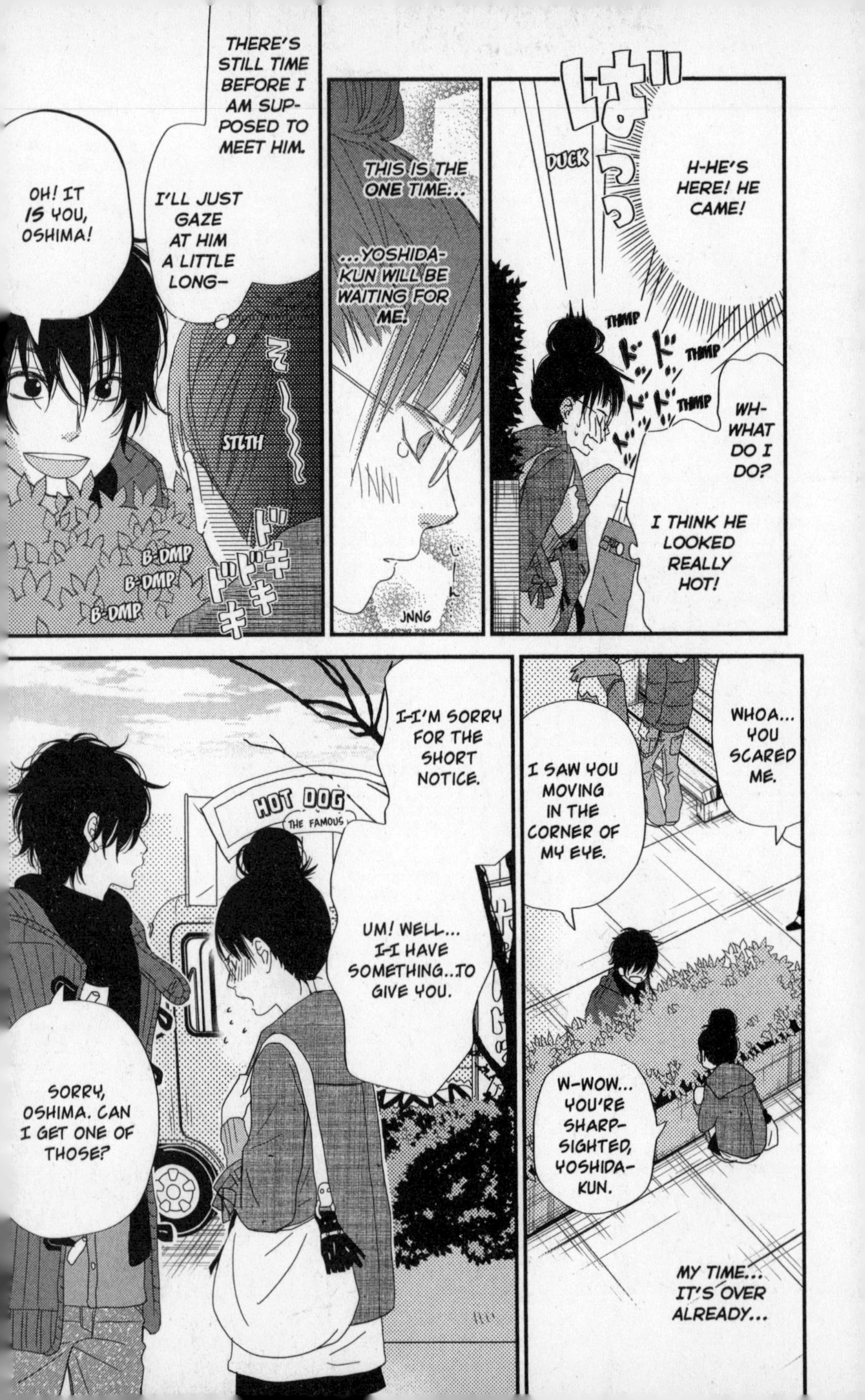
DUCK
H-HE'S HERE! HE CAME!
THMP
THMP
THMP
WH-WHAT DO I DO?
I THINK HE LOOKED REALLY HOT!
THIS IS THE ONE TIME...
...YOSHIDA-KUN WILL BE WAITING FOR ME.
JNNG
THERE'S STILL TIME BEFORE I AM SUPPOSED TO MEET HIM.
I'LL JUST GAZE AT HIM A LITTLE LONG–
STLTH
OH! IT IS YOU, OSHIMA!
B-DMP
B-DMP
B-DMP
WHOA... YOU SCARED ME.
I SAW YOU MOVING IN THE CORNER OF MY EYE.
W-WOW... YOU'RE SHARP-SIGHTED, YOSHIDA-KUN.
MY TIME... IT'S OVER ALREADY...
I-I'M SORRY FOR THE SHORT NOTICE.
UM! WELL... I-I HAVE SOMETHING...TO GIVE YOU.
HOT DOG
THE FAMOUS
SORRY, OSHIMA. CAN I GET ONE OF THOSE?

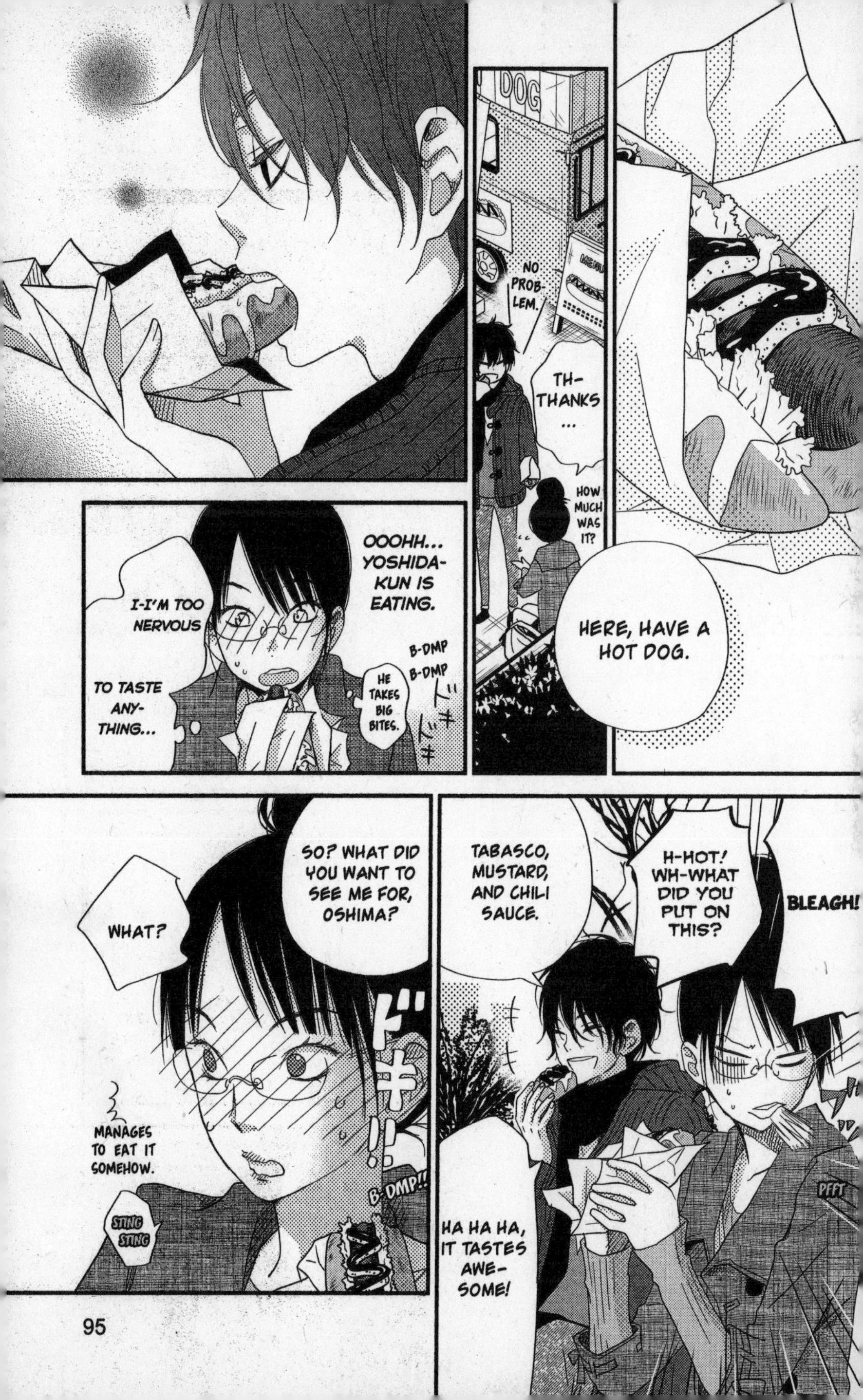
HERE, HAVE A HOT DOG.
DOG
MENU
HOW MUCH WAS IT?
NO PROB-LEM.
TH-THANKS...
OOOHH... YOSHIDA-KUN IS EATING.
B-DMP B-DMP
HE TAKES BIG BITES.
I-I'M TOO NERVOUS
TO TASTE ANY-THING...
BLEAGH!
H-HOT! WH-WHAT DID YOU PUT ON THIS?
TABASCO, MUSTARD, AND CHILI SAUCE.
HA HA HA, IT TASTES AWE-SOME!
PFFT
SO? WHAT DID YOU WANT TO SEE ME FOR, OSHIMA?
WHAT?
B-DMP!!
MANAGES TO EAT IT SOMEHOW.
STING STING

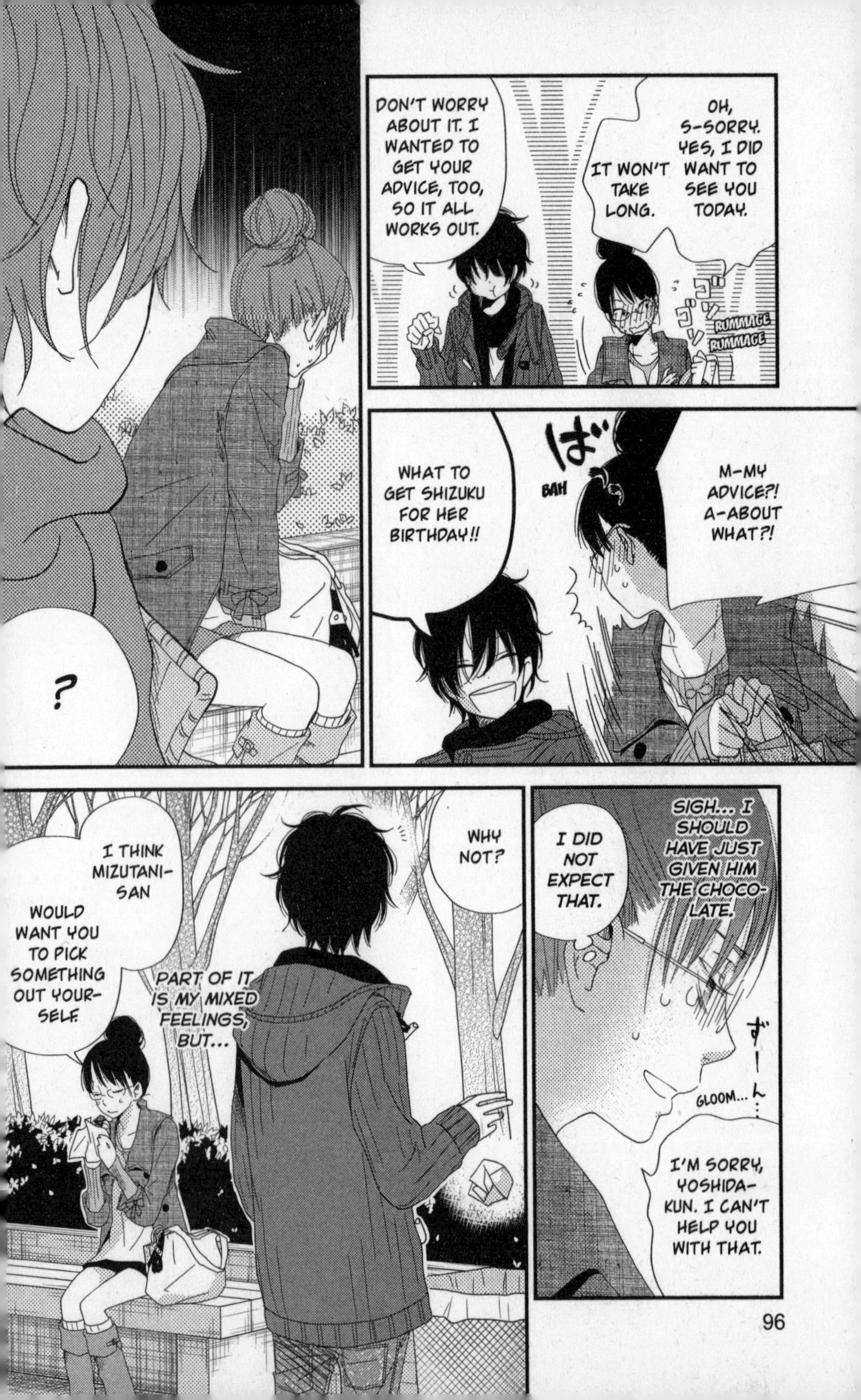
OH, S-SORRY. YES, I DID WANT TO SEE YOU TODAY.
IT WON'T TAKE LONG.
ゴソゴソ RUMMAGE RUMMAGE
DON'T WORRY ABOUT IT. I WANTED TO GET YOUR ADVICE, TOO, SO IT ALL WORKS OUT.
M-MY ADVICE?! A-ABOUT WHAT?!
ば BAH
WHAT TO GET SHIZUKU FOR HER BIRTHDAY!!
?
SIGH... I SHOULD HAVE JUST GIVEN HIM THE CHOCOLATE.
I DID NOT EXPECT THAT.
ずーん… GLOOM...
I'M SORRY, YOSHIDA-KUN. I CAN'T HELP YOU WITH THAT.
WHY NOT?
I THINK MIZUTANI-SAN
WOULD WANT YOU TO PICK SOMETHING OUT YOURSELF.
PART OF IT IS MY MIXED FEELINGS, BUT...

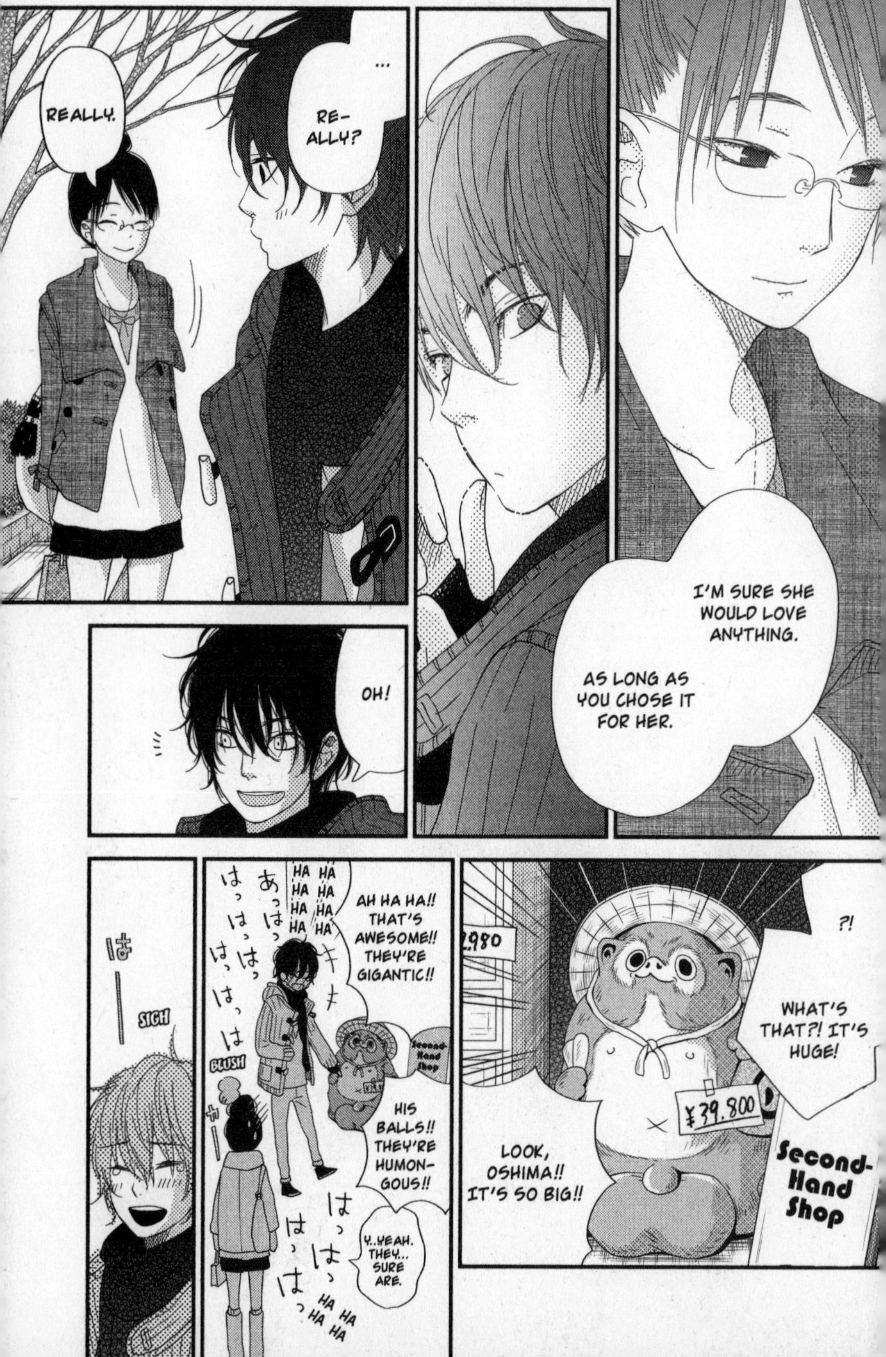
I'M SURE SHE WOULD LOVE ANYTHING.
AS LONG AS YOU CHOSE IT FOR HER.
...
RE-ALLY?
REALLY.
OH!
?!
WHAT'S THAT?! IT'S HUGE!
Second-Hand Shop
2,980
¥39,800
LOOK, OSHIMA!! IT'S SO BIG!!
あっはっはっはっはっは
HA HA HA HA HA HA HA HA
AH HA HA!! THAT'S AWESOME!! THEY'RE GIGANTIC!!
キャ
Second-Hand Shop
HIS BALLS!! THEY'RE HUMONGOUS!!
はっはっはっ
HA HA HA HA
Y..YEAH. THEY... SURE ARE.
カー
BLUSH
はー
SIGH

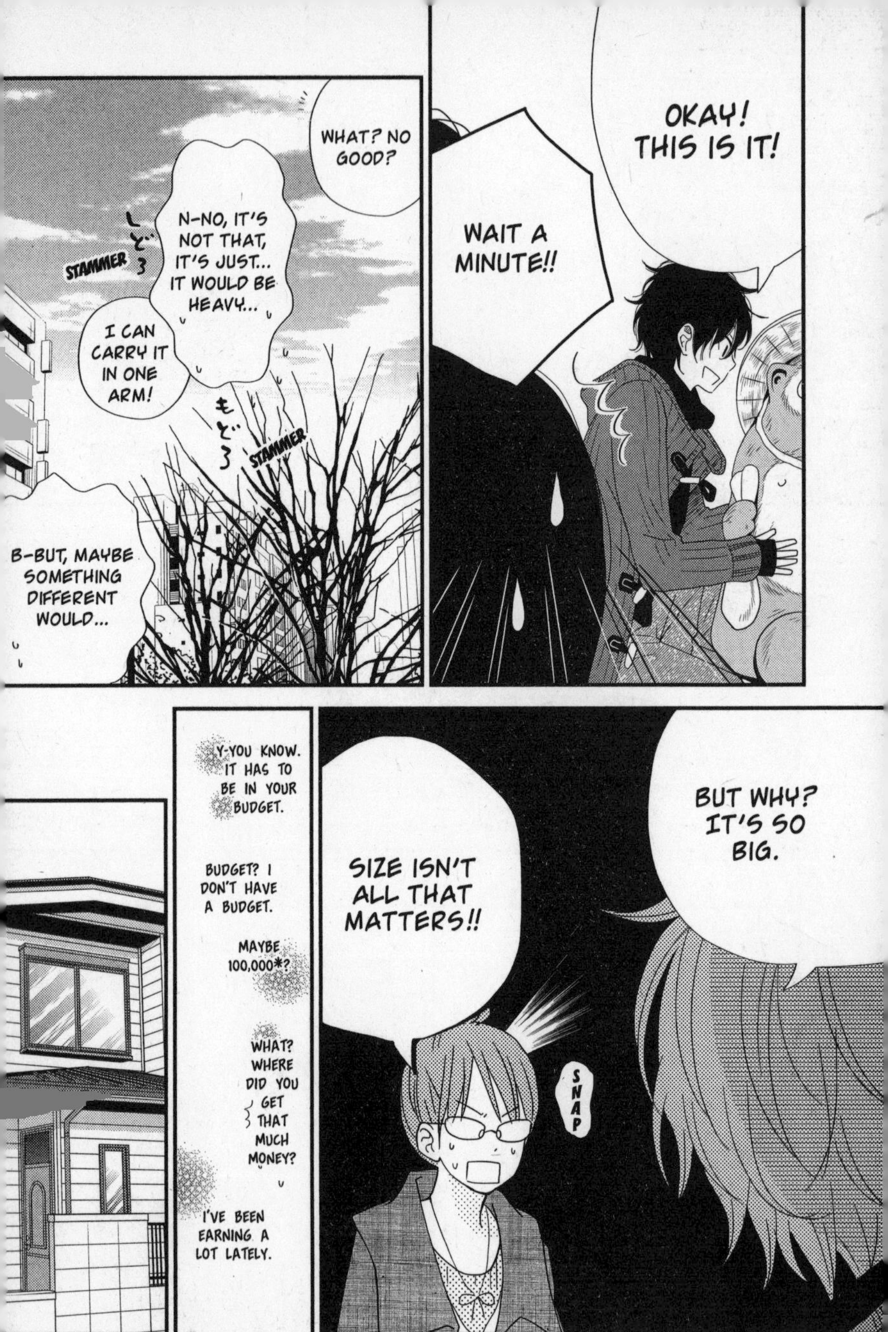
OKAY! THIS IS IT!
WAIT A MINUTE!!
WHAT? NO GOOD?
N-NO, IT'S NOT THAT, IT'S JUST... IT WOULD BE HEAVY...
しどろ
STAMMER
I CAN CARRY IT IN ONE ARM!
もどろ
STAMMER
B-BUT, MAYBE SOMETHING DIFFERENT WOULD...
BUT WHY? IT'S SO BIG.
SIZE ISN'T ALL THAT MATTERS!!
SNAP
Y-YOU KNOW. IT HAS TO BE IN YOUR BUDGET.
BUDGET? I DON'T HAVE A BUDGET.
MAYBE 100,000*?
WHAT? WHERE DID YOU GET THAT MUCH MONEY?
I'VE BEEN EARNING A LOT LATELY.

*About $1,000

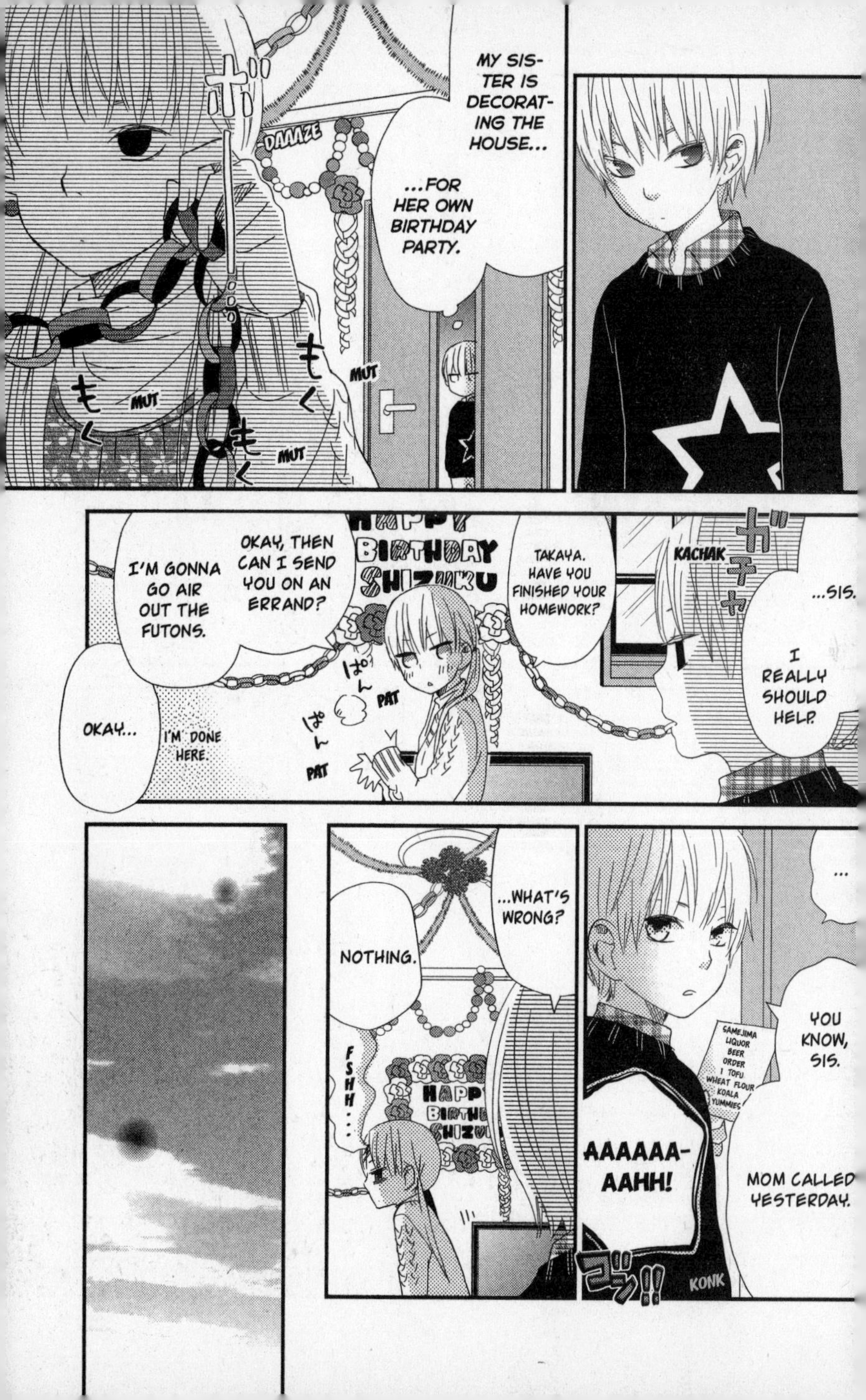
MY SISTER IS DECORATING THE HOUSE...
...FOR HER OWN BIRTHDAY PARTY.
DAAAZE
MUT
MUT
MUT
KACHAK
...SIS.
I REALLY SHOULD HELP.
TAKAYA. HAVE YOU FINISHED YOUR HOMEWORK?
HAPPY BIRTHDAY SHIZUKU
PAT
PAT
OKAY, THEN CAN I SEND YOU ON AN ERRAND?
I'M GONNA GO AIR OUT THE FUTONS.
I'M DONE HERE.
OKAY...
...
YOU KNOW, SIS.
SAMEJIMA LIQUOR BEER ORDER 1 TOFU WHEAT FLOUR KOALA YUMMIES
MOM CALLED YESTERDAY.
AAAAAA-AAHH!
KONK
...WHAT'S WRONG?
NOTHING.
FSHH...

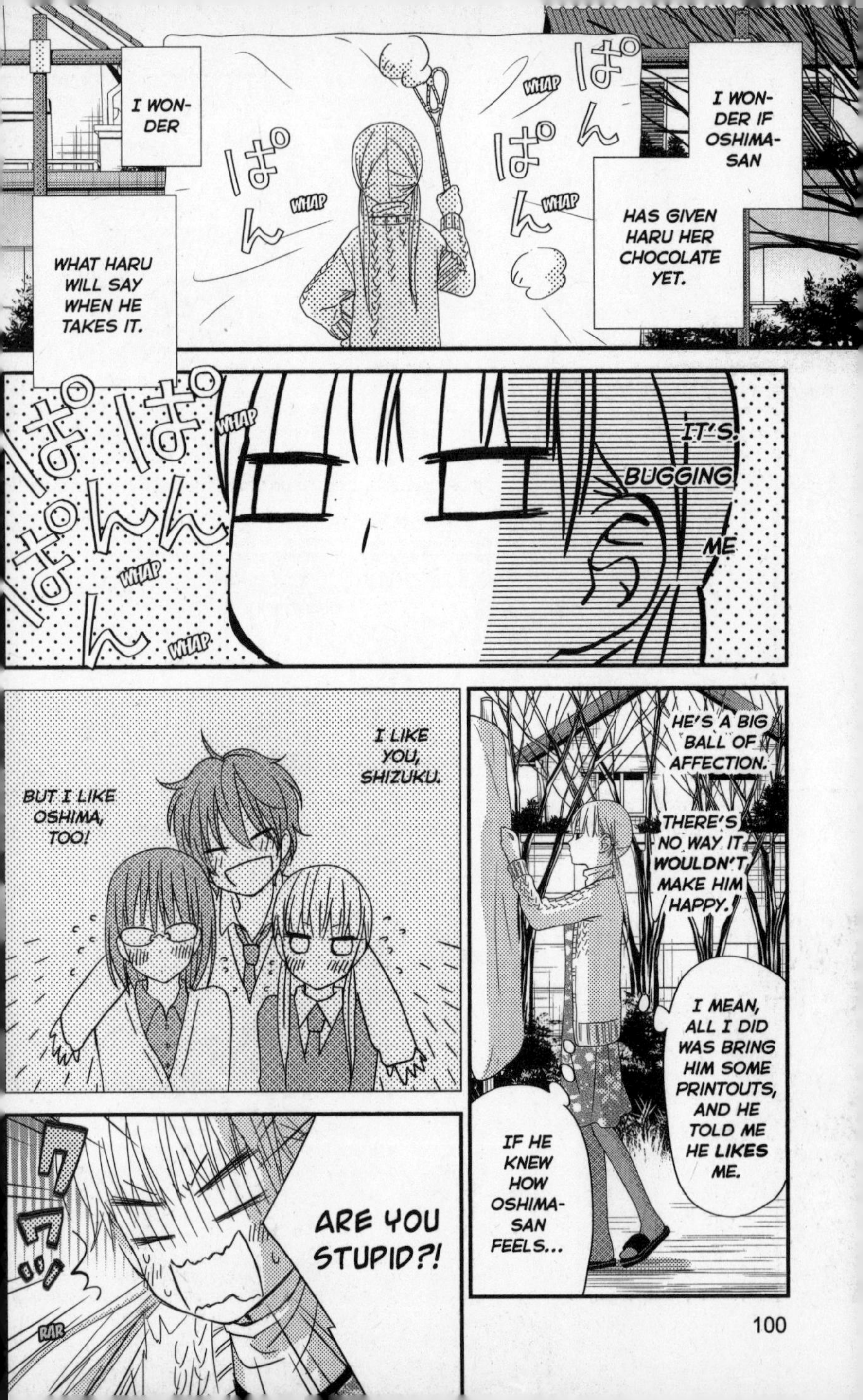
I WONDER IF OSHIMA-SAN
HAS GIVEN HARU HER CHOCOLATE YET.
ぱんぱん
WHAP
WHAP
ぱん
WHAP
I WONDER
WHAT HARU WILL SAY WHEN HE TAKES IT.
IT'S BUGGING ME
ぱんぱん
WHAP
ぱんぱん
WHAP
WHAP
HE'S A BIG BALL OF AFFECTION.
THERE'S NO WAY IT WOULDN'T MAKE HIM HAPPY.
I MEAN, ALL I DID WAS BRING HIM SOME PRINTOUTS, AND HE TOLD ME HE LIKES ME.
IF HE KNEW HOW OSHIMA-SAN FEELS...
I LIKE YOU, SHIZUKU.
BUT I LIKE OSHIMA, TOO!
ARE YOU STUPID?!
RAR

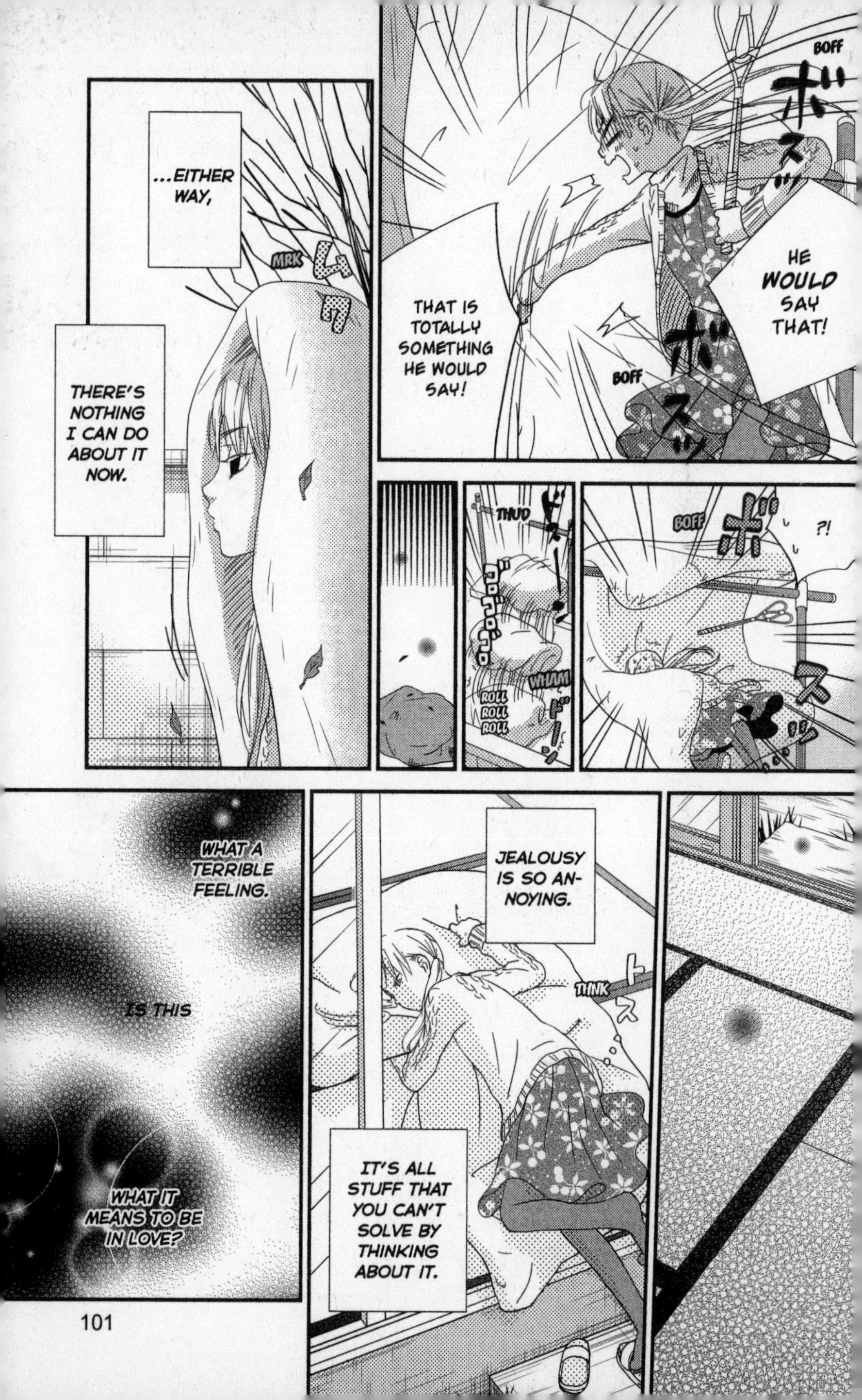
BOFF
HE WOULD SAY THAT!
THAT IS TOTALLY SOMETHING HE WOULD SAY!
BOFF
BOFF
?!
THUD
WHAM
ROLL
ROLL
ROLL
...EITHER WAY,
MRK
THERE'S NOTHING I CAN DO ABOUT IT NOW.
JEALOUSY IS SO AN-NOYING.
THINK
IT'S ALL STUFF THAT YOU CAN'T SOLVE BY THINKING ABOUT IT.
WHAT A TERRIBLE FEELING.
IS THIS
WHAT IT MEANS TO BE IN LOVE?

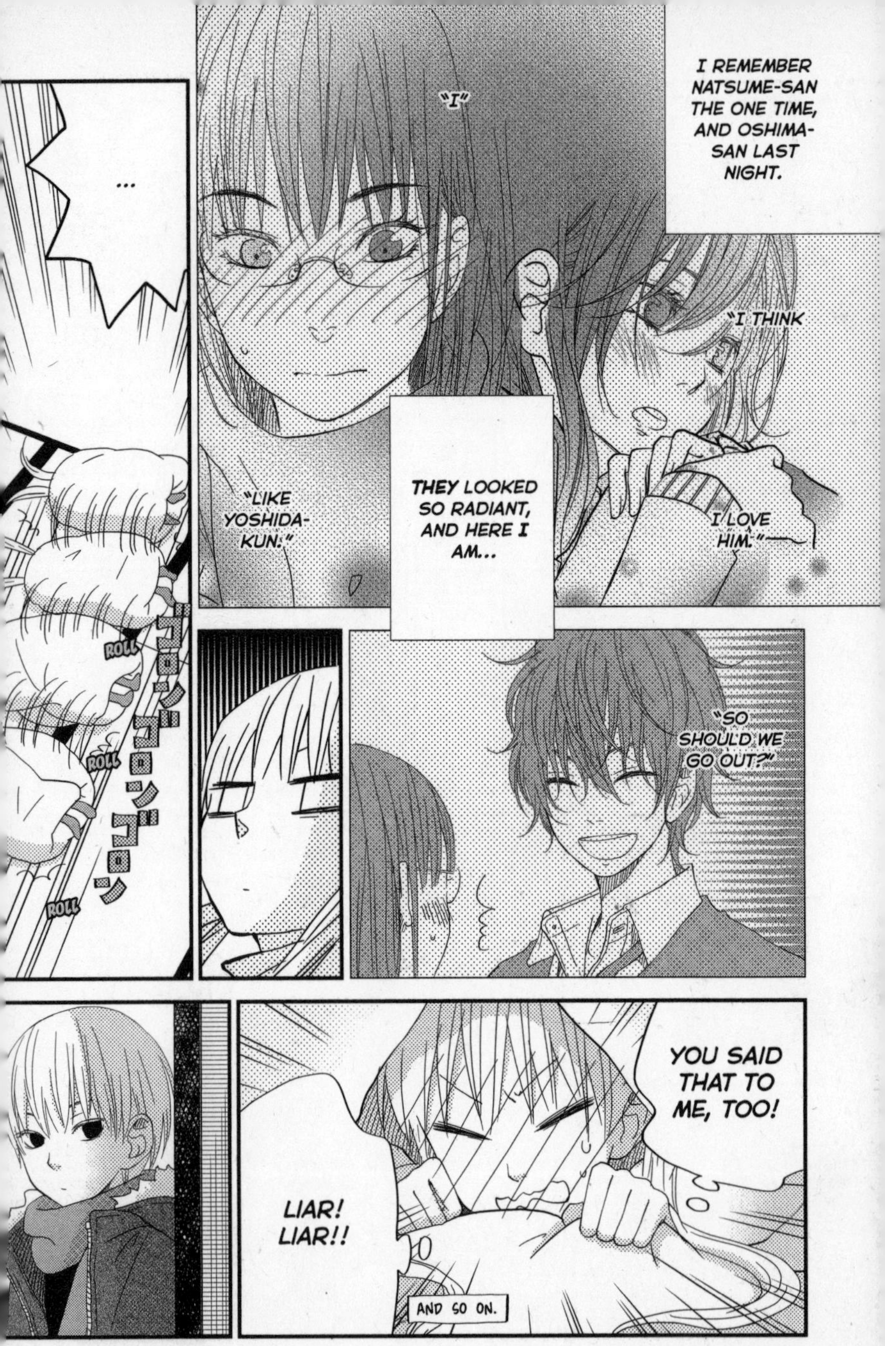

I REMEMBER NATSUME-SAN THE ONE TIME, AND OSHIMA-SAN LAST NIGHT.
"I THINK
I LOVE HIM."
"I"
"LIKE YOSHIDA-KUN."
THEY LOOKED SO RADIANT, AND HERE I AM...
"SO SHOULD WE GO OUT?"
...
ROLL
ROLL
ROLL
ゴロンゴロンゴロン
YOU SAID THAT TO ME, TOO!
LIAR! LIAR!!
AND SO ON.

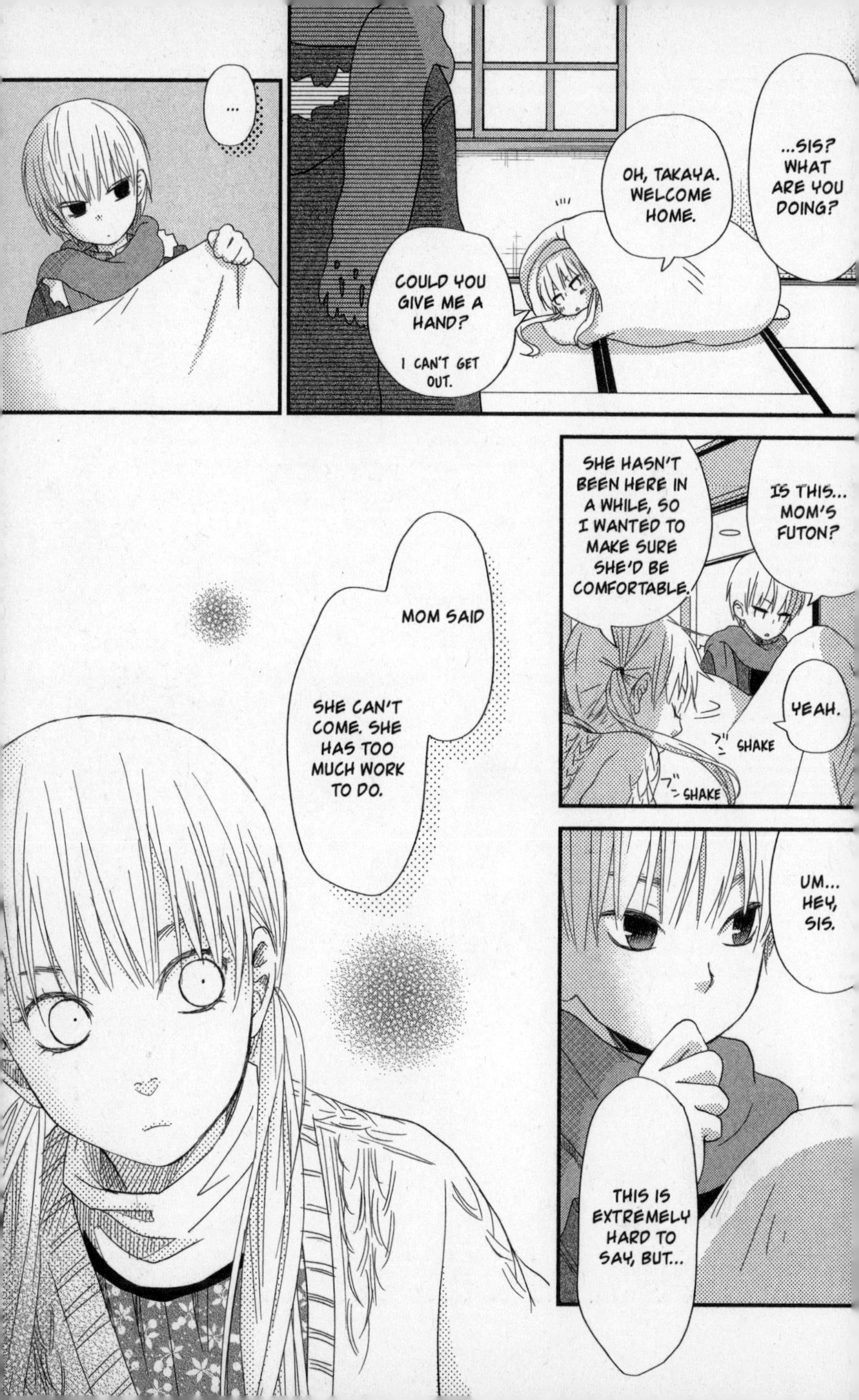
...SIS? WHAT ARE YOU DOING?
OH, TAKAYA. WELCOME HOME.
COULD YOU GIVE ME A HAND?
I CAN'T GET OUT.
...
IS THIS... MOM'S FUTON?
SHE HASN'T BEEN HERE IN A WHILE, SO I WANTED TO MAKE SURE SHE'D BE COMFORTABLE.
YEAH.
SHAKE
SHAKE
UM... HEY, SIS.
THIS IS EXTREMELY HARD TO SAY, BUT...
MOM SAID
SHE CAN'T COME. SHE HAS TOO MUCH WORK TO DO.

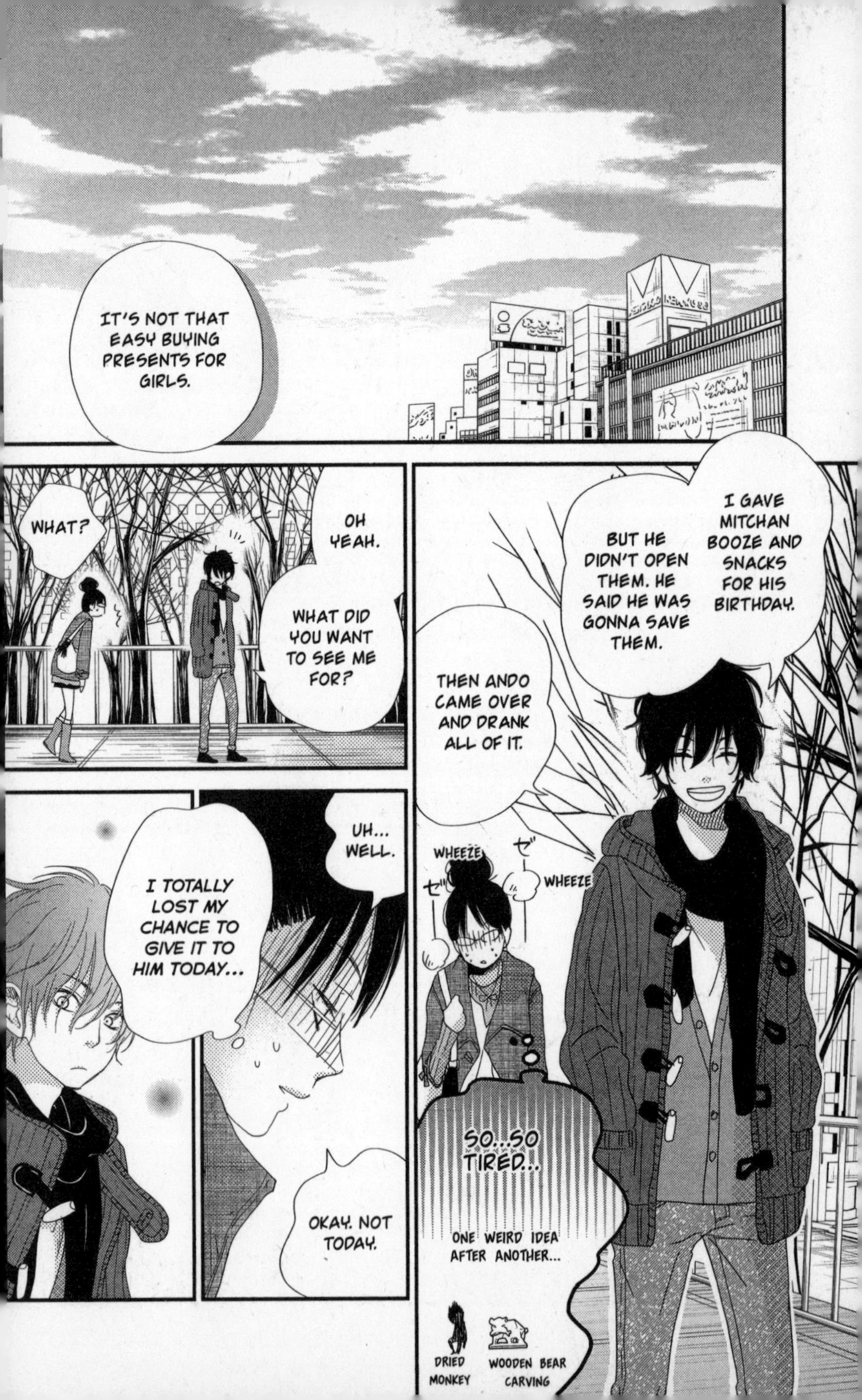
IT'S NOT THAT EASY BUYING PRESENTS FOR GIRLS.
I GAVE MITCHAN BOOZE AND SNACKS FOR HIS BIRTHDAY.
BUT HE DIDN'T OPEN THEM. HE SAID HE WAS GONNA SAVE THEM.
THEN ANDO CAME OVER AND DRANK ALL OF IT.
ゼー
WHEEZE
ゼ
WHEEZE
SO...SO TIRED...
ONE WEIRD IDEA AFTER ANOTHER...
DRIED MONKEY
WOODEN BEAR CARVING
OH YEAH.
WHAT DID YOU WANT TO SEE ME FOR?
WHAT?
UH... WELL.
OKAY. NOT TODAY.
I TOTALLY LOST MY CHANCE TO GIVE IT TO HIM TODAY...

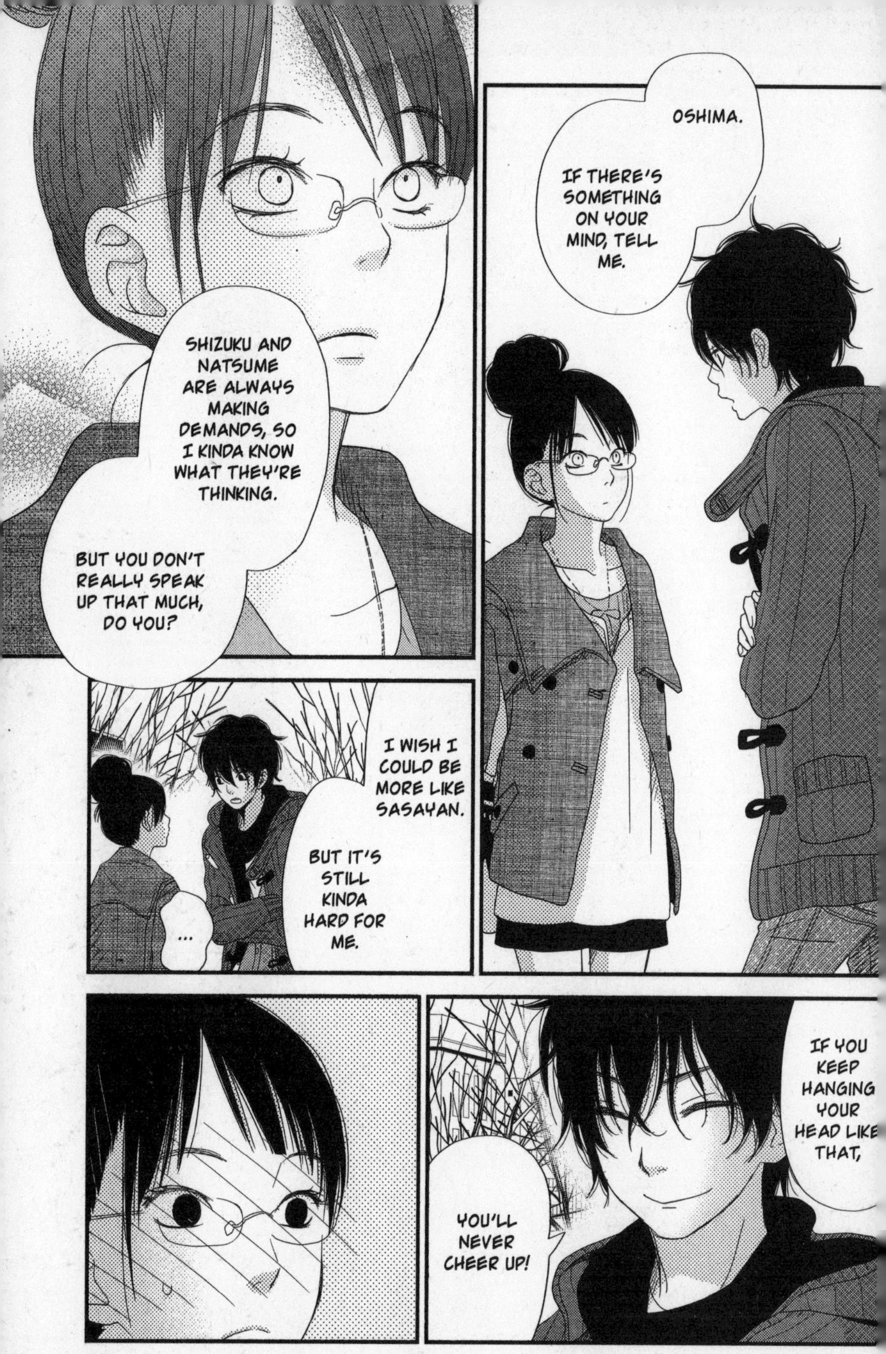
OSHIMA.
IF THERE'S SOMETHING ON YOUR MIND, TELL ME.
SHIZUKU AND NATSUME ARE ALWAYS MAKING DEMANDS, SO I KINDA KNOW WHAT THEY'RE THINKING.
BUT YOU DON'T REALLY SPEAK UP THAT MUCH, DO YOU?
I WISH I COULD BE MORE LIKE SASAYAN.
BUT IT'S STILL KINDA HARD FOR ME.
...
IF YOU KEEP HANGING YOUR HEAD LIKE THAT,
YOU'LL NEVER CHEER UP!

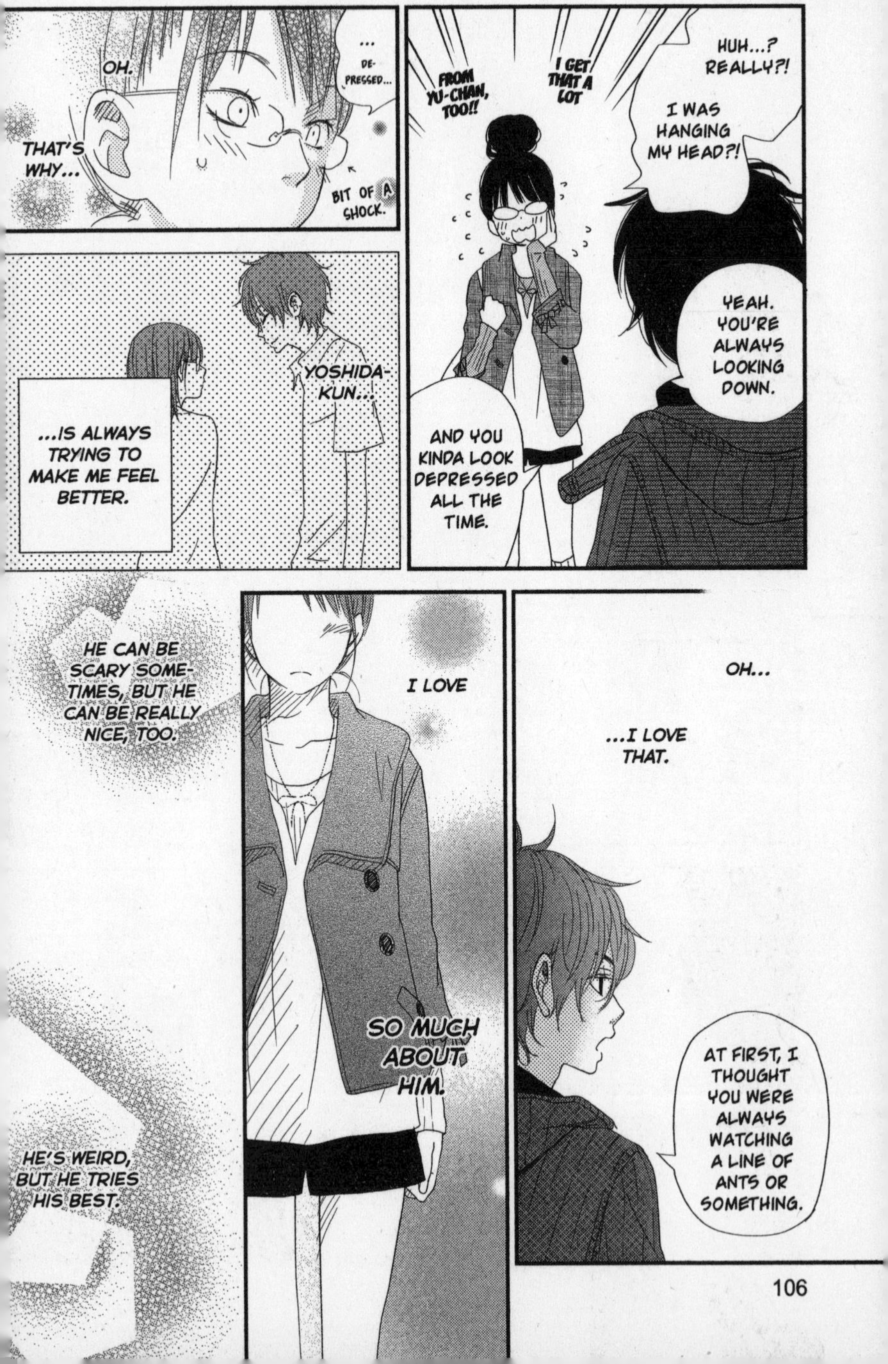

HUH...? REALLY?!
I WAS HANGING MY HEAD?!
I GET THAT A LOT
FROM YU-CHAN, TOO!!
YEAH. YOU'RE ALWAYS LOOKING DOWN.
AND YOU KINDA LOOK DEPRESSED ALL THE TIME.
... DE-PRESSED...
OH.
THAT'S WHY...
BIT OF A SHOCK.
YOSHIDA-KUN...
...IS ALWAYS TRYING TO MAKE ME FEEL BETTER.
OH...
...I LOVE THAT.
AT FIRST, I THOUGHT YOU WERE ALWAYS WATCHING A LINE OF ANTS OR SOMETHING.
I LOVE
SO MUCH ABOUT HIM.
HE CAN BE SCARY SOME-TIMES, BUT HE CAN BE REALLY NICE, TOO.
HE'S WEIRD, BUT HE TRIES HIS BEST.

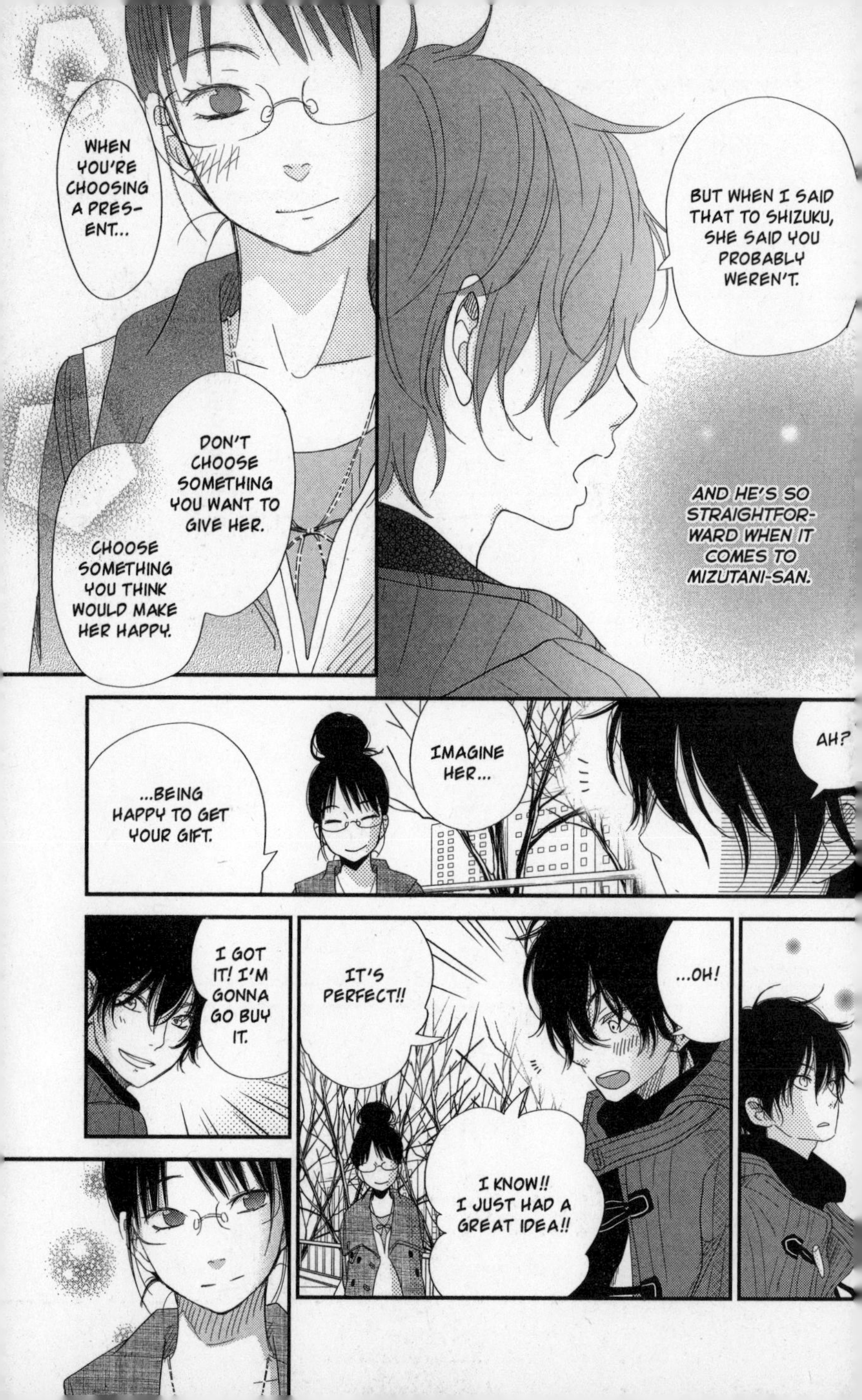
BUT WHEN I SAID THAT TO SHIZUKU, SHE SAID YOU PROBABLY WEREN'T.
AND HE'S SO STRAIGHTFORWARD WHEN IT COMES TO MIZUTANI-SAN.
WHEN YOU'RE CHOOSING A PRES-ENT...
DON'T CHOOSE SOMETHING YOU WANT TO GIVE HER.
CHOOSE SOMETHING YOU THINK WOULD MAKE HER HAPPY.
AH?
IMAGINE HER...
...BEING HAPPY TO GET YOUR GIFT.
...OH!
I KNOW!! I JUST HAD A GREAT IDEA!!
IT'S PERFECT!!
I GOT IT! I'M GONNA GO BUY IT.

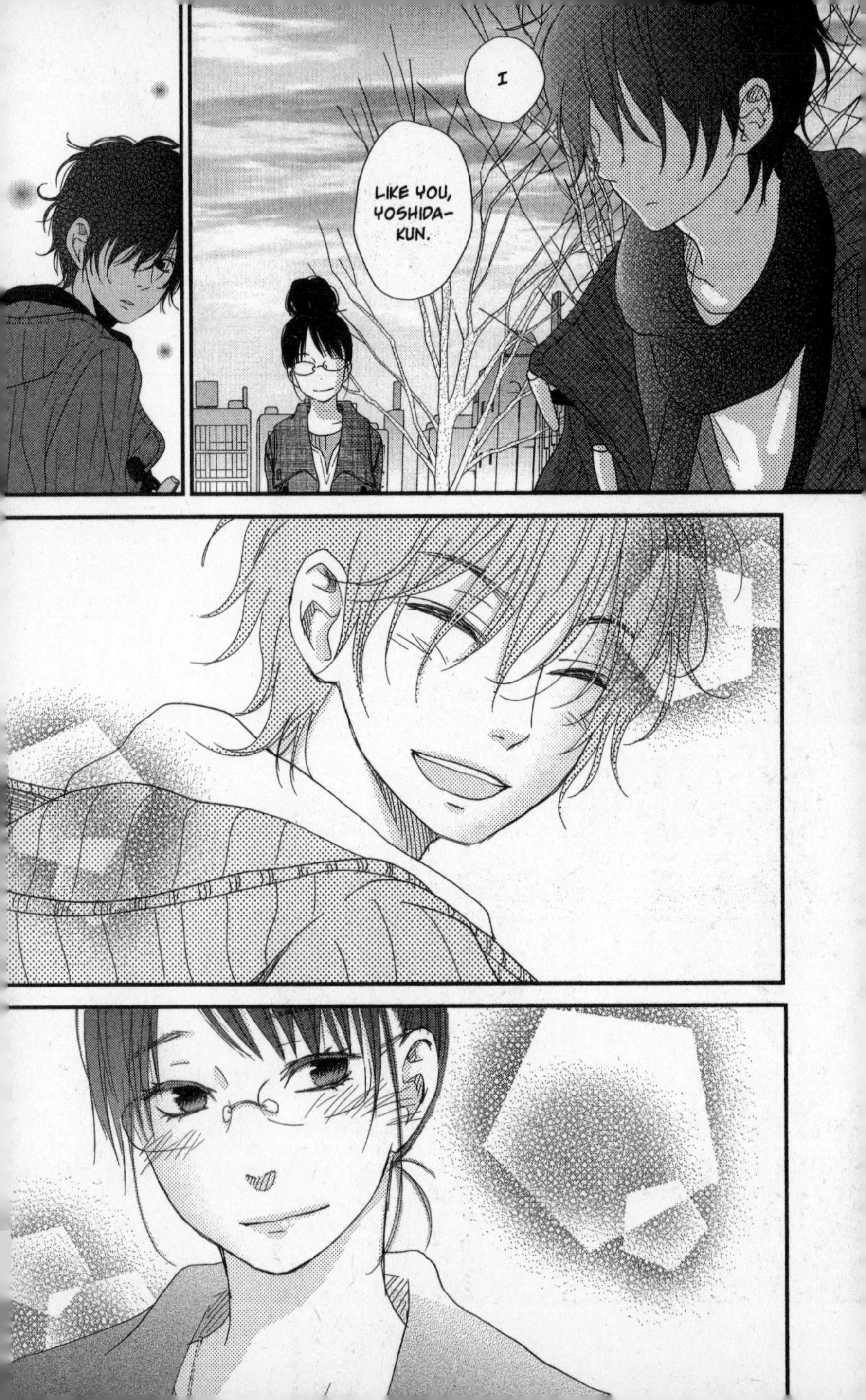
I
LIKE YOU, YOSHIDA-KUN.

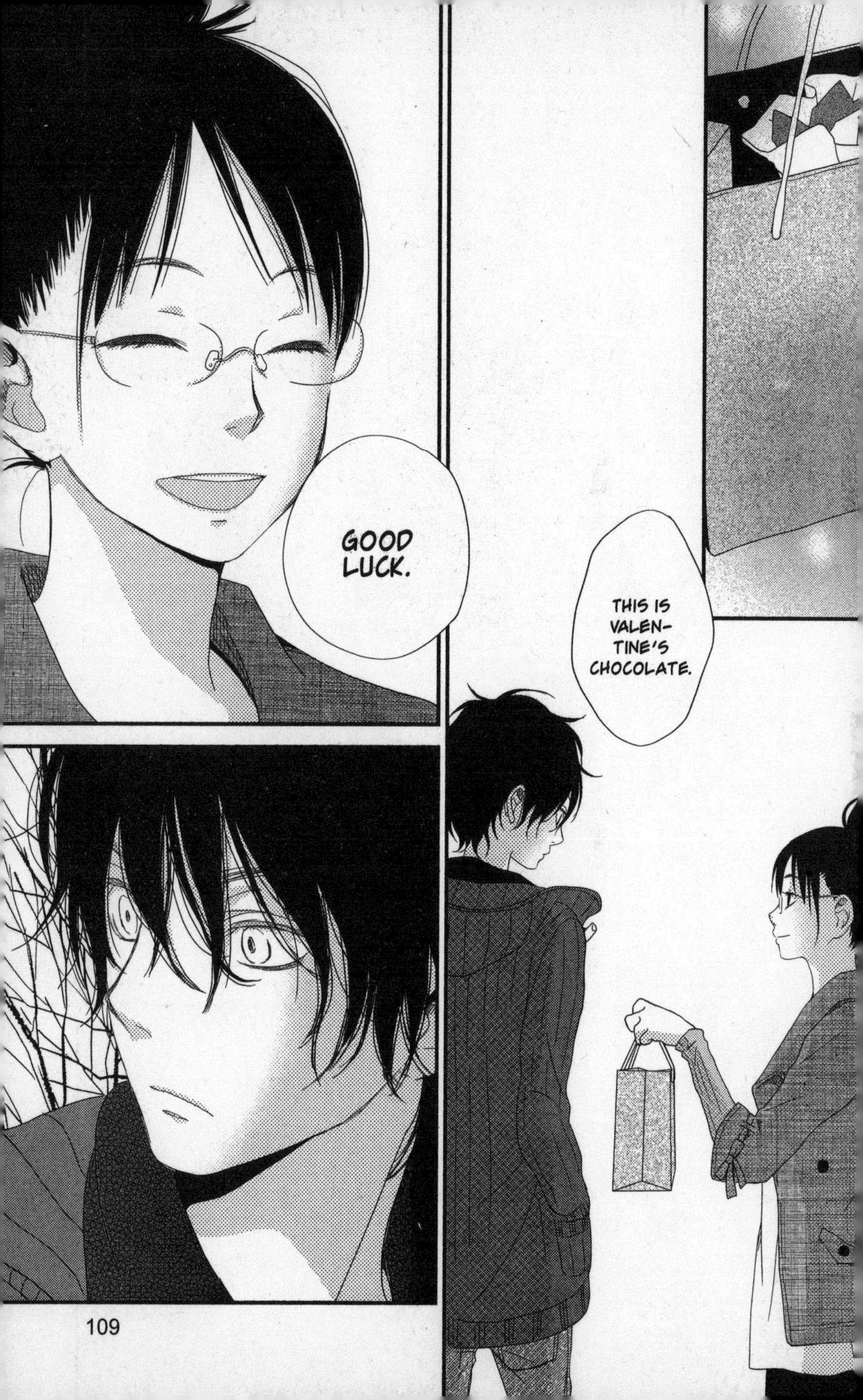
THIS IS VALENTINE'S CHOCOLATE.
GOOD LUCK.

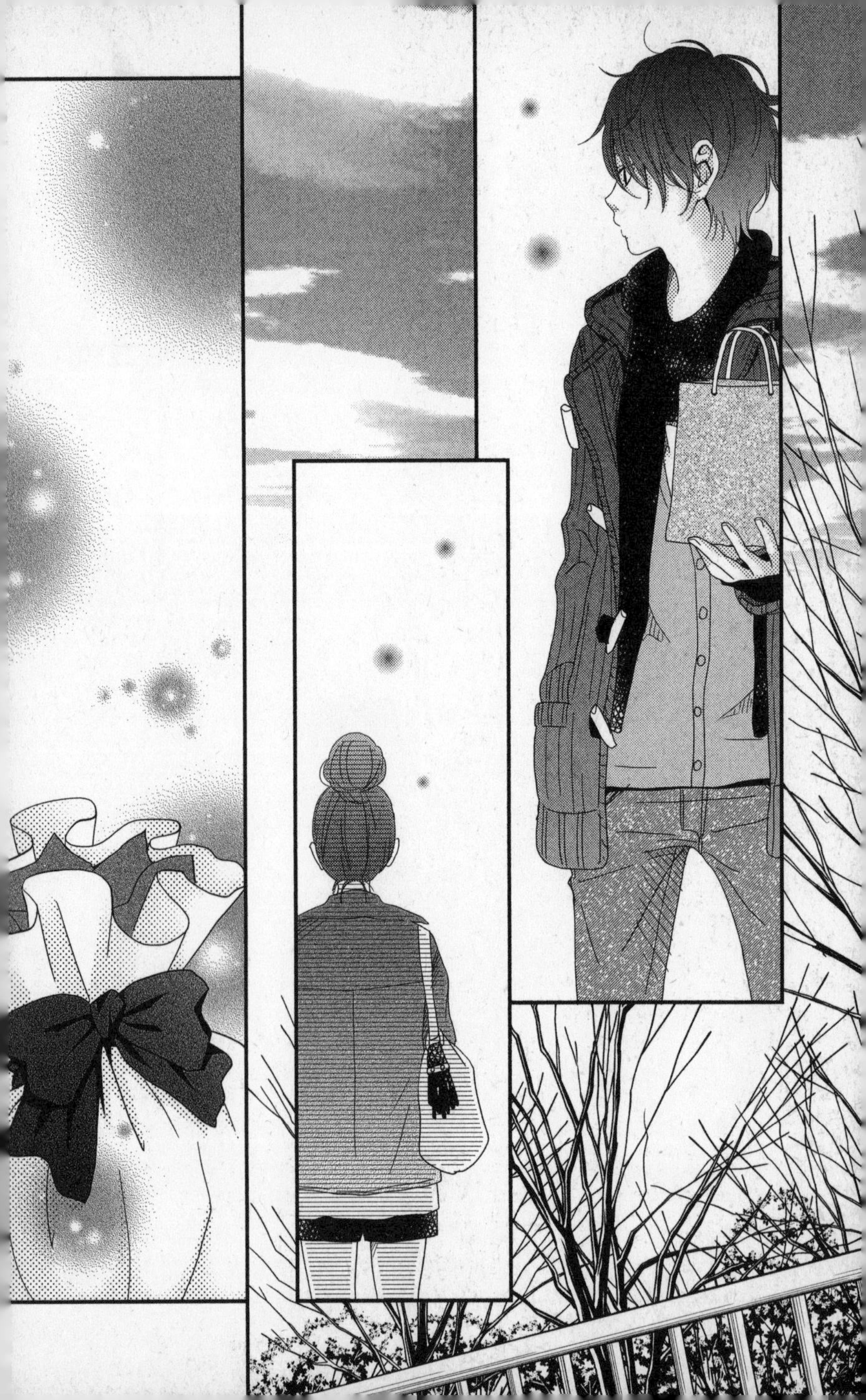

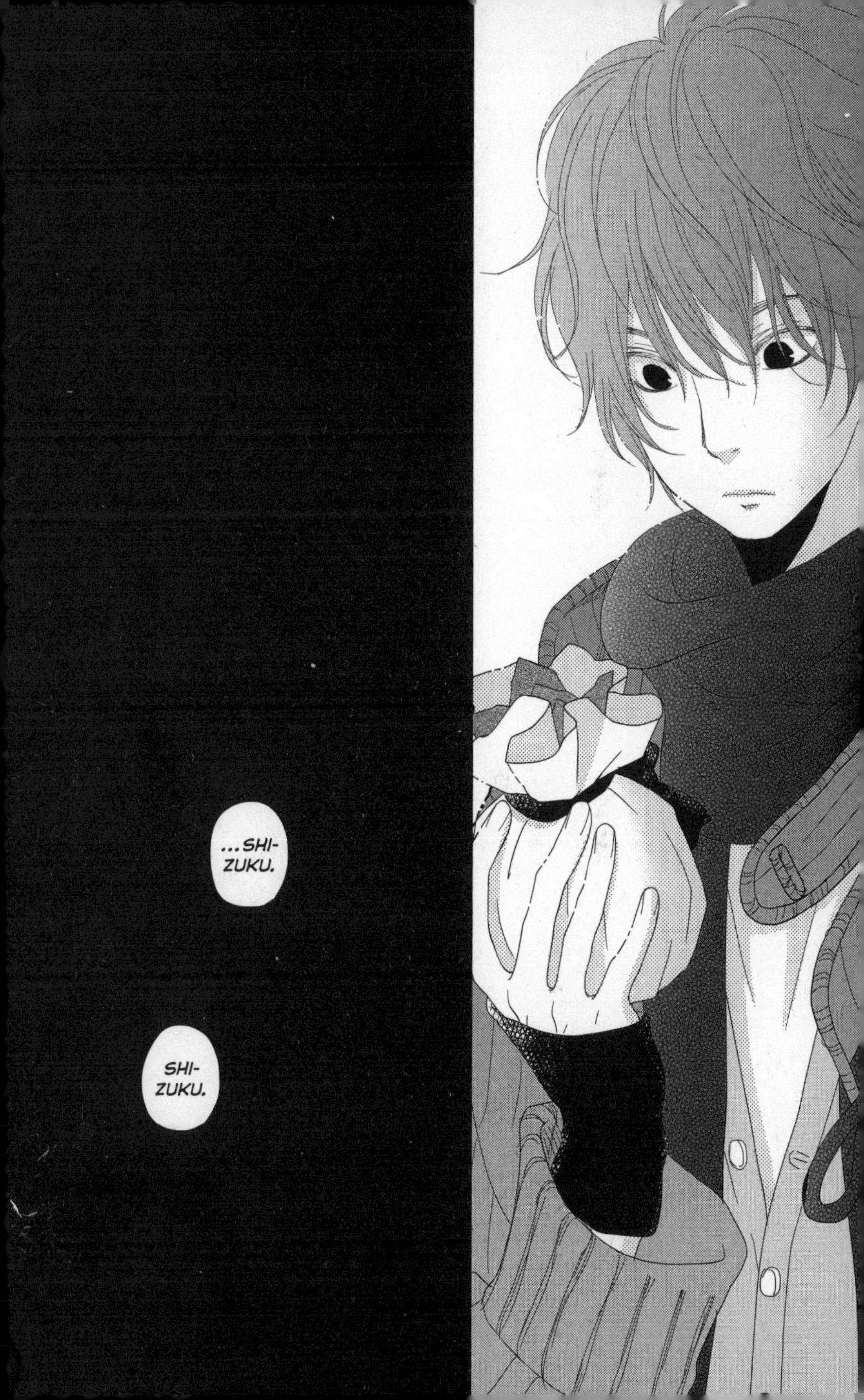
...SHI-
ZUKU.
SHI-
ZUKU.

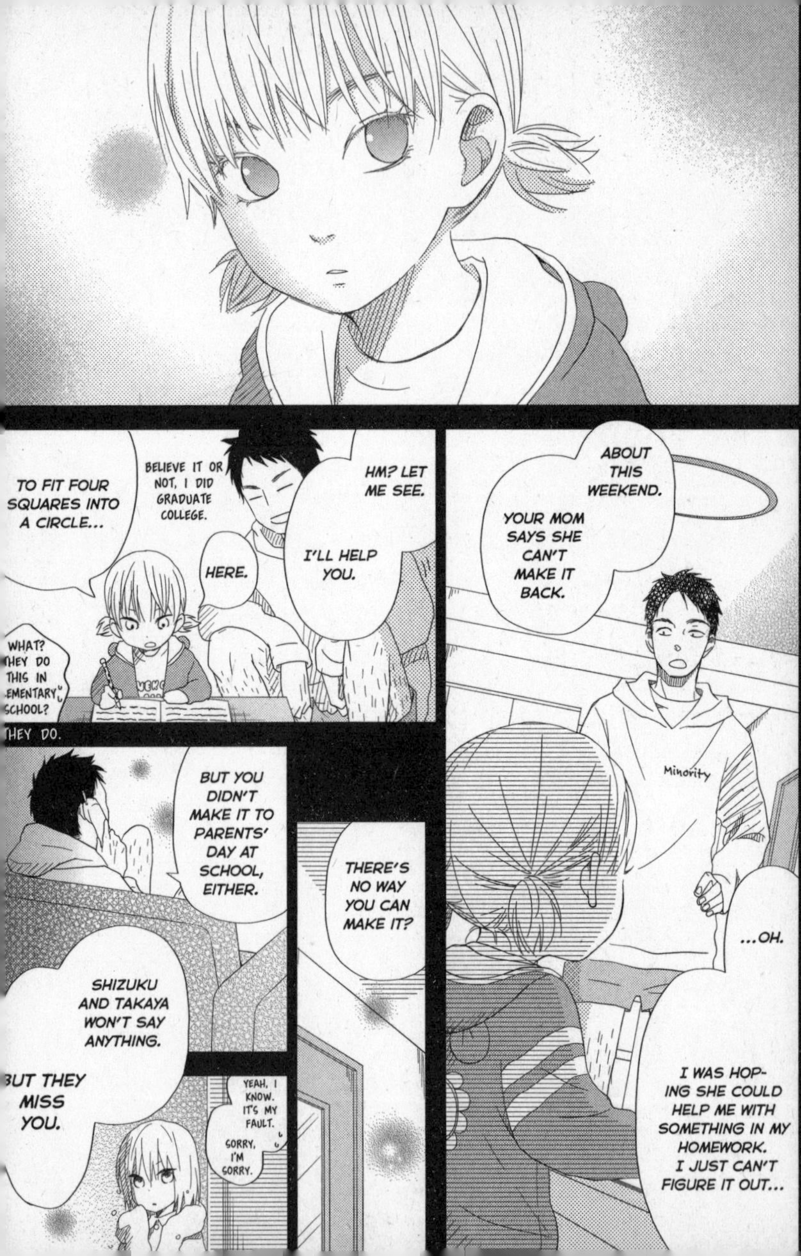
ABOUT THIS WEEKEND.
YOUR MOM SAYS SHE CAN'T MAKE IT BACK.
...OH.
I WAS HOP-ING SHE COULD HELP ME WITH SOMETHING IN MY HOMEWORK. I JUST CAN'T FIGURE IT OUT...
HM? LET ME SEE.
I'LL HELP YOU.
HERE.
BELIEVE IT OR NOT, I DID GRADUATE COLLEGE.
TO FIT FOUR SQUARES INTO A CIRCLE...
WHAT? HEY DO THIS IN EMENTARY SCHOOL?
HEY DO.
THERE'S NO WAY YOU CAN MAKE IT?
BUT YOU DIDN'T MAKE IT TO PARENTS' DAY AT SCHOOL, EITHER.
SHIZUKU AND TAKAYA WON'T SAY ANYTHING.
UT THEY MISS YOU.
YEAH, I KNOW. IT'S MY FAULT.
SORRY, I'M SORRY.

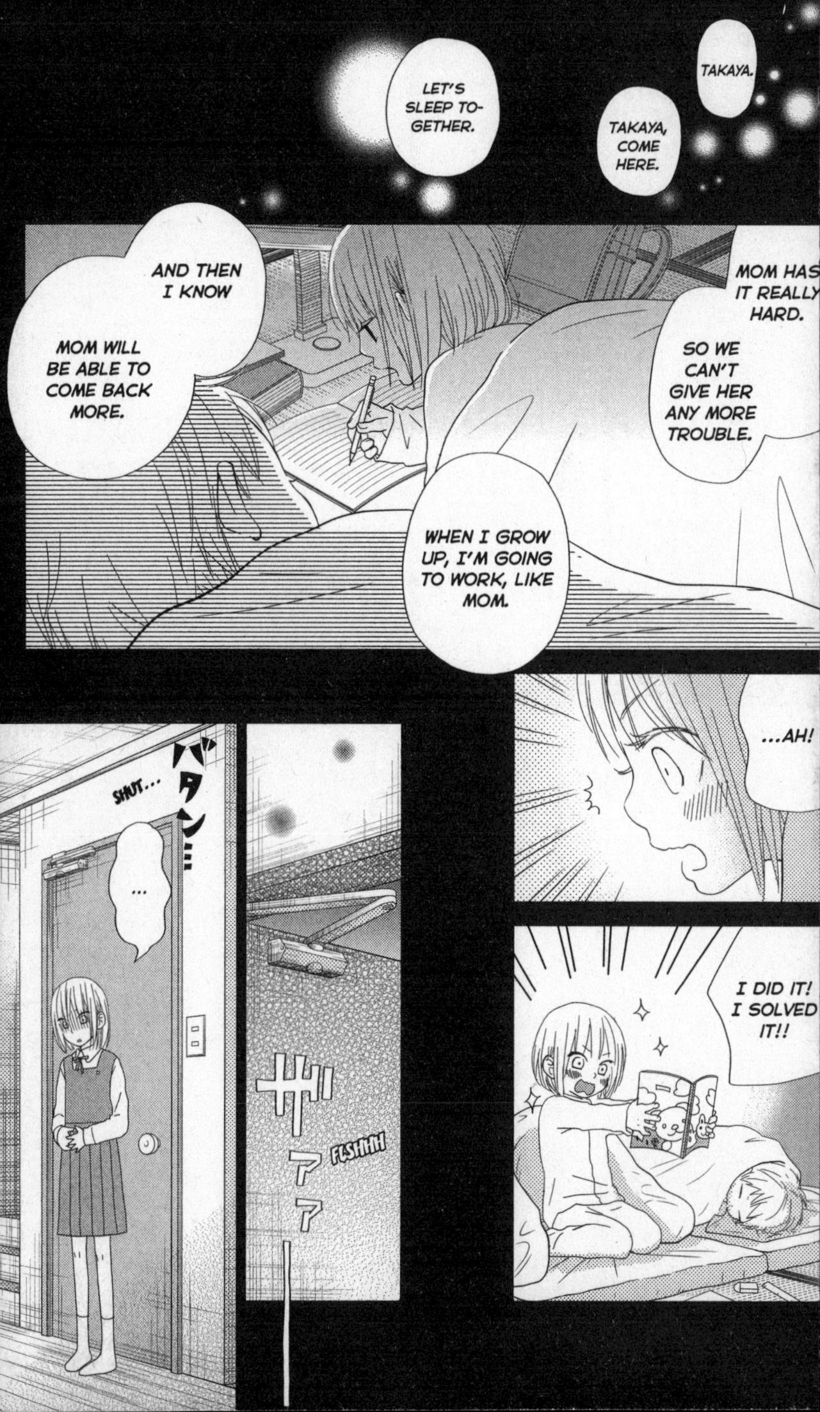
TAKAYA.
TAKAYA, COME HERE.
LET'S SLEEP TOGETHER.
MOM HAS IT REALLY HARD.
SO WE CAN'T GIVE HER ANY MORE TROUBLE.
WHEN I GROW UP, I'M GOING TO WORK, LIKE MOM.
AND THEN I KNOW
MOM WILL BE ABLE TO COME BACK MORE.
...AH!
I DID IT! I SOLVED IT!!
ザァァァ
FLSHHH
バタン
SHUT...
...

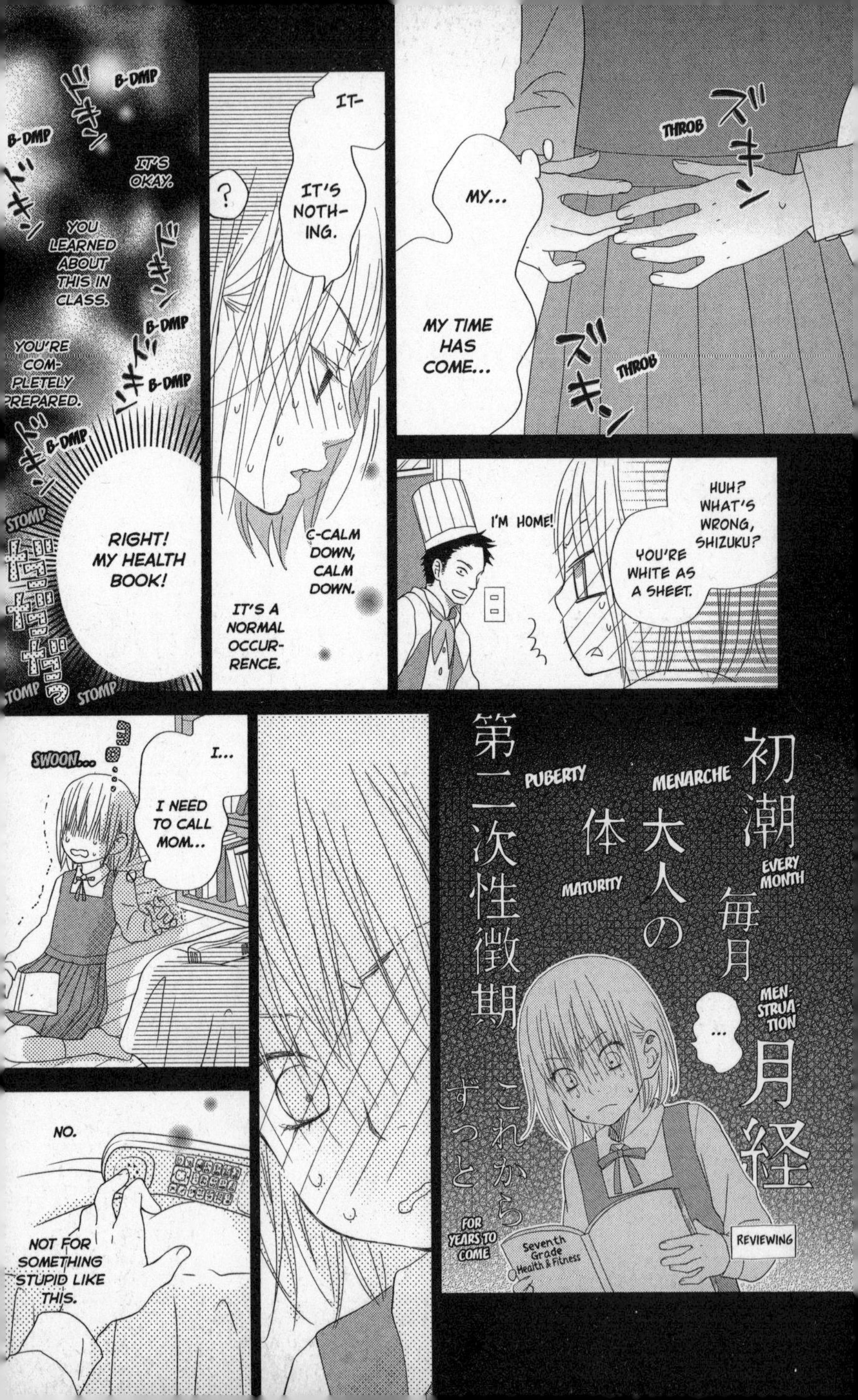
ズキン
THROB
MY...
MY TIME HAS COME...
ズキン
THROB
HUH? WHAT'S WRONG, SHIZUKU?
YOU'RE WHITE AS A SHEET.
I'M HOME!
IT-
?
IT'S NOTHING.
C-CALM DOWN, CALM DOWN.
IT'S A NORMAL OCCURRENCE.
B-DMP
ドキン
B-DMP
IT'S OKAY.
YOU LEARNED ABOUT THIS IN CLASS.
B-DMP
YOU'RE COMPLETELY PREPARED.
B-DMP
B-DMP
RIGHT! MY HEALTH BOOK!
STOMP
STOMP
STOMP
初潮
MENARCHE
大人の体
MATURITY
毎月
EVERY MONTH
第二次性徴期
PUBERTY
...
月経
MENSTRUATION
これからずっと
FOR YEARS TO COME
REVIEWING
Seventh Grade Health & Fitness
SWOON...
I...
I NEED TO CALL MOM...
NO.
NOT FOR SOMETHING STUPID LIKE THIS.

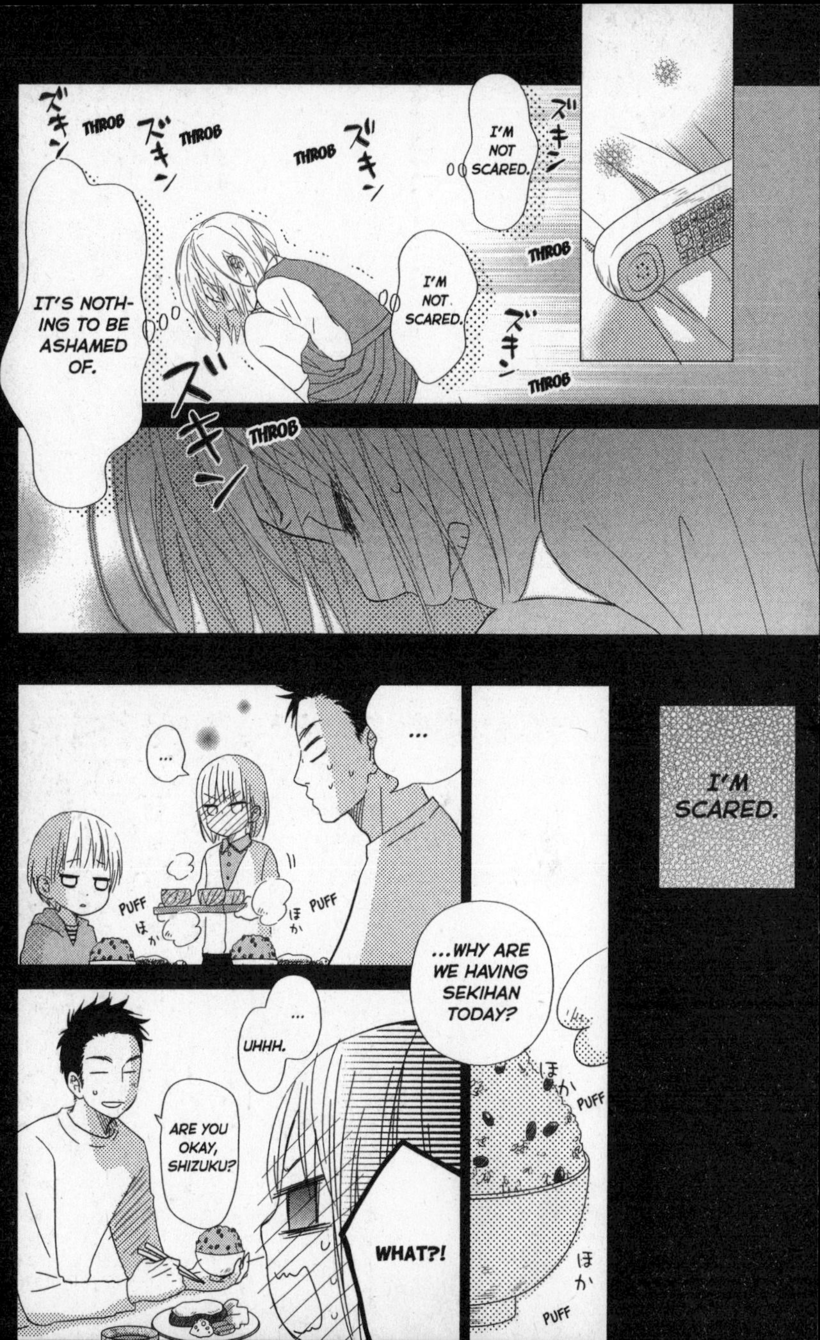
ズキン
THROB
I'M NOT SCARED.
ズキン
THROB
I'M NOT SCARED.
ズキン
THROB
ズキン
THROB
ズキン
THROB
ズキン
THROB
IT'S NOTHING TO BE ASHAMED OF.
ズキン
THROB
I'M SCARED.
...
...
ほか
PUFF
ほか
PUFF
...WHY ARE WE HAVING SEKIHAN TODAY?
ほか
PUFF
WHAT?!
ほか
PUFF
...
UHHH.
ARE YOU OKAY, SHIZUKU?

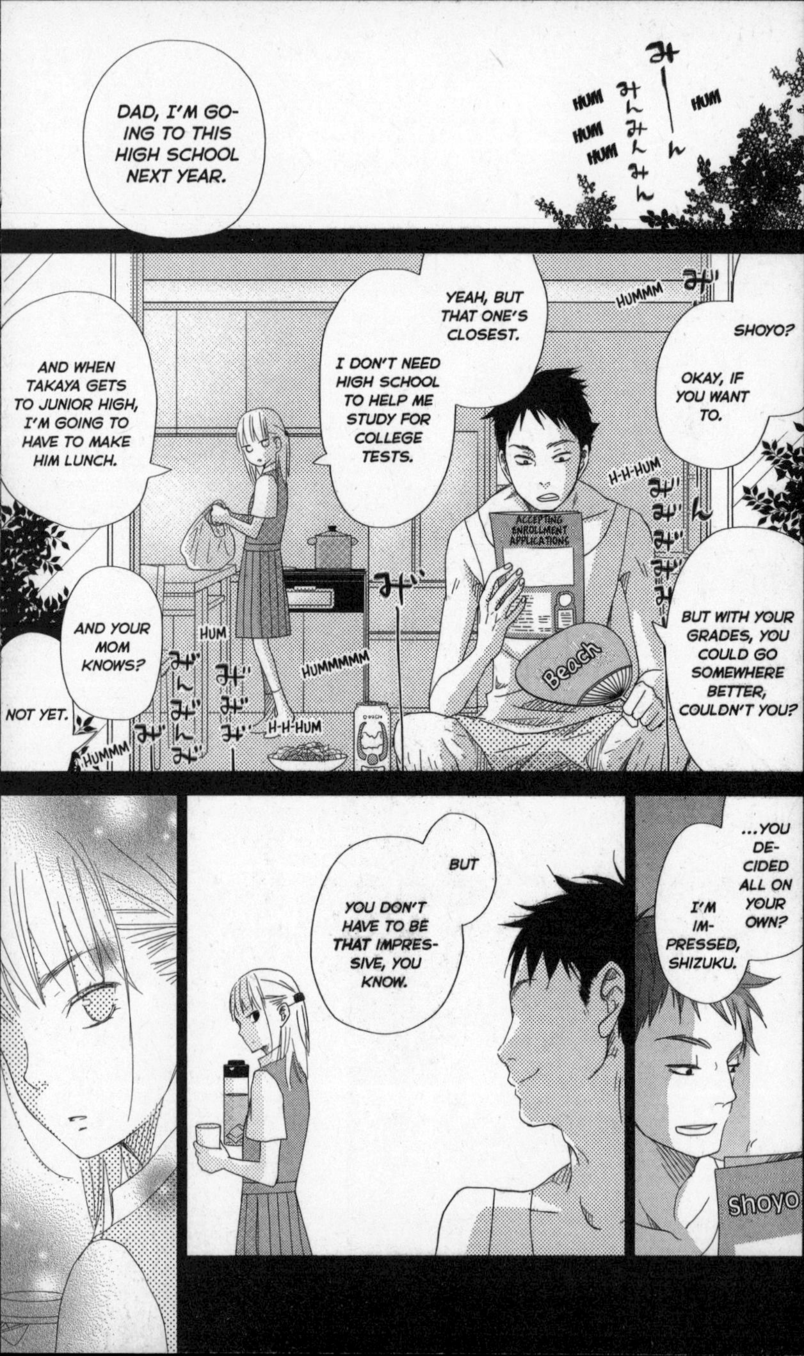
みーーん
みんみんみん
HUM
HUM
HUM
HUM
DAD, I'M GO-ING TO THIS HIGH SCHOOL NEXT YEAR.
みﾞ
HUMMM
SHOYO?
OKAY, IF YOU WANT TO.
H-H-HUM
みﾞんみﾞみﾞみﾞみﾞ
BUT WITH YOUR GRADES, YOU COULD GO SOMEWHERE BETTER, COULDN'T YOU?
ACCEPTING ENROLLMENT APPLICATIONS
Beach
YEAH, BUT THAT ONE'S CLOSEST.
I DON'T NEED HIGH SCHOOL TO HELP ME STUDY FOR COLLEGE TESTS.
みﾞ
HUMMMMM
H-H-HUM
AND WHEN TAKAYA GETS TO JUNIOR HIGH, I'M GOING TO HAVE TO MAKE HIM LUNCH.
AND YOUR MOM KNOWS?
HUM
NOT YET.
HUMMM
...YOU DECIDED ALL ON YOUR OWN?
I'M IM-PRESSED, SHIZUKU.
shoyo
BUT
YOU DON'T HAVE TO BE THAT IMPRES-SIVE, YOU KNOW.

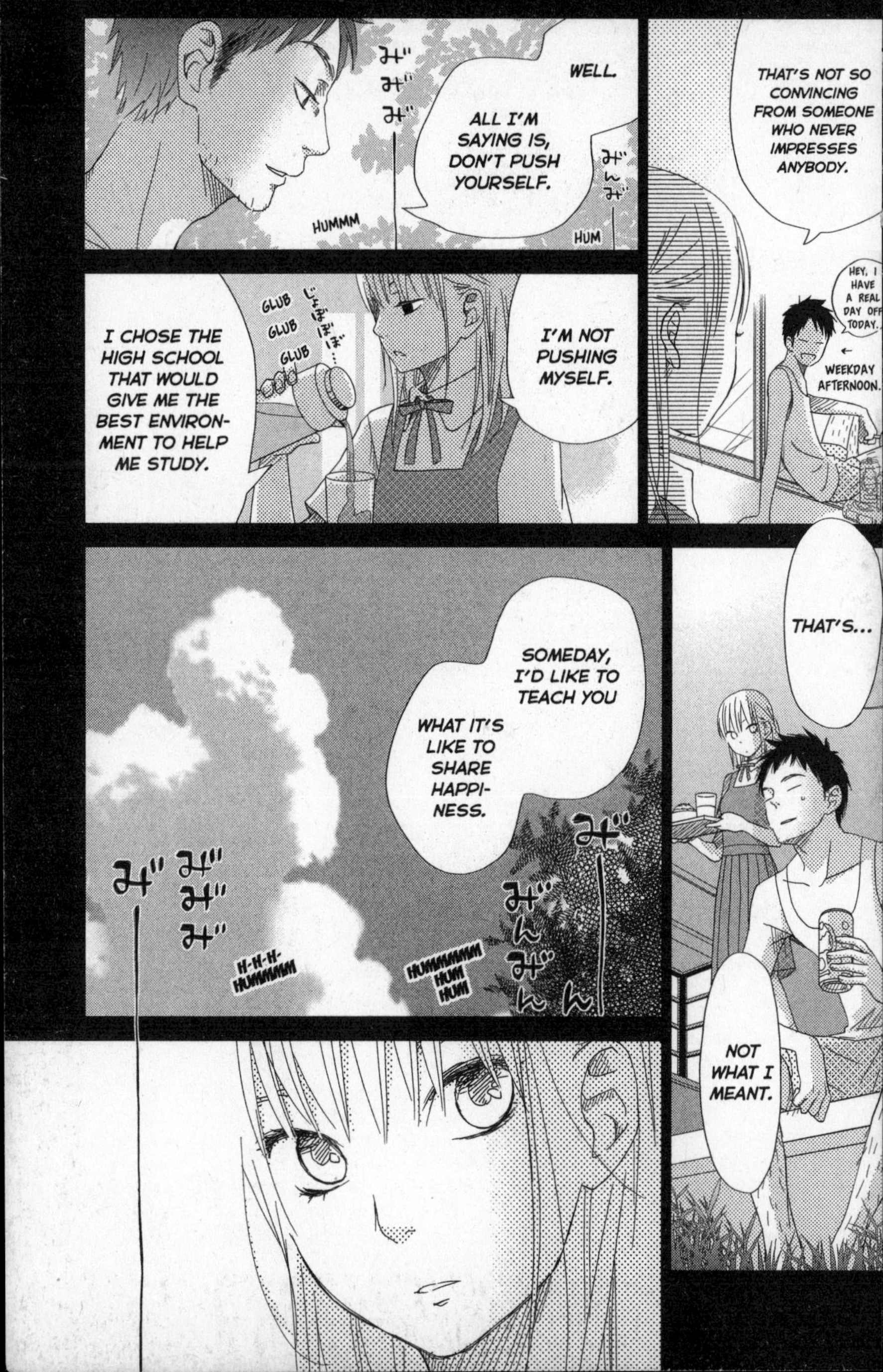
THAT'S NOT SO CONVINCING FROM SOMEONE WHO NEVER IMPRESSES ANYBODY.
HEY, I HAVE A REAL DAY OFF TODAY.
← WEEKDAY AFTERNOON.
WELL.
ALL I'M SAYING IS, DON'T PUSH YOURSELF.
みんみ
HUM
みゞみゞみゞ
HUMMM
I'M NOT PUSHING MYSELF.
じょぼぼぼ…
GLUB GLUB GLUB
I CHOSE THE HIGH SCHOOL THAT WOULD GIVE ME THE BEST ENVIRONMENT TO HELP ME STUDY.
THAT'S…
NOT WHAT I MEANT.
SOMEDAY, I'D LIKE TO TEACH YOU
WHAT IT'S LIKE TO SHARE HAPPINESS.
みゞー みんみんみん
HUMMMMM HUM HUM
みゞみゞみゞみゞ
H-H-H-HUMMMM

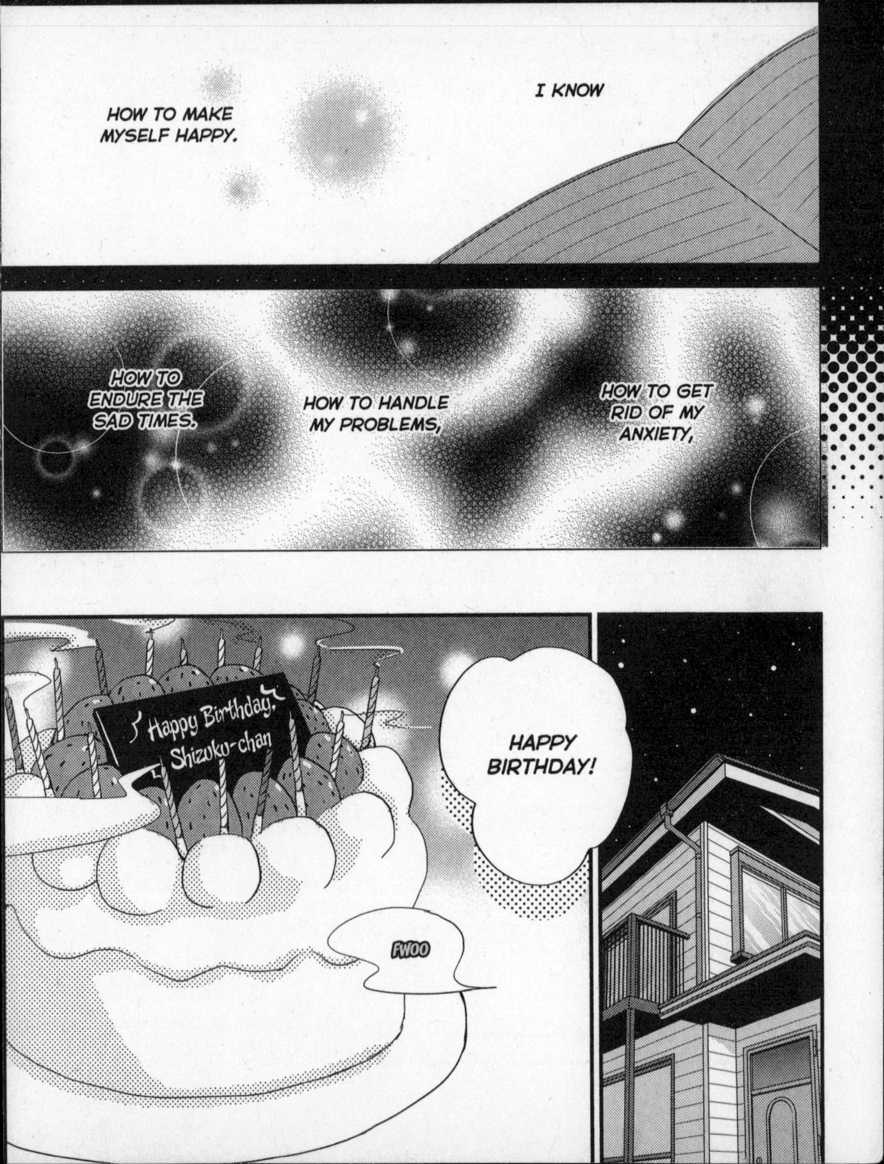
I KNOW
HOW TO MAKE MYSELF HAPPY.
HOW TO GET RID OF MY ANXIETY,
HOW TO HANDLE MY PROBLEMS,
HOW TO ENDURE THE SAD TIMES.
HAPPY BIRTHDAY!
Happy Birthday, Shizuku-chan
FWOO

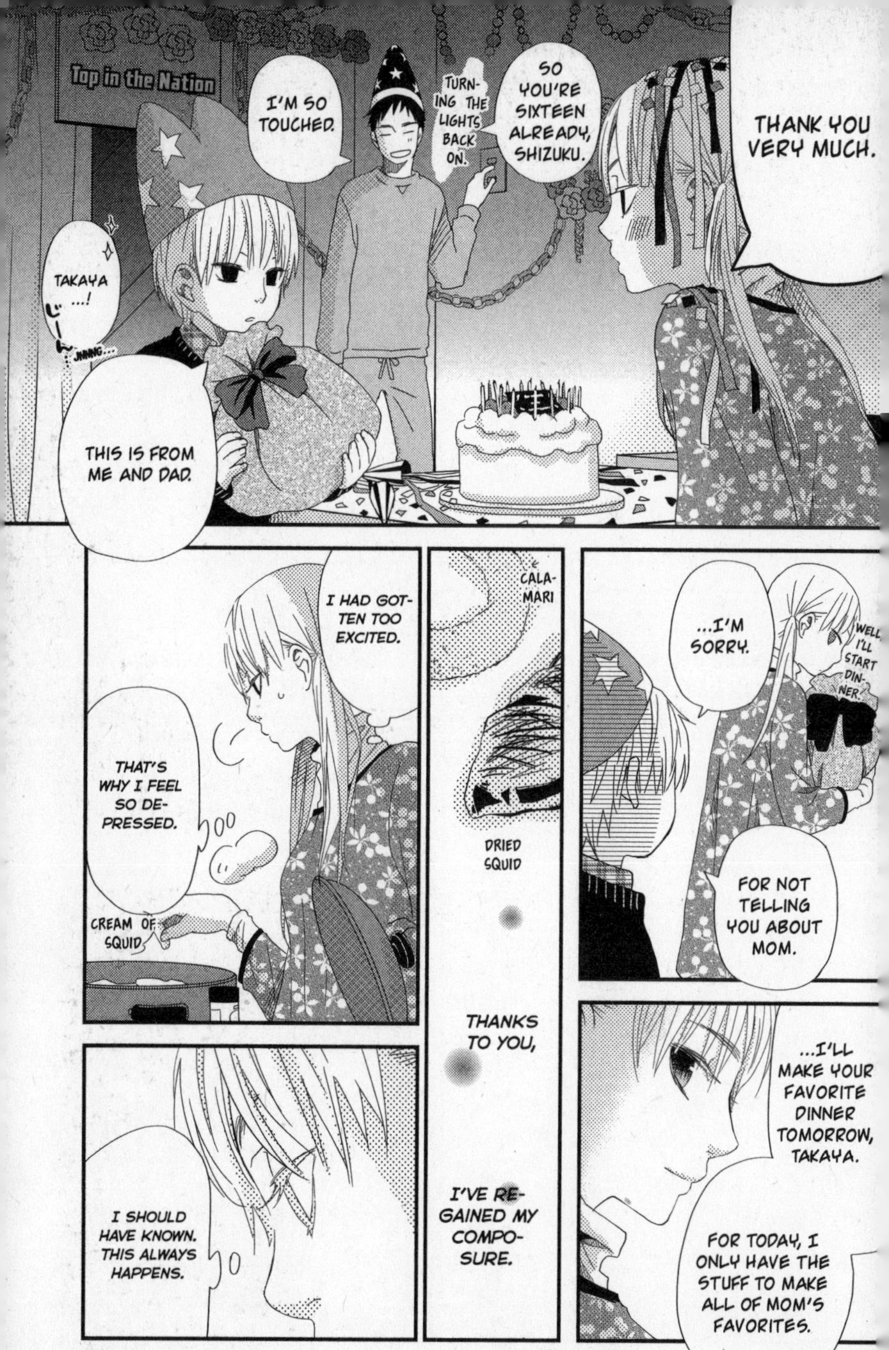
Top in the Nation
THANK YOU VERY MUCH.
SO YOU'RE SIXTEEN ALREADY, SHIZUKU.
TURNING THE LIGHTS BACK ON.
I'M SO TOUCHED.
TAKAYA ...!
JNNNG...
THIS IS FROM ME AND DAD.
...I'M SORRY.
WELL I'LL START DINNER.
FOR NOT TELLING YOU ABOUT MOM.
...I'LL MAKE YOUR FAVORITE DINNER TOMORROW, TAKAYA.
FOR TODAY, I ONLY HAVE THE STUFF TO MAKE ALL OF MOM'S FAVORITES.
CALAMARI
DRIED SQUID
THANKS TO YOU,
I'VE REGAINED MY COMPOSURE.
I HAD GOTTEN TOO EXCITED.
THAT'S WHY I FEEL SO DEPRESSED.
CREAM OF SQUID
I SHOULD HAVE KNOWN. THIS ALWAYS HAPPENS.

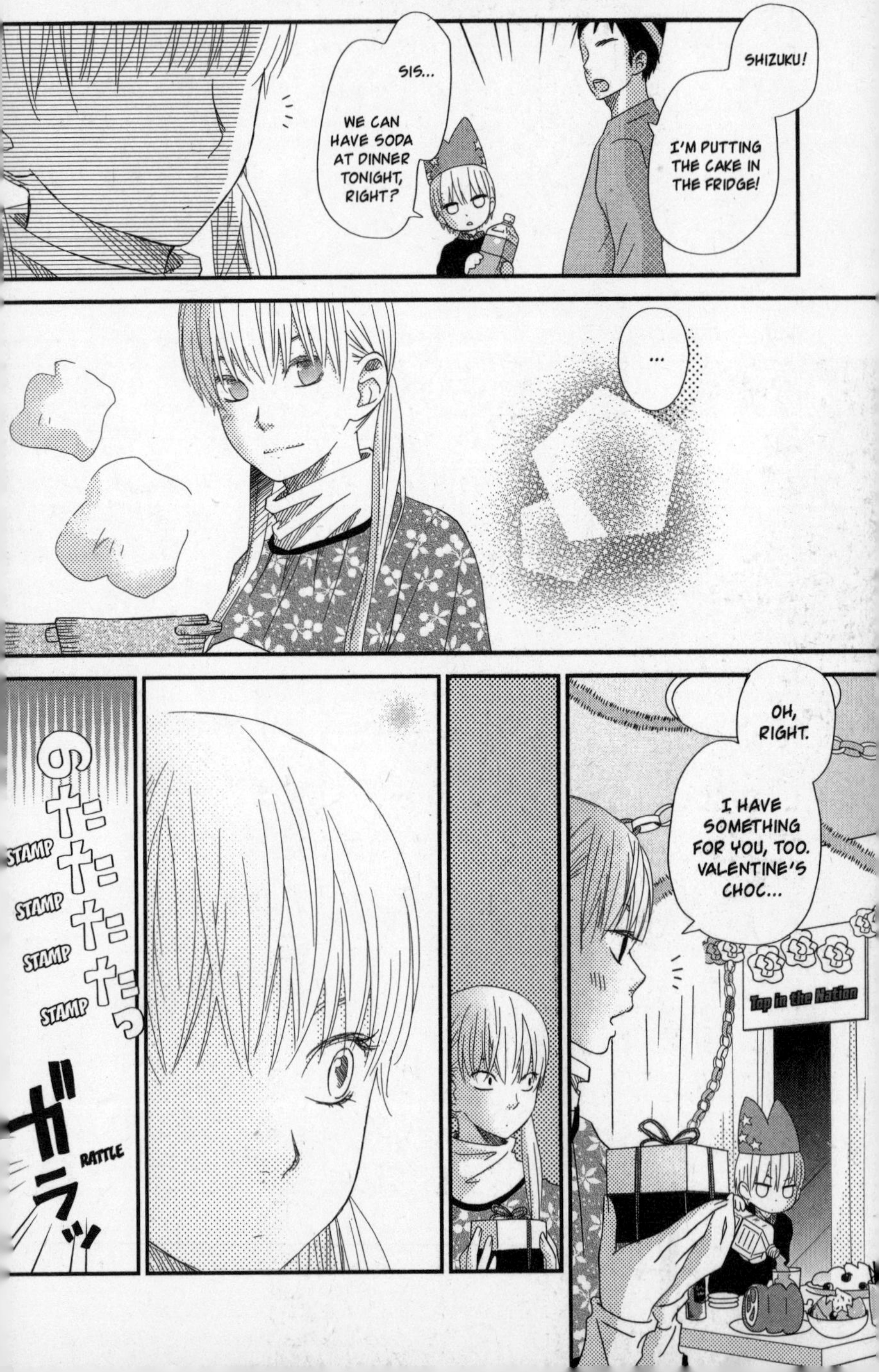
SHIZUKU!
I'M PUTTING THE CAKE IN THE FRIDGE!
SIS...
WE CAN HAVE SODA AT DINNER TONIGHT, RIGHT?
...
OH, RIGHT.
I HAVE SOMETHING FOR YOU, TOO. VALENTINE'S CHOC...
Top in the Nation
のたたたたっ
STAMP
STAMP
STAMP
STAMP
ガラッ
RATTLE

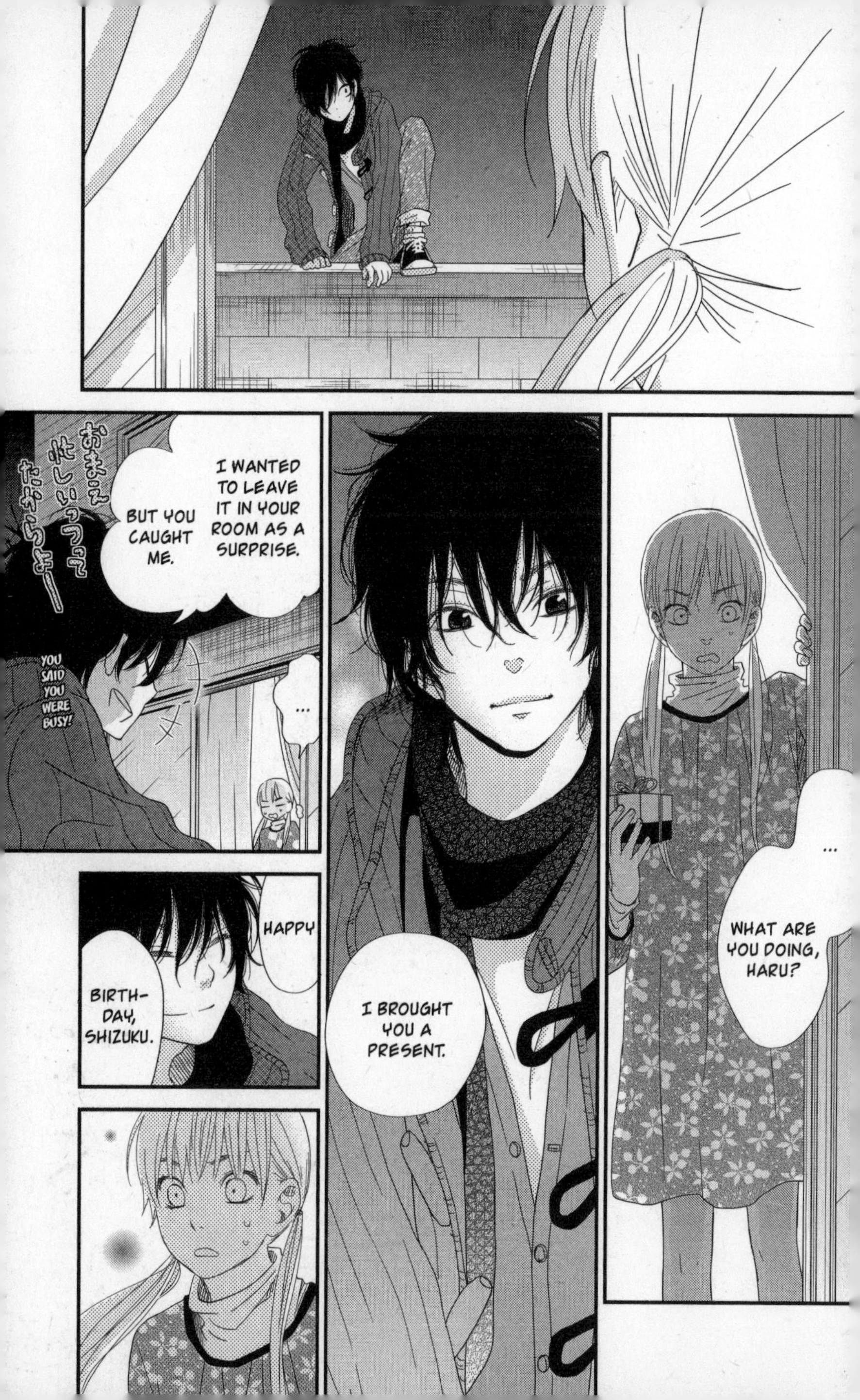
...
WHAT ARE YOU DOING, HARU?
I BROUGHT YOU A PRESENT.
I WANTED TO LEAVE IT IN YOUR ROOM AS A SURPRISE.
BUT YOU CAUGHT ME.
YOU SAID YOU WERE BUSY!
...
HAPPY
BIRTH-DAY, SHIZUKU.

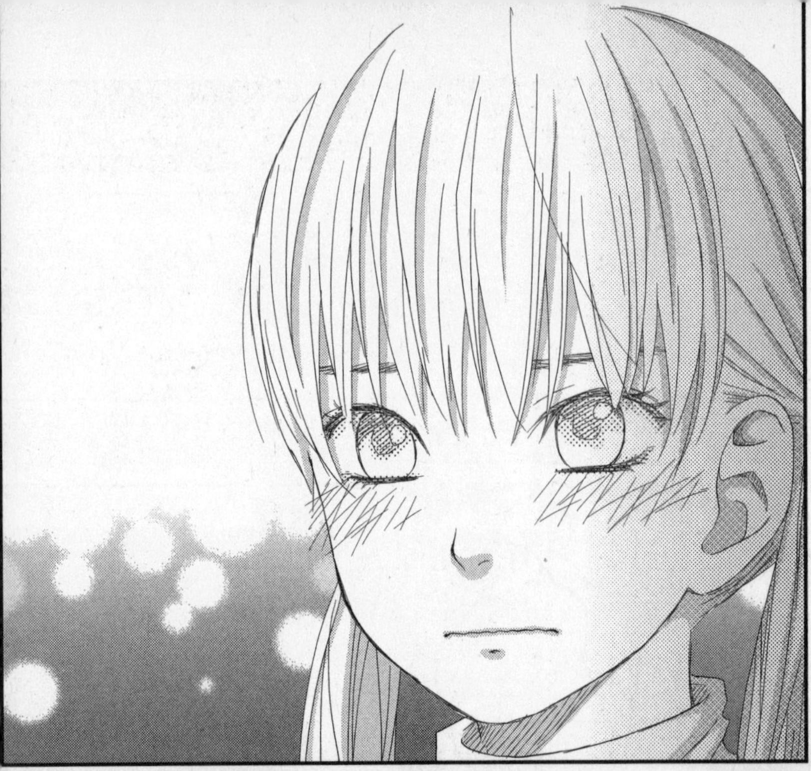

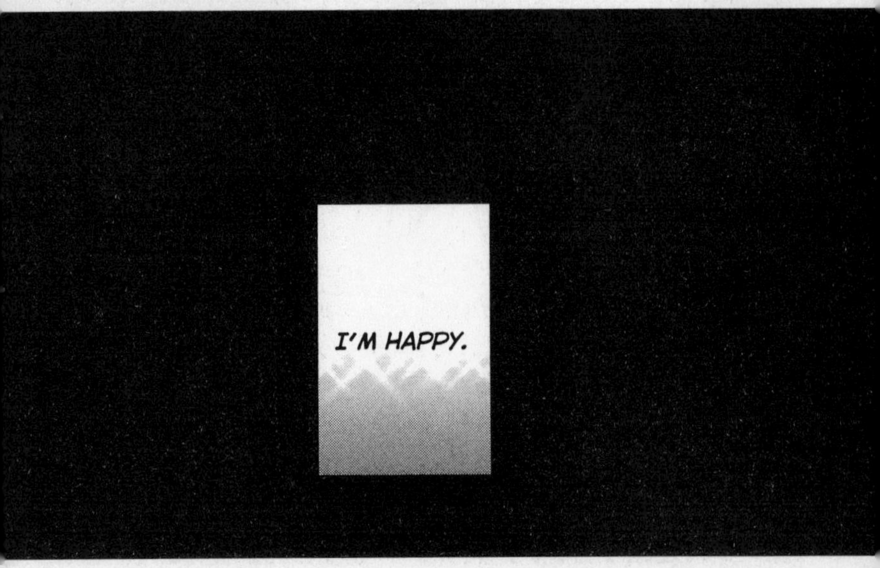
I'M HAPPY.

Round and Round

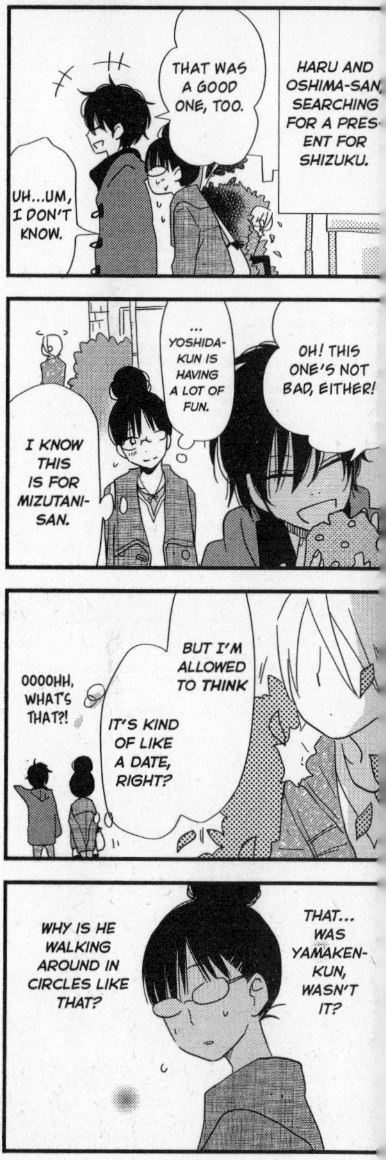
HARU AND OSHIMA-SAN, SEARCHING FOR A PRESENT FOR SHIZUKU.
THAT WAS A GOOD ONE, TOO.
UH...UM, I DON'T KNOW.
OH! THIS ONE'S NOT BAD, EITHER!
...YOSHIDA-KUN IS HAVING A LOT OF FUN.
I KNOW THIS IS FOR MIZUTANI-SAN.
BUT I'M ALLOWED TO THINK
IT'S KIND OF LIKE A DATE, RIGHT?
OOOOHH, WHAT'S THAT?!
THAT... WAS YAMAKEN-KUN, WASN'T IT?
WHY IS HE WALKING AROUND IN CIRCLES LIKE THAT?

Bumping into Each Other

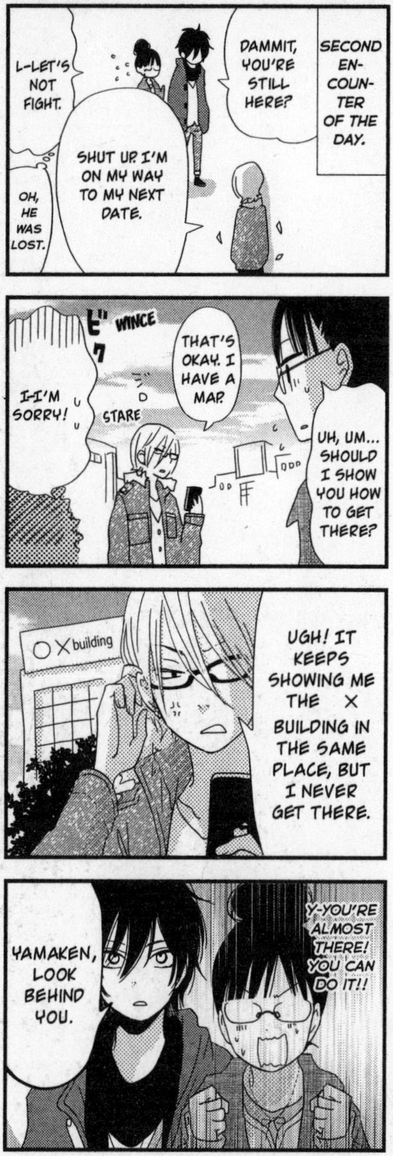
SECOND ENCOUNTER OF THE DAY.
DAMMIT, YOU'RE STILL HERE?
L-LET'S NOT FIGHT.
SHUT UP. I'M ON MY WAY TO MY NEXT DATE.
OH, HE WAS LOST.
UH, UM... SHOULD I SHOW YOU HOW TO GET THERE?
THAT'S OKAY. I HAVE A MAP.
WINCE
STARE
I-I'M SORRY!
UGH! IT KEEPS SHOWING ME THE X BUILDING IN THE SAME PLACE, BUT I NEVER GET THERE.
○X building
Y-YOU'RE ALMOST THERE! YOU CAN DO IT!!
YAMAKEN, LOOK BEHIND YOU.

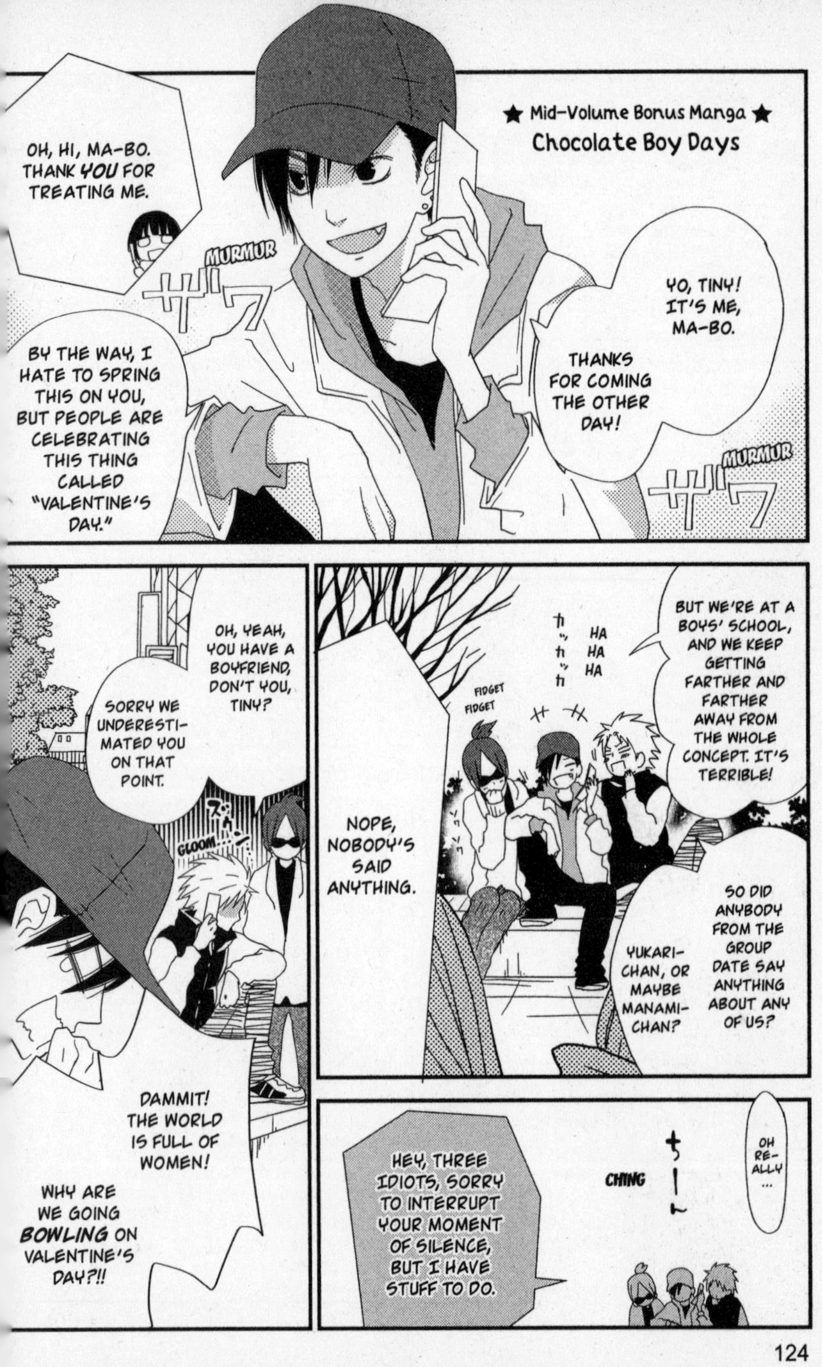
★ Mid-Volume Bonus Manga ★
Chocolate Boy Days
YO, TINY! IT'S ME, MA-BO.
THANKS FOR COMING THE OTHER DAY!
MURMUR
ザワ
OH, HI, MA-BO. THANK *YOU* FOR TREATING ME.
MURMUR
ザワ
BY THE WAY, I HATE TO SPRING THIS ON YOU, BUT PEOPLE ARE CELEBRATING THIS THING CALLED "VALENTINE'S DAY."
BUT WE'RE AT A BOYS' SCHOOL, AND WE KEEP GETTING FARTHER AND FARTHER AWAY FROM THE WHOLE CONCEPT. IT'S TERRIBLE!
HA HA HA
FIDGET FIDGET
SO DID ANYBODY FROM THE GROUP DATE SAY ANYTHING ABOUT ANY OF US?
YUKARI-CHAN, OR MAYBE MANAMI-CHAN?
NOPE, NOBODY'S SAID ANYTHING.
OH RE-ALLY ...
CHING
HEY, THREE IDIOTS, SORRY TO INTERRUPT YOUR MOMENT OF SILENCE, BUT I HAVE STUFF TO DO.
OH, YEAH, YOU HAVE A BOYFRIEND, DON'T YOU, TINY?
SORRY WE UNDERESTI-MATED YOU ON THAT POINT.
GLOOM
DAMMIT! THE WORLD IS FULL OF WOMEN!
WHY ARE WE GOING **BOWLING** ON VALENTINE'S DAY?!!

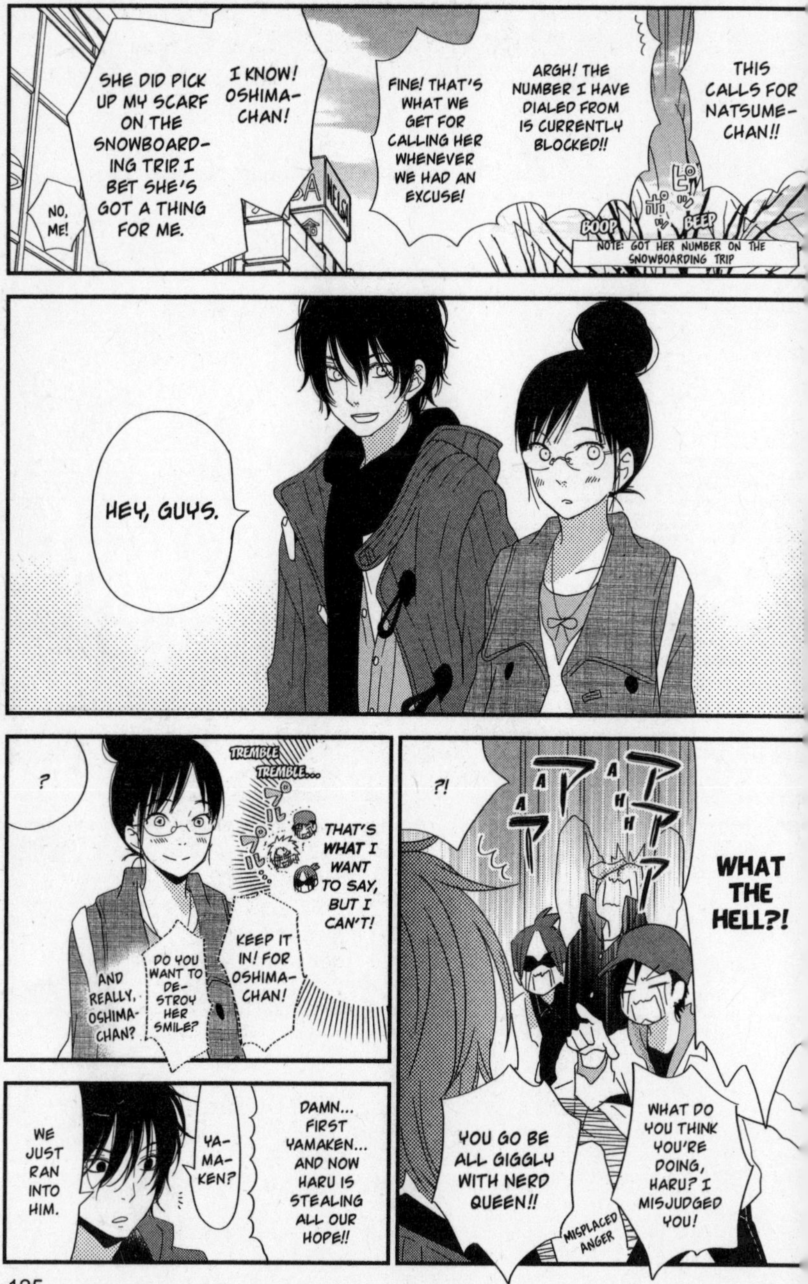
THIS CALLS FOR NATSUME-CHAN!!
BOOP
BEEP
NOTE: GOT HER NUMBER ON THE SNOWBOARDING TRIP
ARGH! THE NUMBER I HAVE DIALED FROM IS CURRENTLY BLOCKED!!
FINE! THAT'S WHAT WE GET FOR CALLING HER WHENEVER WE HAD AN EXCUSE!
I KNOW! OSHIMA-CHAN!
SHE DID PICK UP MY SCARF ON THE SNOWBOARDING TRIP. I BET SHE'S GOT A THING FOR ME.
NO, ME!
HEY, GUYS.
WHAT THE HELL?!
AHHH
?!
WHAT DO YOU THINK YOU'RE DOING, HARU? I MISJUDGED YOU!
MISPLACED ANGER
YOU GO BE ALL GIGGLY WITH NERD QUEEN!!
?
TREMBLE TREMBLE...
THAT'S WHAT I WANT TO SAY, BUT I CAN'T!
KEEP IT IN! FOR OSHIMA-CHAN!
DO YOU WANT TO DESTROY HER SMILE?
AND REALLY, OSHIMA-CHAN?
DAMN... FIRST YAMAKEN... AND NOW HARU IS STEALING ALL OUR HOPE!!
YAMAKEN?
WE JUST RAN INTO HIM.

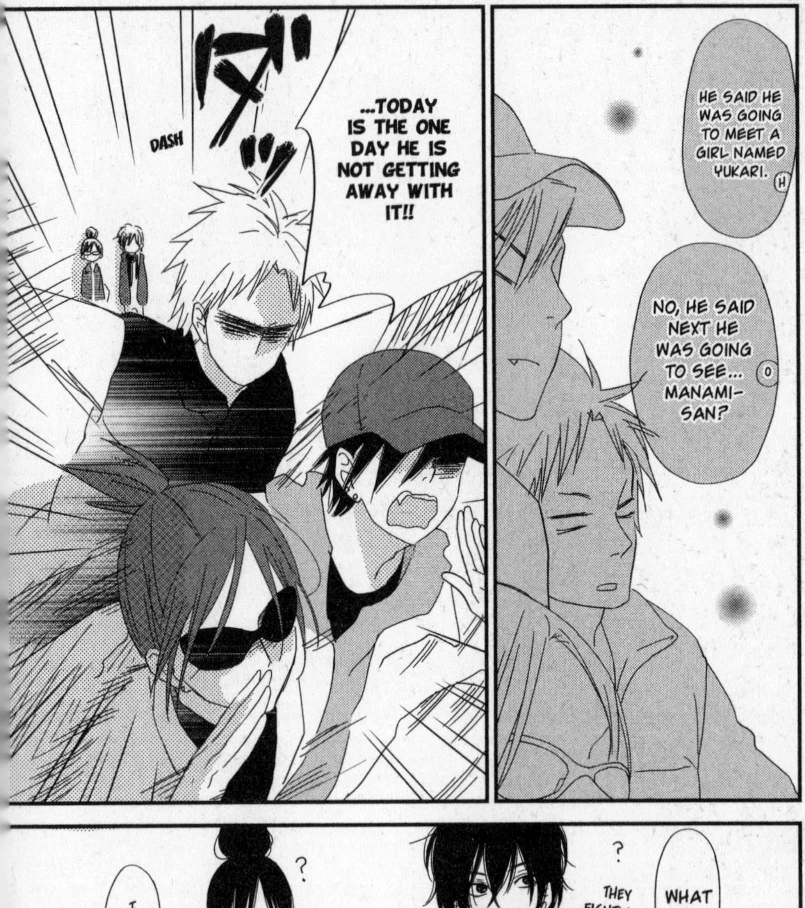
HE SAID HE WAS GOING TO MEET A GIRL NAMED YUKARI.
NO, HE SAID NEXT HE WAS GOING TO SEE... MANAMI-SAN?
DASH
...TODAY IS THE ONE DAY HE IS NOT GETTING AWAY WITH IT!!
WHAT THE?
THEY FIGHTING?
I DON'T KNOW...

Chocolate Boy Days ★ End ★

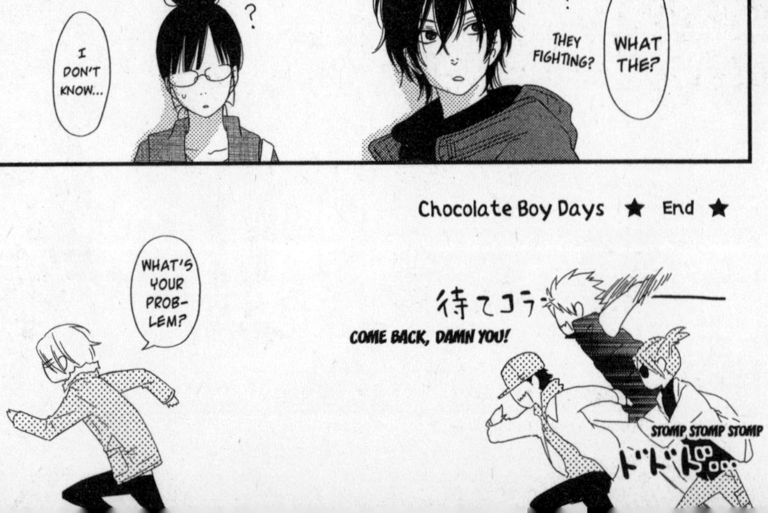
待てコラー
COME BACK, DAMN YOU!
STOMP STOMP STOMP
WHAT'S YOUR PROB-LEM?

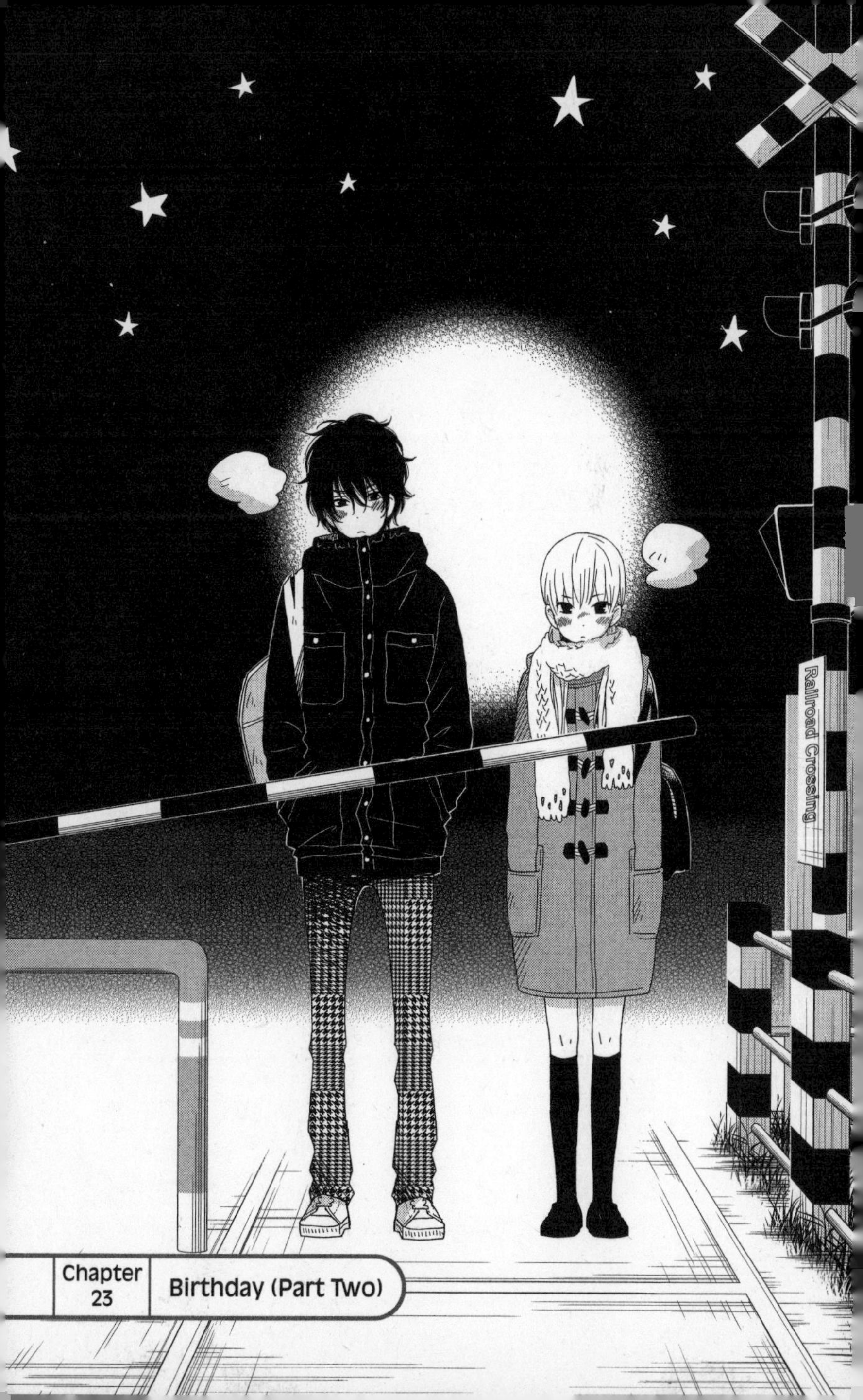
Railroad Crossing

Chapter 23 Birthday (Part Two)

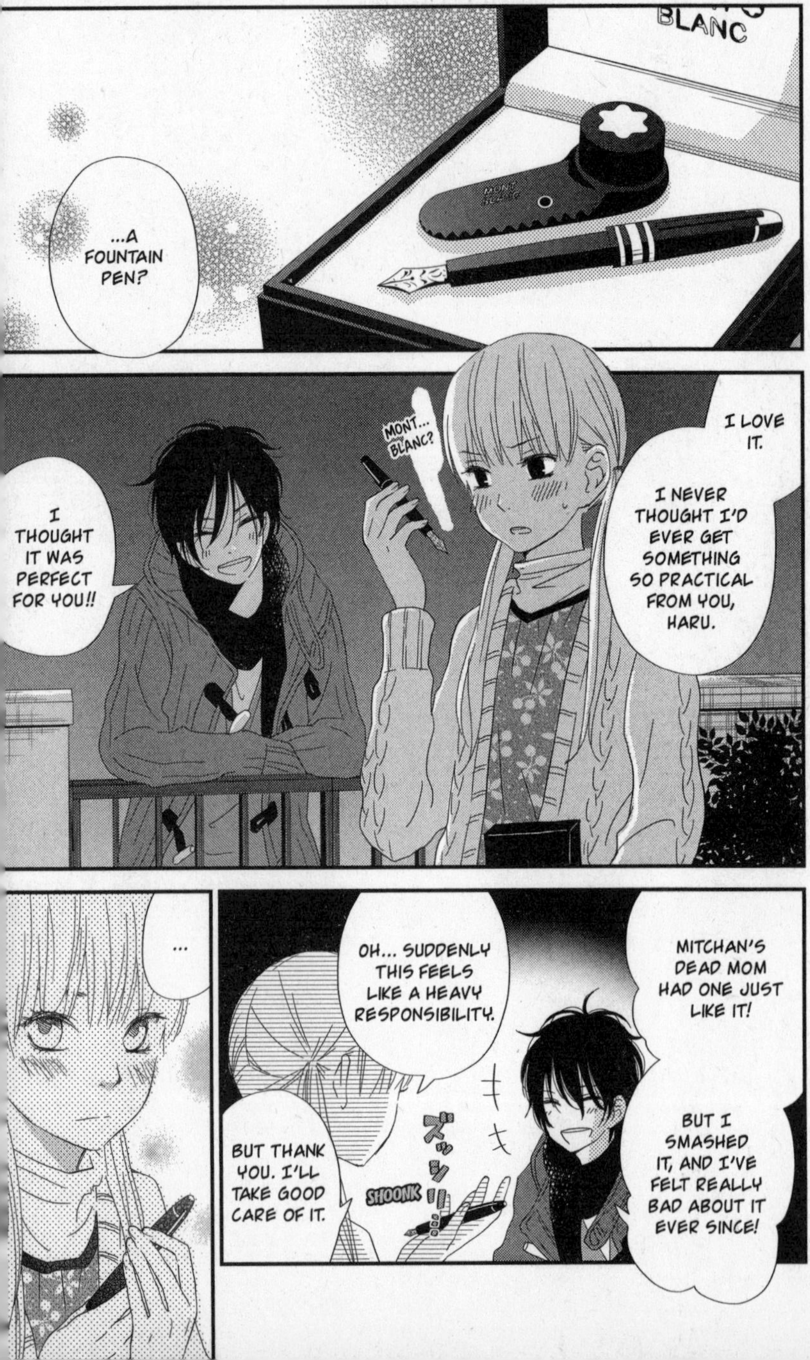
BLANC
...A FOUNTAIN PEN?
I LOVE IT.
I NEVER THOUGHT I'D EVER GET SOMETHING SO PRACTICAL FROM YOU, HARU.
MONT... BLANC?
I THOUGHT IT WAS PERFECT FOR YOU!!
MITCHAN'S DEAD MOM HAD ONE JUST LIKE IT!
OH... SUDDENLY THIS FEELS LIKE A HEAVY RESPONSIBILITY.
BUT I SMASHED IT, AND I'VE FELT REALLY BAD ABOUT IT EVER SINCE!
SHOONK
BUT THANK YOU. I'LL TAKE GOOD CARE OF IT.
...

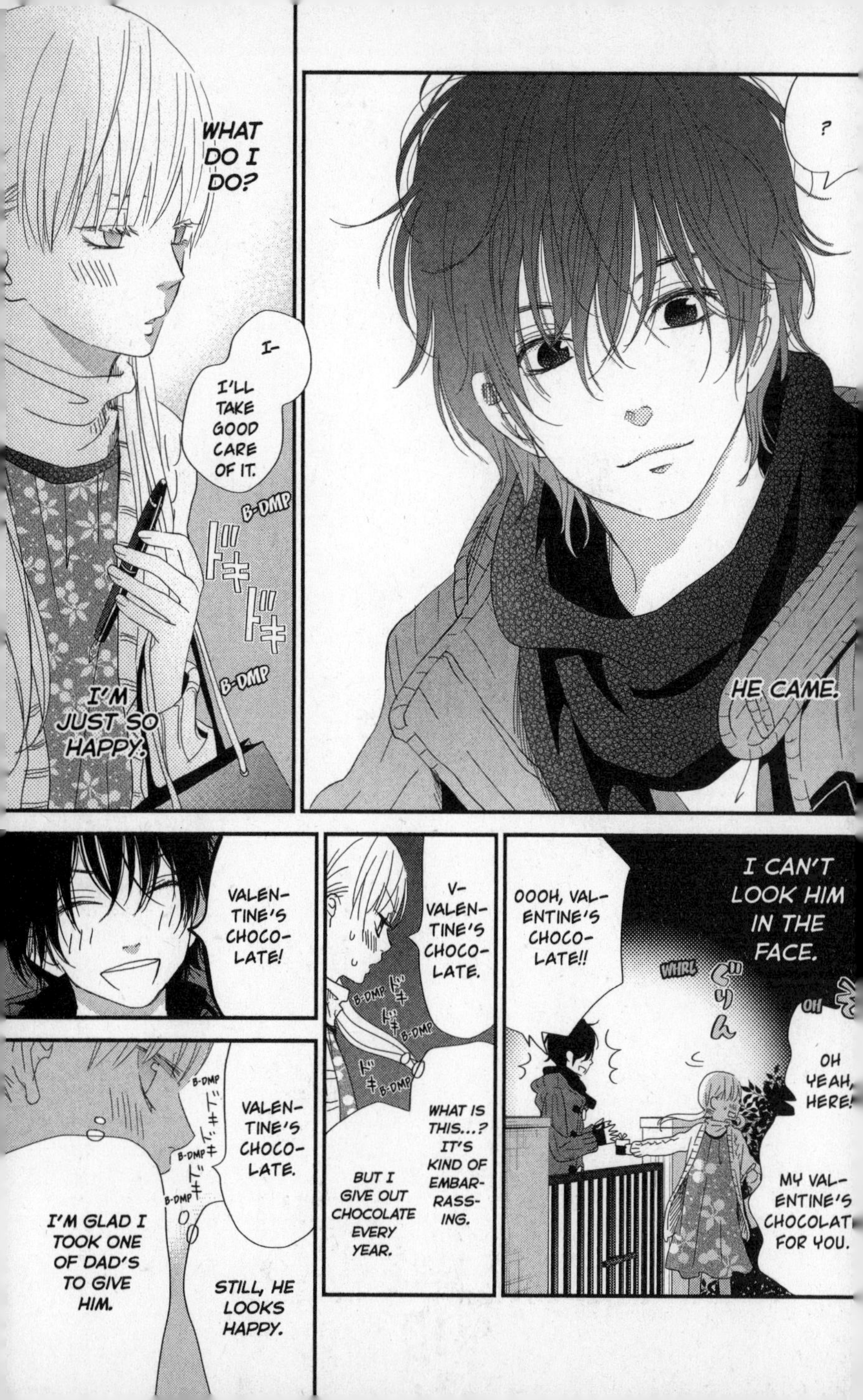
?
HE CAME.
WHAT DO I DO?
I-
I'LL TAKE GOOD CARE OF IT.
B-DMP ドキ
ドキ B-DMP
I'M JUST SO HAPPY.
I CAN'T LOOK HIM IN THE FACE.
WHRL ぐりん
OH そ
OH YEAH, HERE!
MY VALENTINE'S CHOCOLAT FOR YOU.
OOOH, VAL-ENTINE'S CHOCO-LATE!!
V- VALEN-TINE'S CHOCO-LATE.
B-DMP ドキ
ドキ B-DMP
ドキ B-DMP
WHAT IS THIS...? IT'S KIND OF EMBAR-RASS-ING.
BUT I GIVE OUT CHOCOLATE EVERY YEAR.
VALEN-TINE'S CHOCO-LATE!
B-DMP ドキ
B-DMP ドキ
B-DMP ドキ
VALEN-TINE'S CHOCO-LATE.
STILL, HE LOOKS HAPPY.
I'M GLAD I TOOK ONE OF DAD'S TO GIVE HIM.

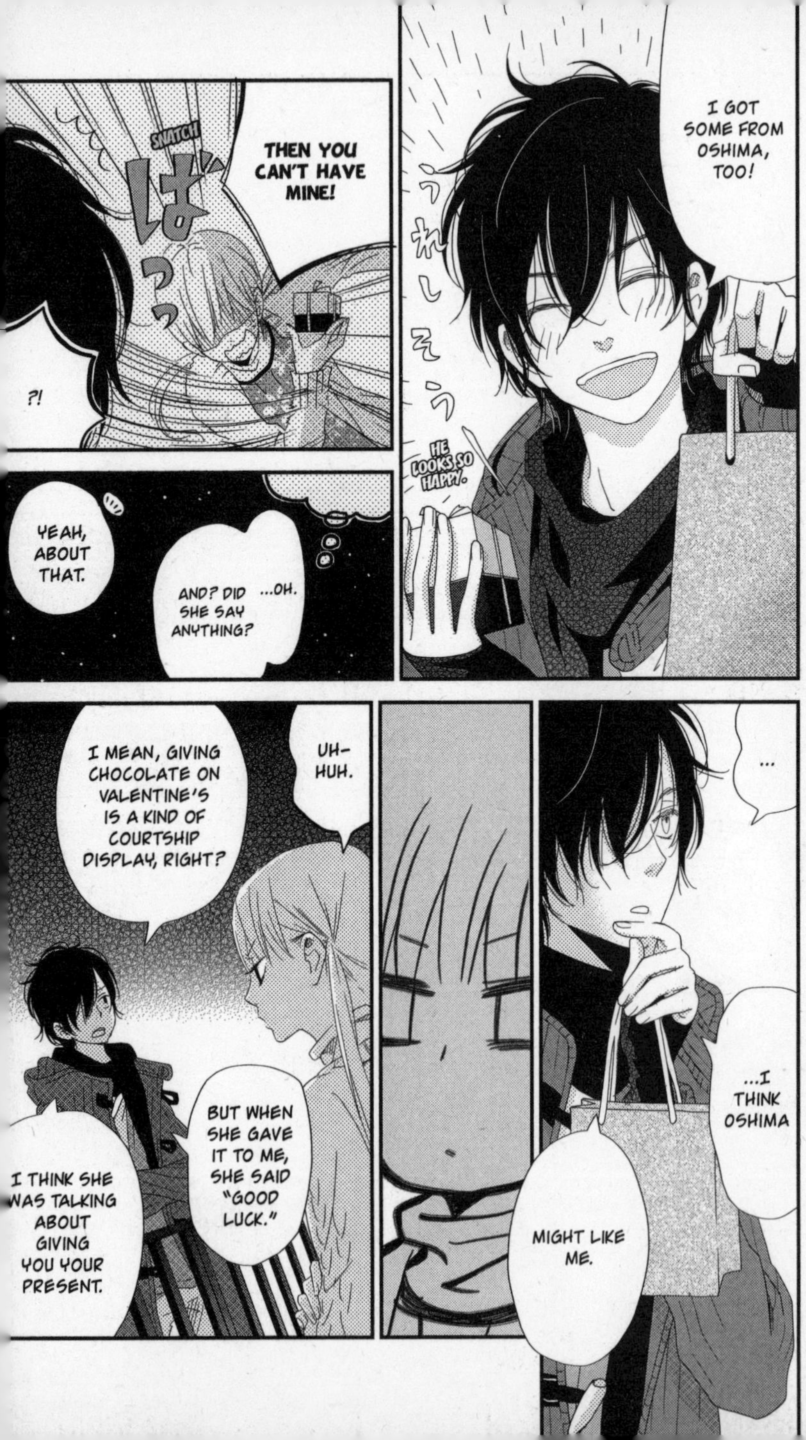
I GOT SOME FROM OSHIMA, TOO!
HE LOOKS SO HAPPY.
SNATCH
THEN YOU CAN'T HAVE MINE!
?!
AND? DID SHE SAY ANYTHING?
...OH.
YEAH, ABOUT THAT.
...
...I THINK OSHIMA
MIGHT LIKE ME.
UH-HUH.
I MEAN, GIVING CHOCOLATE ON VALENTINE'S IS A KIND OF COURTSHIP DISPLAY, RIGHT?
BUT WHEN SHE GAVE IT TO ME, SHE SAID "GOOD LUCK."
I THINK SHE WAS TALKING ABOUT GIVING YOU YOUR PRESENT.

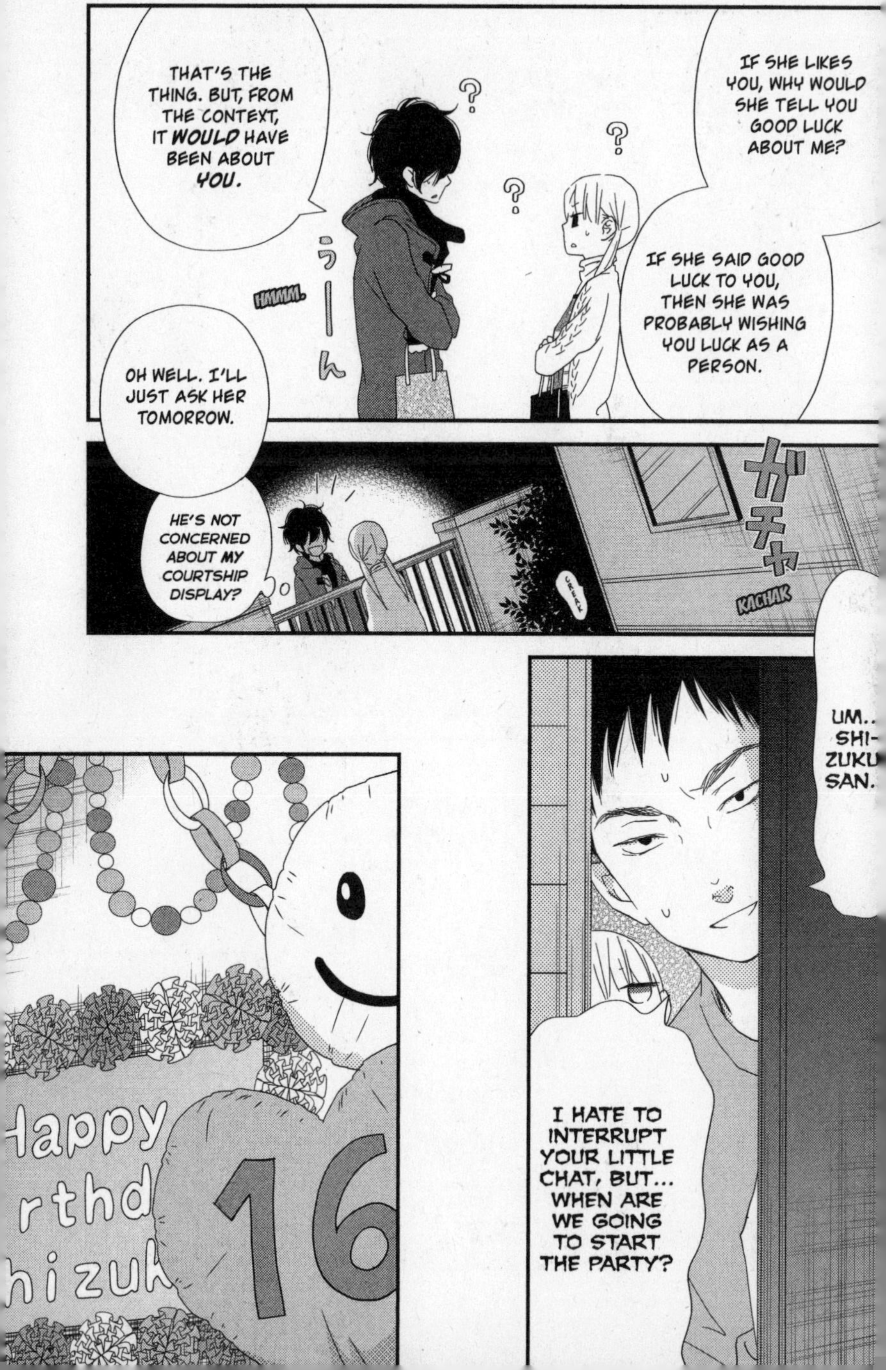
IF SHE LIKES YOU, WHY WOULD SHE TELL YOU GOOD LUCK ABOUT ME?
IF SHE SAID GOOD LUCK TO YOU, THEN SHE WAS PROBABLY WISHING YOU LUCK AS A PERSON.
THAT'S THE THING. BUT, FROM THE CONTEXT, IT WOULD HAVE BEEN ABOUT YOU.
うーん
HMMM.
OH WELL. I'LL JUST ASK HER TOMORROW.
ガチャ
KACHAK
CREAK
HE'S NOT CONCERNED ABOUT MY COURTSHIP DISPLAY?
UM... SHI-ZUKU SAN.
I HATE TO INTERRUPT YOUR LITTLE CHAT, BUT... WHEN ARE WE GOING TO START THE PARTY?
Happy
rthd
hizuk
16

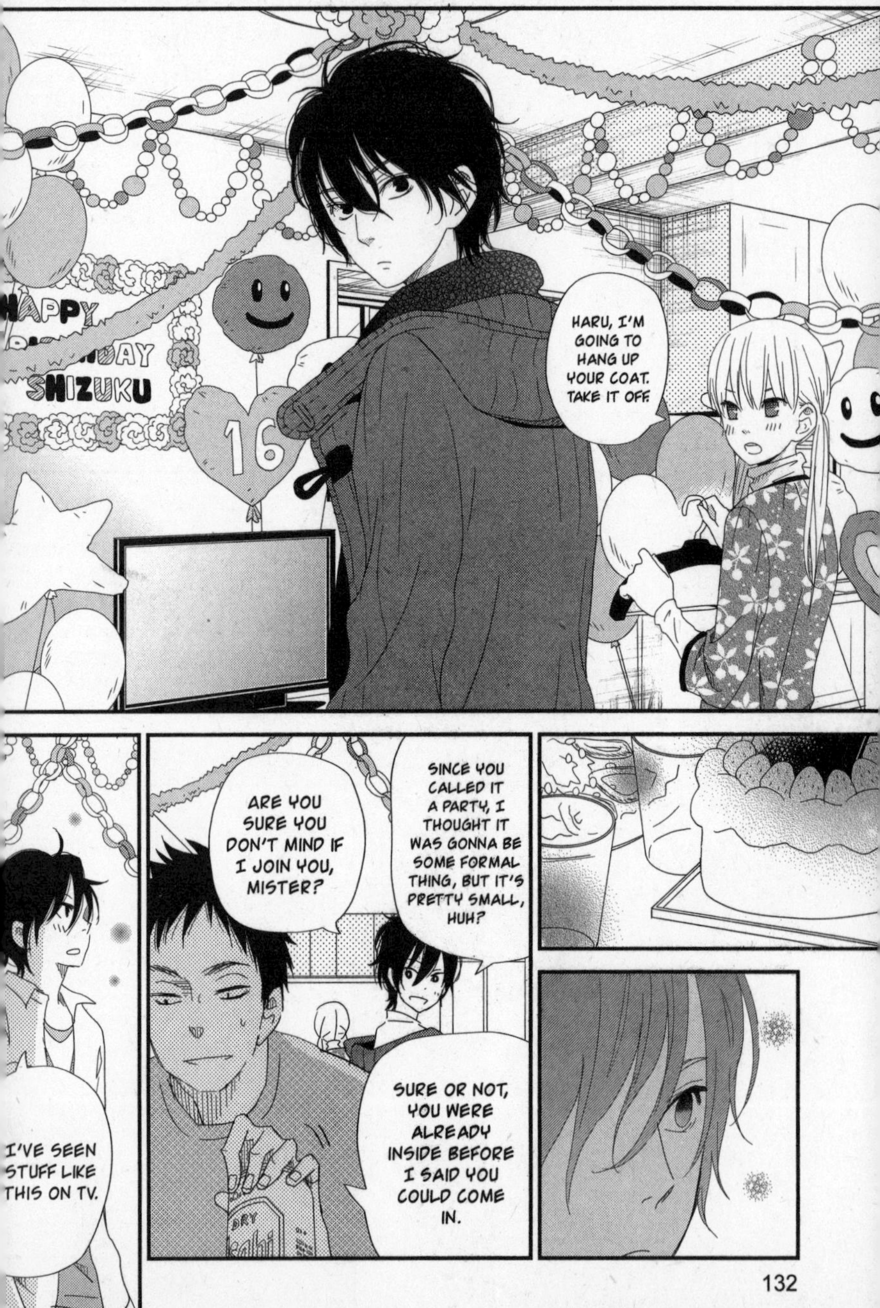
HAPPY
SHIZUKU
16
HARU, I'M GOING TO HANG UP YOUR COAT. TAKE IT OFF.
SINCE YOU CALLED IT A PARTY, I THOUGHT IT WAS GONNA BE SOME FORMAL THING, BUT IT'S PRETTY SMALL, HUH?
ARE YOU SURE YOU DON'T MIND IF I JOIN YOU, MISTER?
SURE OR NOT, YOU WERE ALREADY INSIDE BEFORE I SAID YOU COULD COME IN.
I'VE SEEN STUFF LIKE THIS ON TV.

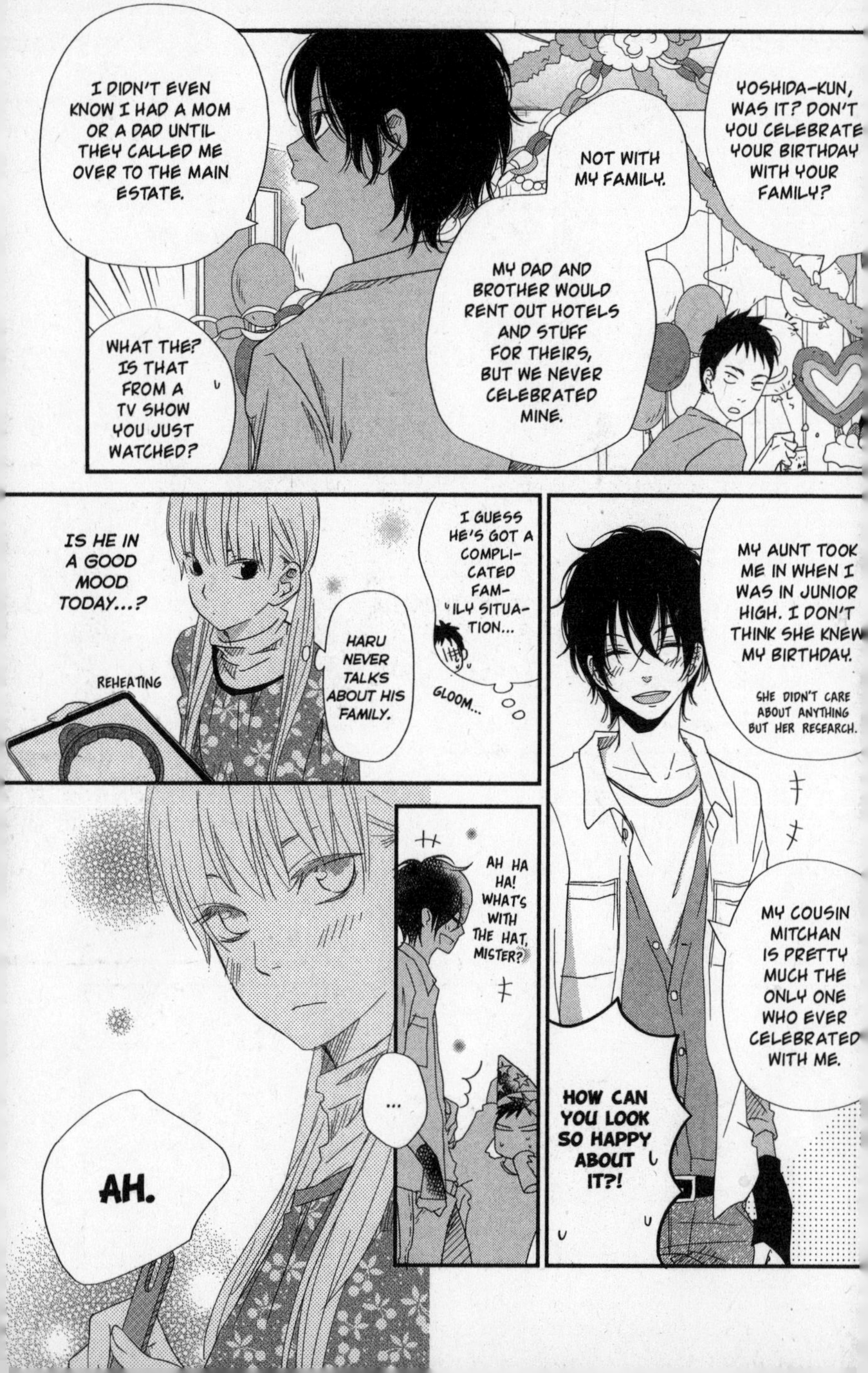

YOSHIDA-KUN, WAS IT? DON'T YOU CELEBRATE YOUR BIRTHDAY WITH YOUR FAMILY?
NOT WITH MY FAMILY.
MY DAD AND BROTHER WOULD RENT OUT HOTELS AND STUFF FOR THEIRS, BUT WE NEVER CELEBRATED MINE.
I DIDN'T EVEN KNOW I HAD A MOM OR A DAD UNTIL THEY CALLED ME OVER TO THE MAIN ESTATE.
WHAT THE? IS THAT FROM A TV SHOW YOU JUST WATCHED?
MY AUNT TOOK ME IN WHEN I WAS IN JUNIOR HIGH. I DON'T THINK SHE KNEW MY BIRTHDAY.
SHE DIDN'T CARE ABOUT ANYTHING BUT HER RESEARCH.
MY COUSIN MITCHAN IS PRETTY MUCH THE ONLY ONE WHO EVER CELEBRATED WITH ME.
HOW CAN YOU LOOK SO HAPPY ABOUT IT?!
I GUESS HE'S GOT A COMPLICATED FAMILY SITUATION...
GLOOM...
HARU NEVER TALKS ABOUT HIS FAMILY.
IS HE IN A GOOD MOOD TODAY...?
REHEATING
AH HA HA! WHAT'S WITH THE HAT, MISTER?
...
AH.

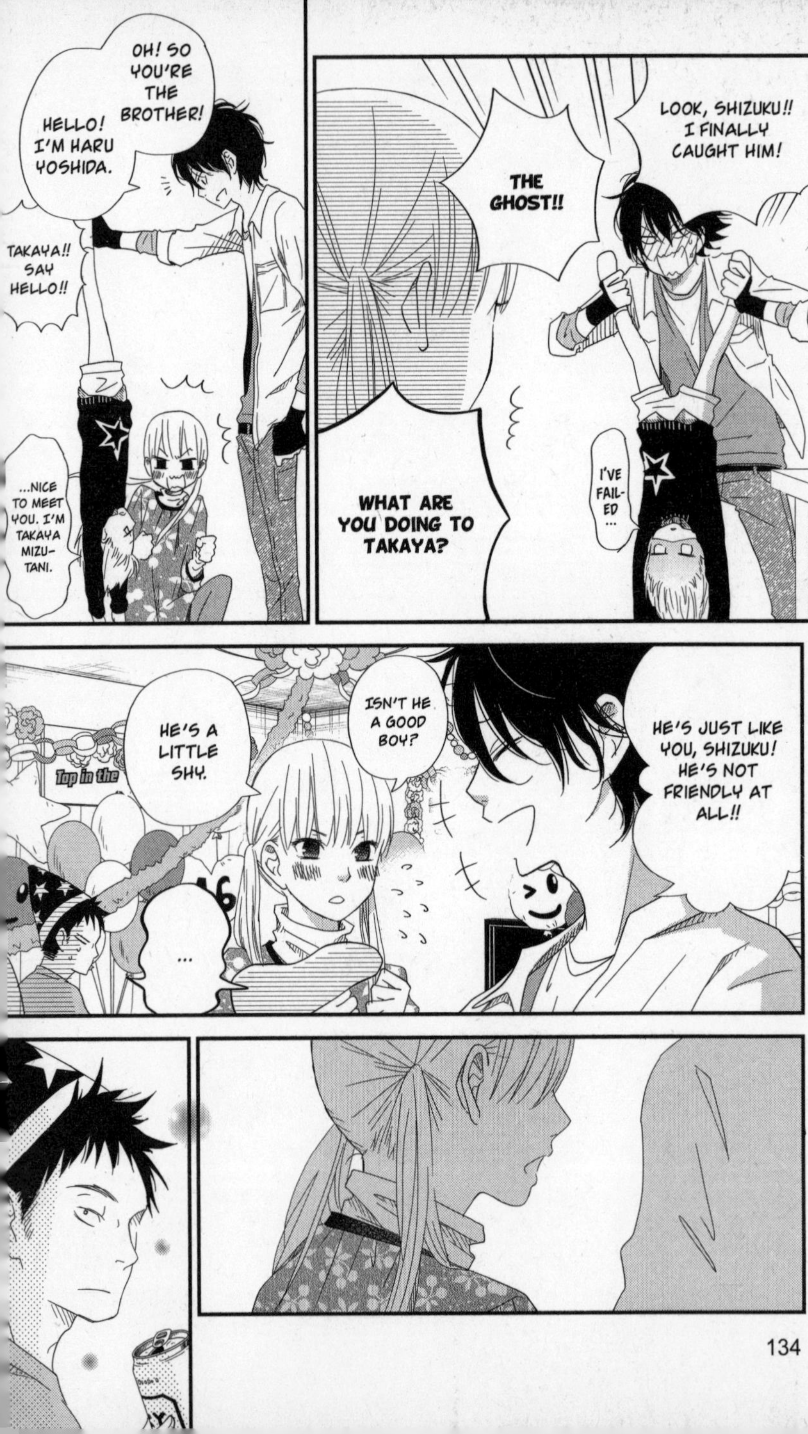
LOOK, SHIZUKU!! I FINALLY CAUGHT HIM!
THE GHOST!!
I'VE FAIL-ED ...
WHAT ARE YOU DOING TO TAKAYA?
OH! SO YOU'RE THE BROTHER!
HELLO! I'M HARU YOSHIDA.
TAKAYA!! SAY HELLO!!
...NICE TO MEET YOU. I'M TAKAYA MIZU-TANI.
HE'S JUST LIKE YOU, SHIZUKU! HE'S NOT FRIENDLY AT ALL!!
ISN'T HE A GOOD BOY?
HE'S A LITTLE SHY.
Top in the
...

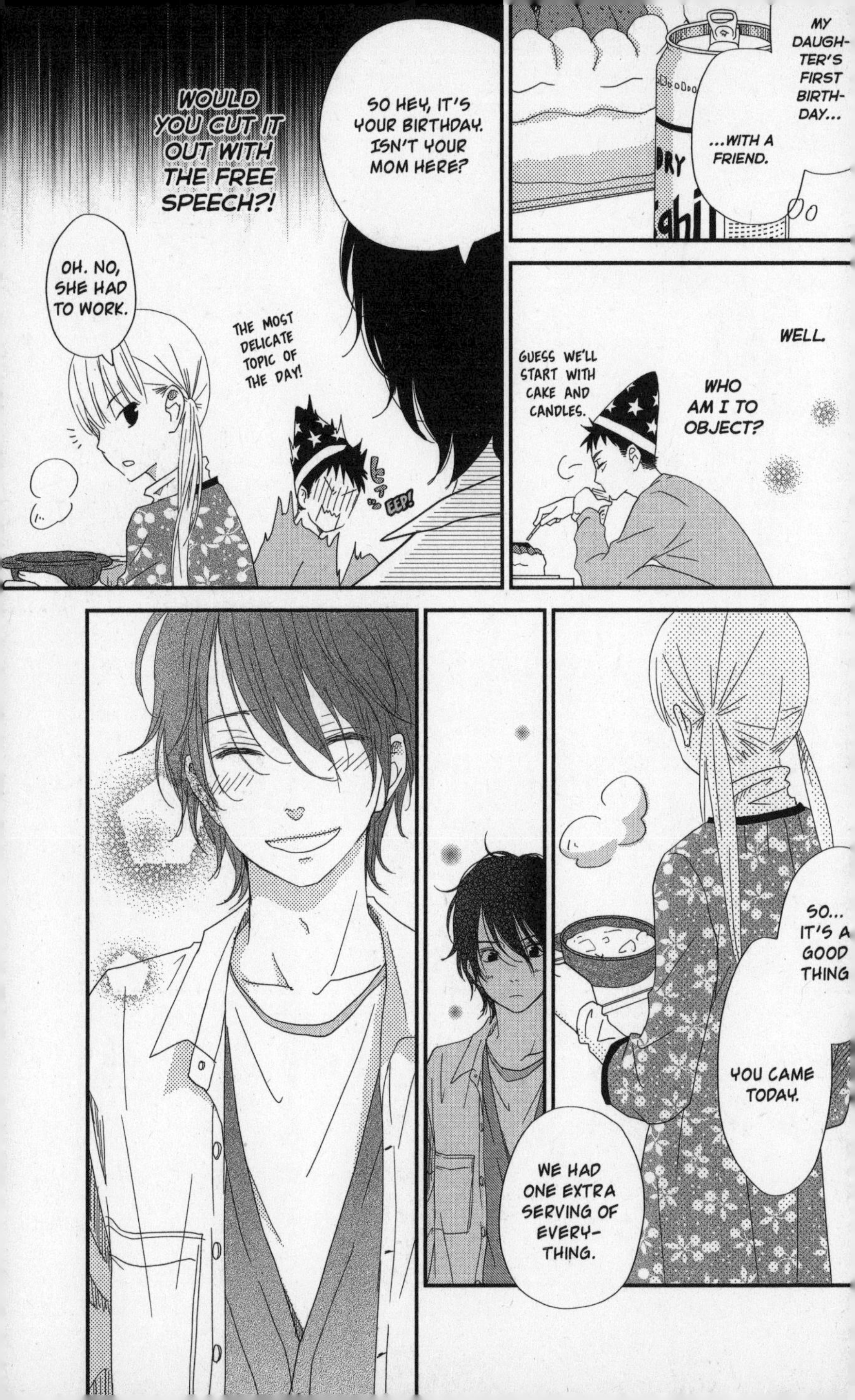
MY DAUGHTER'S FIRST BIRTHDAY...
...WITH A FRIEND.
WELL.
WHO AM I TO OBJECT?
GUESS WE'LL START WITH CAKE AND CANDLES.
SO HEY, IT'S YOUR BIRTHDAY. ISN'T YOUR MOM HERE?
WOULD YOU CUT IT OUT WITH THE FREE SPEECH?!
OH. NO, SHE HAD TO WORK.
THE MOST DELICATE TOPIC OF THE DAY!
EEP!
SO... IT'S A GOOD THING
YOU CAME TODAY.
WE HAD ONE EXTRA SERVING OF EVERYTHING.

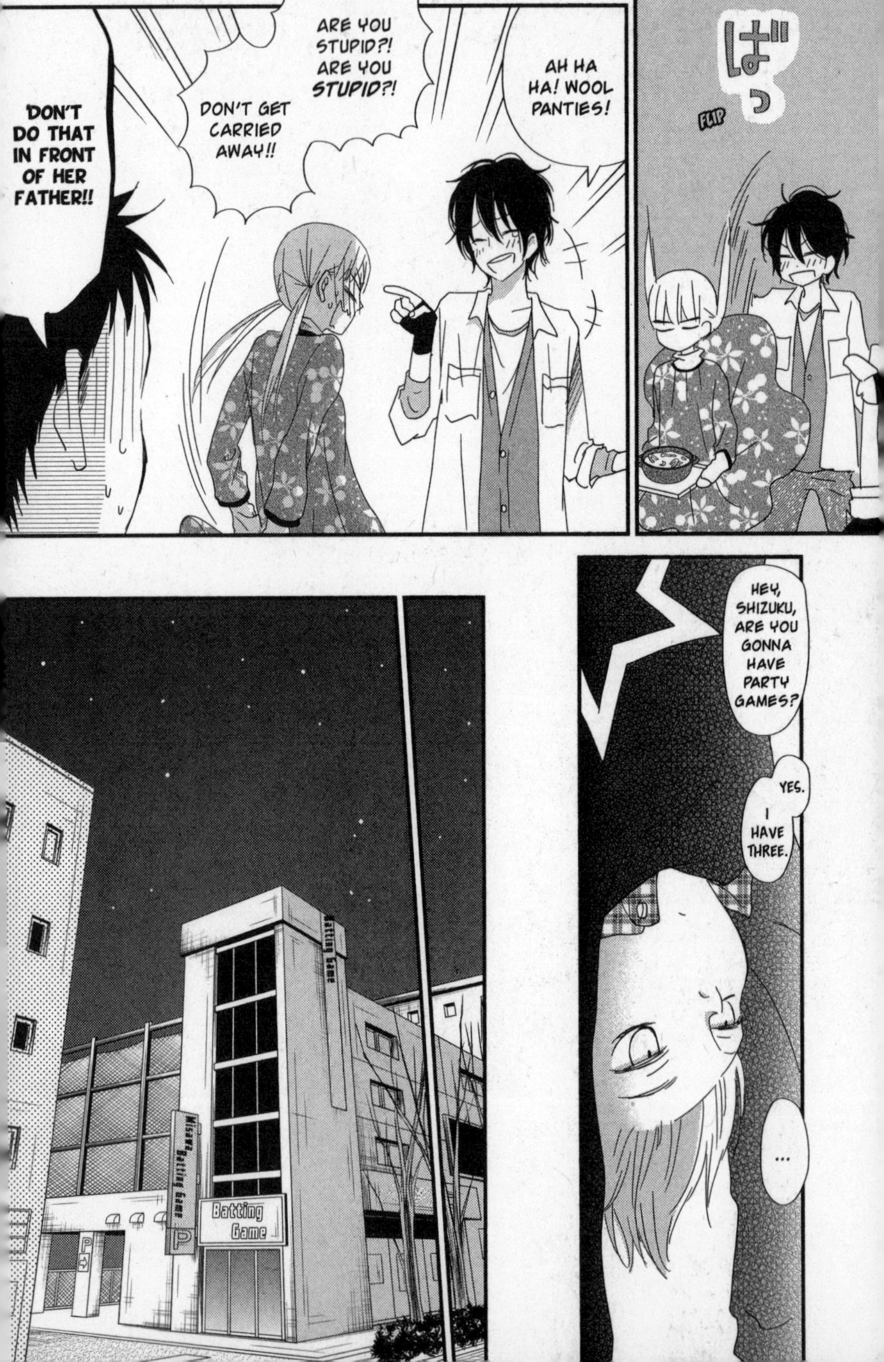
ばっ
FLIP
AH HA HA! WOOL PANTIES!
ARE YOU STUPID?! ARE YOU STUPID?!
DON'T GET CARRIED AWAY!!
DON'T DO THAT IN FRONT OF HER FATHER!!
HEY, SHIZUKU, ARE YOU GONNA HAVE PARTY GAMES?
YES. I HAVE THREE.
...
Batting Game
Misawa Batting Game
Batting Game

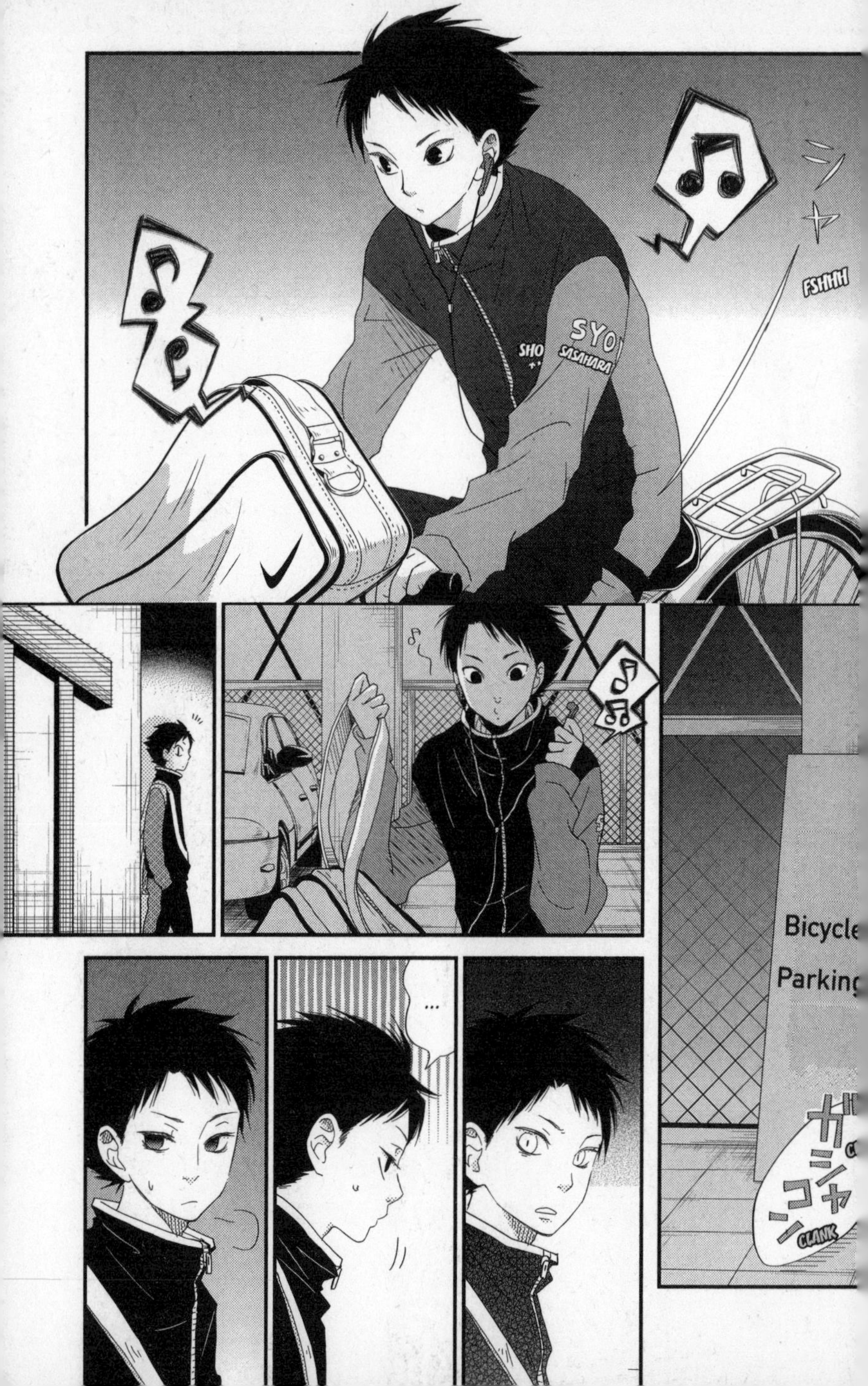
SYO
SHO
SASAHARA
FSHHH
Bicycle
Parking
ガシャン
CLANK
...

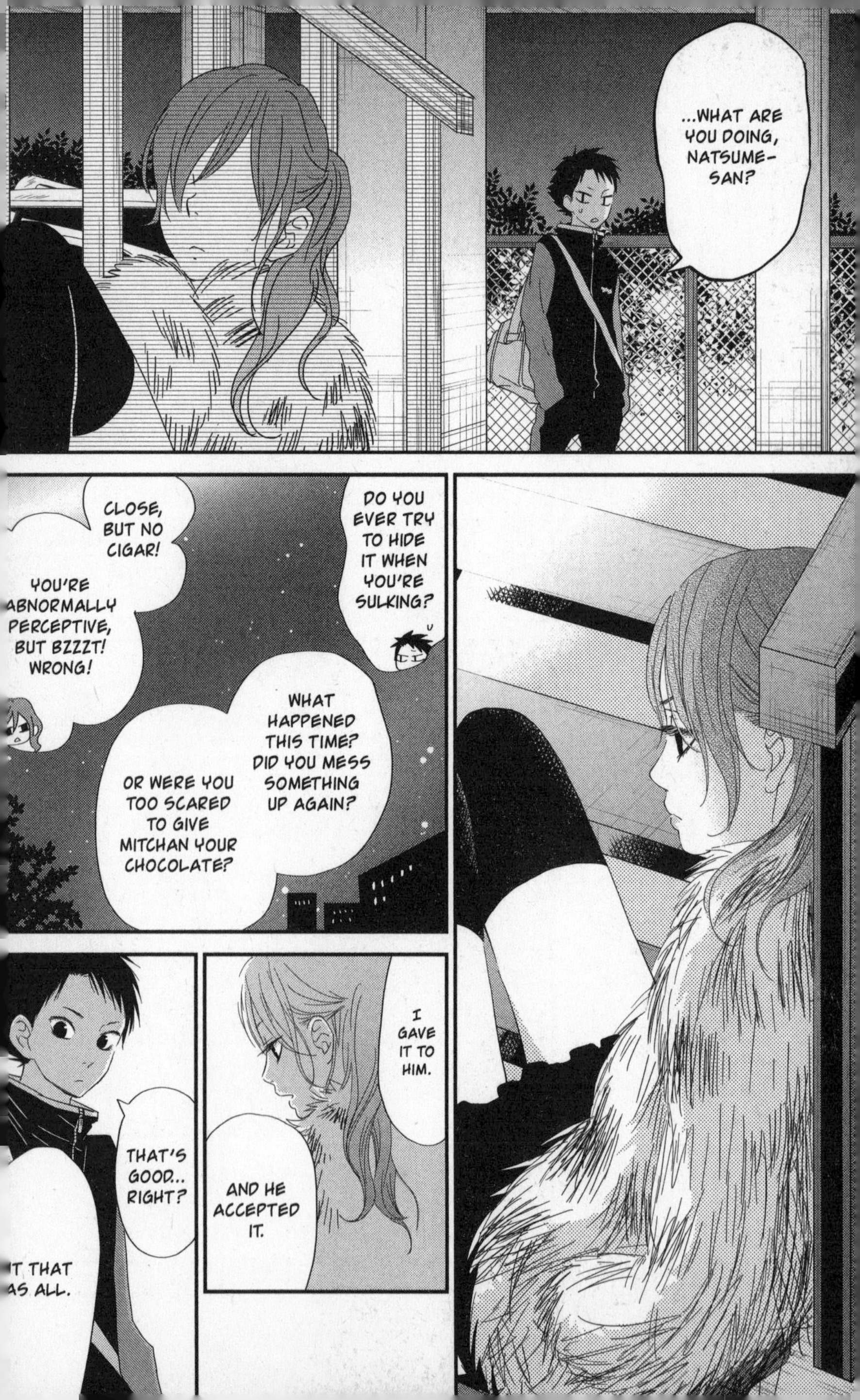
...WHAT ARE YOU DOING, NATSUME-SAN?
DO YOU EVER TRY TO HIDE IT WHEN YOU'RE SULKING?
WHAT HAPPENED THIS TIME? DID YOU MESS SOMETHING UP AGAIN?
OR WERE YOU TOO SCARED TO GIVE MITCHAN YOUR CHOCOLATE?
CLOSE, BUT NO CIGAR!
YOU'RE ABNORMALLY PERCEPTIVE, BUT BZZZT! WRONG!
I GAVE IT TO HIM.
AND HE ACCEPTED IT.
THAT'S GOOD... RIGHT?
IT THAT
AS ALL.

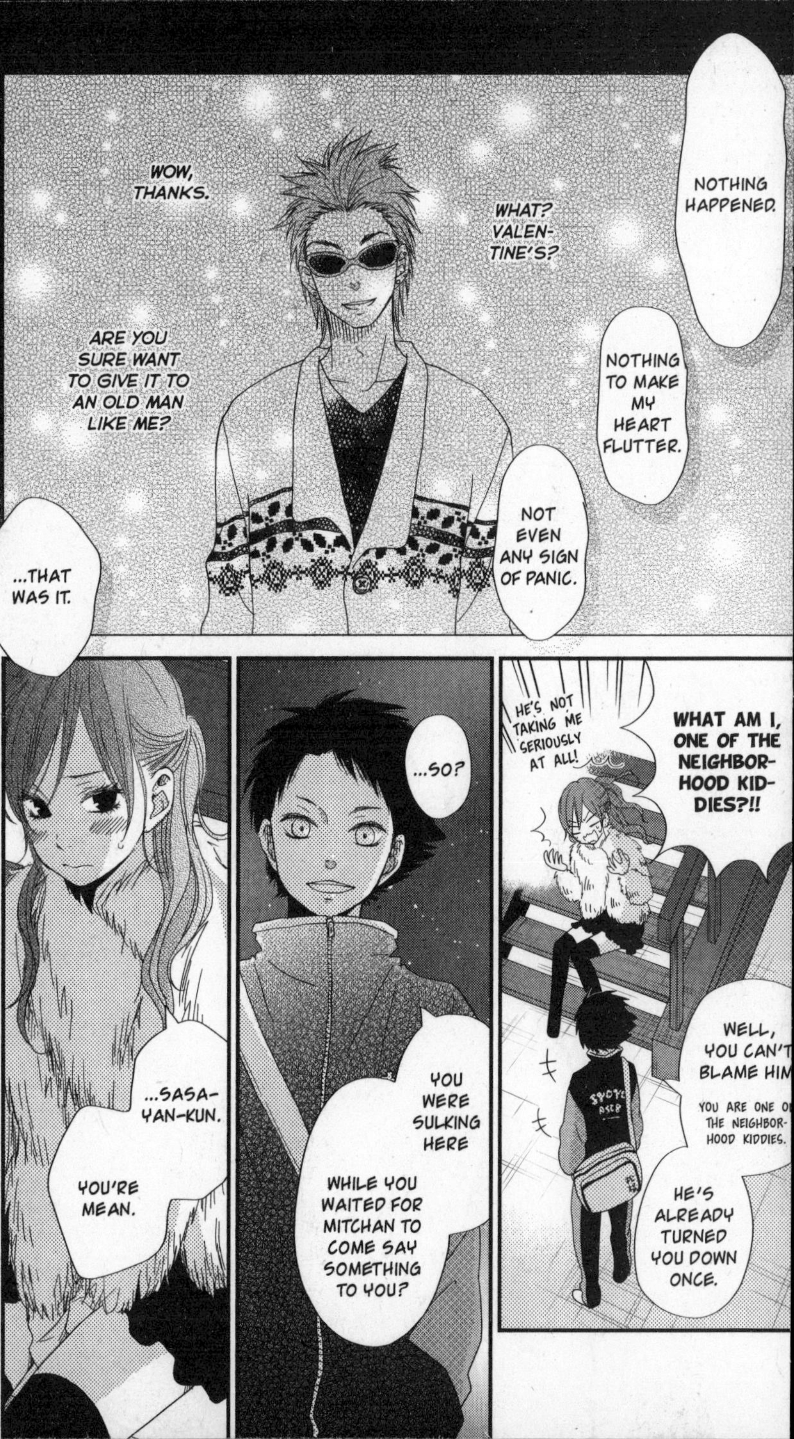
NOTHING HAPPENED.
NOTHING TO MAKE MY HEART FLUTTER.
WHAT? VALEN-TINE'S?
WOW, THANKS.
ARE YOU SURE WANT TO GIVE IT TO AN OLD MAN LIKE ME?
NOT EVEN ANY SIGN OF PANIC.
...THAT WAS IT.
WHAT AM I, ONE OF THE NEIGHBOR-HOOD KIDDIES?!!
HE'S NOT TAKING ME SERIOUSLY AT ALL!
WELL, YOU CAN'T BLAME HIM
YOU ARE ONE OF THE NEIGHBOR-HOOD KIDDIES.
HE'S ALREADY TURNED YOU DOWN ONCE.
...SO?
YOU WERE SULKING HERE
WHILE YOU WAITED FOR MITCHAN TO COME SAY SOMETHING TO YOU?
...SASA-YAN-KUN.
YOU'RE MEAN.

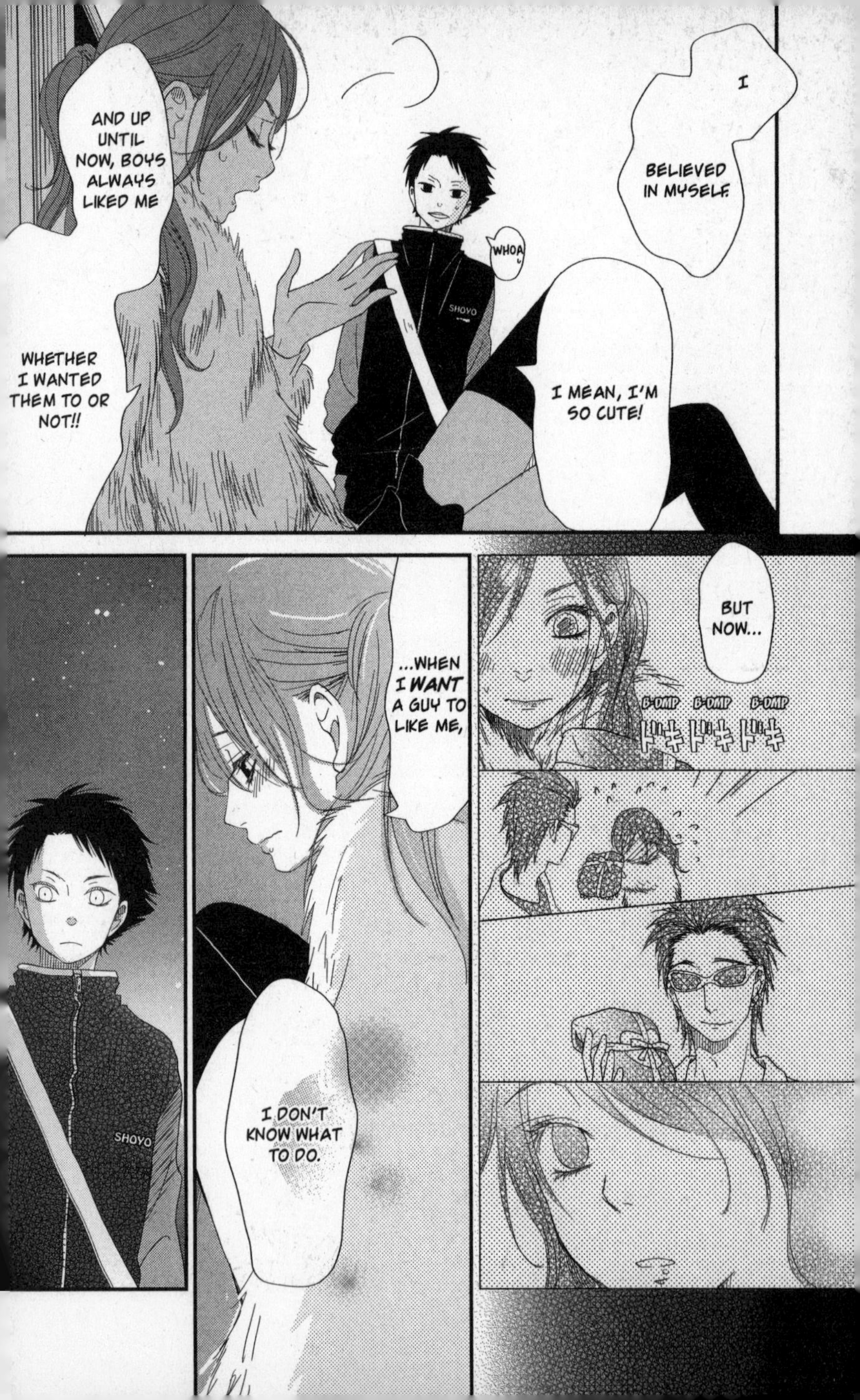
I
BELIEVED IN MYSELF.
I MEAN, I'M SO CUTE!
WHOA
AND UP UNTIL NOW, BOYS ALWAYS LIKED ME
WHETHER I WANTED THEM TO OR NOT!!
BUT NOW...
B-DMP B-DMP B-DMP
ドキドキドキ
...WHEN I WANT A GUY TO LIKE ME,
I DON'T KNOW WHAT TO DO.

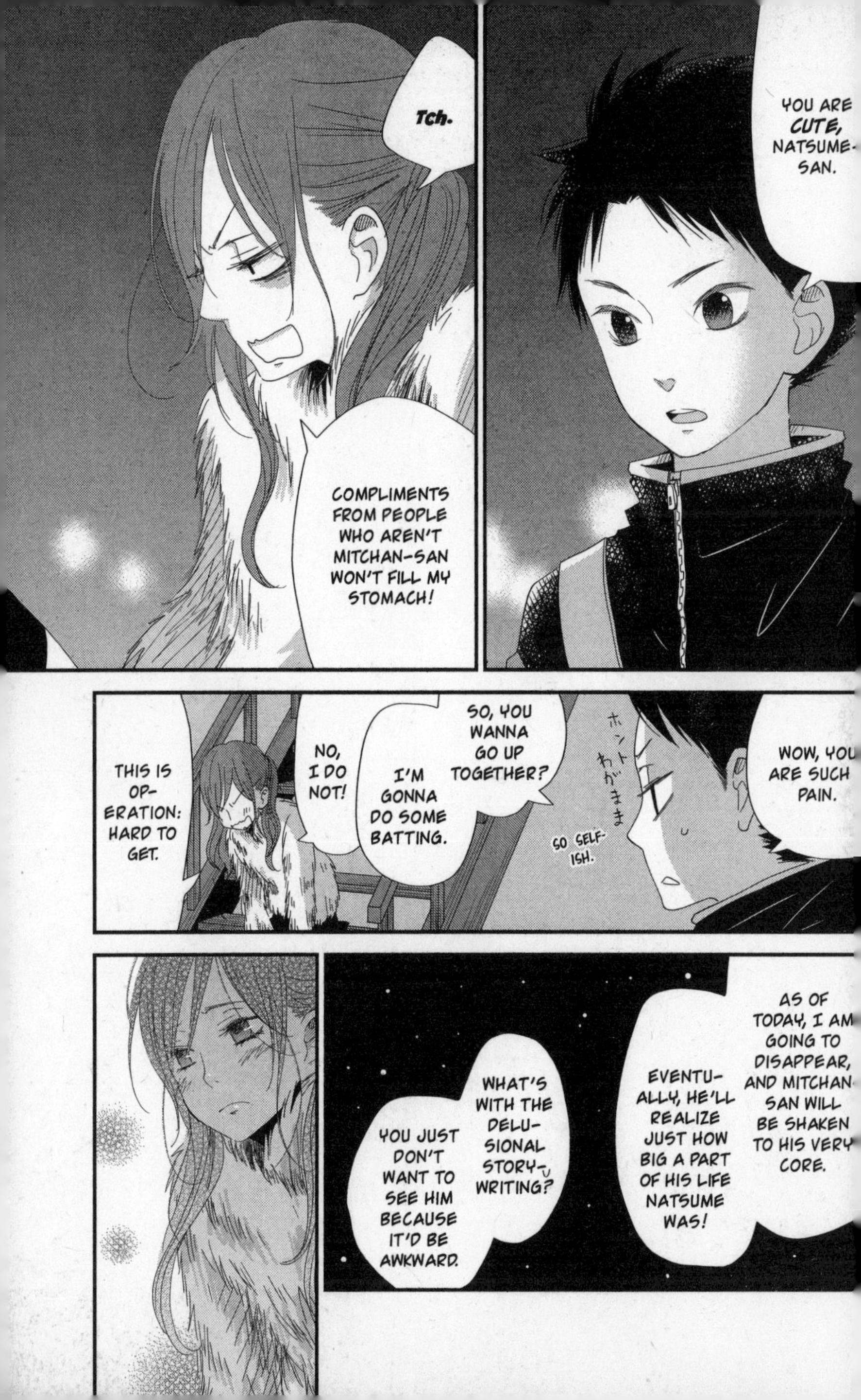
YOU ARE CUTE, NATSUME-SAN.
Tch.
COMPLIMENTS FROM PEOPLE WHO AREN'T MITCHAN-SAN WON'T FILL MY STOMACH!
WOW, YOU ARE SUCH PAIN.
ホントわがまま
SO SELFISH.
SO, YOU WANNA GO UP TOGETHER?
NO, I DO NOT!
I'M GONNA DO SOME BATTING.
THIS IS OPERATION: HARD TO GET.
AS OF TODAY, I AM GOING TO DISAPPEAR, AND MITCHAN-SAN WILL BE SHAKEN TO HIS VERY CORE.
EVENTUALLY, HE'LL REALIZE JUST HOW BIG A PART OF HIS LIFE NATSUME WAS!
WHAT'S WITH THE DELUSIONAL STORY-WRITING?
YOU JUST DON'T WANT TO SEE HIM BECAUSE IT'D BE AWKWARD.

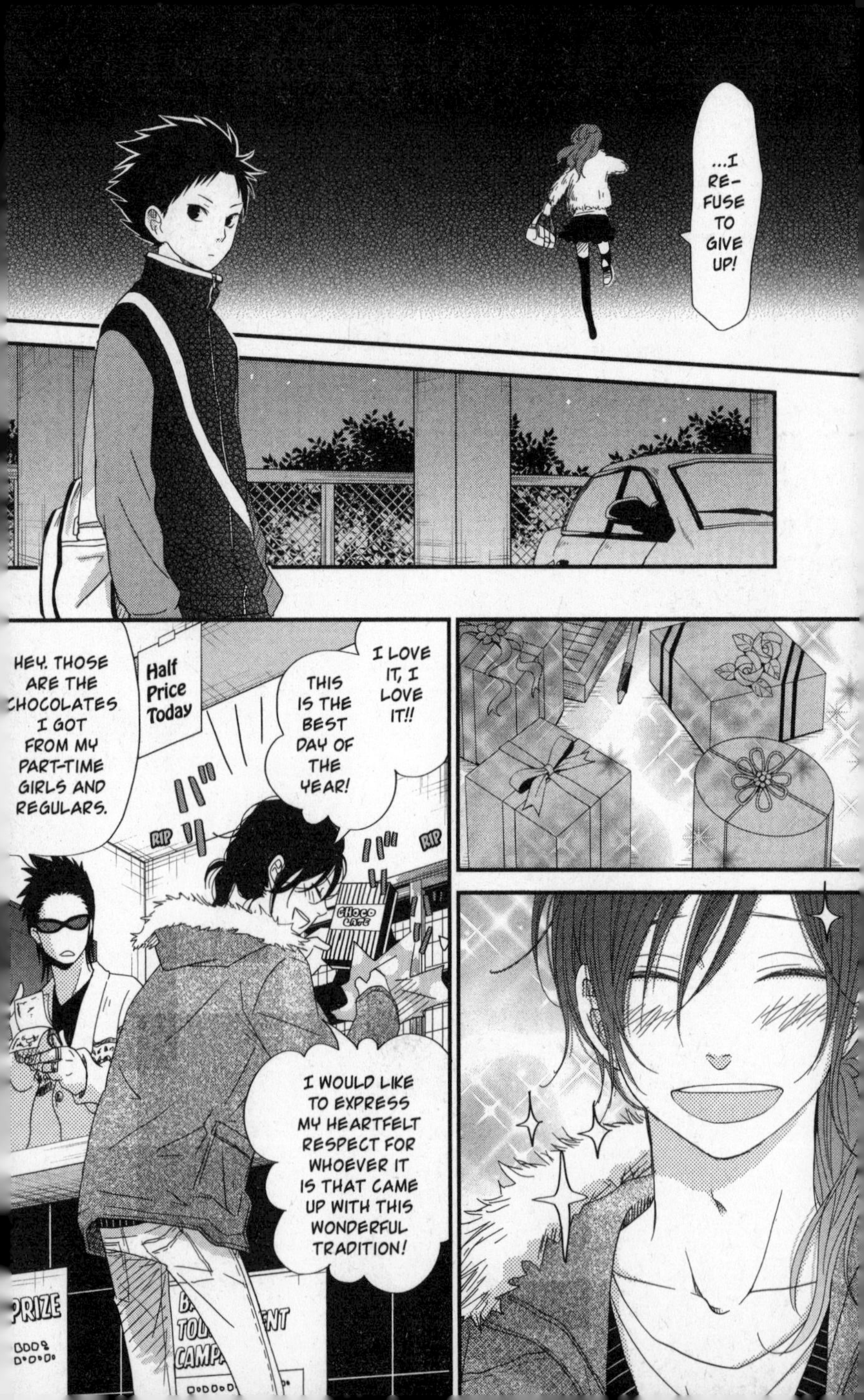
...I RE-FUSE TO GIVE UP!
I LOVE IT, I LOVE IT!!
THIS IS THE BEST DAY OF THE YEAR!
Half Price Today
HEY. THOSE ARE THE CHOCOLATES I GOT FROM MY PART-TIME GIRLS AND REGULARS.
RIP
RIP
CHOCO LATE
I WOULD LIKE TO EXPRESS MY HEARTFELT RESPECT FOR WHOEVER IT IS THAT CAME UP WITH THIS WONDERFUL TRADITION!
PRIZE

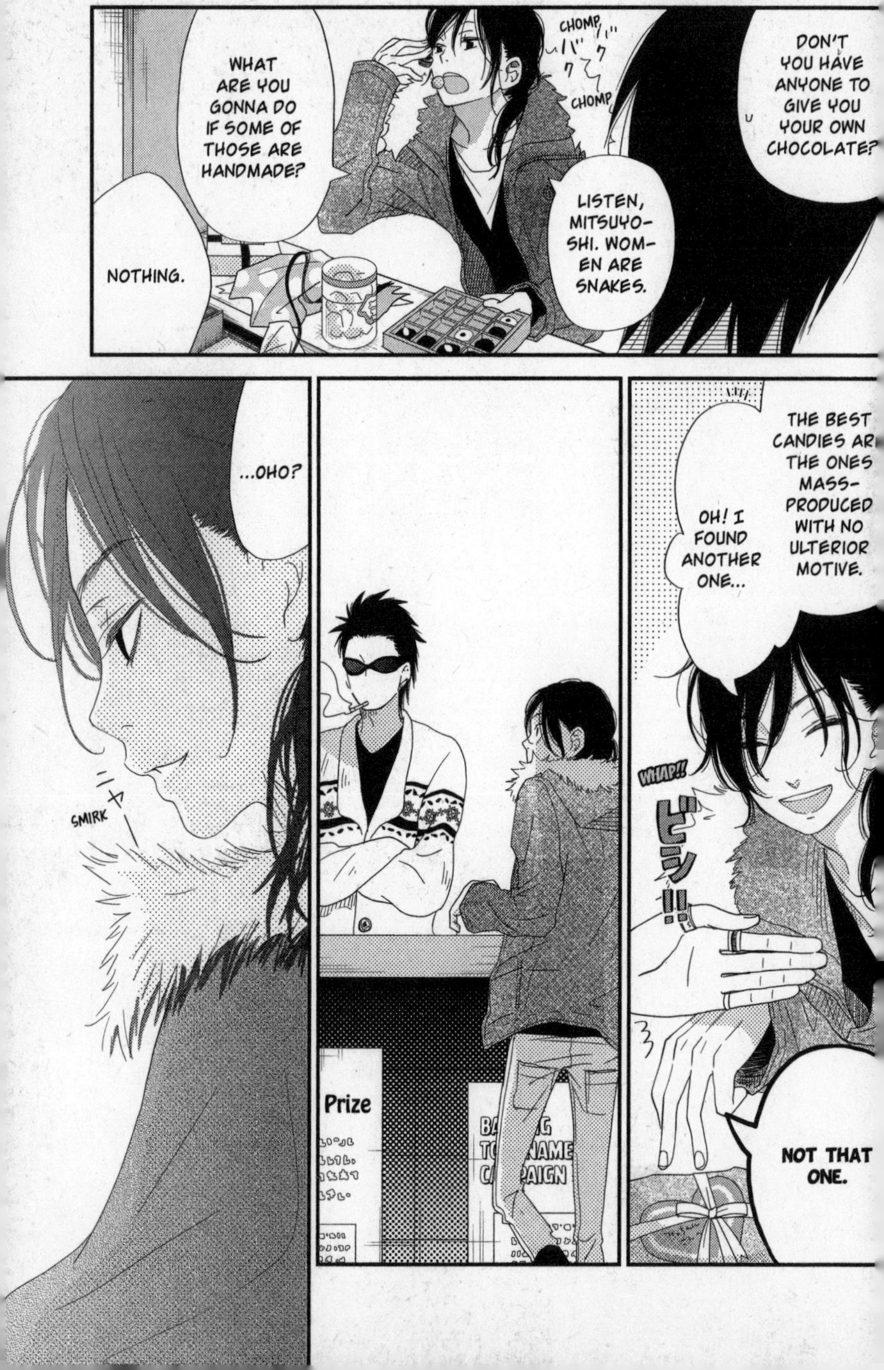
DON'T YOU HAVE ANYONE TO GIVE YOU YOUR OWN CHOCOLATE?
CHOMP
CHOMP
WHAT ARE YOU GONNA DO IF SOME OF THOSE ARE HANDMADE?
LISTEN, MITSUYO-SHI. WOM-EN ARE SNAKES.
NOTHING.
THE BEST CANDIES AR THE ONES MASS-PRODUCED WITH NO ULTERIOR MOTIVE.
OH! I FOUND ANOTHER ONE...
WHAP!!
NOT THAT ONE.
Prize
...OHO?
SMIRK

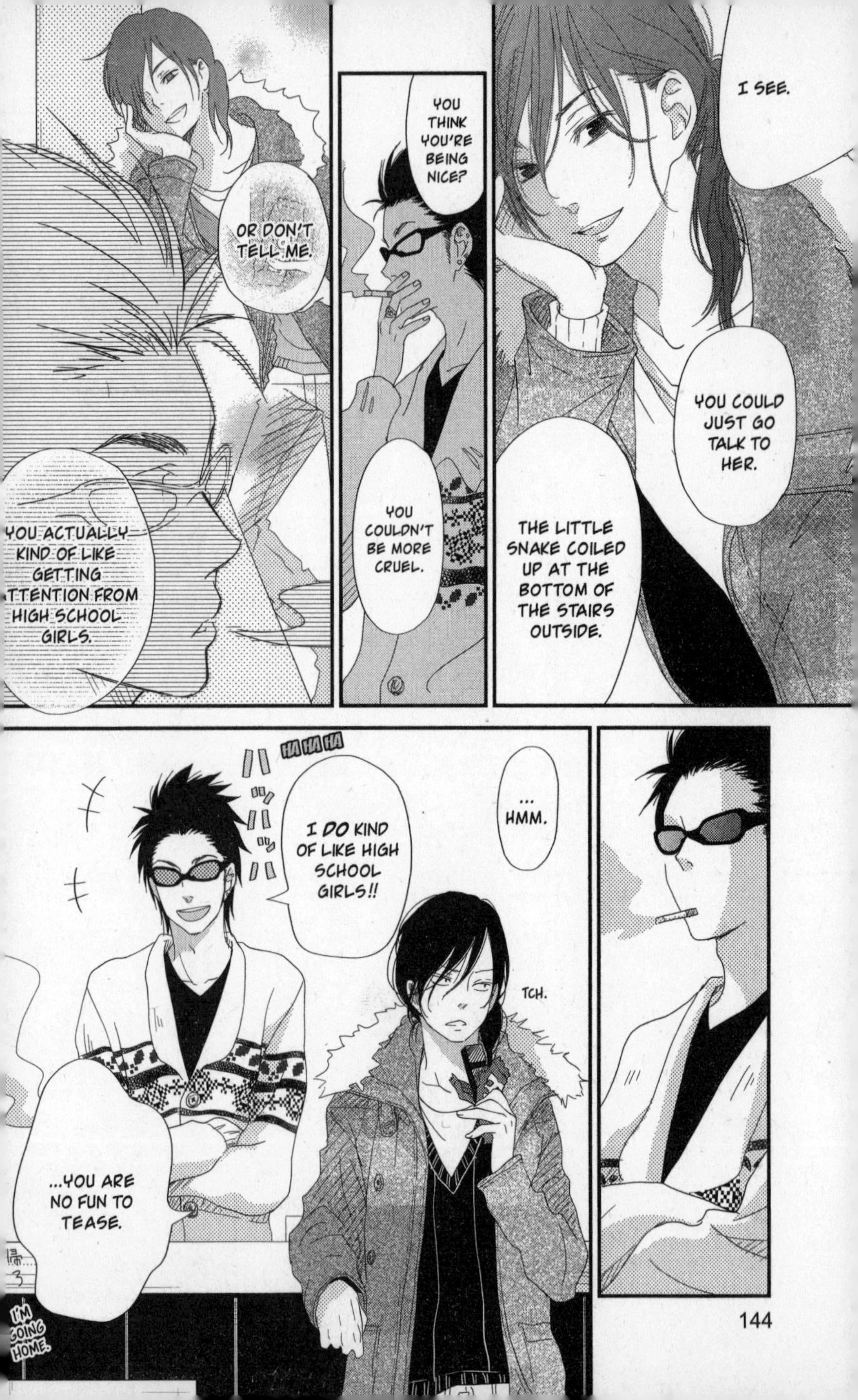
I SEE.
YOU COULD JUST GO TALK TO HER.
THE LITTLE SNAKE COILED UP AT THE BOTTOM OF THE STAIRS OUTSIDE.
YOU THINK YOU'RE BEING NICE?
YOU COULDN'T BE MORE CRUEL.
OR DON'T TELL ME.
YOU ACTUALLY KIND OF LIKE GETTING TTENTION FROM HIGH SCHOOL GIRLS.
... HMM.
HA HA HA
I DO KIND OF LIKE HIGH SCHOOL GIRLS!!
TCH.
...YOU ARE NO FUN TO TEASE.
I'M GOING HOME.

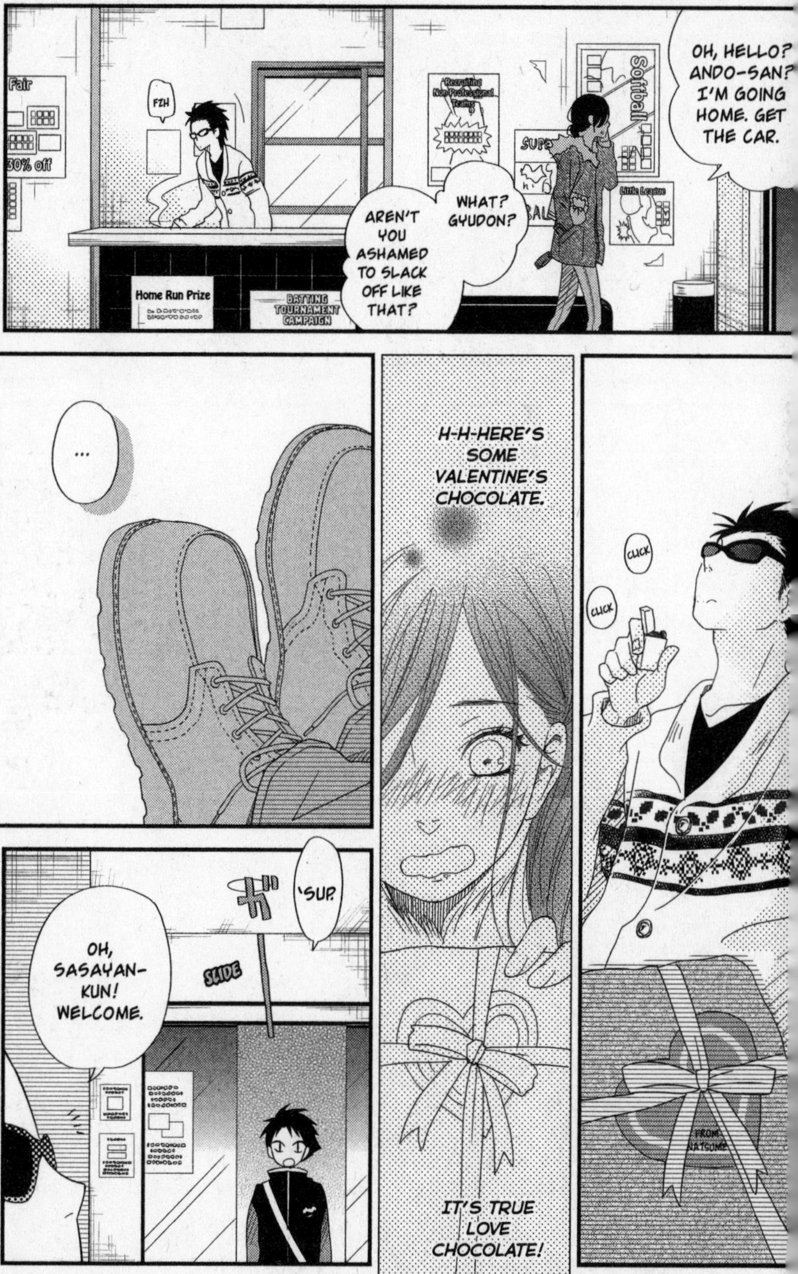
OH, HELLO? ANDO-SAN? I'M GOING HOME. GET THE CAR.
Softball
Little League
Recruiting Non-Professional Teams
WHAT? GYUDON?
AREN'T YOU ASHAMED TO SLACK OFF LIKE THAT?
FZH
Fair
30% off
Home Run Prize
BATTING TOURNAMENT CAMPAIGN
CLICK
CLICK
FROM NATSUME
H-H-HERE'S SOME VALENTINE'S CHOCOLATE.
IT'S TRUE LOVE CHOCOLATE!
...
'SUP.
OH, SASAYAN-KUN! WELCOME.
SLIDE

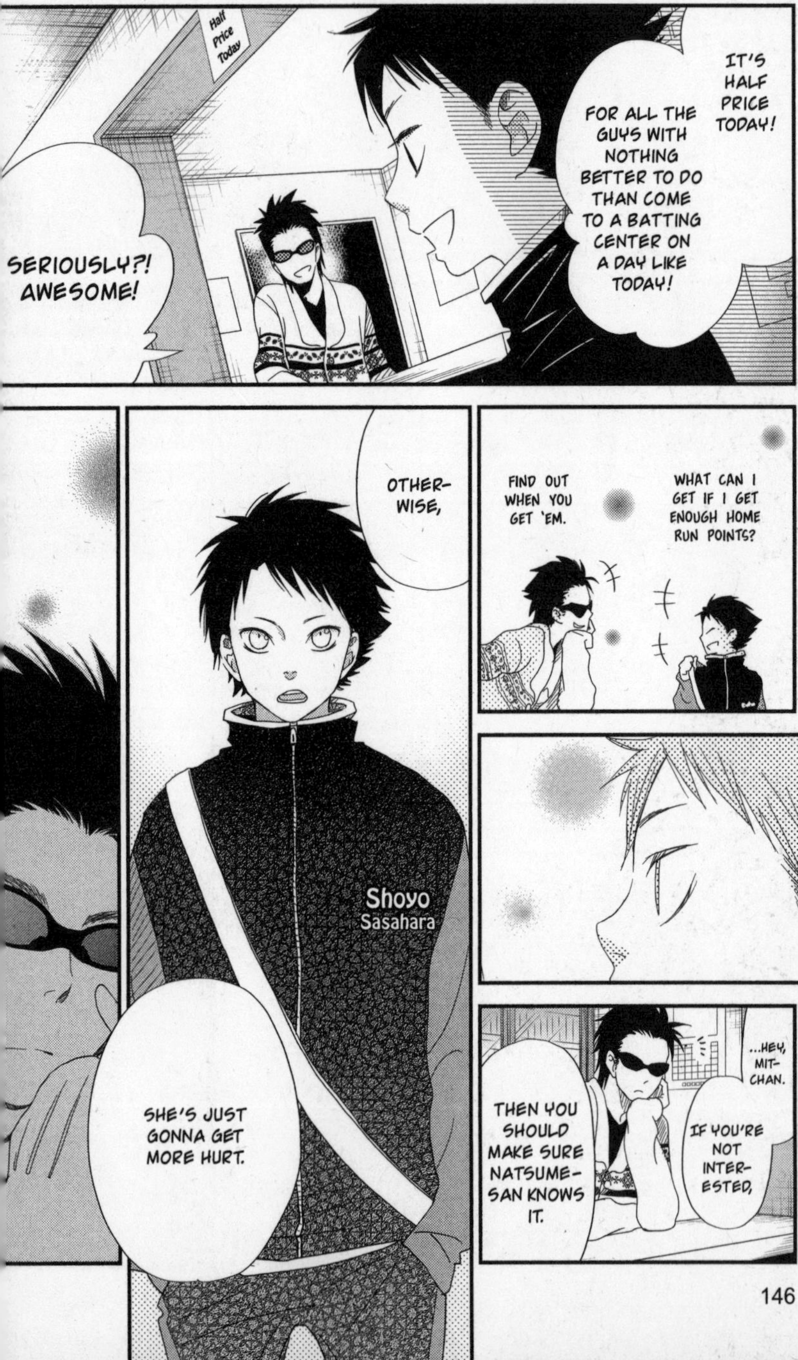
IT'S HALF PRICE TODAY!
FOR ALL THE GUYS WITH NOTHING BETTER TO DO THAN COME TO A BATTING CENTER ON A DAY LIKE TODAY!
Half Price Today
SERIOUSLY?! AWESOME!
WHAT CAN I GET IF I GET ENOUGH HOME RUN POINTS?
FIND OUT WHEN YOU GET 'EM.
...HEY, MIT-CHAN.
IF YOU'RE NOT INTER-ESTED,
THEN YOU SHOULD MAKE SURE NATSUME-SAN KNOWS IT.
OTHER-WISE,
Shoyo Sasahara
SHE'S JUST GONNA GET MORE HURT.

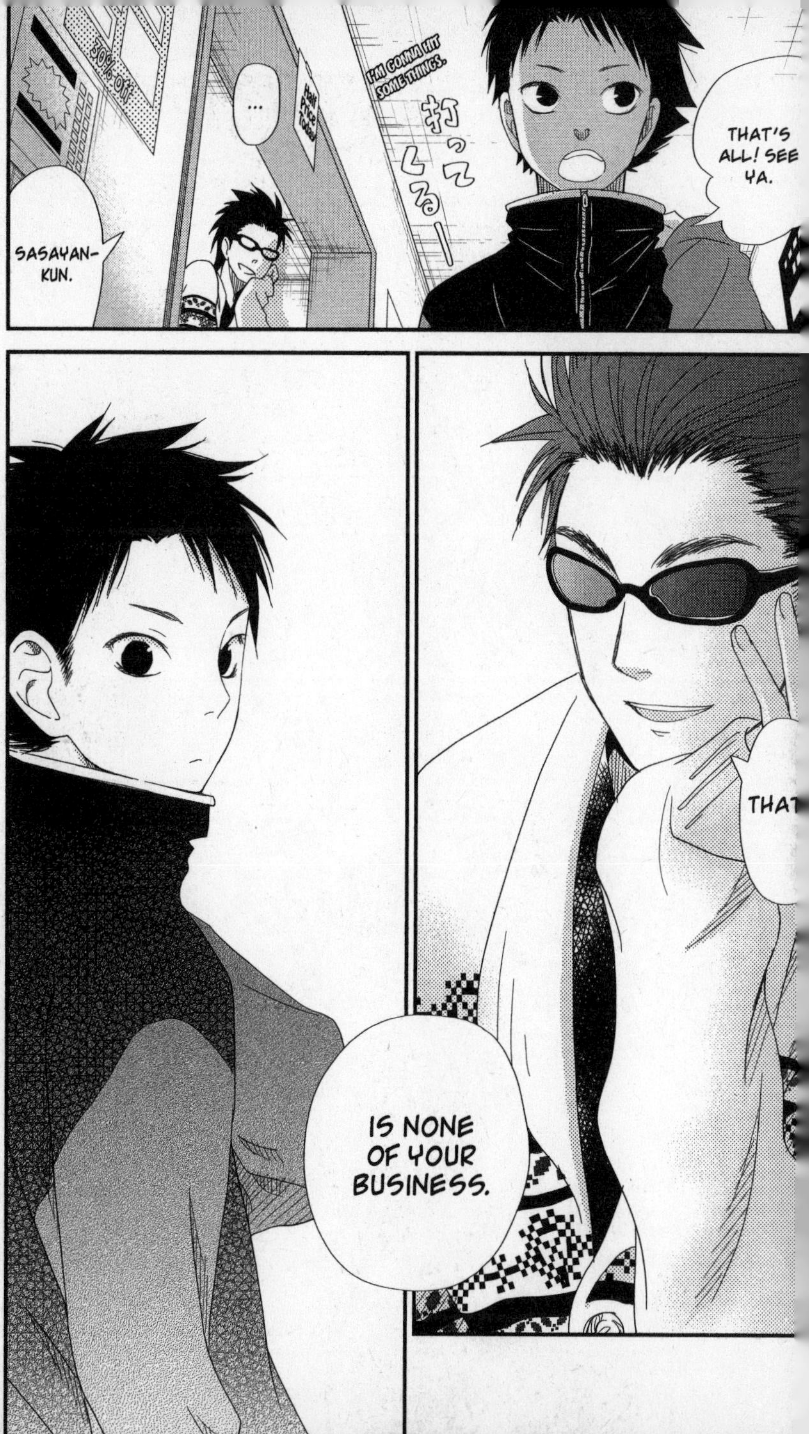
THAT'S ALL! SEE YA.
I'M GONNA HIT SOME THINGS.
打ってくるー
...
Half Price Today
30% off
SASAYAN-KUN.
THAT
IS NONE OF YOUR BUSINESS.

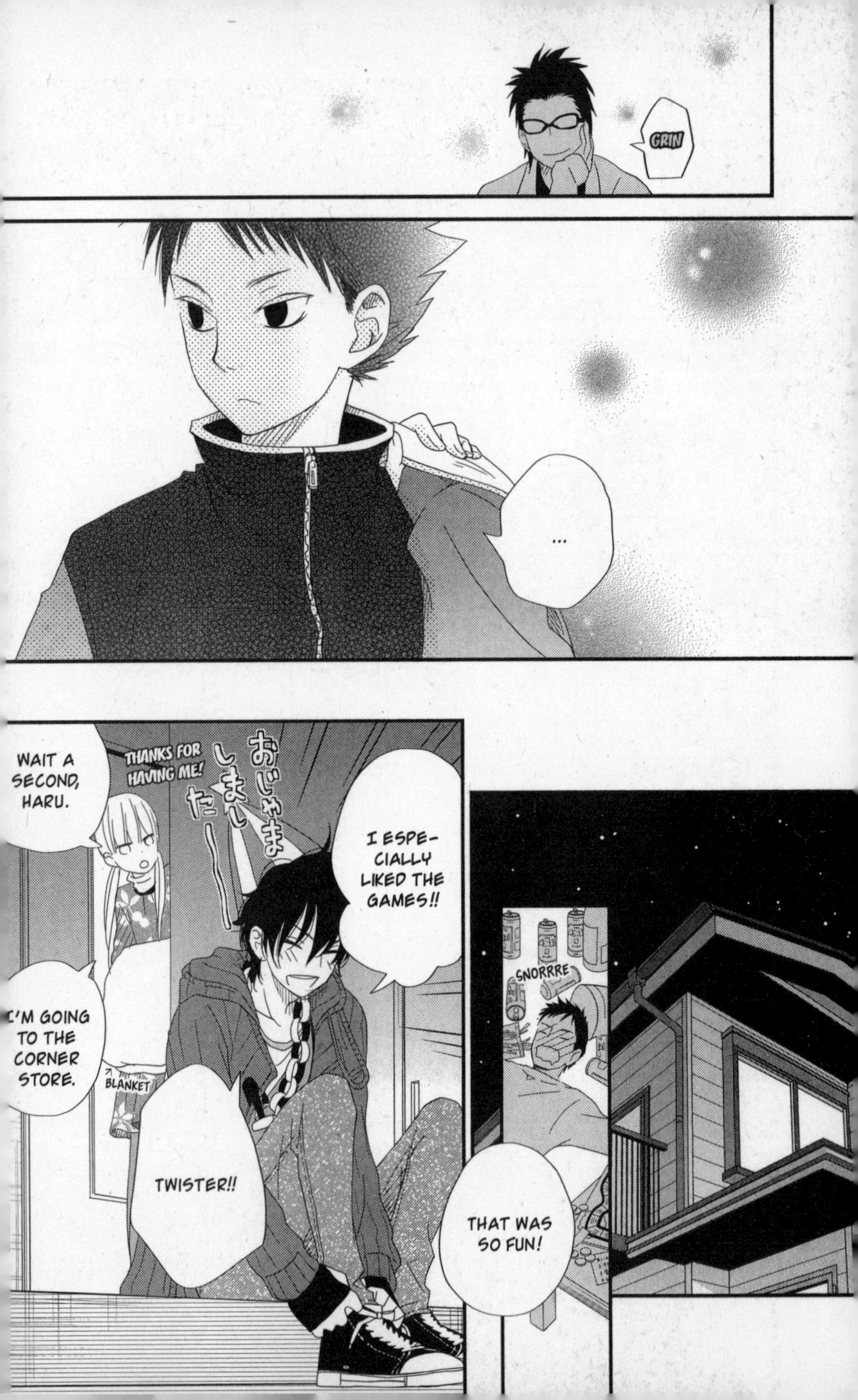
GRIN
...
SNORRRE
THAT WAS SO FUN!
I ESPE-CIALLY LIKED THE GAMES!!
TWISTER!!
おじゃましましたー
THANKS FOR HAVING ME!
WAIT A SECOND, HARU.
I'M GOING TO THE CORNER STORE.
BLANKET

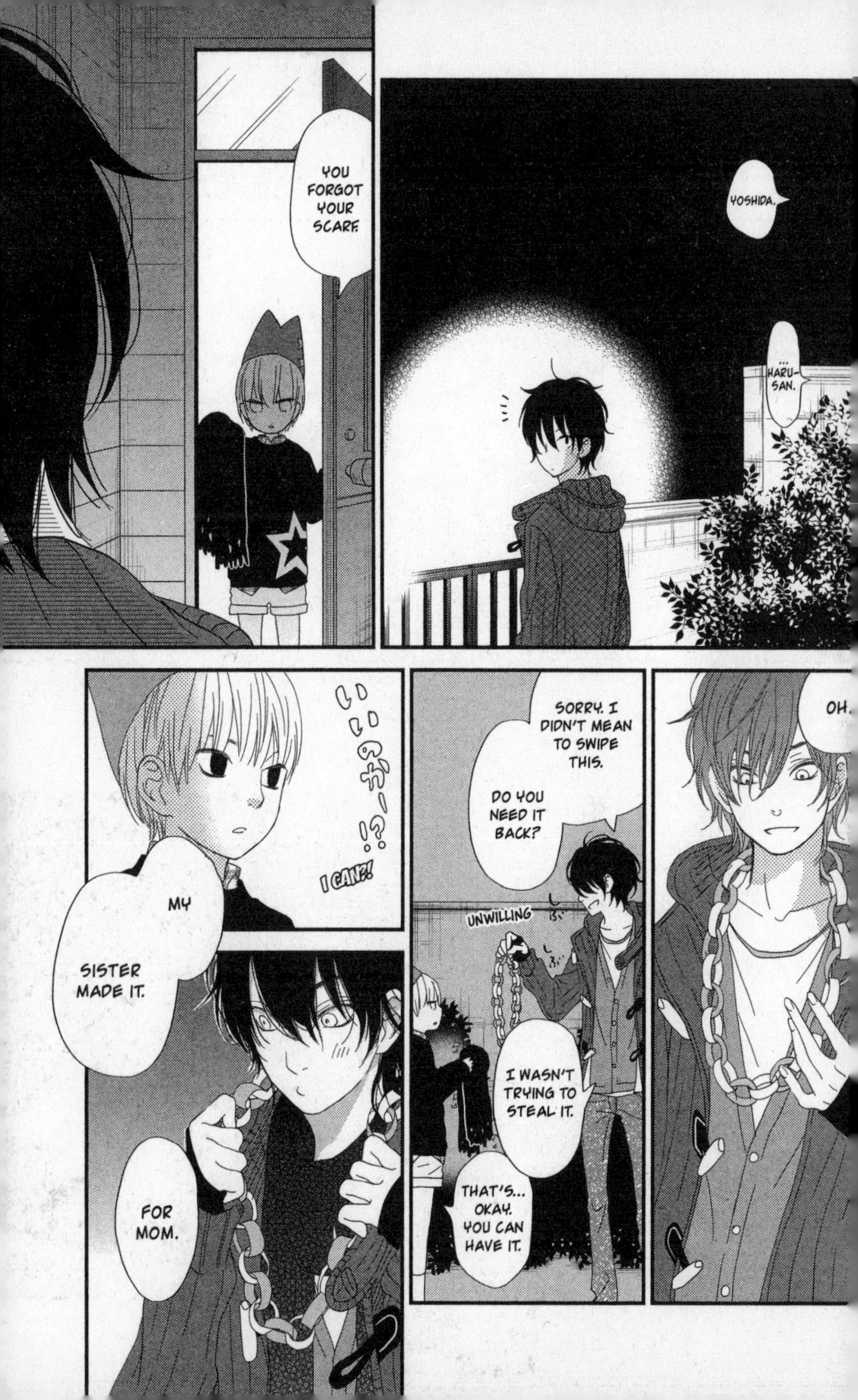

YOSHIDA.
...HARU-SAN.
YOU FORGOT YOUR SCARF.
OH.
SORRY. I DIDN'T MEAN TO SWIPE THIS.
DO YOU NEED IT BACK?
しぶしぶ
UNWILLING
I WASN'T TRYING TO STEAL IT.
THAT'S... OKAY. YOU CAN HAVE IT.
いいのかー!?
I CAN?!
MY SISTER MADE IT.
FOR MOM.

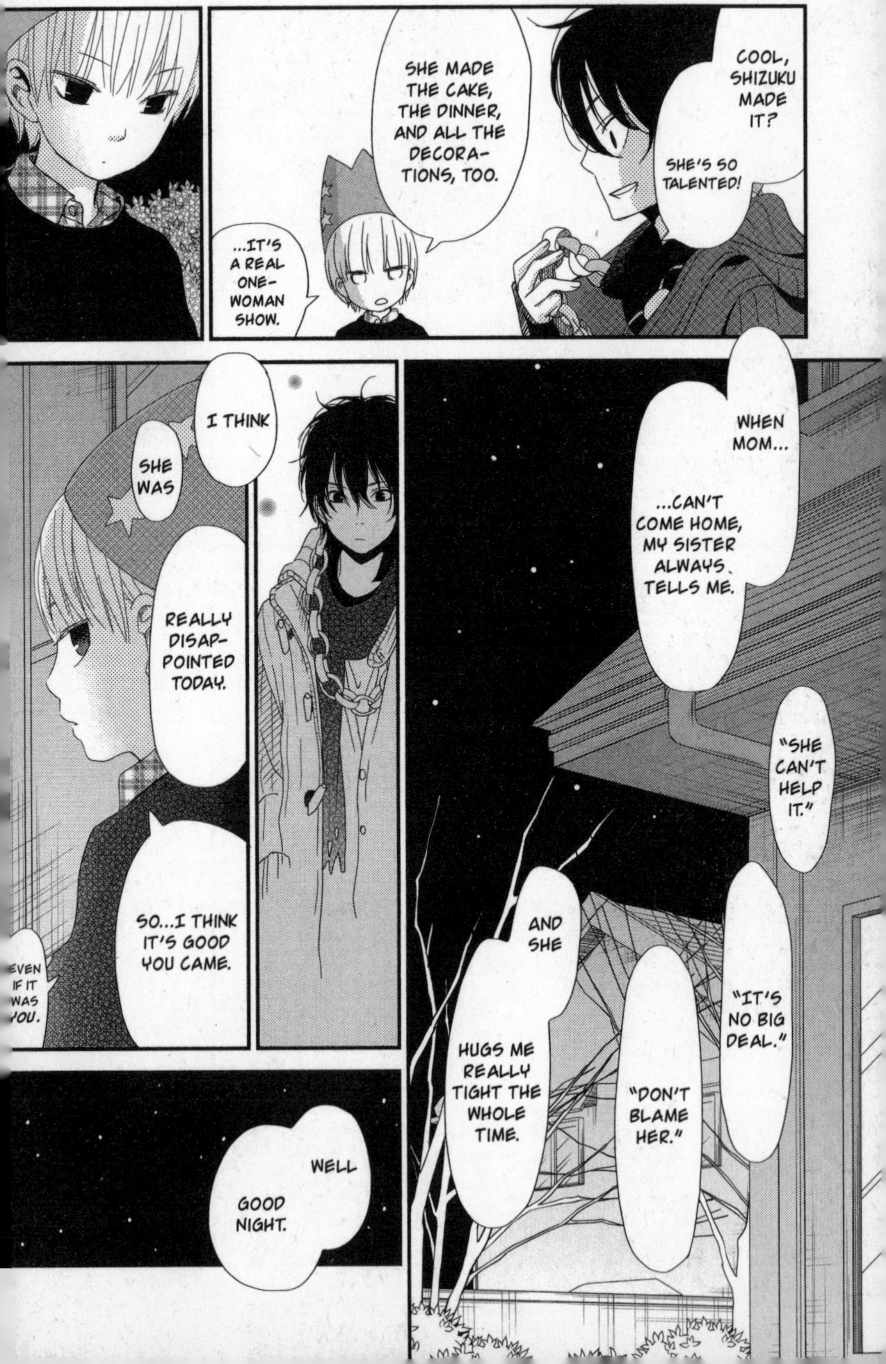
COOL, SHIZUKU MADE IT?
SHE'S SO TALENTED!
SHE MADE THE CAKE, THE DINNER, AND ALL THE DECORA-TIONS, TOO.
...IT'S A REAL ONE-WOMAN SHOW.
WHEN MOM...
...CAN'T COME HOME, MY SISTER ALWAYS TELLS ME.
"SHE CAN'T HELP IT."
"IT'S NO BIG DEAL."
"DON'T BLAME HER."
AND SHE
HUGS ME REALLY TIGHT THE WHOLE TIME.
I THINK
SHE WAS
REALLY DISAP-POINTED TODAY.
SO...I THINK IT'S GOOD YOU CAME.
EVEN IF IT WAS YOU.
WELL
GOOD NIGHT.

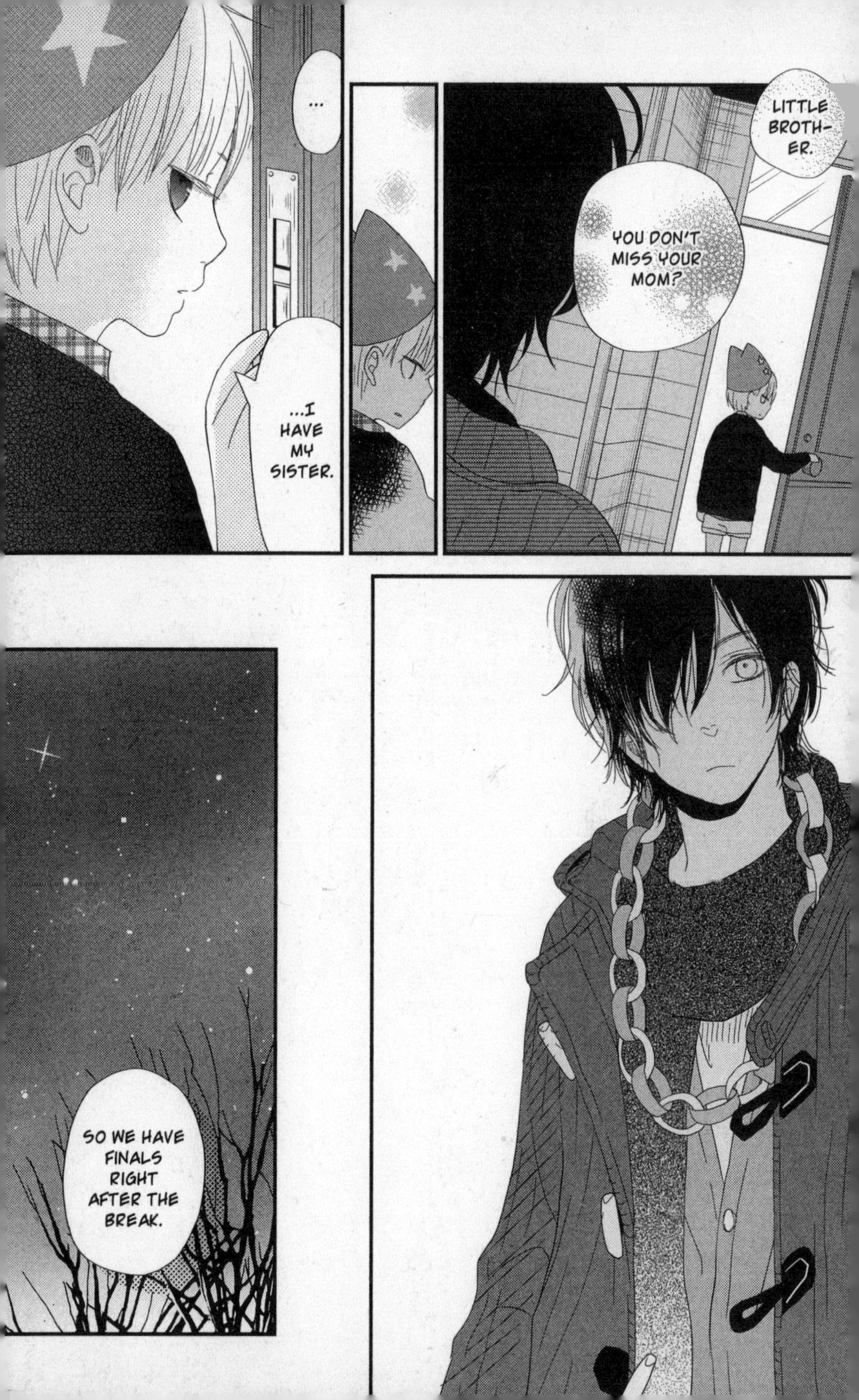
LITTLE BROTHER-ER.
YOU DON'T MISS YOUR MOM?
...
...I HAVE MY SISTER.
SO WE HAVE FINALS RIGHT AFTER THE BREAK.

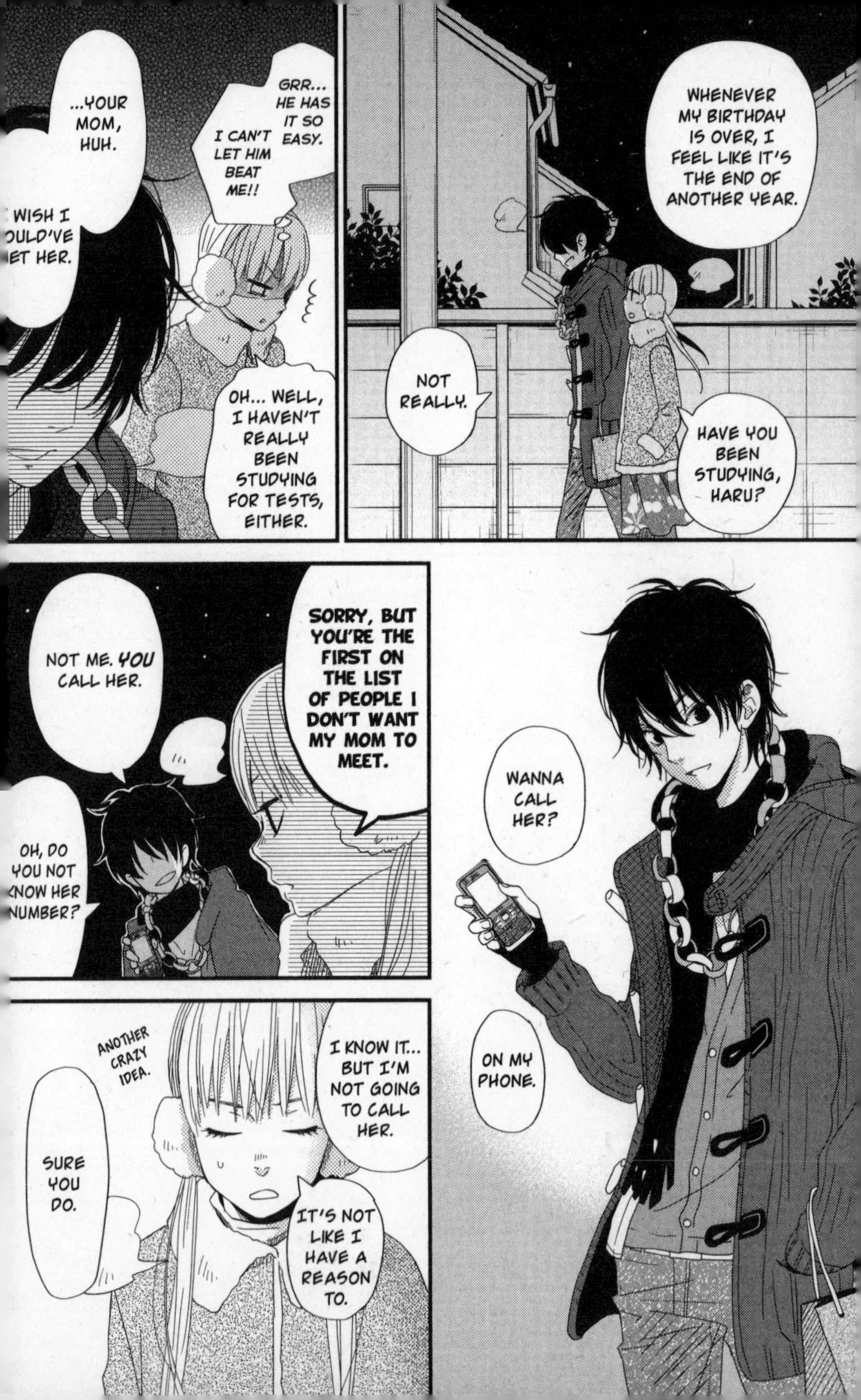
WHENEVER MY BIRTHDAY IS OVER, I FEEL LIKE IT'S THE END OF ANOTHER YEAR.
HAVE YOU BEEN STUDYING, HARU?
NOT REALLY.
GRR... HE HAS IT SO EASY.
I CAN'T LET HIM BEAT ME!!
...YOUR MOM, HUH.
OH... WELL, I HAVEN'T REALLY BEEN STUDYING FOR TESTS, EITHER.
WISH I OULD'VE ET HER.
WANNA CALL HER?
ON MY PHONE.
SORRY, BUT YOU'RE THE FIRST ON THE LIST OF PEOPLE I DON'T WANT MY MOM TO MEET.
NOT ME. YOU CALL HER.
OH, DO YOU NOT KNOW HER NUMBER?
I KNOW IT... BUT I'M NOT GOING TO CALL HER.
ANOTHER CRAZY IDEA.
IT'S NOT LIKE I HAVE A REASON TO.
SURE YOU DO.

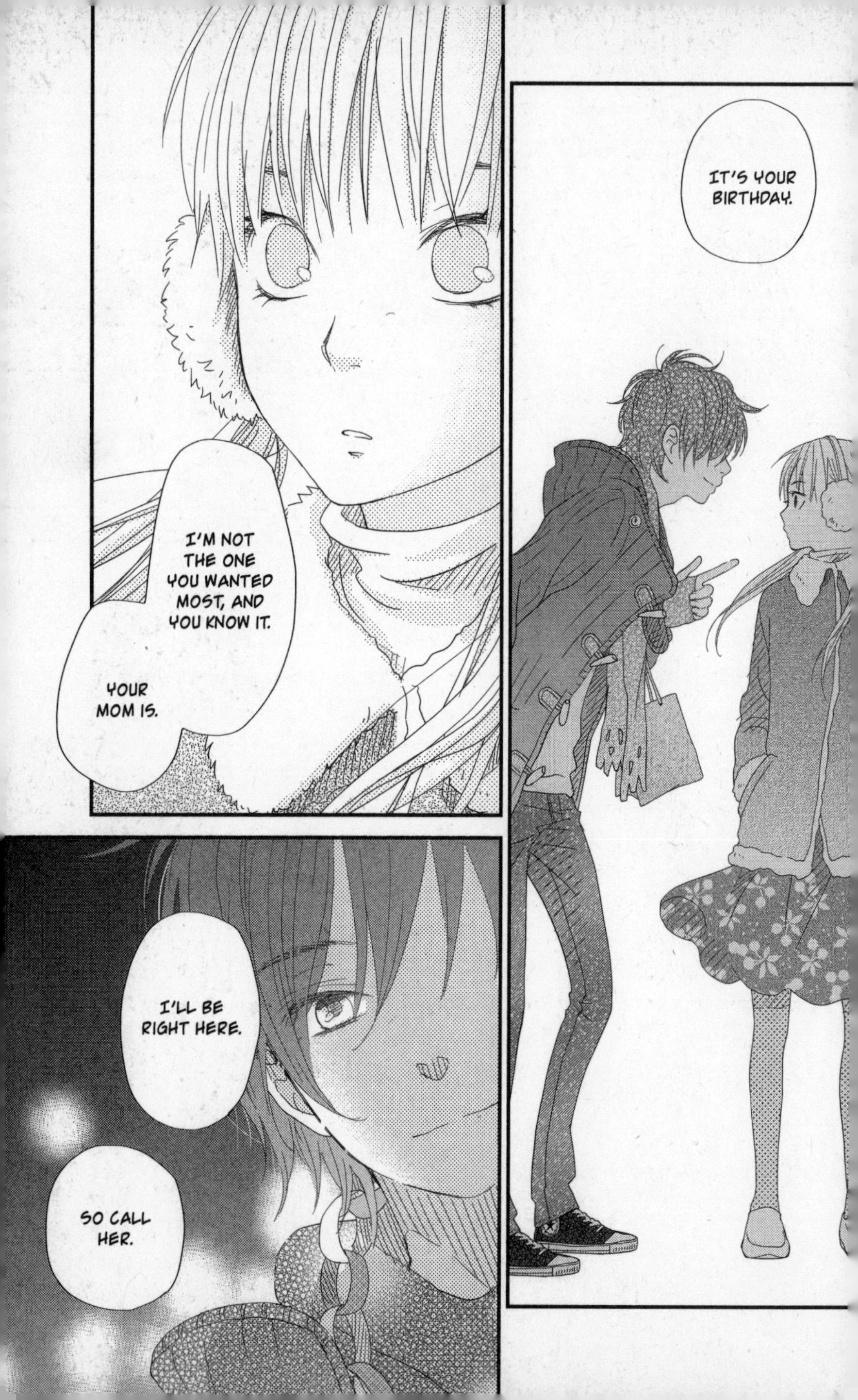
IT'S YOUR BIRTHDAY.
I'M NOT THE ONE YOU WANTED MOST, AND YOU KNOW IT.
YOUR MOM IS.
I'LL BE RIGHT HERE.
SO CALL HER.

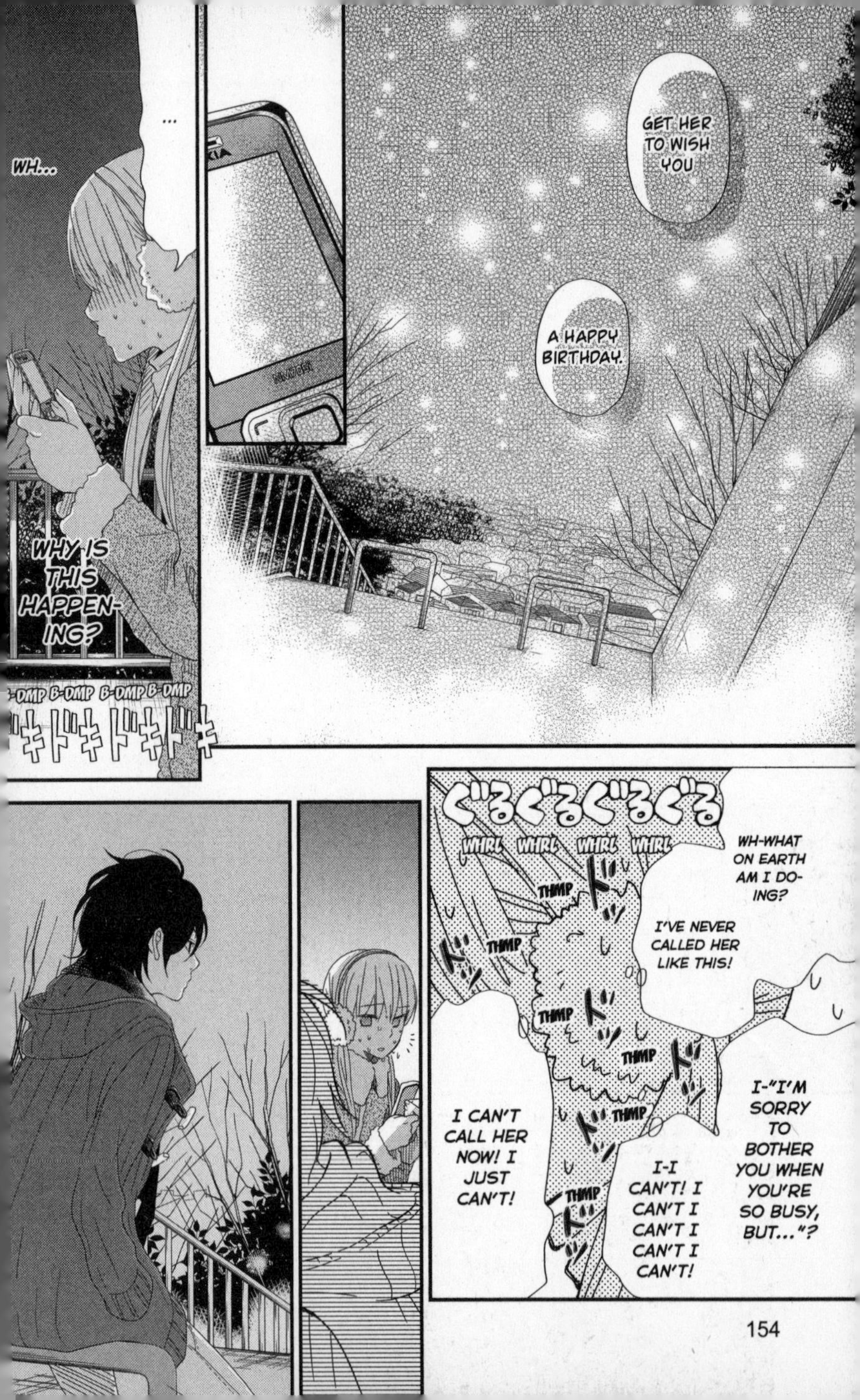
GET HER TO WISH YOU
A HAPPY BIRTHDAY.
...
WH...
WHY IS THIS HAPPEN-ING?
B-DMP B-DMP B-DMP B-DMP
ドキドキドキドキ
ぐるぐるぐるぐる
WHRL WHRL WHRL WHRL
THMP THMP THMP THMP THMP THMP
WH-WHAT ON EARTH AM I DO-ING?
I'VE NEVER CALLED HER LIKE THIS!
I-"I'M SORRY TO BOTHER YOU WHEN YOU'RE SO BUSY, BUT..."?
I-I CAN'T! I CAN'T I CAN'T I CAN'T I CAN'T!
I CAN'T CALL HER NOW! I JUST CAN'T!

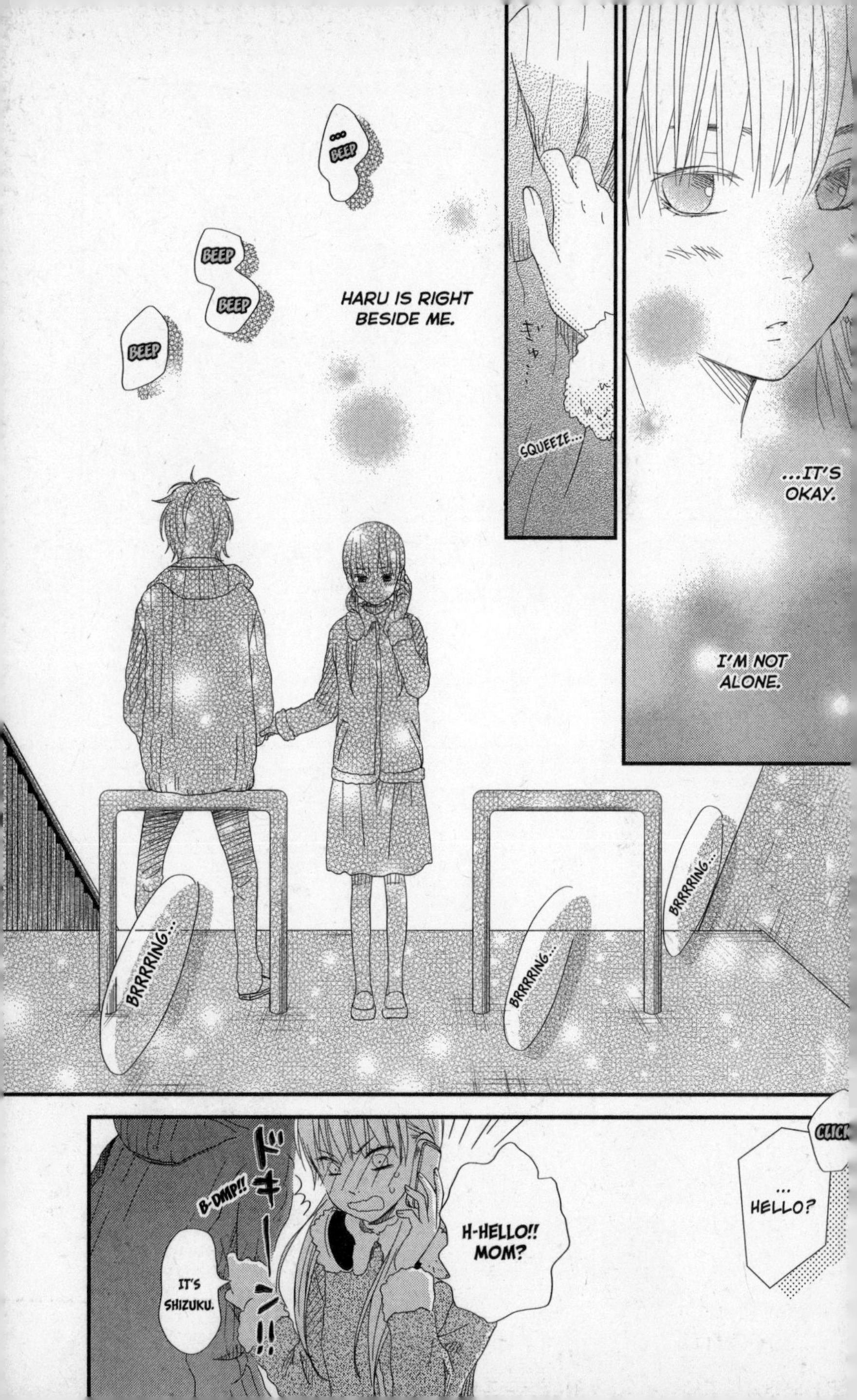
...IT'S OKAY.
I'M NOT ALONE.
ぎゅ...
SQUEEZE...
... BEEP
BEEP
BEEP
BEEP
HARU IS RIGHT BESIDE ME.
BRRRRING...
BRRRRING...
BRRRRING...
CLICK
... HELLO?
H-HELLO!! MOM?
B-DMP!!
ドキーン!!
IT'S SHIZUKU.

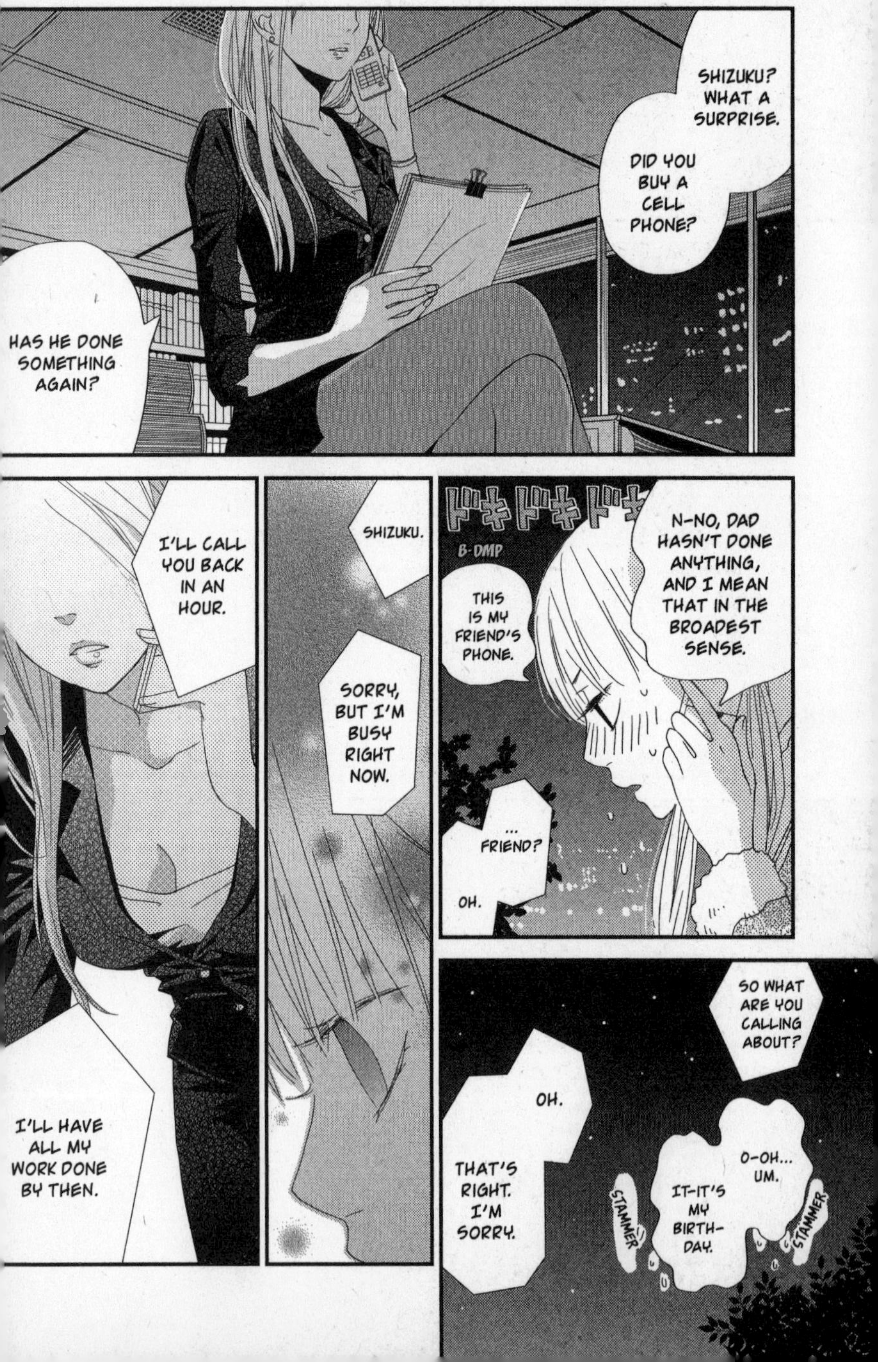
SHIZUKU? WHAT A SURPRISE.
DID YOU BUY A CELL PHONE?
HAS HE DONE SOMETHING AGAIN?
ドキドキドキ
B-DMP
N-NO, DAD HASN'T DONE ANYTHING, AND I MEAN THAT IN THE BROADEST SENSE.
THIS IS MY FRIEND'S PHONE.
...FRIEND?
OH.
SO WHAT ARE YOU CALLING ABOUT?
O-OH... UM.
IT-IT'S MY BIRTH-DAY.
STAMMER
STAMMER
OH.
THAT'S RIGHT. I'M SORRY.
SHIZUKU.
SORRY, BUT I'M BUSY RIGHT NOW.
I'LL CALL YOU BACK IN AN HOUR.
I'LL HAVE ALL MY WORK DONE BY THEN.

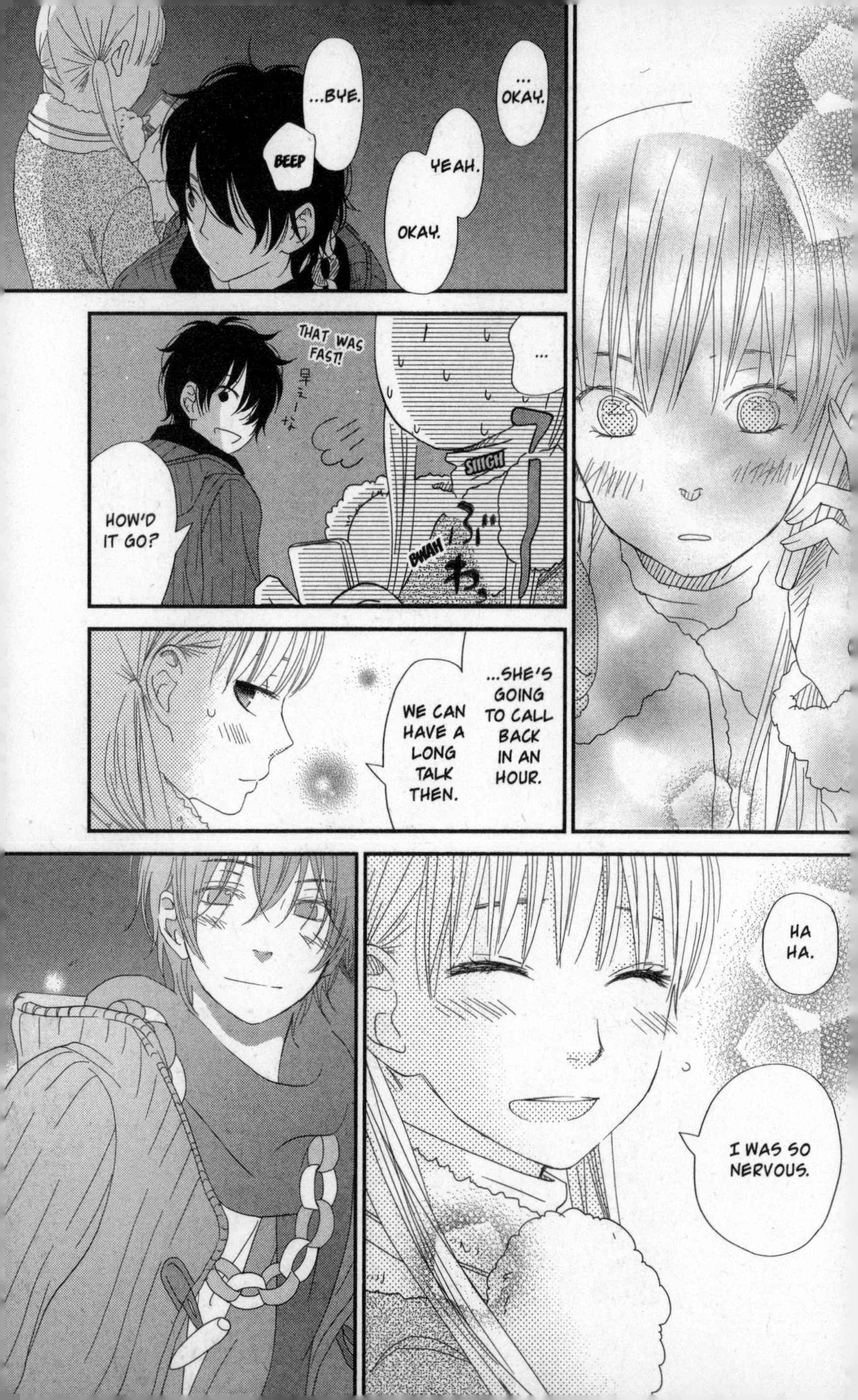
...
OKAY.
YEAH.
OKAY.
...BYE.
BEEP
...
SIIIGH
BWAH
THAT WAS FAST!
HOW'D IT GO?
...SHE'S GOING TO CALL BACK IN AN HOUR.
WE CAN HAVE A LONG TALK THEN.
HA HA.
I WAS SO NERVOUS.

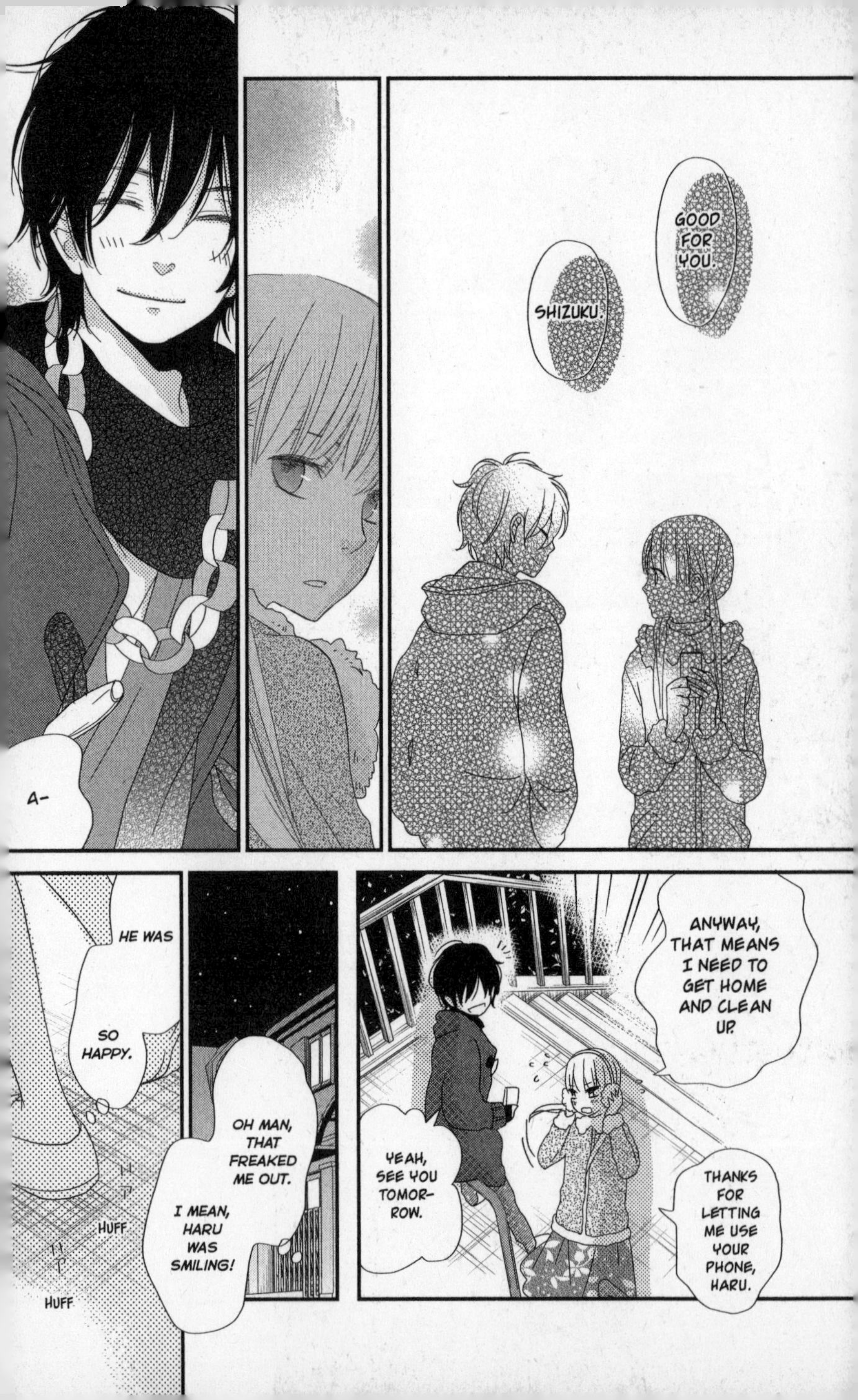

GOOD FOR YOU.
SHIZUKU.
A-
ANYWAY, THAT MEANS I NEED TO GET HOME AND CLEAN UP.
THANKS FOR LETTING ME USE YOUR PHONE, HARU.
YEAH, SEE YOU TOMOR-ROW.
OH MAN, THAT FREAKED ME OUT.
I MEAN, HARU WAS SMILING!
HE WAS
SO HAPPY.
HUFF
HUFF

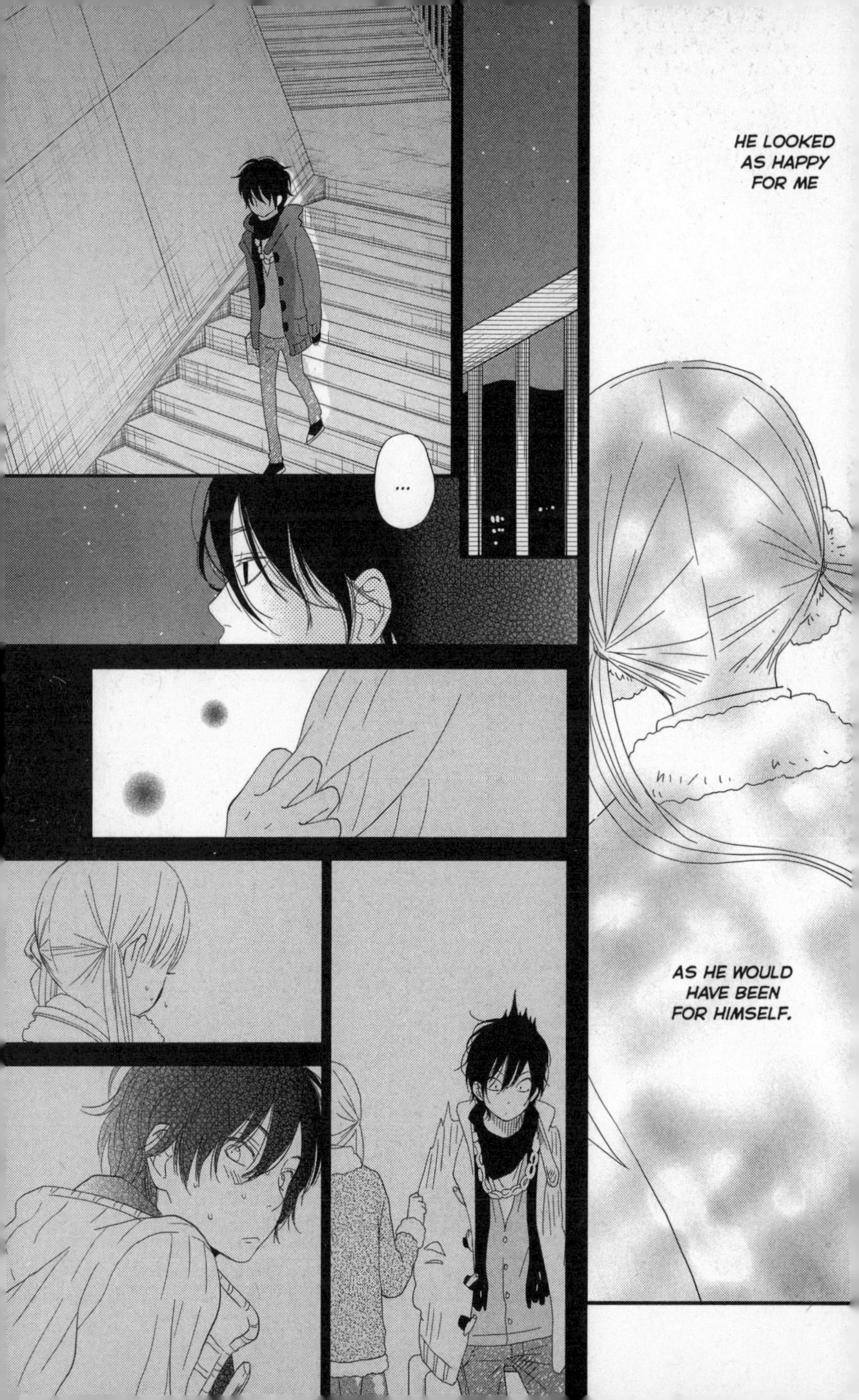
HE LOOKED AS HAPPY FOR ME
AS HE WOULD HAVE BEEN FOR HIMSELF.
...

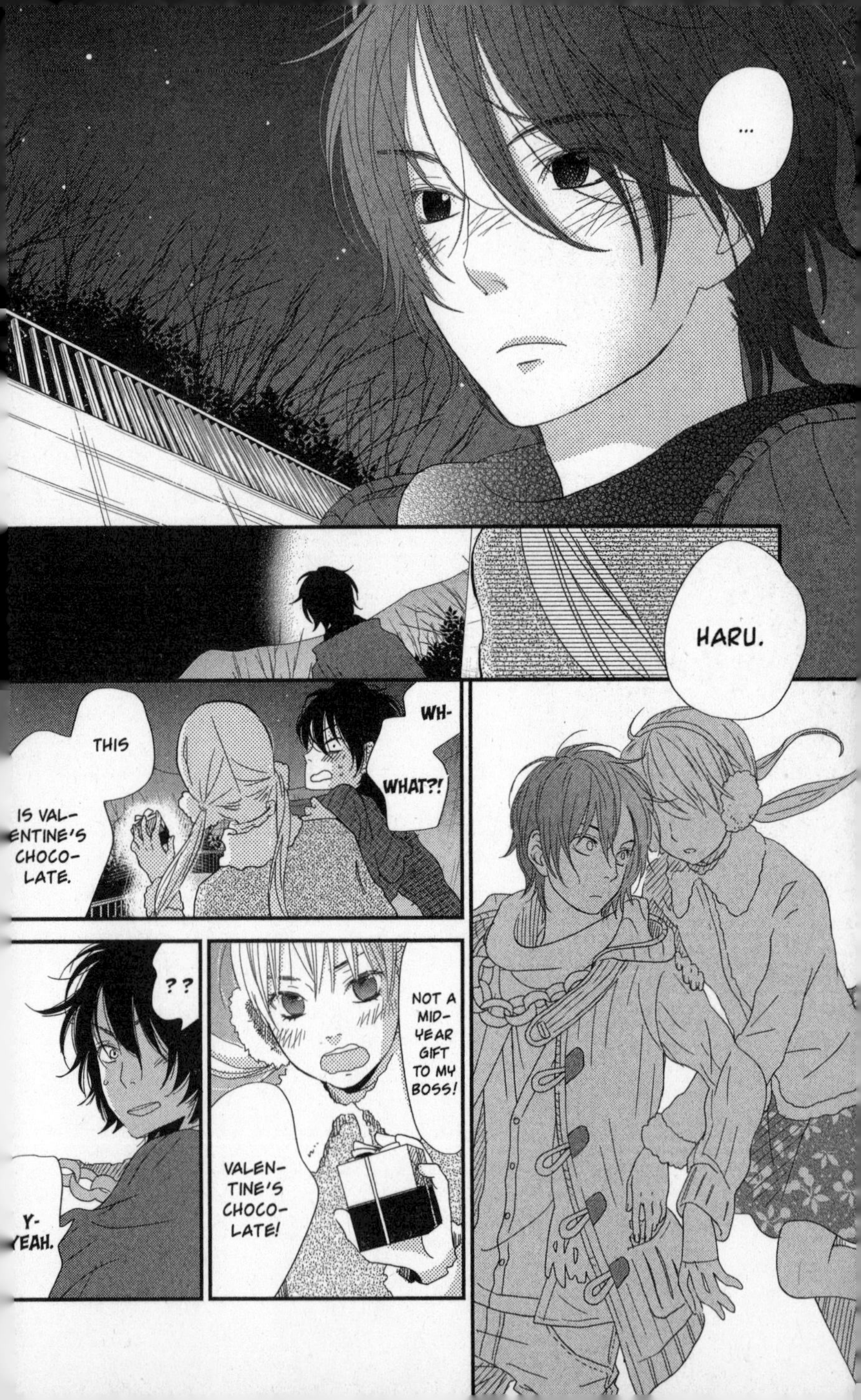
...
HARU.
WH- WHAT?!
THIS IS VAL-ENTINE'S CHOCO-LATE.
NOT A MID-YEAR GIFT TO MY BOSS!
VALEN-TINE'S CHOCO-LATE!
??
Y-YEAH.

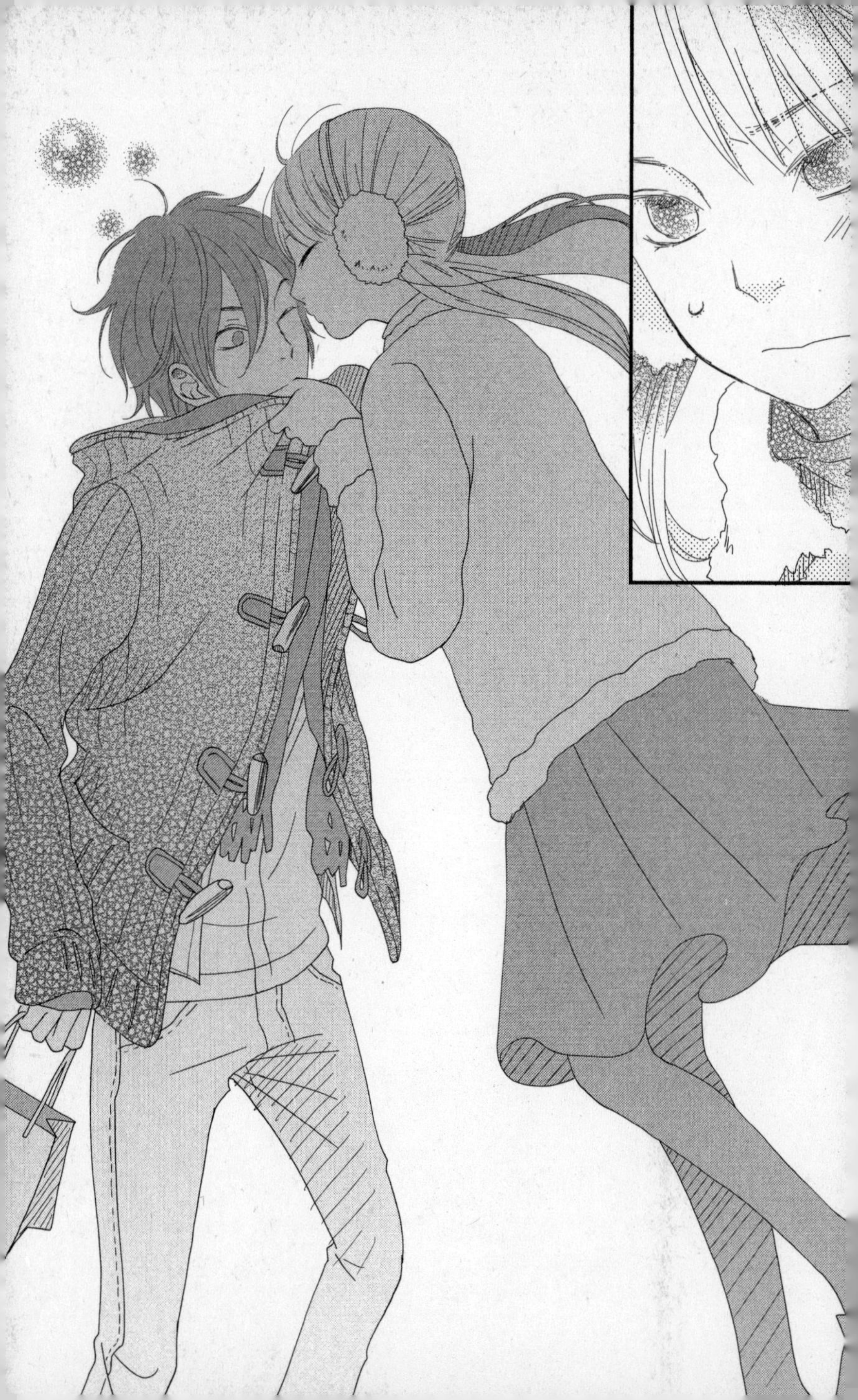

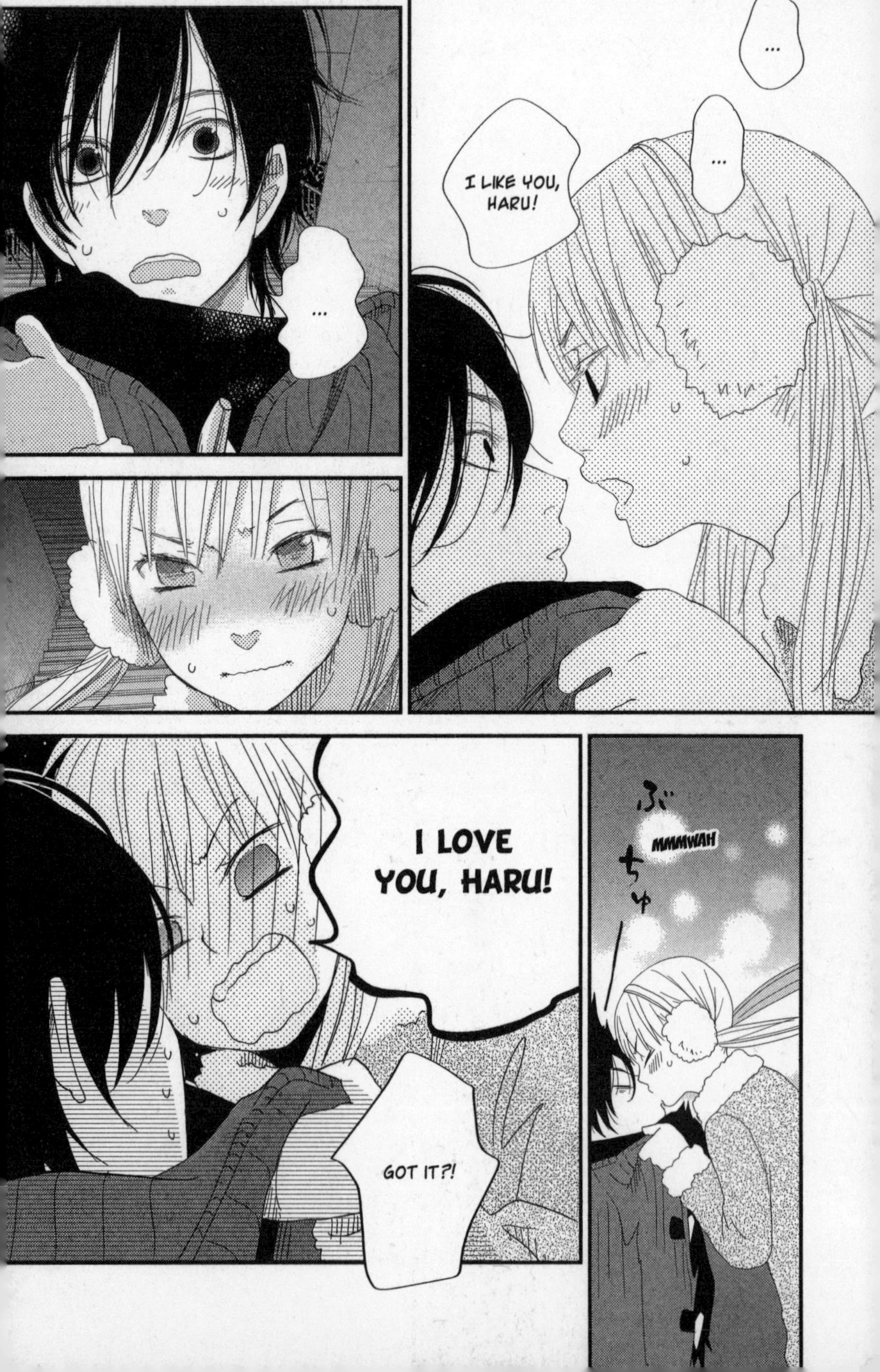
...
...
I LIKE YOU, HARU!
...
ぶちゅ
MMMWAH
I LOVE YOU, HARU!
GOT IT?!

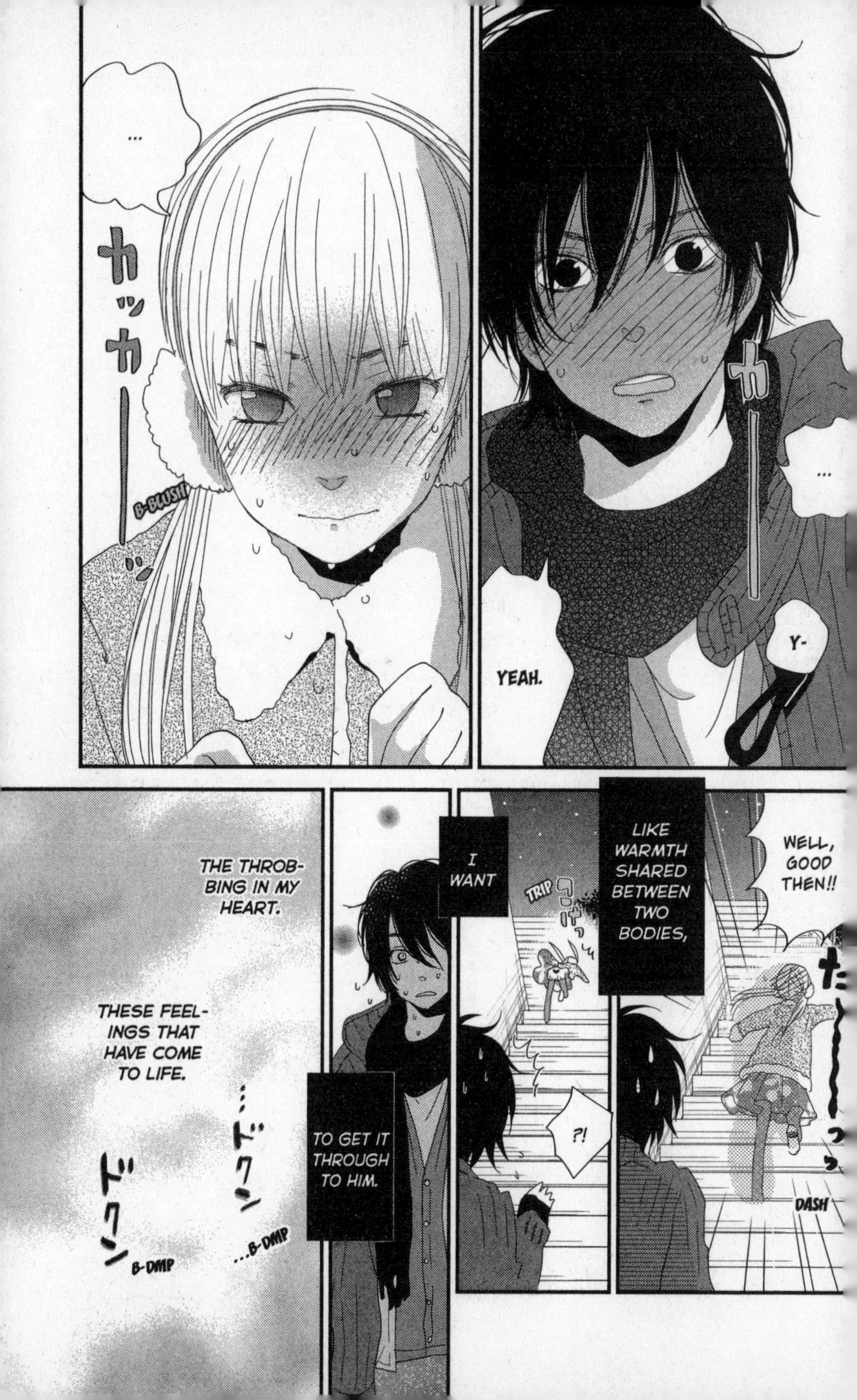
…
Y-
YEAH.
…
カッカー
B-BLUSH!
WELL, GOOD THEN!!
DASH
LIKE WARMTH SHARED BETWEEN TWO BODIES,
TRIP
?!
I WANT
TO GET IT THROUGH TO HIM.
THE THROB-BING IN MY HEART.
THESE FEEL-INGS THAT HAVE COME TO LIFE.
…ドクン
…B-DMP
ドクン
B-DMP

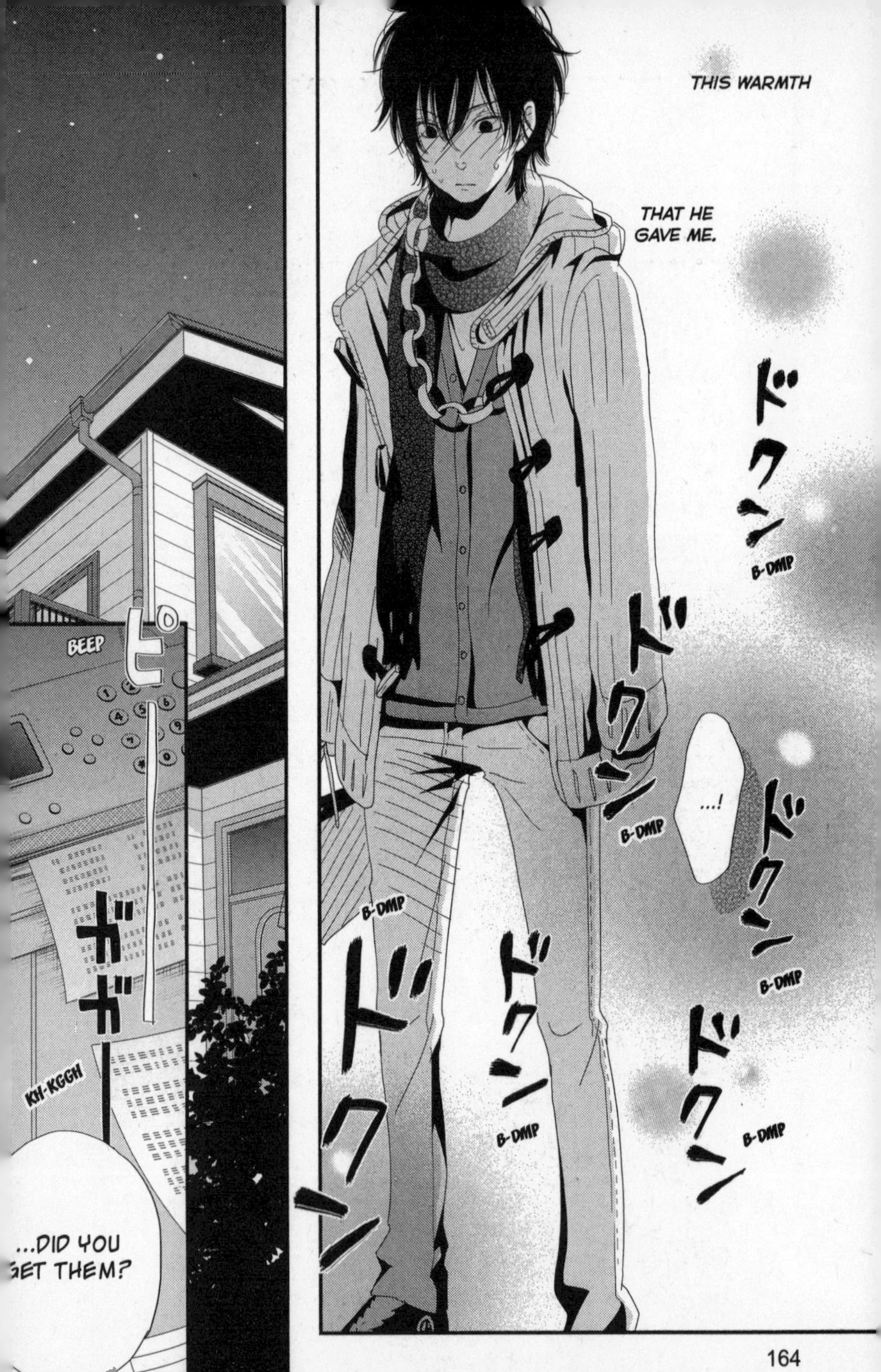
THIS WARMTH
THAT HE GAVE ME.
ドクン
B-DMP
ドクン
B-DMP
...!
ドクン
B-DMP
ドクン
B-DMP
ドクン
B-DMP
ドクン
B-DMP
ドクン
ピー
BEEP
ガガ
KH-KGGH
...DID YOU GET THEM?

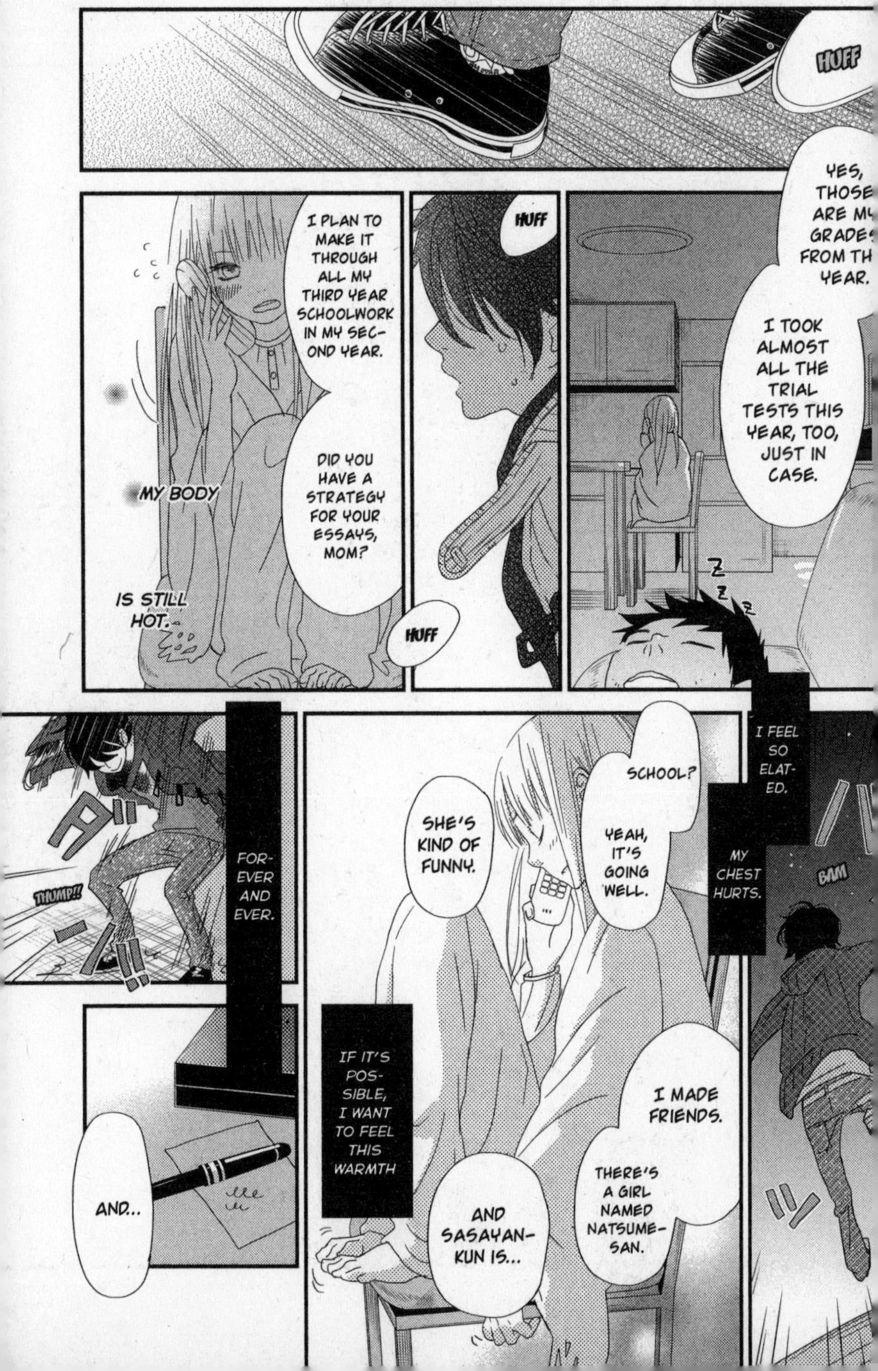
HUFF
YES, THOSE ARE MY GRADES FROM TH YEAR.
I TOOK ALMOST ALL THE TRIAL TESTS THIS YEAR, TOO, JUST IN CASE.
Z Z Z
HUFF
HUFF
I PLAN TO MAKE IT THROUGH ALL MY THIRD YEAR SCHOOLWORK IN MY SECOND YEAR.
DID YOU HAVE A STRATEGY FOR YOUR ESSAYS, MOM?
MY BODY
IS STILL HOT.
I FEEL SO ELATED.
MY CHEST HURTS.
BAM
SCHOOL?
YEAH, IT'S GOING WELL.
SHE'S KIND OF FUNNY.
I MADE FRIENDS.
THERE'S A GIRL NAMED NATSUME-SAN.
AND SASAYAN-KUN IS...
IF IT'S POSSIBLE, I WANT TO FEEL THIS WARMTH
FOREVER AND EVER.
THUMP!!
AND...

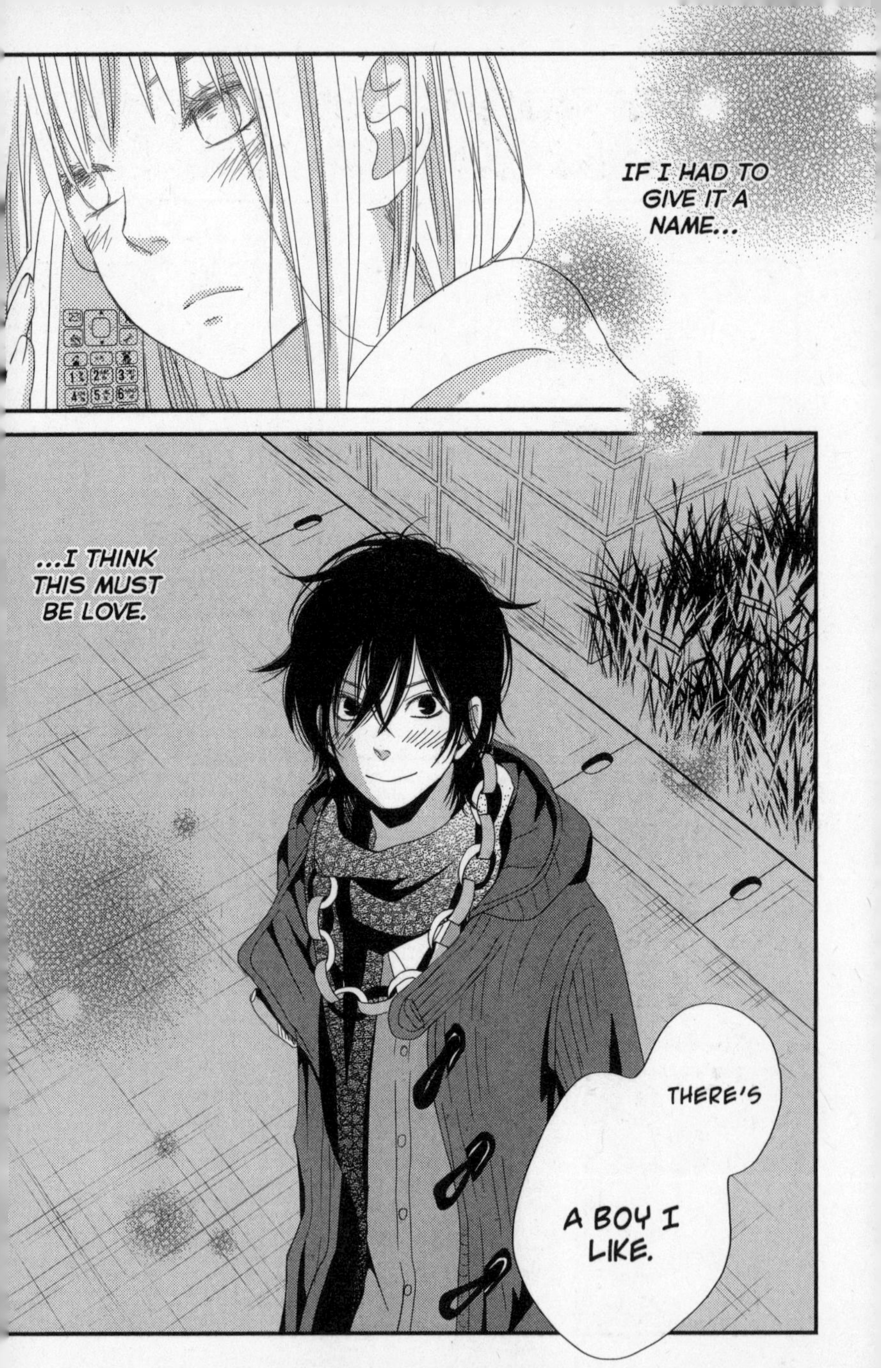
IF I HAD TO GIVE IT A NAME...
...I THINK THIS MUST BE LOVE.
THERE'S
A BOY I LIKE.

Continued in Volume 7!!

Mother and Daughter (Part One)

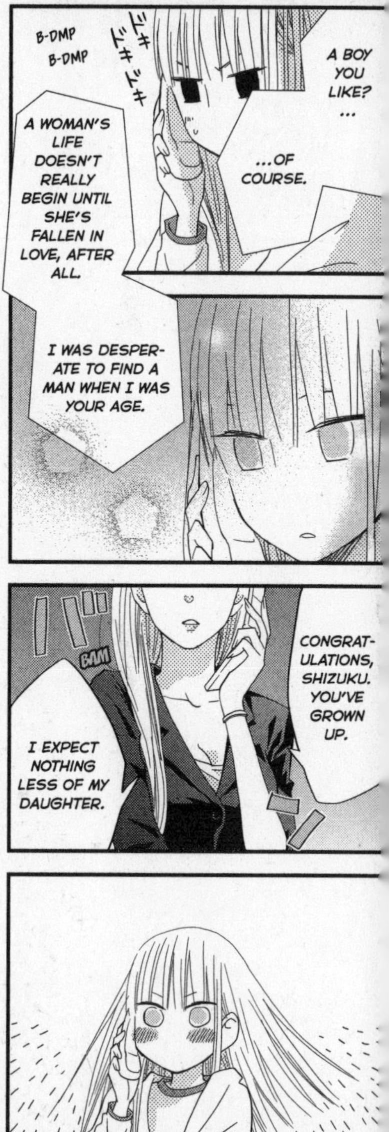
A BOY YOU LIKE? ...
...OF COURSE.
ドキドキ
B-DMP
B-DMP
A WOMAN'S LIFE DOESN'T REALLY BEGIN UNTIL SHE'S FALLEN IN LOVE, AFTER ALL.
I WAS DESPERATE TO FIND A MAN WHEN I WAS YOUR AGE.
CONGRATULATIONS, SHIZUKU. YOU'VE GROWN UP.
BAM
I EXPECT NOTHING LESS OF MY DAUGHTER.

Mother and Daughter (Part Two)

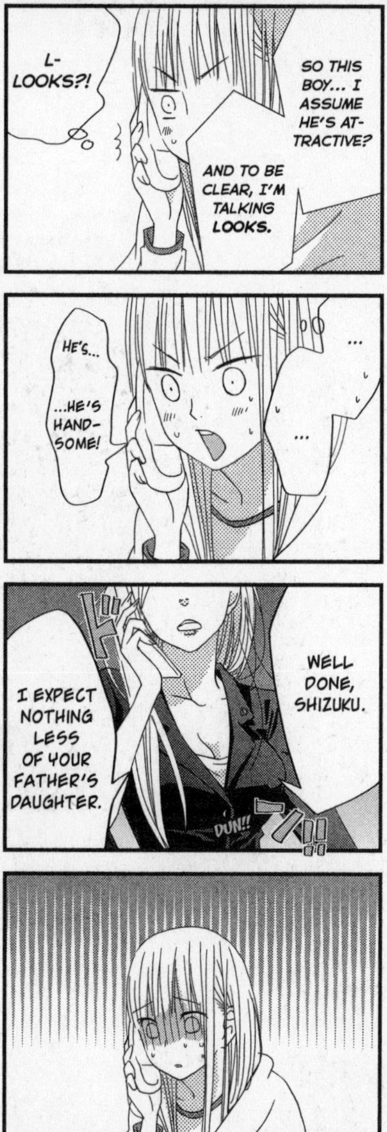
SO THIS BOY... I ASSUME HE'S ATTRACTIVE?
AND TO BE CLEAR, I'M TALKING LOOKS.
L- LOOKS?!
...
...
HE'S...
...HE'S HANDSOME!
WELL DONE, SHIZUKU.
I EXPECT NOTHING LESS OF YOUR FATHER'S DAUGHTER.
DUN!!

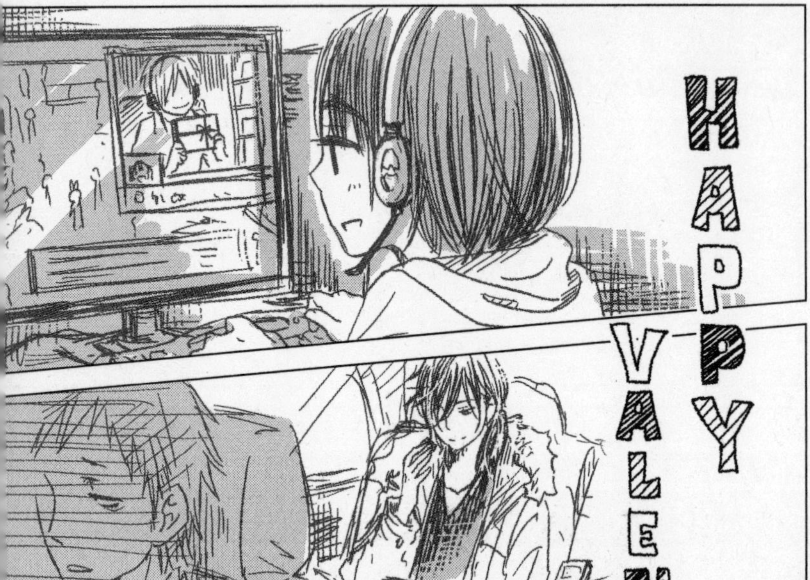
HAPPY VALENTINE'S

Continued in Volume 7

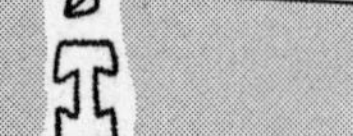

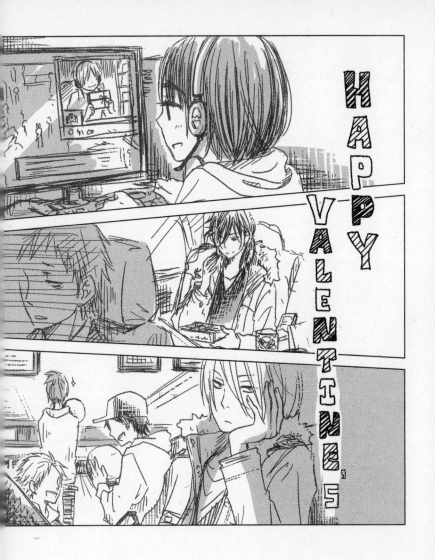

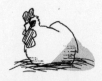

C O M M E N T

Robico

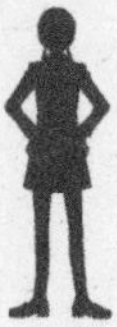

I have a really hard time writing comments, like, for this book and in the magazine's sidebars. But nobody ever wanted any comments from me until I started drawing manga, so I'm very grateful for this honor, but I'm still bad at it. We made it to volume six. I hope you enjoyed it.

Translation Notes

Japanese is a tricky language for most Westerners, and translation is often more art than science. For your edificaiton and reading pleasure, here are notes on some of the places where we could have gone in a different direction with our translation of this book, or where a Japanese cultural reference is used.

One of these days is none of these days, page 21

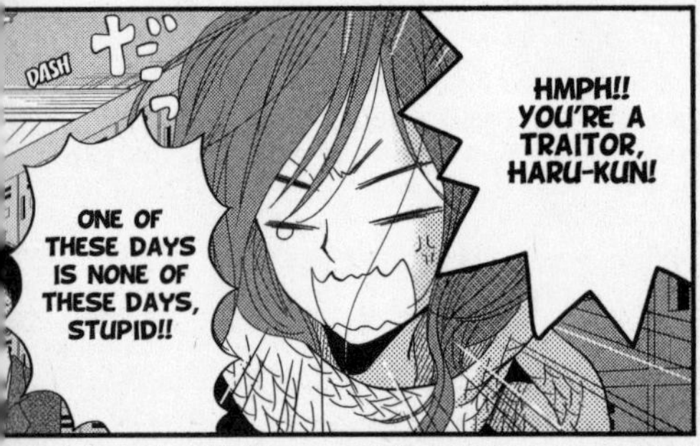
DASH
HMPH!! YOU'RE A TRAITOR, HARU-KUN!
ONE OF THESE DAYS IS NONE OF THESE DAYS, STUPID!!

This quote is attributed to the British publisher H.G. Bohn, and, as you may have guessed, not quite what Asako said in the Japanese version of the text. Asako originally quoted a Japanese drama, *Operation Love*, in which a grandfather advises his son that, "ashita yarō wa baka-yarō da." This is a play on words, which means roughly, "Anyone who says 'I'll do it tomorrow' is a fool," the pun being in yarō which means "I'll do it [tomorrow]" or "[stupid] guy." To maintain the insulting tone of Asako's line, the translators added a "stupid" for good(?) measure.

Guri-Gura, page 24

Guri-Gura gets his name from the picture books that inspired Shimoyanagi-kun to get him in the first place: the series Guri and Gura are about twin mice. Guri-Gura is big enough that he might really be a rat, but in Japanese, the word is *nezumi* for either one (so the original Guri and Gura might actually be rats, as well). In the first book, Guri and Gura make a cake, which has inspired numerous dessert recipes, many of which take the form of giant pancakes.

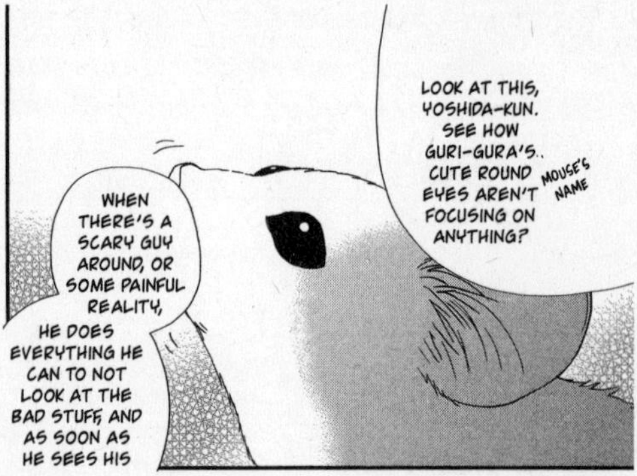
LOOK AT THIS, YOSHIDA-KUN. SEE HOW GURI-GURA'S.. CUTE ROUND EYES AREN'T FOCUSING ON ANYTHING?
MOUSE'S NAME
WHEN THERE'S A SCARY GUY AROUND, OR SOME PAINFUL REALITY,
HE DOES EVERYTHING HE CAN TO NOT LOOK AT THE BAD STUFF AND AS SOON AS HE SEES HIS

Mid-year gift to your boss, page 53

More specifically, Asako says that her Valentine's chocolate is not a summer oseibo. Oseibo means "end of the year," and is often used to refer to the end-of-the-year gifts traditionally given at New Year's. In July, there is a summer end-of-the-year, also known as chūgen, or "mid-year." On this holiday, it is traditional to give gifts to relatives and people who have done good things for the giver, such as doctors, teachers, bosses, etc. In other words, it's a gift of obligation and/or gratitude, rather than a gift of passion.

True love chocolate, page 53

In Japan, they do Valentine's Day a little bit differently than in the West. It is a day for women to give chocolate to the men in their lives, often as a way to let a man know that she is fond of him. However, if a woman has several male friends and relatives, she may give chocolate to all of them, so none of them feels left out. This chocolate is called giri-choko, or "obligation chocolate," as it is given out of a sense of obligation (much like a mid-year gift to a boss). The man whose attention a woman wants most is called her honmei, which means "favorite" or "number one candidate." He is given the honmei-choko, translated here as "true love chocolate."

Hunt Raths, page 60

Yu-chan is talking about hunting a certain type of creature in *Monster Hunter*, which is a phenomenally popular video game (with many sequels) in Japan. Oddly, the *Monster Hunter* series has not enjoyed as much success in non-Japanese markets.

Sekihan, page 115

Sekihan, or red rice, is sticky rice cooked with azuki beans. It is usually eaten to celebrate special occasions, like birthdays and weddings. In this case, they are celebrating Shizuku's becoming a woman.

Takaya the ghost, page 134

To be more precise, Haru thinks Takaya is a *zashiki-warashi*, which is a type of supernatural creature in Japanese folklore. It takes the form of a child, and can be mischievous, but is a protector of the house.

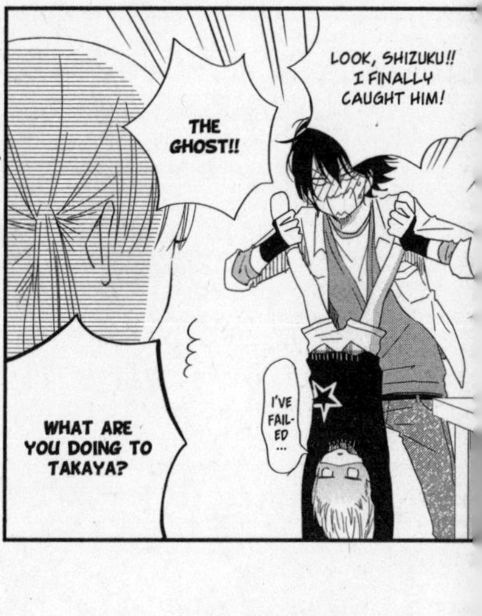
LOOK, SHIZUKU!! I FINALLY CAUGHT HIM!
THE GHOST!!
I'VE FAIL-ED...
WHAT ARE YOU DOING TO TAKAYA?

HOYO HIGH SCHOOL BASEBALL TEAM! ~ FIRST YEAR PRACTICE MATCH, TOP OF THE THIRD ~

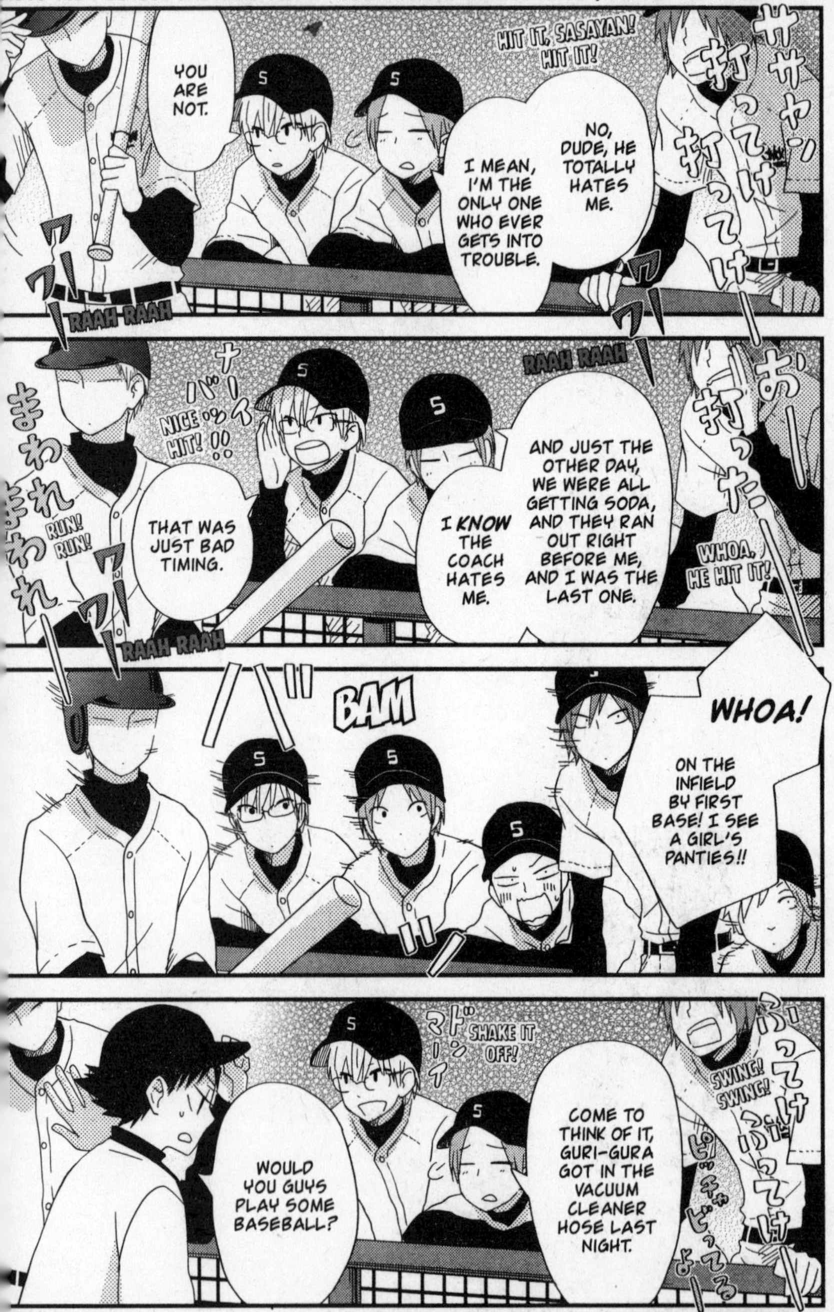

HIT IT, SASAYAN! HIT IT!
NO, DUDE, HE TOTALLY HATES ME.
I MEAN, I'M THE ONLY ONE WHO EVER GETS INTO TROUBLE.
YOU ARE NOT.
RAAH RAAH
WHOA, HE HIT IT!
RAAH RAAH
AND JUST THE OTHER DAY, WE WERE ALL GETTING SODA, AND THEY RAN OUT RIGHT BEFORE ME, AND I WAS THE LAST ONE.
I KNOW THE COACH HATES ME.
NICE HIT!!
THAT WAS JUST BAD TIMING.
RUN! RUN!
RAAH RAAH
WHOA!
ON THE INFIELD BY FIRST BASE! I SEE A GIRL'S PANTIES!!
BAM
SWING! SWING!
COME TO THINK OF IT, GURI-GURA GOT IN THE VACUUM CLEANER HOSE LAST NIGHT.
SHAKE IT OFF!
WOULD YOU GUYS PLAY SOME BASEBALL?

THE PITCHER'S SCARED!

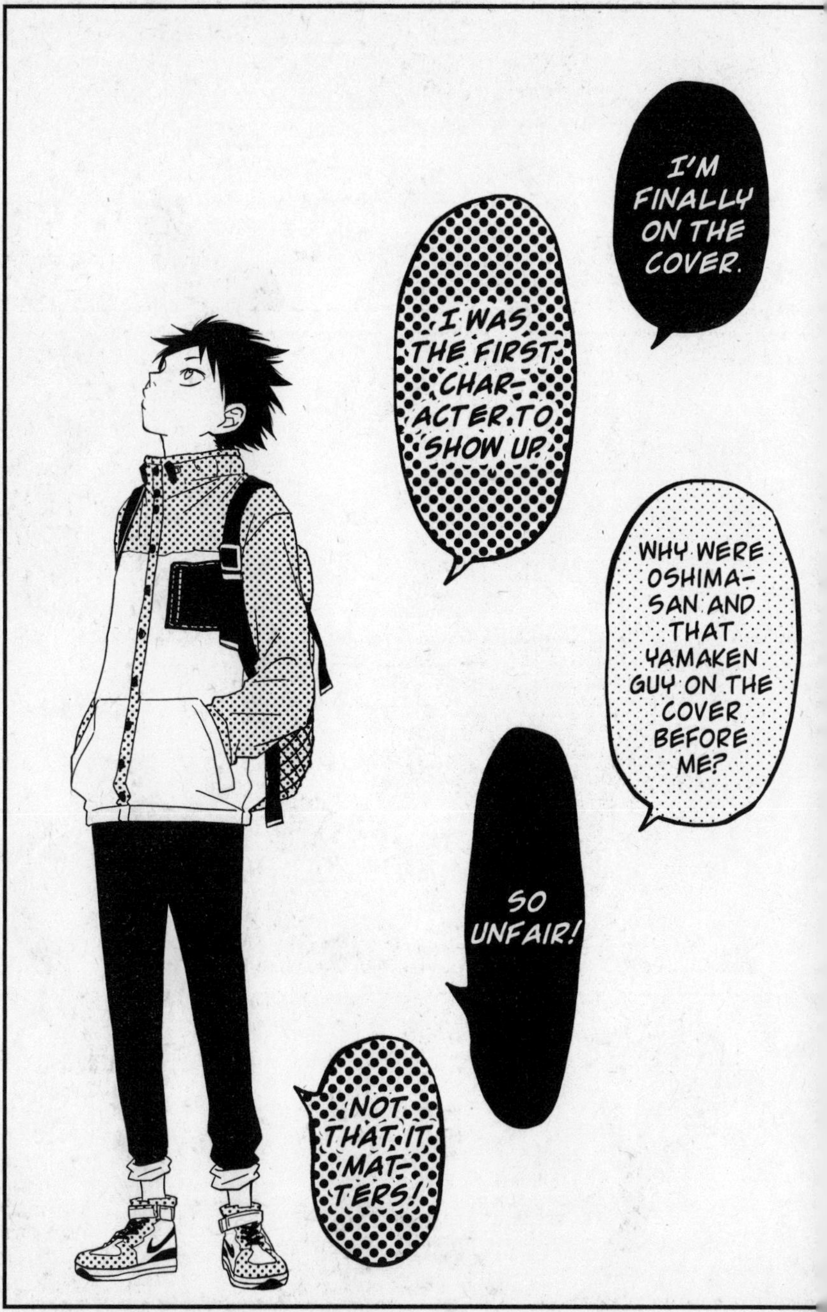
I'M FINALLY ON THE COVER.
I WAS THE FIRST CHAR-ACTER TO SHOW UP.
WHY WERE OSHIMA-SAN AND THAT YAMAKEN GUY ON THE COVER BEFORE ME?
SO UNFAIR!
NOT THAT IT MAT-TERS!

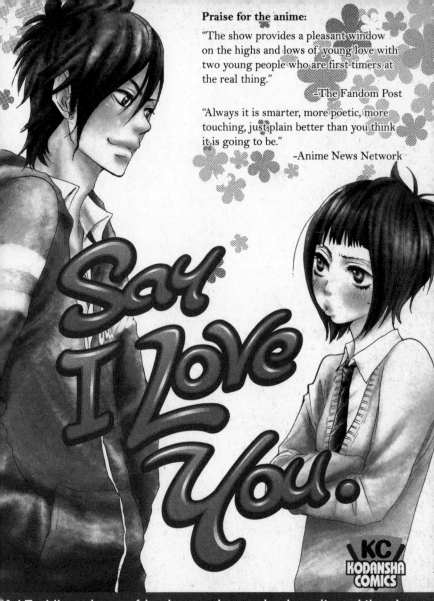

KC
KODANSHA
COMICS

Mei Tachibana has no friends — and says she doesn't need them!

But everything changes when she accidentally roundhouse kicks the most popular boy in school! However, Yamato Kurosawa isn't angry in the slightest— in fact, he thinks his ordinary life could use an unusual girl like Mei. But winning Mei's trust will be a tough task. How long will she refuse to say, "I love you"?

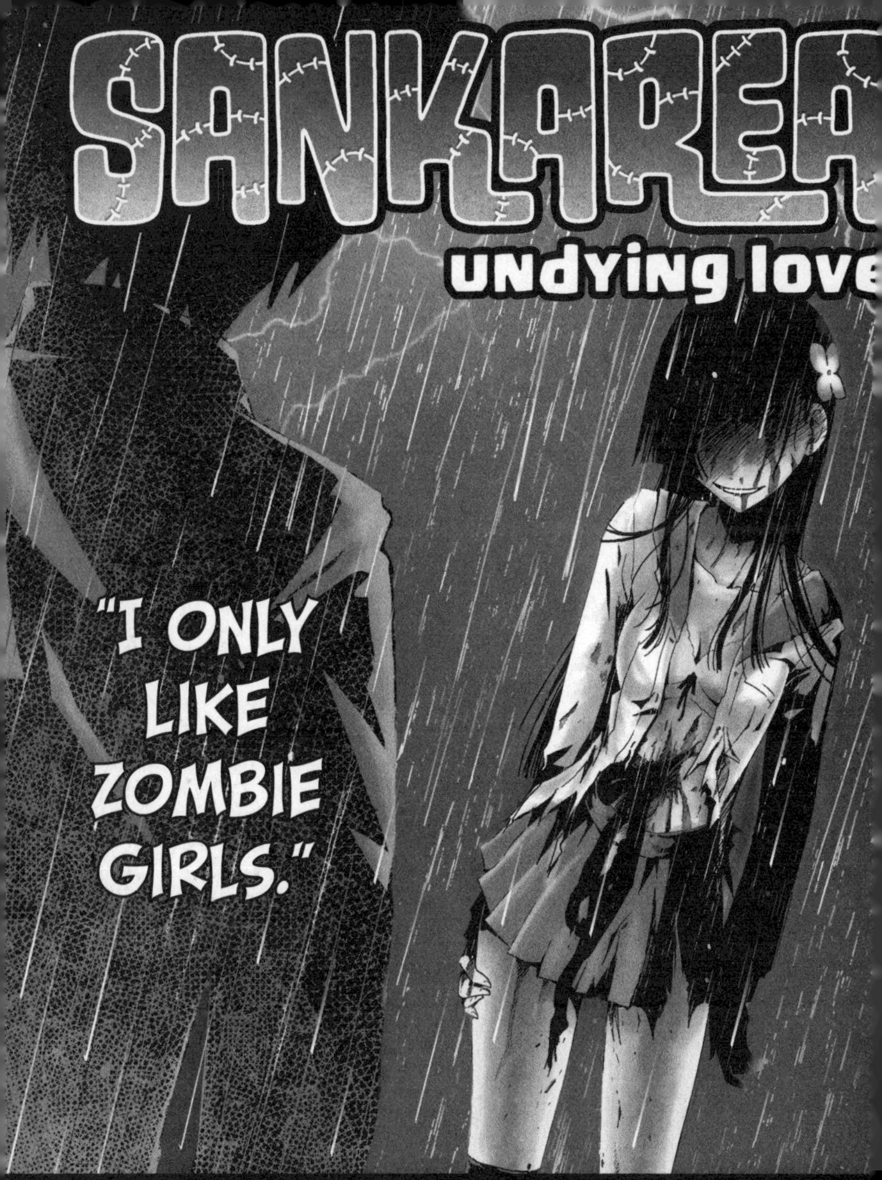

SANKAREA
undying love

"I ONLY LIKE ZOMBIE GIRLS."

Chihiro has an unusual connection to zombie movies. He doesn't feel bad the survivors – he wants to comfort the undead girls they slaughter! Whe his pet passes away, he brews a resurrection potion. He's discovered by local heiress Sanka Rea, and she serves as his first test subject!

KOD CO.

My Little Monster volume 6 is a work of fiction. Names, characters, places, and incidents are the products of the author's imagination or are used fictitiously. Any resemblance to actual events, locales, or persons, living or dead, is entirely coincidental.

A Kodansha Comics Trade Paperback Original.

Published in the United States by Kodansha Comics, an imprint of Kodansha USA Publishing, LLC, New York.

Publication rights for this English edition arranged through Kodansha Ltd., Tokyo.

First published in Japan in 2010 by Kodansha Ltd., Tokyo as *Tonari no Kaibutsu-kun*, volume 6.

ISBN 978-1-61262-800-4

Printed in the United States of America.

www.kodanshacomics.com

9 8 7 6 5 4 3 2 1

Translator: Alethea Nibley & Athena Nibley
Lettering: Kiyoko Shiromasa